THE

BANGLADESH

READER

HISTORY, CULTURE, POLITICS

Meghna Guhathakurta and Willem van Schendel, eds.

DUKE UNIVERSITY PRESS　*Durham and London*　2013

Library of Congress Cataloging-in-Publication Data
The Bangladesh reader : history, culture, politics /
Meghna Guhathakurta and Willem van Schendel, eds.
p. cm.—(The world readers)
Includes bibliographical references and index.
ISBN 978-0-8223-5304-1 (cloth : alk. paper)
ISBN 978-0-8223-5318-8 (pbk. : alk. paper)
1. Bangladesh—History. 2. Bangladesh—Civilization.
3. Bangladesh—Politics and government.
I. Guhathakurata, Meghana.
II. Schendel, Willem van.
III. Series: World readers.
DS394.5.B364 2013
954.92—dc23
2012044744

Contents

List of Illustrations

Acknowledgments

We are very grateful for the many kinds of help we received in putting together this book. Its publication would not have been possible without the support of many different copyright holders who gave us permission to use images and excerpts of text. We would like to thank them for their cooperation.

We are also grateful to Abu Faisal Md. Khaled for his enthusiastic assistance in collecting copyright permissions. In addition we thank the following for help, information, comments, advice, and much more: Hana Shams Ahmed, M. M. Akash, Rasheda Akhter, Ellen Bal, Suraiya Begum, Bhaswati Bhattacharya, Apurba Kumar Bose, Timour Claquin, Khushi Kabir, Utpal Kanti Khisa, Nienke Klompmaker, NETZ Bangladesch, Md. Mahbubar Rahman, Saifuzzaman Rana, Niko Richter, Bianca Son, and Eef Vermeij. At Duke University Press, Valerie Millholland made the project possible and Gisela Fosado, Vanessa Doriott Anderson, Lorien Olive, and China Medel skillfully guided us through it; we are grateful to all of them.

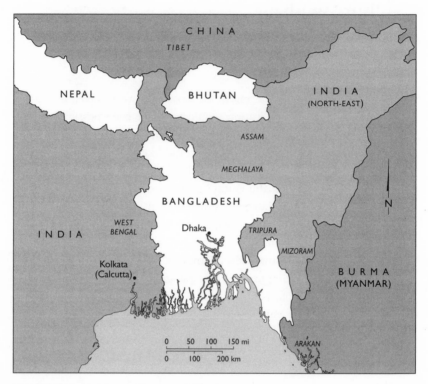

Bangladesh and its surroundings. By Bill Nelson.

Introduction

Bangladesh is the eighth most populous country on earth. It has more inhabitants than Russia or Japan, and its national language—Bengali—ranks sixth in the world in terms of native speakers. And yet, Bangladesh remains a great unknown. It rarely figures in global affairs or the media, and when it does we usually hear dismal stories about floods, mass poverty, or political turmoil. These stark portrayals do no justice at all to the rich historical, cultural, and political permutations that have created contemporary Bangladesh. Without a deeper understanding of these processes, Bangladesh will remain a riddle.

There are good reasons for this weak international presence. Bangladesh is a newcomer: as a sovereign unit, it is only some forty years old. Before it gained independence, it was known as East Pakistan (1947–71) and before that as the eastern half of Bengal. Still, it has always been a region with a strong identity because its ecology is distinct from that of the surrounding areas. Bangladesh comprises the world's largest delta, formed by multiple rivers flowing from the Himalayas. The Ganges and the Brahmaputra are the largest of these rivers but there are dozens of others. Annual silt deposits make the soil of the Bengal Delta extremely fertile, and the tropical monsoon climate allows for lush vegetation. From the earliest recorded history to the present day, rice cultivation has been the bedrock of human existence here. Intensive agriculture has resulted in a population that is among the most densely packed in the world. With more than 150 million inhabitants and an area the size of Wisconsin or Greece, Bangladesh has a population density that is three times higher than that of neighboring India.

It would be wrong, however, to think of Bangladesh as an inward-looking agricultural society. On the contrary, openness to the outside world has been its historical hallmark. From the earliest times the society has been a crossroads of trade routes where ideas, people, and goods mingled. Here Tibetan wares were dispatched to ancient Rome, traders from the Maldives met their Armenian counterparts, African kings ruled, and Europeans gradually rose from positions as mercenaries and pirates to colonial overlords. In precolonial times, rice from the Bengal Delta fed populations as far apart as the Moluccas in eastern Indonesia and Goa in western India, and its silk fabrics traveled even farther. The delta was a major stronghold of Buddhist learning—and has many remains to show for it—before Hindu and Muslim identities came to dominate the cultural scene. Linguistic, religious, and regional diversity have been a feature of Bangladeshi history as much as the mobility of its population.

Modern identities in Bangladesh are the outcome of this long-lasting openness and incessant renewal. And this includes the very idea of Bangladesh itself, the unexpected outcome of a unique and spectacular double decolonization, first from British rule in 1947 and then from Pakistani rule in 1971. These historical vicissitudes must be understood if we are to make any sense of the intensity of contemporary identity politics in Bangladesh—and why these revolve round cultural distinctions such as Bengali Muslim versus Muslim Bengali, or Bengali versus indigenous people.

The Bangladesh Reader provides an introduction to this huge, old, multi-faceted, and little-known society. But it is not a history of Bangladesh—there are other books that provide analyses of the country's history (see "Suggestions for Further Reading"). *The Bangladesh Reader* approaches its subject in a different way. Think of it as a choir performing a grand oratorio, a multitude of voices evoking social life and aspirations past and present. Its main aim is to convey the ambiance, complexity, texture, and excitement of Bangladesh to a broad readership. First-time visitors, students, and others seeking an introduction to the country will find much that is new and interesting, and so will Bangladeshis and scholars of the region.

We hope to surprise readers with unusual angles and thus inspire them to explore further. To this end we have selected both classic contributions that are familiar to many Bangladeshis—and essential reading for those who want to know the country—and quirky ones that are much less known. We aim for a lively, broad, and entertaining collection that brings out the cultural richness of Bangladesh from its earliest history to the present day.

This book assembles an array of entries, including eyewitness accounts, historical documents, speeches, treaties, essays, poems, songs, autobiography, photographs, cartoons, paintings, posters, advertisements, a recipe, maps, and short stories. Many of these contributions have not been accessible to English-speaking readers before, or are very hard to get hold of. We offer translations not only from Bengali but also from a range of other languages, including Prakrit, Sanskrit, Arabic, Chinese, Greek, Chakma, Dutch, Urdu, Portuguese, French, Sak, and German. We have abridged some selections for readability.

The *Reader* chronicles Bangladeshi history and culture over two and a half millennia by letting a great diversity of actors speak in their own words. We encounter rich and poor Bangladeshis, women and men, kings and poets, colonizers and colonized, rebels and saints, urban and rural folk, and scholars and laborers. Our introductory notes to individual entries provide context, but the focus is on how participants tell the story of Bangladesh—in a format that is readable, welcoming, and eclectic. The intended result is a tapestry of facts, opinions, emotions, and perspectives that evoke the thrill of life in Bangladesh from ancient times through colonial and postcolonial transmutations to the present day. To use a Bangladeshi expression, the book is as variegated as an embroidered quilt.

We hope that *The Bangladesh Reader* will provide a much-needed boost to the study of Bangladesh and South Asia. The book engages with themes and debates that challenge conventional ideas about Bangladeshi culture and history. For example, the contributions of the country's many non-Bengali communities tend to be ignored in the existing literature because Bangladesh history tends to be written as either the emancipation of downtrodden Muslims or the inexorable emergence of the Bengali nation-state. Both are highly problematic; there is nothing monolithic or preordained in the multiple histories and many social worlds that have created contemporary Bangladesh. Our contributors hint at local accommodations, popular perceptions, political processes, and transnational connections that challenge scholars of South Asia to advance more-insightful explanations. We hope the book will open up new avenues in Bangladesh studies.

The Bangladesh Reader follows a largely chronological order, but we are less concerned with providing a historical timeline than with conveying the feel of Bangladesh. In our selection of pieces we have applied a number of criteria. Brevity and accessibility were very important. We have avoided long pieces and readings that require much prior knowledge. We have given priority to pieces that are crucially important but presently unavailable in English or difficult to find. We have aimed for a mix of different types of materials, most of them originally intended for a general audience. Finally, we have chosen a very broad variety of voices and contributions that we hope will pique the reader's curiosity and challenge existing clichés about Bangladesh. These choices dictated the omission, purely owing to considerations of space, of many works that are of great significance to our understanding of Bangladesh. Naturally, some of these are included in the list of further readings at the end of the book.

The *Reader* consists of chronologically ordered parts, preceded by selections that present some contemporary voices from Bangladesh. What are Bangladeshis discussing today? How do they see themselves? Where do they think their country is heading?

We then look at the long period from the earliest surviving writings to the eighteenth century in part II. What people were living in the Bengal delta in those long-gone times? Can we still connect with their experiences? We hear the voices of poets, pilgrims, and kings, as well as those of adventurers from many lands.

Part III takes us to the 190-year period of British rule (1757–1947). We read fragments from the first Bengali autobiography; accounts of politics, revolt, and famine; a call to holy war; a satire on gender relations; a Nobel laureate's short story; and much more. A section of images of Bangladesh's past is included in this part.

Next, we consider the period when the Bengal Delta became part of the new state of Pakistan and was known as East Pakistan (1947–71). We read about the partitioning of British India: joy at the passing of colonial rule, puzzled officials trying to find the new international border, a lament for lost unity, and the story of a migrant. We then turn to the gradual unraveling of the state of Pakistan and trace how language emerged as the main rallying theme in East Pakistan politics. We also hear about new lifestyles, minority issues, and more.

The war of 1971, which enabled Bangladesh to break away from Pakistan, forms the focus of part V. A period of abiding significance in contemporary Bangladesh, it is the attention of much historical writing. Here we present contrasting voices and perspectives. We hear popular leaders declaring independence, Pakistani army men denouncing the betrayal of East Pakistan, and people from many walks of life articulating their feelings about the maelstrom in which they were caught up. The war was followed by the exuberance of independence and the constitution of a new state, and we include an introduction to the early years of Bangladesh. A gallery of images of politics is included in this part.

Then we explore national identity, a vexed issue in Bangladesh today, in part VI. Since independence the idea of the nation has been at the center of swirling debates and contestations: what makes us, inhabitants of Bangladesh, a nation? A question like "Are we Bengali or Bangladeshi?" may sound strange to untutored ears but it is being debated daily all over the country—and devotees of Bengali culture, Islamist activists, secular thinkers, and people from the many ethnic minorities provide different answers.

Part VII looks at an aspect of Bangladesh that is still astonishingly little known abroad: its vibrant cultural life. This is a society that displays its cultural creativity, from popular arts to fine arts, in many and surprising ways. Poetry has always been a major art form. It is deeply appreciated and widely practiced but rarely reaches an international audience. We provide some examples. Painting, dance, creative writing, filmmaking, artistic parades, pop music, food, and rickshaw art are some of the other cultural expressions that are briefly introduced. A section of images of cultural diversity is included in this part.

The next part explores *development*, a term that became omnipresent in public discourse in Bangladesh and continues to be the lens through which most outsiders try to understand the country. We encounter development practitioners and their critics, sketches of lives in poverty and wealth, and the power dynamics surrounding the implementation of development projects. We learn what it is like to be a patient in a Bangladeshi hospital, or a migrant in a provincial town, or a rich person in the capital city Dhaka. And we hear Bangladeshis comment on the development regime that has such deep roots in their society.

In the *Reader*'s final part, we explore some of the links that connect Bangladesh's society to the wider world. Millions of people have left the country to find a livelihood abroad, and many of these migrants maintain strong emotional (and sometimes economic and political) ties with their former home. We hear about the fate of refugees from the partition of India, well-established Londoners of Bangladeshi origin, and unauthorized settlers in India. We also learn how the state of Bangladesh became part of the world state system, how the idea of microfinance became one of the country's best-known exports, and how Bangladeshi chic may have a global future.

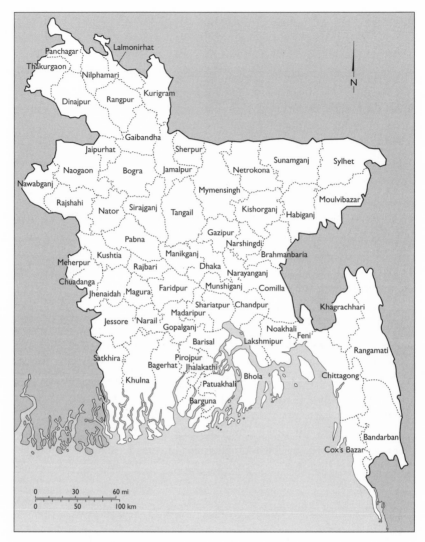

Districts of Bangladesh. By Bill Nelson.

I

Voices from Bangladesh

We begin *The Bangladesh Reader* with a few contemporary voices—Bangladeshis speaking their minds about issues that are important to them today: their work, their hopes for the future, their dissatisfactions, and their spiritual aspirations. These voices stand for the tens of millions of articulate citizens of Bangladesh and give a taste of one of their great talents: self-expression.

Becoming a Village Photographer

Sabina Yasmin Sathi

The media image of Bangladesh tends toward the somber, if not tragic. Floods, cyclones, mass poverty, political instability, corruption, and underdevelopment figure prominently in most media coverage of the country. To challenge this unbalanced view, a group of young media activists started a quest to find positive stories about Bangladesh, stories that spoke to the remarkable achievements of ordinary people in rural Bangladesh. In their quest they came across physically handicapped people who started a green revolution by using natural fertilizers, women who took to repairing cycles to send their children to school, and singers who claimed that their mystical songs eased two kinds of hunger: physical and mental. Here is the story of a teenage girl who refused to believe that her destiny should be determined by anyone but herself.

My name is Sabina Yasmin Sathi and I am seventeen years old. I come from the village of Akua, located in the union of Shohodebpur, in Kalihati *upazila* [subdistrict], Tangail district. My father was a poor *madrasha* [Islamic school] teacher. He wanted me to study in the madrasha as well. My mother and I did not want that. So I got admitted to the local high school instead. In the year 2001, I took a course in photography under the science curriculum of the mass education program. Later I took a loan, bought my own camera, and started to take pictures.

At first my father objected because he feared social pressure. But later he relented. Besides, my mother supported me all the time and that was my strength. Many neighbors spread the word that I was engaging in un-Islamic behavior. Taking pictures is against Islam, they said. But others saw that I was spending the money I earned toward my own education. I no longer depended on my parents to pay for my schooling.

At a certain point in time I became the pride of my village. I am now called to photograph many events in my village and also villages around me. When young girls seek admission to a school or college, they need a passport-size photograph. They seek my help. UNICEF did a photo essay on me once.

Translated from Bengali by Meghna Guhathakurta.

Wait for a While, Death!

Abdul Gofur Hali

In this poem—written in 1997—Abdul Gofur Hali addresses death and evokes life as a chance to reach for the divine. He follows a poetic tradition in Bangladesh when he describes himself as "crazy." Gofur is a well-known representative of a popular mystical Islamic (Sufi) movement known as Maijbhandari. This movement venerates the Muslim saint of Maijbhandar, a small town in the southeastern district of Chittagong.

Wait for a while, death,
Let me behold my true self a little longer.

My soul has found its playmate
And is still busy playing,
Don't be so harsh as to destroy
The mating of soul and god.

When the soul comes home after playing,
Then go and show yourself.
Don't you remember your own words?
This bond abides through ages.

Crazy Gofur wonders:
What did I do in the name of playing?
Human life quivers
Like a drop of water on a taro leaf.

Translated from Bengali by Hans Harder.

Telephone Ladies and Social Business

Muhammad Yunus

The Grameen Bank (gram means village in Bengali) is an institution that pro-
vides small loans to poor people who do not qualify for traditional bank loans be-
cause they lack collateral. Its founder, Muhammad Yunus, has been exceptionally
successful in promoting his ideas about microcredit (or microfinance) and social
business worldwide. Today his method is widely eulogized and also criticized. The
Grameen approach spawned one of Bangladesh's most powerful conglomerates of
institutions, and Yunus became one of the country's best-known citizens. In 2006
the Grameen Bank and Yunus shared the Nobel Peace Prize. In this excerpt from the
speech he gave to accept another prize, the World Information Society Award, he
explains some of his ideas.

All you need to do is to find a business model where ICT [information and
communication technology] can become an income-generating activity to
the poor. I tried this through [putt]ing mobile phones in the hands of the
poor women in Bangladesh. It worked beautifully. Almost everybody that
I shared my thoughts [with] about getting poor women involved in mobile
phone business thought: this is an idea which may fit into a science fiction,
but not in a real situation of Bangladesh.

But poor women responded to my idea with enthusiasm. They learned
quickly how to handle the phone, and the business. Today there are 200,000
telephone ladies in Bangladesh, earning a good income for their families
and contributing USD 11 million worth of revenue per month to Grameen
Phone, the mobile phone company.

Grameen Phone found the women in Grameen Bank network so reliable as business partners, that it has now launched another programme
with them. This time . . . poor women [not only will sell the airtime, they
will also sell telephone connections for new subscribers, receive money
on behalf of the company from the subscribers for replenishment of their
accounts, and replace their prepaid card completely. This is a case of win-

win-win situation from all three sides, the mobile phone company, the subscribers and the poor women.

Grameen Bank now serves over 6 million borrowers, 96 per cent of whom are women. The number of these borrowers will reach 8 million by the end of this year [2006], and 12 million by the end of 2010. The number of telephone ladies is expected to reach 400,000 by the end of this year, and exceed one million by 2010. . . .

We have been emphasizing the importance of sending the children to school since we began our work in the mid seventies. Our social programme, known as "Sixteen Decisions," includes this. Not only 100 per cent of the children of Grameen families started going to school, now many of them are going to medical schools, engineering schools, universities, etc. Grameen Bank provides them with student loans. There are more than 10,000 students at high levels of education who are financed by Grameen Bank's education loans.

We are in the process of setting up a technology promotion fund in collaboration with Mr Mohammed Abdul Latif Jameel of Saudi Arabia, to provide financing to innovative adaptation of already designed technology, provide venture capital and loans to produce and market these technologies. I am expecting that ICT will be an area of technology, which the innovators will give high priority.

Two years back, Grameen Bank launched a special programme to give loans to beggars. We did not impose any of our existing rules on them. Their loans are interest-free. They can pay whatever amount they wish, whenever they want to pay. When the first loan is repaid they can take a second loan, usually a bigger loan, and so on. With this money they turn themselves into door-to-door sales persons. It is up to them to decide when they should give up begging. We now have over 70,000 beggars in this programme and it will reach 100,000 by the end of the year. . . .

I strongly feel that we can create a poverty-free world. The basic ingredient of overcoming poverty is packed inside each of the individual human beings, including the poorest human being. All we need to do is to help the person to unleash this energy and creativity. Once this can be done, poverty will be history. It will disappear very fast. The only place in the world where poverty may exist will be the poverty museums, no longer in human society.

We need to reconceptualize the business world to make sure it contributes to the creation of a humane society, not aggravate the problems around us. We need to recognize two types of businesses, not one, and offer equal opportunities to both. These two types of businesses are: One which is already known, business to make money, that is conventional business, the principle of whom is to maximize profit. And the other new kind, business to do good to people, or social business.

Social business enterprises are a new kind of non-loss non-dividend enterprises, which aim at solving social, health and environmental problems, utilizing the market mechanism. We need to give opportunities to the social business entrepreneurs [that are] similar to the institutional and policy support system that the world has built over the years for the conventional businesses. One such new institution to help social business entrepreneurs will be the creation of "social stock market" to bring the social business entrepreneurs and social investors to come in contact with each other and solve the problem of finding investment money for this new type of business.

I Work in a Clothing Factory

Shana K.

Factories making ready-made clothes for export first appeared in Bangladesh's towns and cities in the 1980s. They spread rapidly and became the country's major export industry. Today these factories give employment to hundreds of thousands of workers, mostly women. One of them is Shana. Here she gives us a brief sketch of what life is like for workers in the ready-made textile industry.

June 15, 2010

My name is Shana K—. I am 18 years old and work as a sewing operator at the Meridian Garments factory. I started working three years ago at several different sewing factories. My duty at Meridian starts at 8:00 A.M. and regularly ends at 10:00 P.M. or 12:00 midnight. There are also 14 to 15 all-night shifts [per month] to 3:00 A.M. Management allows workers to leave at 8:00 P.M., to go home to eat supper and rest before starting the night shift at 10:00 P.M. I don't get any weekly day off. On Saturdays, management allows us to leave work at 8:00 P.M. On average, we can enjoy just one day off in two or three months. I studied up to the ninth grade, but unfortunately, could not continue my studies due to financial hardship.

My salary is 3,100 taka ($44.60) a month, but I can earn 5,000–6,000 taka ($71.94–$86.33) including overtime [OT] work. We work an average of five or six hours of overtime each day and the rate for OT duty is 22 taka (32 cents) per hour. I haven't married yet. We are only two in our family. My father died when I was nine years old. I have one brother, who lives in a village with my uncle. He is studying in the ninth grade. My mom has been living with me. My mother is also working in a garment factory at Savar, as a sewing operator. She is earning 4,000–5,000 taka ($57.55–$71.94) per month including overtime duty. Often we get paid late.

We have rented one small room in the Mirpur neighborhood, which costs 1,500 taka ($21.58). The house is very simple, made of corrugated iron

Laborers in a garment factory. Photograph by Jenneke Arens. Used by permission of the photographer.

sheets. Inside the house it is very hot. There is some garbage around the house which smells bad. We rented this house a few months ago since it was too difficult to pay the 2,600 taka ($37.41) rent for our old room. We have a single wooden bed, a mirror, a hanger for keeping clothes and a rack for keeping plates and glasses.

For the two of us, we spend 5,000 taka ($71.94) a month for the simplest food. We eat rice three times a day with mashed or fried potatoes, or other kinds of vegetables and lentils. We can eat fish just once a week and meat or cheap broiler chicken just one day a month. The prices of all commodities have increased more than 100 percent in the last two or three years, but our salary has not increased at all. We have to spend 2,500 taka ($25.97) a month for my brother for his education and other costs. My uncle takes care of him, but we have to provide the expenditures for his education, food, clothing, etc.

We have no opportunity for recreation or entertainment. There is a 17-inch black-and-white television, but we cannot manage the time to watch it. When we return home, it is around 11:00 P.M. or 12:00 midnight. When we return from the factory, we have to cook food and we eat supper at midnight. We have no energy to watch TV then. My mom has one day off per week on Fridays. When relatives from our village visit our room, they usually come on Fridays.

We have to spend 2,500 taka ($35.97) for medical treatment. My mom is 45 years old. She became very weak after she suffered an electric shock about three years ago. She needs medicines regularly that cost more than 1,500 ($21.58) per month. My mother is planning to arrange a marriage for me after two years from now. But we need to save 70,000 to 100,000 taka ($1,007–$1,439) for arranging this marriage, for ornaments and the feast for guests.

There is also no security in our life. We do not have any health insurance. A few months back when I was coming from the factory at 12:00 midnight with my pay, some thieves attacked me and grabbed all my wages. I cried out that we are very poor and will starve without this money, but the robbers did not pay heed to me.

I walk to the factory, but my mother takes the bus to the factory. For transportation, she needs to spend 1,000 taka ($14.39) a month.

Due to our poor income, our lives are gradually getting ruined. We are trapped living in a small room with no facilities. There are only two gas burners, one toilet and one water pump for five families. So we have to wait in a queue for cooking or using the toilet. The bed we use is very uncomfortable, but we cannot buy a better one due to the shortage of money.

My brother is living far from us with my uncle in our village back home. We cannot bring him to live with us as the expenditure for education is much higher in Dhaka and we would need to rent a larger room if he comes. We have a small piece of land in our village, but there is no house. We had to sell our house after the death of my father. The food we are consuming every day is very poor. If the minimum wage is raised to 6,200 taka ($89.21) my wage would be higher, including overtime, and as a result we could eat fish once or twice a week and meat once a week. A wage increase would help us take care of our health. Right now we are always anxious about whether we can manage money to buy food or for medical treatment. We have never been able to save money for the future. In fact, we sometimes have to borrow money just to eat or for medicine. In truth, we live just from hand to mouth.

Translated from Bengali; translator not identified.

Bengali New Year

Shamsuzzaman Khan and Kajalie Shehreen Islam

Since 1989, Bengali New Year (Pohela Boishakh) has been celebrated publicly as never before. The Bengali year begins on April 14, which is the first day of the month of Boishakh. One of the holiday's high points in Dhaka is a festive parade featuring floats with enormous, colorful animals—peacocks, owls, frogs, tigers, elephants—as well as music and theater performances and food. Although Bengali New Year has long been important because it marked the festive annual settling of debts, the parade is a new tradition. Today it is a celebration of Bengali culture as well as a symbolic statement against communal (religious sectarian) politics, as this interview explains.

Every year on April 14, thousands of people in white-red saris and colourful *panjabis* [shirts] brave the heat to join the parades, *melas* [fairs] or family-and-friends gatherings around *panta-ilish* [soaked rice and hilsa fish] and a variety of *bharta* [mashed dishes]. Their faces painted, terra-cotta crafts and bright masks in hand, they celebrate the advent of the Bengali New Year. But has the day always been celebrated in this manner and what social relevance do these rituals have in our lives today?

Professor Shamsuzzaman Khan, Director-General of Bangla Academy, has spent most of his life studying Bengali culture and folklore. He has served as Director-General of the National Museum and Shilpakala Academy; taught at National University, Jagannath College and Bangladesh Agricultural University, Mymensingh[;] and edited and continues to edit journals and magazines.

On the occasion of Pahela Boishakh, Professor Khan talks to Kajalie Shehreen Islam of *The Daily Star* about the traditions surrounding the festivities, how they came about and their social significance for Bengalis.

How did the Bengali new year, that is, the Bengali calendar, come about?

The history of the Bengali new year and calendar is somewhat unclear and it is difficult to say exactly when it came about, but some assumptions can be made based on circumstantial evidence. The fact that it is called Bangla *san* or *saal*, which are Arabic and Parsee words respectively, suggests that it was introduced by a Muslim king or sultan. Some historians suggest Moghul emperor Akbar, as he had reformed the Indian calendar—with the help of his royal astronomer Fatehullah Shirajee—in line with the Iranian *nawroj* or new day. Others suggest it was the seventh-century king Sasanka.

I personally believe it was Nawab Murshid Quli Khan who was a *subedar* or Moghul governor and later a Nawab, who celebrated Bengali traditions such as the *Punyaha*, a day for ceremonial land tax collection. I believe he used Akbar's new year framework, revenue reforms and fiscal policy and started the Bangla calendar.

Why is Nababarsho [Bengali New Year] *celebrated on different days in Bangladesh and West Bengal?*

An expert committee headed by Professor SP Pandya, after much scientific deliberation, set the date and their report was published in the *Indian Journal of History of Science* in 2004, where it was clearly stated that "The year shall start with the month of Vaishakha when the sun enters nirayana Mesa rasi, which will be 14th April of the Gregorian Calendar." The Indian government accepted this in 2002 but has not been able to convince West Bengal to adopt it.

How do Pahela Boishakh *celebrations today compare to those you remember from your childhood?*

The main element back then was the *halkhata* or the ceremonial opening of a fresh ledger by businesses. In our agriculture-based society, people were short of cash and would often buy on credit. On the first day of the New Year, shop owners would decorate their shops with paper flowers and *dhoop* (incense) and lay out sweets for the customers who would repay their debts in full or at least in part. It was a matter of social prestige to do so.

In this context, I would like to quote Bangabandhu Sheikh Mujibur Rahman. I remember Bangabandhu, after forming the Planning Commission following the country's independence, saying that the members who were scholars trained in the west understood little about the lives of the rural people of Bangladesh, about the local context, geography, economy. "In our agriculture-based society, people do not have cash all

New Year's Day parade in Dhaka. Photograph by Palash Khan, © Palash Khan / leadfoto.com. Used by permission of the photographer.

year. Even our fathers and uncles would buy a sari for their wives and *hilsa* fish on the new year," said Bangabandhu.

Other *Nababarsho* traditions included the *lathi khela* [fighting with bamboo clubs] and of course the *mela* or fair which would begin a day early on *Chaitra Shankranti*, the last day of the Bengali year, and continue for two to three and up to seven days. The *mela* was a source of entertainment as well as a place to shop and stock up on necessities, mainly kitchen utensils such as *da, boti, kurol*, wooden crafts, children's toys, etc., which were all available at these fairs.

Then there were the *gorur larai* (bullfight), *morog larai* (cock fight), *putul naach* (puppet show), *jatra*, etc., some of which still take place in certain parts of the country, though not as much. For example, some people in far-flung *haor* areas [wetlands] of the country still invest in expensive bulls and raise them to be able to win the bullfight at the new year.

From where did we derive and what is the significance of traditions such as eating panta-ilish *on* Nababarsho?

Panta-ilish is, I think, an unfortunate joke towards the poor.

However, there was a tradition called *Amani*, according to which the woman of the house would, the night before, soak rice and the twig of a mango tree in a pot of water and on the morning of the new year, sprinkle it on everyone in the family. This was based on a magical belief that the water would wash away the mistakes and negative aspects of the past year and bring peace to the family. This tradition is also empowering for women as they have the responsibility of this *mangolik* or wishing-well ritual.

Some aspects are also taken from early *Nababarsho* festivals, namely, *Nabanno utshab*, which is a thanksgiving ritual in which *payesh* [sweet rice porridge] is laid out by the river or for birds to have and which is also believed to bring peace.

How do you see the way in which Pahela Boishakh *is celebrated today?*

I see it very positively. I think the celebrations are a sign of national cohesion regardless of religion, caste and creed. It is a national festival. It has taken positive aspects from *Amani, Nabanno*, etc., and is a wonderful mixture of several traditions. The parade brought out by the Institute of Fine Arts, for example, is an extension of the *michhil* or processions that used to be brought out in the villages. The parade with masks of owls, snakes and more have a multidimensional meaning and metaphor. They are a symbol of protest. They first began in 1989 when, under the autocratic rule of General Ershad, people could not protest openly and this was a symbolic way of doing so. Even today, they are symbols of protest against governments and political parties which are communal, oppressive, etc. Bengali culture is a mixed, secular culture and the *Pahela Boishakh* celebrations are a reflection of this, invigorating our culture even more.

Do you think Bengali culture is in the face of any threats?

There are the threats of globalisation, satellite culture, etc., but I believe our culture is so powerful that it will survive the onslaught of these. It has had to be accepted even by these elements, which use, for example, Baul songs, in perhaps a different form and of course for their own profit, but the important thing is that they are not being able to deny its presence and power. Bengali culture has the strength to adjust to new situations, and it is based on human values. The phrase that parents are always telling their children, *"Manush hou,"* cannot be translated into English; "be human" does not carry the same connotations that it does in Bengali. But the original phrase is proof of how humans and human values are put above everything else and that is the essence of our culture.

The Fundamentalist

Abdul Qader Mullah

A senior member of the Islamic Assembly (Jama'at-e-Islami, the most prominent Islamist political party of Bangladesh) criticizes national politics. He explains that following "Islamic ideology" will bring about a perfect society.

In our country, democracy is not there. The Prime Minister [Sheikh Hasina] would never be where she is if she were not the daughter of Sheikh Mujib. She has no political background. She is a housewife. Khaleda Zia, too, was never a political worker. If she were not the widow of Zia [President Ziaur Rahman], she would not be head of the party. The behaviour and mode of expression of these two women are not those of normal ladies. One is busy with revenge, the other with her husband's killing. Hasina thinks those entangled in her father's killing should be punished by any means. Women are emotional anyway, but how can these two be normal, think of the common people?

We cannot go back to the feelings of 20 years ago. History is important for learning and improving the future. We, in Jama'at, are free of this emotion. We work for an ideology which seeks to improve the social, judicial and economic system, even the political system.

What is written in the Koran is not practised by our leaders or by the common people. The ruling class prevents non-Muslim communities from understanding Islamic ideology. It was Bernard Shaw who said, "When I go through the Koran, it offers the best ideology for the improvement of human society, but when I see the society of the Muslims, this is the worst." If someone like Mohamad were dictator, he would remove all evils from the world, and people could live in heaven.

Sixty per cent of wealth of the world is in the hands of Muslims. Yet we have so many poor. More than 90 per cent of the world's homeless are Muslims—how will they say our religion, our ideology are the best? The Prophet says "If a Muslim has everything and allows his neighbour to pass his night without food, that man is not a Muslim." Whether the neighbour is Muslim or not is not important. Social inequality is against Islam. Those who have their money in the USA, their children educated there, their dogs have meat while the man who lives under his building has not 100 grammes in a month. Most of our wealth has been captured by a few, spread through corruption, illegal business. When they go to the Baitul Mokarram Masjid on Friday, that is hypocrisy.

This Land Is Your Land,
This Land Is Our Land

Farah Mehreen Ahmad

A young member of an activist writers' collective chides fellow Bangladeshis for keeping silent about human rights abuses and the treatment of minorities.

There are a few things I want to say to my peers.

Dost [friends], we the "new-new" don't know much about our history other than the heroism of our relatives, the brutality of the *hanadar bahini* [occupying forces], some specific dates, some illustrious names, and some songs.

When we wear a Che T-shirt, he looks like Michael Jackson. Most of us haven't read his biography. Most of us are unaware of his flaws. Yes, he had some. You'd know if you dug beyond the translation of "hasta la victoria siempre" [until victory, forever].

When we buy a T-shirt with "Joy Bangla" [Victory to Bangladesh] printed on it, we kind of know what it means. To us it resonates as something parallel to a "carpe diem/noctem" or "veni, vidi, vici" sort of deal or even a yin-yang tattoo.

History is not a thing of the past for us to relish on particular days. It is what we make every day, whether we know it or not—just by virtue of existing. When we were too busy being the Converse All-Star, Old Navy hoodie, and *gaamchha* [thin cotton towel] clad "casually classy" generation, Bengali settlers burnt down over two hundred homes of Bangladeshis who don't look like us. The army joined in and [killed several of them by brush fire]. And we were here making history—once again—with our silence.

We are going down in the books, babe, as the one that didn't speak up; as the one that when asked to attend a rally to protest said, "Kintu dost, oita toh plan a chhilona" [But that wasn't in the plan, buddy]. Sorry for the disruption, bud, but I don't think being subjected to this kind of atrocity *oder plan a chhilo* [was part of their plan].

Some elders tell us this land really isn't ours; that we don't respect our history and are too west bound and east wounded; that we really don't know what it means to be Bangladeshi since the *desh* [nation] was fed to us with a silver spoon. We resentfully worship the rubble we stand on, as if it's all over, as if there is nothing else to fight.

But there is one more thing left to be defined though. We have that one more [line] that shows when we say "us" we mean "them" too. Why did we vote in 2008, in what was arguably the most monumental political event we witnessed in our two-decades-and-then-some-old lives? I thought we took a few vows:

To not only chuckle when our friend laughingly tells us that his dad, an army officer, asked him to "stop acting like a bloody civilian" when he was disappointed, but be alarmed by how people who are paid to protect us see us.

To be repulsed by their gunshots and read it as *rokkhok* [protectors] morphing into homicidal *tokkhoks* [venomous beings], disrupting the silence we choose to bury those darn *paharis* [hill people] under.

To not only high-five me when I tell you how I walked into the checkpoint to give that officer a piece of my mind for winking at me, but remember how you especially loved the part where I told him that he gets paid to protect me and I have the right to make him surrender his uniform if he makes me feel vulnerable. Since playing poker is your favourite after-work pastime, can you [muster] that same [enthusiasm for] the hills and raise it a thousand notches?

To not forget to notice the face some several inches above the *pinon* [hill women's skirt] your sister was wondering where she could buy.

To notice the human being whose dancing feet you watched admiringly while saying "era kintu ektu Thai-der moton, na?" [They look a bit like Thais, don't they?].

To cringe at the patronizing generalization when the aunty asked for a Chakma [one of Bangladesh's hill minority communities] cook because "ora khub sincere hoy" [they're so honest] or a night guard of the same because "ora khub teji hoy" [they're so spirited]. To burst this greedy and exploitative bubble of fantasy traits attributed to those who are forced to be third-class citizens for our needs and convenience, as if their sole purpose is to serve us—the Raj.

To slap our friend who has a crush on his Chakma classmate and calls her "minority" behind her back as if that's her name, and allows his friends to do the same. "Dost, Minority'r shathe khub mojaye asos na?" [Hey, bud, having a swell time with Minority, I see?].

To not pervert "majority rule" to mean the rule of a power tripping, vile, and nonchalant majority, but the rule of a conscientious majority. To put an end to those darn [categories]—"foreign" . . . "stranger" . . . "unknown" . . . "different" . . . "them."

To harness a Bangladesh that isn't exclusively for Bangalis.

Can we vow to not allow evil to defecate all over our Home? Can we fix our radars to catch their [hill people's] corpses though we have skipped their lives? One of these days during one of those *addas* [chats] at one of those coffee joints, can we touch on their plight? Maybe just throw in a "dost, oi paharigulir na life a onek para . . . purai bad buzz" [Buddy, those hill people have a raw deal . . . a real bad buzz], for good measure?

How They Discriminate Me

Roshni Rani

There are roughly eleven million Hindus in Bangladesh, the largest Hindu popula-
tion in any country except India and Nepal. Hindus are an important minority in
Bangladesh and they are highly differentiated. In this firsthand account, Roshni
Rani, a woman from Kushtia (a town in western Bangladesh), speaks of gender
discrimination among her low-caste community—and how hard it is for women to
take part in decision making.

"Boy or girl, two is enough"—that statement has failed to make its way
into the Harijan [Dalit, the lowest caste] community. Boys are assets and
girls are a burden—this is currently the predominant conception among
the Harijans. When a male child is born, the whole community rejoices.
But when a girl is born, a completely different emotion prevails. This is the
first barrier in the development of a girl child. Parents of a boy think about
every minute aspect of their child's future. But parents of a girl do not even
give a passing thought to planning their little daughter's future. "Health is
wealth." When children are healthy, both their bodies and their minds are
alert. If a child, whether a boy or girl, does not get care, love, nutritious
food, and the freedom to play from childhood, then his or her development
is stunted.

From their earliest childhood, girls are not allowed to play with boys.
Moreover, parents think if girls go outside they will be spoiled, if they are
allowed to play outside it will degrade the reputation of the family . . . "people will talk," they whisper. In this way, girls are discriminated from their
very birth. Although my brother is younger than I, he has more chances to
play than I. When my brother is playing or going to school, I am busy working in the household. Most Harijan girls are involved in child labour. Not
only that, they are also engaged in risky and injurious work. For example,
a girl of seven, eight years old should play but she has to cook and do other
heavy household chores. Moreover, their parents do not give them any directions or advice when they go through the physical and mental changes of

Harijan women demonstrating in the streets of Kushtia town. Photograph by Willem van Schendel, 2006.

puberty. Even when someone from outside tries to educate us, our parents do not welcome such advice but become suspicious. For example, a senior woman from FAIR [a local NGO] came to educate us in reproductive health, but our parents declared that she had come to spoil and corrupt us girls. Her intervention would make the girls unruly, they thought. But later they were properly briefed and they allowed the session to begin. Those of us who attended the workshop understood that to protect ourselves we should have a thorough knowledge about reproductive healthcare.

There is will, but no way, among Harijan women. A girl may think that she will grow up to be something better and be successful in life but her wish remains unfulfilled. Education is not approved of for girls, though many desire it. Parents think that it is a waste of money to pay for a girl's education. They think a girl belongs to the family of her future husband and will leave her father's home once she is married. As a result, child marriage is very common in the Harijan community. Parents want to marry off their daughters early so that some of their financial burdens are relieved. Therefore, when the girl goes to her in-laws' house at a young age, she faces physical, mental, and sexual oppression. Moreover, she becomes a mother at a very young age and, due to lack of adequate knowledge, both mother and child suffer from malnutrition. Most efforts of Harijan women to attain conjugal bliss tend to end in disaster. Sometimes it becomes difficult for them even to stay in a marital relationship. Usually, after a long day, her husband arrives at night, completely drunk. And then he begins bout after bout of physical and mental torture. He beats up his wife, uses foul language, and, without any proof, accuses her of suspicious behaviour. The Harijan community has a social council but there is no participation of women in its decision making, even when the woman is a plaintiff or an accused.

I think that women should participate in the social council because otherwise women's rights will always be violated. Why is there so much discrimination against women in our society? Can't we find a way out of this?

Translated from Bengali by Sushmita Hossain Natasha.

II

Early Histories

As a sovereign country, Bangladesh is only forty years old, but people have been living in this great delta and its surrounding hills for hundreds of generations. Archaeological findings show that agriculture was introduced early on and that around 500 BCE an important shift occurred when rice cultivation on permanent, irrigated fields spread across the region. This allowed for much higher population densities and the growth of urban centers. The tropical monsoon climate and a scarcity of durable building material—there are no stone quarries in the delta, so bamboo, wood, mud, and adobe were the materials of choice—means that relatively few buildings and artifacts survived from early times. As a result, there is much uncertainty about Bangladesh's earliest societies.

What we now call Bangladesh has been known under many other names in the past. Among these are East Bengal and East Pakistan, but for the earlier periods it is best to speak of the Bengal Delta and its surrounding hill country. The Bengal Delta has always been a crossroads, linking enormous river systems (notably the Ganges and Brahmaputra) with the Indian Ocean. Its cities were important nodes of long-distance trade and cultural exchange. Here traders from Tibet, north India, Persia, Southeast Asia, China, Sri Lanka, the Maldives, and Arabia met on a regular basis, and the goods that the Bengal Delta exported could be found from ancient Greece and Rome to Central Asia and China. In addition to trade, politics and administration showed the openness of the delta. Over the centuries, state power was sometimes in the hands of local rulers but often it was not. Non-Bengali rulers included Afghans, Turks, north Indians, Arakanese, and Ethiopians.

This part contains some clues to trace developments from about 300 BCE to 1750 CE: the early introduction of writing, observations by visitors from foreign lands, the development of the Bengali language (now the national language), important religious and ethnic permutations, and the rise and fall of states. Together the pieces introduce the regional specificity of the

There is a centuries-old tradition of excavating large rectangular ponds in Bangladesh. Here we see the huge Horse Pond (Ghora Dighi) that was created in the fifteenth century in the southern town of Bagerhat. Photograph by Willem van Schendel, 2006.

cultures that emerged in what is now Bangladesh. Set in the middle of this collection is a powerful interpretation (by Richard M. Eaton) of the ultimate expression of that regional specificity: over the centuries the Bengal Delta—unlike any of the regions surrounding it—saw most of its inhabitants adopt Islamic identities.

The Earliest Inscription

Anonymous

In November 1931, Baru Faqir of Bogra district found a piece of stone that turned out to contain the oldest inscription found so far in Bangladesh. Baru Faqir lived in Mahasthan, a village located on the earliest and largest archaeological site of Bangladesh. Today the monumental brick walls of the ancient city of Pundranagara (or Pudanagala) can still be seen here, and archaeologists continue to excavate the site, which has been occupied continuously for several millennia.

The inscription soon became known as the Mahasthan Brahmi Inscription. Written in the Prakrit language and the Brahmi script, it dates from about 300 BCE. The text reveals an urban administration handing out food from its granary to victims of natural disasters. It also shows that the local economy was monetized. The Gandaka mentioned in the text may have been a coin worth four cowries—small shells imported from the faraway Maldive Islands. Cowries continued to be used as currency in Bangladesh up to the nineteenth century.

Some archaeologists have suggested that the inscription supports the idea that Pundranagara was an eastern outpost of the Maurya Empire, which ruled over large tracts of India at the time.

The Mahasthan Brahmi inscription, c. 300 BCE. From *Banglapedia: National Encyclopedia of Bangladesh*, vol. 6 (Dhaka: Asiatic Society of Bangladesh, 2003), 350. Image © Banglapedia Trust. Used by permission.

To Gobardhana of the Samvamgiyas [ethnic or religious group] was granted by order sesamum and mustard seeds. The Sumatra [group of people] will cause it to be carried out from the prosperous city of Pundranagara. [And likewise] will cause paddy to be granted to the Samvamgiyas. In order to tide over the outbreak of distress caused by flood [or fire, or superhuman agency] and insects [parrots?] in the city, this granary and treasury will have to be replenished with paddy and Gandaka coins.

Translated from Prakrit/Magadhi by Jean-François Salles.

A View from the Sea

Anonymous

The ancient Greeks used to write what they called periploi, *documents that listed the seaports and landmarks that the captain of a ship would find along a shore. In the first century* CE, *a Greek in Egypt wrote one of these for the Red Sea and the Indian Ocean. Fortunately, a copy of this unique text survives in a Byzantine manuscript from the tenth century. It describes the coast of India up until the region that we now call Bangladesh.*

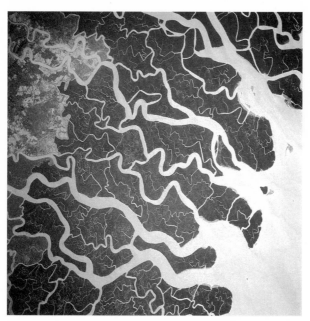

In early times mangrove forests covered most of the unstable coastal islands of Bangladesh. Today the remaining mangroves, the most extensive in the world, are known as the Sundarbans. Here they are observed from space. Photography by the Science & Analysis Laboratory, NASA Johnson Space Center, Houston, 1997. Courtesy of nasaimages.org.

Sailing with the ocean to the right and the shore remaining beyond to the left, Ganges [a town] comes into view, and near it the very last land towards the east, Chryse. There is a river near it called the Ganges, and it rises and falls in the same way as the Nile. On its bank is a market town that has the same name as the river, Ganges. Through this place are brought malabathrum [cassia leaves or *tej pata*] and Gangetic spikenard [muskroot or *jatamangshi*] and pearls, and muslins of the finest sort, which are called Gangetic. It is said that there are gold mines near these places, and there is a gold coin which is called *caltis*. And just opposite this river there is an island in the ocean, the last part of the inhabited world towards the east, under the rising sun itself; it is called Chryse, and it has the best tortoise-shell of all places on the Erythraean Sea [Indian Ocean].

Translated from Greek by Wilfred H. Schoff.

Jackfruits and a Jade Buddha

Xuanzang

Over the centuries, many Chinese pilgrims visited India to receive instruction in the Buddhist faith and to visit holy places. Perhaps the most famous is Xuanzang, who traveled widely in Central and South Asia in the early seventh century CE. His fame is based on the observant account of his travels that he wrote after his return to China. In his book, Buddhist Records of the Western World, *he describes his visits to two centers of Buddhist learning in Bangladesh around 640 CE. The capital of the first center, Pundravarddhana, is Mahasthan—the city in northern Bangladesh that also yielded Bangladesh's earliest inscription. The capital of the second, Samatata, is Mainamati (then known as Devaparvata), near contemporary Comilla town. Xuanzang describes how he finds devotees of different religious traditions living together in these cities, and he is much impressed by a huge Buddha image made of green jade. Finally, like many visitors to Bangladesh before and after him, he marvels at the sight and taste of the ubiquitous jackfruit.*

Pu-na-fa-tan-na (Pundravarddhana)

This country is about 4,000 li [six hundred kilometers] in circuit. Its capital is about 30 li [twelve kilometers] round. It is thickly populated. Offices connected with river navigation, with their surrounding flowers and groves, occur at regular intervals. The soil is flat and loamy, and rich in all kinds of grain produce. The jackfruit, though plentiful, is highly esteemed. The fruit is as large as a pumpkin. When it is ripe it is of a yellowish-red colour. When divided, it has in the middle many tens of little fruits of the size of a pigeon's egg; breaking these, there comes forth a juice of a yellowish-red colour and of delicious flavour. The fruit sometimes collects on the tree branches as other clustering fruits, but sometimes at the tree roots, as in the case of the earth-growing *fu ling* [China root].

The climate is temperate; the people esteem learning. There are about twenty monasteries, with some three thousand priests; they study both the Little and Great Vehicle [the two main branches of Buddhism: Theravada

Gold-plated statue of a *bodhisattva* (a being on the path to enlightenment) from Mahasthan (Pundravarddhana) in northern Bangladesh, seventh to eighth century. From the Kern Special Collections at the Leiden University Library, University of Leiden. Photograph © Leiden University Library, Kern Institute, P-038529. Used by permission.

and Mahayana]. There are some hundred Dêva [Brahmanical] temples, where sectaries of different schools congregate. The naked Nirgranthas [Jains] are the most numerous.

Some 20 li [eight kilometers] to the west of the capital is the Po-chi-p'o [Vasibha] monastery. Its courts are light and roomy; its towers and pavilions are very lofty. The priests are about seven hundred in number; they study the law according to the Great Vehicle. Many renowned priests from Eastern India dwell here.

Not far from this is a stupa built by King Asoka. Here Tathâgata [Buddha], in old days, preached the law for three months for the sake of the Dêvas. Occasionally, on fast-days, there is a bright light visible around it.

By the side of this, again, is a place where the four past Buddhas walked for exercise and sat down. The bequeathed traces are still visible.

Not far from this there is a monastery in which there is a statue of Kwan-tsz'-tsai Bodhisattva. Nothing is hid from its divine discernment; its spiritual perception is most accurate; men far and near consult [this being] with fasting and prayers.

San-mo-ta-cha (Samatata)

This country is about 3000 li [twelve hundred kilometer] in circuit and borders on the great sea. The land is low and is rich. The capital is about 20 li [eight kilometers] round. It is regularly cultivated, and is rich in crops, and the flowers and fruits grow everywhere. The climate is soft and the habits of the people agreeable. The men are hardy by nature, small of stature, and of black complexion; they are fond of learning, and exercise themselves diligently in the acquirement of it. There are believers both of false and true doctrines. There are thirty or so monasteries with about two thousand priests. They are all of the Sthavira [Theravada Buddhist] school. There are some hundred Dêva temples, in which sectaries of all kinds live. The naked ascetics called Nirgranthas are most numerous.

Not far out of the city is a stupa, which was built by King Asoka. In this place Buddha [Tathâgata] in former days preached the deep and mysterious law for seven days for the good of the Dêvas. By the side of it [the stupa] are traces where the four Buddhas sat and walked for exercise.

Not far from this, in a monastery, is a figure of Buddha of green jade. It is eight feet high, with the marks on its person perfectly shown, and with a spiritual power which is exercised from time to time.

Translated from Chinese by Samuel Beal.

Songs of Realization

Bhusuku-pada, Sabara-pada, and Kukkuri-pada

In Bangladesh, ritual forms of worship and spiritual practices that aim at liberation from ignorance and rebirth have been popular for a very long time. Practitioners of these "tantric" traditions may seek liberation by performing dances during which they improvise "songs of realization." These charya *songs give expression to the mystics' heightened clarity and bliss.*

A collection of such songs, composed by numerous poets between the eighth and eleventh centuries CE *and recorded on palm leaf, was discovered in the library of the royal court of Nepal in 1907. The collection, named* Charyapada, *turned out to be a major find because it contained the earliest written examples of the Bengali language. Similarly, other major modern languages such as Assamese, Oriya, and Maithili trace their histories to songs in the* Charyapada.

Little is known about the composers of these songs except that they were all Buddhist monks. Bhusuku-pada, Sabara-pada, and Kukkuri-pada, whose mystic songs of realization appear here, are thought to have been from Bengal and to have lived in the eighth or ninth century CE.

CHARYAPADA 6, *by Bhusuku-pada*
Who have I accepted and who have I given up?
All sides are surrounded by the cries of the hunter.
The deer's own flesh is his enemy.
Bhusuku the hunter does not spare him for a moment.
The deer touches no green, nor drinks water.
He does not know where the doe lives.
The doe tells the deer: leave this forest, and free yourself.
Thus the deer sped for his life, leaving no hoof-marks behind.
Bhusuku says "this does not reach the heart of the unwise."

CHARYAPADA 28, *by Sabara-pada*
The mountains are high, the Sabari [hunter] girl lives there.
She wears peacock feathers.

One of the Charyapada songs, written on palm leaf. From Hasna Jasimuddin Moudud. *A Thousand Year Old Bengali Mystic Poetry* (Dhaka: University Press Limited, 1992). Used by permission of The University Press Limited.

Her neck is adorned with a necklace of *gunja* [rosary pea] berries.
O wild Sabara, o mad Sabara,
Do not cry or make a noisy complaint.
Your own wife is the Sahaja Sundari [a goddess].
The tree blossomed into flowers, the branch touched the sky.
Sabari wears ear-ornaments and *vajra* [ritual thunderbolt].
She wanders in this forest alone.
The bed of three metals is placed.
Sabara spreads the bed with great pleasure.
Sabara the lover and Sabari his mistress made love into the morning.
The heart is a betel leaf, eating camphor with great enjoyment.
By embracing the Void in his neck he passes the night in bliss.
Consider the Guru's advice as your bow and, with you mind as the
    arrow,
Pierce through Nirvana in one try.

CHARYAPADA 48, *by Kukkuri-pada*
Kulish and Karuna are united.
The army is in deep sleep.
The senses are won over.
Great bliss becomes king of the Void.
The shell played the *anahata* [unplayed] sound.
The magic tree and the worldly powers fled away.
Kukkuri-pa raised his finger aloft and said:
In the City of Bliss all has been won over.
The three worlds became filled with great bliss.
So says Kukkuri-pa in great content.

Translated from old Bengali by Hasna Jasimuddin Moudud.

A King's Gift of Land

Anonymous

In the past, the territory we now know as Bangladesh bore many different names. In recent centuries it was best known as eastern Bengal but in ancient texts, such as the one reprinted here, we come across other terms. Scholars think that these refer to various regions of the country. It is impossible to be sure, however, where exactly these regions were located: different historical sources contradict each other, the meaning of the terms has changed over the centuries, and the political geography of the region has been volatile. Nevertheless, it is generally assumed that Pundra was in northern Bangladesh, Vanga (or Vangala) was in central Bangladesh, Samatata was in southeastern Bangladesh, and Harikela was in eastern Bangladesh.

The modern term Bangla is derived from Vangala. It refers to both the region (Bengal) and its dominant language (Bengali). Inhabitants of the region are known as Bangali (Bengali in English). Today Bengal is divided. Its eastern parts are administered by the state of Bangladesh (desh means country) and its western parts by India.

At the time of the land gift described here, a lineage known as the Chandra dynasty ruled over eastern and central Bangladesh. The capital was in Vikramapura (Bikrampur), near contemporary Dhaka. This copperplate inscription dates from the middle of the tenth century CE. It publicly announces that King Srichandra ("an excellent follower of the Buddha") had donated land in perpetuity to Srikaradatta Sarman ("protector of Brahmans"). The inscription warns that the gift must be respected, by (future) kings as well as "by farmers dwelling there, who are obliged to hear this command." The inscription gives us a glimpse of power relations, religious diversity, landlordism, and royal style in Bangladesh a thousand years ago.

Siddham, success to you! Venerable is the blessed Victor, the single vessel of mercy, and victorious, furthermore, is the law, the single light to the world, through the worship of both of which the whole great community of monks attains the end of the cycle of existence. Now, in the lineage of the powerful and prosperous Chandras, rulers of Rohitagiri, was one like the full moon who was celebrated in the world as the blessed Purnachandra. He was mentioned before his descendants in the pedestals of images [as well as] on victory columns, which had freshly chisel-hewn benedictions, and on copperplates. His son, Suvarnachandra, a Buddhist, was renowned in the world as if because he was born into the respectable family of the Moon, that is, the Lord possessing beams that are a mine of nectar, who lovingly bears the Buddha's hare incarnation stationed in his spot. It is said that on the new moon day his mother, on account of her pregnancy while desiring to see the orb of the moon rising, was gratified because of [the sight of] the golden moon [*suvarnacandra*] [and] so they call [him] "Suvarnachandra." His son Trailokyachandra, the sanctifier of both families, who was the abode feared by improper conduct, was known in the three worlds [*trailokya*] through his qualities by travellers of all directions.

He who resembled Dilipa became king on the island that has the name "Chandra" prefixed to it, and he was a receptacle of the good fortune that had blossomed under the royal umbrella insignia of the king of Harikela. As Jyotsna to Chandra, Sachi to Jisnu, Gauri to Hara, and Sri to Hari, his beloved—having the splendour of gold [*kancana*]—was to him whose commands were respected [called] 'Srikanchana.' Possessing Indra's radiance [and] understanding prudent policy, he [i.e. Trailokyachandra] at a moment made auspicious through a lunar conjunction attained through her [i.e. Srikanchana] a son, Srichandra, who resembled the moon [and] in whom astrologers observed the marks of [a future] king. Having made the earth embellished with a single umbrella, he [i.e. Srichanda] was not obedient to fools, put his enemies into prisons, and made the four directions fragrant with his fame. You should know that, from the illustrious triumphal-headquarters, which were established at the blessed city of Vikrama [i.e. Vikramapura], he—an excellent follower of the Buddha—is the rightful successor of the blessed lord Trailokyachandra and a king among great kings. Lord Srichandra, the highest Lord, the noble Lord, a king among great kings, is prosperous. With regard to this [one] *pataka* of land, [in the town of] Vyaghravoraka, belonging to the district of Srinagara, in the region of Samatata, in the middle of the great province of Paundra, he [i.e. Srichandra] appropriately honours, addresses, inscribes, and commands all who have gathered together: the queen, noblemen, princes, king's ministers, regional rulers, military planners, ministers of foreign affairs, generals, record keepers, administrators, head of the king's doors, minister of forts, those who catch dangerous robbers, those who remove thieves, officiators over the fleets, elephants, horses, cows, buffaloes, goats, and sheep, etc., commanders of troops, tax inspectors, junior police, sergeants, and police chiefs, governors of districts, and the like, as well as other servants of the

Seated Buddha, Comilla District, Pala period bronze, eighth to early
ninth century CE. From the collection of the Metropolitan Museum of
Art, 1984.486.5. Photograph © 2011 SCALA Group SpA.

king: those said to work as inspectors and those who were not announced
here: members of the communities of Chatas and Bhatas, citizens, farmers,
and leading Brahmans.

   It must be understood by all of you [present] that this land, as inscribed
[in this plate] above, which is limited by its own boundaries, is flanked on
all sides with pastures of *puti*-grass, with its low-lying and elevated land,
along with its mango, breadfruit, betel-nut and cocoa-nut trees, with salt
[derived from sea water], with [fresh] water and dry land, with its salt-rich
soils and caves, with the [removal of] the ten faults, with the eradication of
robbers, with all sorts of impositions removed, it is without interference
from [the communities of] Chatas and Bhatas, free from taxation which is
associated with levies of gold on all royal subsidies [is granted by us], hav-

ing first performed the water ceremony according to the rules, [I grant this land] to the one who officiates the Kotihoma ritual, the blessed Srikaradatta Sarman, who is the son of Varadatta, grandson of Varadatta, great-grandson of Bhattaputravodhadattasarman, and a protector of Brahmans, who hails from the village of Hastipada in the Sravasti region.

He [i.e. Srikaradatta] is a student of the Vedas belonging to the Kuthumin school, part of the Chhandoga school, as well as the ancestry connected to three Risis, and belonging to the Parasara lineage. In the name of the venerable lord Buddha, for the increased merit and fame of our parents, until the time of the destruction of the sun and the moon, [this land] is given by us according to the laws of land-division, recording it in a copperplate grant with the seal of the blessed Dharmachakra. Henceforth, by everyone, this gift of land is to be respected; by future kings, in particular, it is to be recognized and protected, in the case of [attempts at] taking it back, on account of the importance of the potential of the gift and for fear of falling into the Great Hell; and by farmers dwelling there, who are obliged to hear this command, [this gift of land] is to be made to bring about enough yield as is appropriate.

Furthermore, here are some verses in regards to relating the [wisdom of] Dharma: Both the one who receives this land and the one who gives the land produce merit and are sure to go to heaven. Land has been given by many kings from Sagara onwards. Whosoever owns land, that one gains its benefits. He who gives back this gift or who takes [the land] of another man shall be tormented along with his ancestors, after turning into a worm in excrement.

Translated from Sanskrit by Benjamin J. Fleming.

Note

The bracketed material was published in the original translation.

A Visit to Sylhet

Ibn Battutah

In the fourteenth century CE, Bengal was divided among many different kingdoms that vied for regional power. It was also a period in which many visitors, adventurers, and religious messengers arrived from Central and West Asia. One of these was Shah Jalal, probably born in Konya, Turkey, who arrived with a group of followers in Sylhet (northeastern Bangladesh), possibly as part of an army to defeat a local ruler. Shah Jalal settled here and soon became famous for his miraculous acts and spiritual powers. Some thirty years later, in 1346 CE, he received a visit from Ibn Battutah. This traveler from Morocco had heard of Shah Jalal's fame and took a detour to Sylhet after he had been shipwrecked in the Indian Ocean on his way to China. Ibn Battutah wrote the description here (the only eyewitness account of Shah Jalal that we have), which is part of an account of his travels that would make him famous.

Shah Jalal was a Sufi missionary, a member of the Islamic cult that seeks to establish a direct relationship with Allah through meditation, preaching, and asceticism. The first Sufis had arrived in Bengal some 150 years before Shah Jalal and they would continue to trickle into the region for centuries. They were instrumental in spreading Islam in various parts of the region. Shah Jalal died a year after his meeting with Ibn Battutah, and Shah Jalal's tomb became a place where his followers would come to pray for his blessing. Today his shrine is one of the largest and most venerated, drawing thousands of devotees from all over South Asia. The Sufi tradition of turning the grave of a spiritual guide into an object of veneration is highly popular in Bangladesh, even though more scriptural interpretations of Islam frown on it.

I sailed for Bengal, which is an extensive and plentiful country. I never saw a country in which provisions were so cheap. . . . The first town we entered here was Sadkawan [Chittagong], which is large and situated on the sea-shore. . . . From Sadkawan I travelled to the mountains of Kamru [Kamrup], which are at the distance of one month from this place. These are extensive mountains, and they join the mountains of Tibet, where there are musk

Caps for sale at Shah Jalal's shrine in Sylhet. Photograph by Willem van Schendel, 2001.

gazelles. . . . My object in visiting these mountains was to meet one of the saints, namely, [Shah Jalal of Sylhet].[1]

This Sheikh was one of the greatest saints, and one of those singular individuals who had the power of working great and notable miracles. He had also lived to a remarkably great age. He told me that he had seen El Mostaasim, the Caliph in Baghdad [and was there when he was killed in 1258 CE]. . . . [H]is companions told me afterwards that he had died at the age of one hundred and fifty years; that he fasted through a space of about forty years, never breaking his fast till he had fasted throughout ten successive days. He had a cow, on the milk of which he usually breakfasted; and his practice was to [stand] up all night. [He was skinny and tall and he had a thin beard.] It was by his means that the people of these mountains became Mahommedans; and on this account it was, that he resided among them. . . .

When I was on my journey to see this Sheikh, four of his companions met me at the distance of two days [from where he lived], and told me that the Sheikh had said to the Fakeers who were with him, "A Western religious traveller is coming to you: Go out and meet him." "It was," said they, "by the order of the Sheikh that we came to you"—notwithstanding the fact that he had no knowledge whatever of my circumstances, except what he had by divine revelation. I went with them accordingly to his cell [outside] the cave, near which there was no building whatever. The people of this country are partly Mohammedans and partly infidels, both of whom visit the Sheikh and bring valuable presents. On these the Fakeers, and other people who arrive here, subsist. As for the Sheikh himself, he confines himself to the milk of his cow, as already mentioned. When I presented myself to him he arose and embraced me. He then asked me of my country and travels, of which I informed him. He then said to the Fakeers, "Treat him honourably." They accordingly carried me to the cell and kept me as their guest for three days.

On the day I presented myself to the Sheikh he had on a religious garment made of fine goat's hair. I was astonished at it and said to myself, "I wish the Sheikh would give it to me." When I went in to bid him farewell, he arose and went to the side of the cave, took off his goat's hair garment as well as the fillet of his head and his sleeves, and put them on me.

The Fakeers then told me that it was not his practice to put on this garment, and that he had put it on only on the occasion of my coming, for he had said to them, "This garment will be wished for by a Mogrebine [person from the Maghreb] but an infidel king shall take it from him and shall give it to our brother Borhan Oddin of Sagirj, whose it is, and for whose use it has been made."

When I was told this by the Fakeers, I said, "As I have a blessing from the Sheikh, and as he has clothed me with one of his own clothes, I will never enter with them into the presence of any king either infidel or Moslem." . . .

When, however, I had bid farewell to [Shah Jalal], I travelled to the city of Habank [Habiganj?], which is very large and beautiful; it is divided by the river which descends from the mountains of Kamru, called the Blue River [the Meghna?]. By this one may travel to Bengal and the countries of Laknouti. Upon it are gardens, mills and villages, which it refreshes and gladdens like the Nile of Egypt. The inhabitants of these parts are infidels, tributary to the Mohammedans. By this river I travelled for fifteen days, proceeding from road to road, till I came to the city of Sunarkawan [Sonargaon]. Here I found a junk, which was proceeding to Java [Sumatra], between which and this place there is a distance of forty days.

Translated from Arabic by Samuel Lee.

Note

1. Ibn Battutah calls him Shaikh Jalal Uddin of Tabriz but this is clearly an error because this was the name of one of the founders of the Suhrawardi order of Sufis in India, who had died about a century earlier.

The Rise of Islam

Richard M. Eaton

*In his detailed and authoritative study of the emergence of Islam as a popular reli-
gion in Bengal, Richard Eaton takes issue with a widespread notion of Islam as "an
unassimilated 'foreign' intrusion" into Bengal, often seen as the result of conversion
by the sword. On the contrary, he demonstrates that, over a period of centuries,
Bengalis—mostly in the eastern part of Bengal—gradually indigenized Islamic elements by adding them to their preexisting beliefs, creating a completely new blend
of Bengali and Islamic worldviews. In other words, "when figures like Adam, Eve
and Abraham became identified with central leitmotifs of Bengali history and civilization, Islam had become established as profoundly and authentically Bengali."
Eaton's abridged introduction outlines this process, which set eastern Bengal apart
from all surrounding regions—and surprisingly foreshadowed a country called
Bangladesh that would emerge many centuries later.*

Sometime in 1243–44, residents of Lakhnauti, a city in northwestern Bengal,
told a visiting historian of the dramatic events that had taken place there
forty years earlier. At that time, the visitor was informed, a band of several
hundred Turkish cavalry had ridden swiftly down the Gangetic Plain in the
direction of the Bengal delta. Led by a daring officer named Muhammad
Bakhtiyar, the men overran venerable Buddhist monasteries in neighboring Bihar before turning their attention to the northwestern portion of the
delta, then ruled by a mild and generous Hindu monarch. Disguising themselves as horse dealers, Bakhtiyar and his men slipped into the royal city
of Nudiya. Once inside, they rode straight to the king's palace, where they
confronted the guards with brandished weapons. Utterly overwhelmed, for
he had just sat down to dine, the Hindu monarch hastily departed through
a back door and fled with many of his retainers to the forested hinterland of
eastern Bengal, abandoning his kingdom altogether.

This coup d'état inaugurated an era, lasting over five centuries, during which most of Bengal was dominated by rulers professing the Islamic
faith. In itself this was not exceptional, since from about this time until the

eighteenth century, Muslim sovereigns ruled over most of the Indian subcontinent. What was exceptional, however, was that among India's interior
provinces only in Bengal—a region approximately the size of England and
Scotland combined—did a majority of the indigenous population adopt
the religion of the ruling class, Islam. This outcome proved to be as fateful
as it is striking, for in 1947 British India was divided into two independent
states, India and Pakistan, on the basis of the distribution of Muslims. In
Bengal, those areas with a Muslim majority would form the eastern wing
of Pakistan—since 1971, Bangladesh—whereas those parts of the province
with a Muslim minority became the state of West Bengal within the Republic of India. In 1984 about 93 million of the 152 million Bengalis in Bangladesh and West Bengal were Muslims, and of the estimated 96.5 million
people inhabiting Bangladesh, 81 million, or 83 percent, were Muslims; in
fact, Bengalis today comprise the second largest Muslim ethnic population
in the world, after the Arabs.

How can one explain this development? More particularly, why did such
a large Muslim population emerge in Bengal—so distant from the Middle
East, from which Islam historically expanded—and not in other regions of
India? And within Bengal, why did Islamization occur at so much greater
a rate in the east than in the west? Who converted and why? At what time?
What, if anything, did "conversion" mean to contemporary Bengalis? And
finally, between the thirteenth and eighteenth centuries, in what ways did
different generations and different social classes of Muslims in Bengal understand, construe, or even construct, Islamic civilization? In seeking answers to these questions, this study explores processes embedded in the
delta's premodern history that may cast light on the evolution of Bengal's
extraordinary cultural geography.

Bengal's historical experience was extraordinary not only in its widespread reception of Islam but also in its frontier character. In part, the
thirteenth-century Turkish drive eastward—both to Bengal and within
Bengal—was the end product of a process triggered by political convulsions
in thirteenth-century Inner Asia. For several centuries before and after the
Mongol irruption into West Asia, newly Islamicized Turks from Central
Asia and the Iranian Plateau provided a ready supply of soldiers, both as
slaves and as free men, for commanders such as Muhammad Bakhtiyar.
Once within Bengal's fertile delta, these men pushed on until stopped only
by geographical barriers. Surrounded on the north and east by mountains,
and to the south by the sea, Bengal was the terminus of a continent-wide
process of Turko-Mongol conquest and migration. It was, in short, a frontier
zone.

In reality, Bengal in our period possessed not one but several frontiers, each moving generally from west to east. One of these was the political frontier, which defined the territories within which the Turks and their successors, the Bengal sultans and governors of the Mughal Empire, minted coins, garrisoned troops, and collected revenue. A second, the agrarian frontier, divided settled agricultural communities from the forest, Bengal's natural state before humans attacked it with ax and plow. A third was the Islamic frontier, which divided Muslim from non-Muslim communities. A porous phenomenon, as much mental as territorial in nature, this last was the frontier that proved so fateful in 1947. Finally, all three frontiers were superimposed on a much older one, a frontier defined by the long-term eastward march of Sanskritic civilization in the Bengal delta. Characterized either by an egalitarian agrarian society organized around Buddhist monastic institutions or by a hierarchically ordered agrarian society presided over by Brahman priests, Sanskritic civilization in both its Buddhist and its Brahmanic forms had moved down the Gangetic Plain and into the Bengal delta many centuries before Muhammad Bakhtiyar's coup of 1204.

After the establishment of Muslim power in Bengal, the political frontier was extended as the new rulers and their successors overpowered or won over centers of entrenched agrarian interests. As aliens occupying the country by force of arms, Muslim soldiers and administrators were generally concentrated in garrison settlements located in or near pre-conquest urban centers. This was natural in those parts of the delta where the conquerors encountered developed agrarian communities, for by controlling the cities they could control the agriculturally rich hinterland, linked to cities by markets and revenue-paying networks. The Turkish occupation of Bengal thus followed the settlement pattern found throughout the early Delhi sultanate, anticipating in this respect the cantonment city employed by the British in their occupation of India in the nineteenth century.

Of a very different nature was Bengal's agrarian frontier, which divided the delta's cultivated terrain from the wild forests or marshlands that were as yet unpenetrated, or only lightly penetrated, by plow agriculture and agrarian society. Whereas the political frontier was man-made and subject to rapid movement, the agrarian frontier was more stable, slower-moving, and shaped by natural as well as human forces. Prominent among these natural forces was the historic movement of Bengal's rivers, which in the long run caused the northwestern and western delta to decay as their channels shifted increasingly eastward. As new river systems gave access to new tracts of land and deposited on them the silt necessary to fertilize their soil, areas formerly covered by dense forest were transformed into rice fields,

The Sixty Dome Mosque (Shatgumbad Mosjid) in Bagerhat, southern Bangladesh, built c. 1450. Photograph by Willem van Schendel, 2006.

providing the basis for new agrarian communities. Yet, although driven by natural forces, the movement of Bengal's agrarian frontier was also a human phenomenon, since it necessarily involved the arduous work of colonizing and settling new lands.

Our understanding of the third frontier, the cultural one, should not be biased by early Persian histories of the Turkish conquest, which typically speak of a stark, binary opposition between "Islam" and "infidelity" (*kufr*). Use of these terms has often given the impression that the rise of Muslim communities in Bengal was a corollary to, or simply a function of, the expansion of Turkish arms. In fact, however, the terms "Islam" and "infidelity" as used in these sources simply refer to the rulers and the ruled—that is, Persianized Turks who were assumed to be Muslim, and Bengali subjects who were assumed to be non-Muslim. Since large numbers of Bengali Muslims did not emerge until well after the conquest was completed, for the first several centuries after Muhammad Bakhtiyar's invasion, the political and cultural frontiers remained quite distinct geographically.

Each of Bengal's frontiers thus moved by its own dynamics: the Sanskritic frontier by the growth of Buddhist- or Brahman-ordered communities; the political frontier by the force of arms and the articulation and acceptance of the Muslim regime's legitimate authority; the agrarian frontier by the twin processes of riverine movement and colonization; and the

Islamic frontier by the gradual incorporation of indigenous communities into a Muslim-oriented devotional life. Having their own laws of motion, these frontiers overlapped one another in various ways. For example, after having established a base in the northwestern corner of the delta, which for four hundred years remained the epicenter of its rule in Bengal, Turkish power moved swiftly to the revenue-rich southwest. There, where the rulers encountered a dense agrarian society, conquest by Turks did not involve the physical extension of the arable land, but simply the capture of the local revenue structure. On the other hand, in much of the eastern and southern delta, where field agriculture had not yet replaced thick forests, the political and agrarian frontiers collapsed into one. There, the territorial reach of Turkish domination normally stopped at the edge of forests, only penetrating further when the forest itself was cleared. Hence in the east, the expanding Turkish movement involved not only the incorporation of indigenous peoples into a new political system but the physical transformation of the land from marsh or forest into rice fields. The interaction between the delta's Sanskritic, political, agrarian, and Islamic frontiers thus forms one of the great themes of Bengal's history. . . .

This book is written with several audiences in mind. For South Asians who understand Islamic history in the subcontinent in terms of an unassimilated "foreign" intrusion, the study explores how this religion, together with the Perso-Turkic civilization that carried it into the subcontinent, became indigenized in the cultural landscape of premodern Bengal. For Middle Easterners who understand Islam's historical and cultural center of gravity as lying between the Nile and the Oxus rivers, the book examines how and why Islamic civilization in the late medieval period became at least as vibrant and creative on the Bengali "periphery" as in the Middle Eastern "heartland." It also addresses the issue of why so many more Muslims reside outside the Middle East, especially in South Asia, than within it. Finally, this study seeks to reach Western readers for whom Islam's significant expansion was in the direction of Europe—a confrontation that, among other things, bequeathed to Europe and its cultural offshoots an image of Islam as a "militant" religion. I argue that Islam's more significant expansion lay in the direction of India, where Muslims encountered civilizations far more alien than those they met with in the European or Judeo-Christian worlds. Their responses to that encounter, moreover, proved far more creative; and in Bengal, at least, the meeting of Islamic and indigenous cultures led to an exceptional demographic development: the emergence of the world's second-largest Muslim ethnic community. This book is concerned with the nature of that encounter and its extraordinary outcome.

Poor and Rich in Mughal Bengal

Tapan Raychaudhuri

What was everyday life like in Bengal during Mughal rule? The north Indian Mughal state attempted to expand into Bengal beginning in the late sixteenth century and effectively ruled large parts of eastern Bengal from the 1610s to the 1710s.

In a study published in 1953, Tapan Raychaudhuri presented evidence on local lifestyles in Bengal during this period, based on the accounts of assorted observers. These stories vary in reliability. Some are based on decades of personal observance, others on brief visits, and yet others largely on hearsay. The authors include a Mughal court historian (Abul Fazl), Mughal military officers stationed in Bengal (Mirza Nathan, Shihabuddin Talish, and Abdul Latif), and European adventurers and merchants who visited Bengal between the 1580s and the 1670s (Ralph Fitch, Francisco Pelsaert, Sebastien Manrique, Jean-Baptiste Tavernier, Jean de Thévenot, and Thomas Bowrey). Raychaudhuri also refers to the Chandimangala, *a collection of Bengali poems written from the thirteenth century to the nineteenth. Fragmentary as the information is, we do get a sense of the enormous divergence in lifestyles between the rich and the poor and of how seventeenth-century customs differed from contemporary ones.*

The poor man in Bengal in the early days of Mughal rule suffered especially due to the prevalent political insecurity and administrative chaos. Towards the end of our period, peace descended on the land. . . . The poor lived in thatched houses, which were hardly any useful shelters even if there was a light rain. As Tavernier observed with reference to the houses of the carpenters at [Dhaka], these were "properly speaking only miserable huts made of bamboo and mud." Others were made only of mud and clay. Manrique, however, found them very clean and spread with cow-dung. The only furniture of the poor were straw mats, *kanthas* [patchwork bedcovers] and a few earthen pots (Manrique mentioned a specific number: four). The general standard of health was apparently very low. Shihabuddin Talish mentioned the "fatal and loathsome diseases" prevalent in Bengal—leprosy, leucoderma, elephantiasis, cutaneous eruptions, goitre and hydrocele—from which the happier clime of Assam, was free.

As regards food, the poor—according to Manrique—were satisfied with rice and salt, a little *saga* (herbs) and a few simple stews. *Amani* (stale rice-water) was a common and major item of the poor man's diet, and holes were dug into the mud floor to serve as cups for this humble dish. Only the well-to-do could afford milk and milk products. Curd and a cheap sweet made of milk, jaggery [unrefined cane sugar] and oil-seed are, however, mentioned in *Chandimangala* as rare delicacies which the poor could afford on rare occasions. Fish too was not taken either very often or in large quantities, specially by those who lived inland or far from the rivers. But the inventiveness of the Bengali brain sought to relieve the monotony of this simple diet through culinary experiments not entirely without success. Lentil cooked with coconut-water, fried seeds of jackfruit spread with lemon juice, spinach cooked with sour fruits—such were some of the delicacies which even the poorest could afford. So the fate of the poor in Bengal was to some extent better than that of his counterpart in Upper India who, according to Pelsaert, took every day the same unvarying *khichri* [rice and pigeon-peas boiled together] and fried lentils. The poorer classes of the population—or at least some among them—could afford an occasional meat diet, being undeterred by taboo. Burnt mongoose and lizards, ducks, eggs and porcupine flesh were taken by the hunters and, we may assume, also others belonging to the lowest rung of society. The poor man generally could not afford to take any intoxicants, but the distribution of *bhang* [a preparation of cannabis leaves and buds] and opium to encourage sailors and workers, mentioned by Nathan, suggests that the poorer folk were no total strangers to addiction.

The dress of the poor people conformed to their general standard of living, that is to say, it consisted of the irreducible minimum required by conventions of civilised society. Men and women, according to Abul Fazl, for the most part went "naked, wearing only a cloth (*lungi*) about the loins." On festive occasions they, however, wore very clean, white clothes. . . . Women of the poorer classes satisfied their natural instinct for self-adornment with ornaments of bell-metal, and *calai* (tin) and at best wore "silver hoopes about their necks and armes" while their legs were also "ringed with silver and copper and rings made of elephant's teeth."

The recreations which the poor could afford were of course few. Most of these centred round religious festivals or public functions of a semi-religious character. In the open pandals [temporary structures] where *panchalis* [narrative folk songs] were read and sung, or the *kathak* [narrator] told stories from the Puranas, the village folk gathered and constituted the bulk of the audience. The Vaishnava *mahotsavas* [festivals] were open to all and sundry, and the Durga *puja* [worship], arranged by the rich, provided entertainment for the poor as well. The *gajan* or religious procession attended by the beating of drums and ritual dances in honour of Dharma was chiefly a poor man's festival. . . .

Our sources portray in glowing colours the life of the richer classes in that period. The aristocrats, the merchants and the most successful members of the professional classes all lived in great comfort and luxury. . . . Ghoraghat [in Dinajpur district], the best *qasba* (village with market) in Bengal, according to Abdul Latif, had many beautiful mansions and delightful gardens erected and laid by the officers. Islam Khan built a large mosque in the middle of the bazaar and some residences within the fort. . . . Bowrey found [Dhaka], the new capital, to be "an admirable city for its greatness, for its magnificent buildings and multitude of inhabitants," while Thevenot described it as a very narrow town with houses mostly of cane covered with mud. Bakla [in Barisal district] in the days of Ralph Fitch had fair and high-built houses and large streets. . . .

The habitual dress of the upper classes consisted of short *dhoties* [loin-cloths] with no upper garments. But turbans were in use. The fashionable city-dwellers wore tussore [wild silk] *dhoties* and *khassa* [fine cotton] cloth. Well-to-do men also put on a *chaddar* [shawl]. On festive occasions, men wore trousers called *ijars* and a *cabaya* or long tunic of *muslin* after the Mughal style. . . .

Women's dress consisted of *sari* and a brassiere (*kanchali*). On ceremonial occasions an extra piece of cloth (*mekhala*) was wrapped round the upper part of the body, and rich ladies also put on *ijar* [trousers] as underwear. On festive occasions, silk and brocade were worn in profusion. Brassières were embroidered with varied designs, including scenes from mythological stories.

The ornaments worn by women were of great variety. These were of gold, silver, shell and ivory, some being set with costly jewels and coral. . . . Upper-class women also took great care of their toilet. They massaged themselves with *narayana* oil before bath and washed their heads with *amlaki* fruits. Bathing with water drawn from wells or tanks was a particular luxury (going to the river or tank for bath being the more common practice). Round the vermilion mark on the forehead a line would be drawn with sandal-paste, and a dot of collyrium put near it as a sort of foil to beauty. . . .

The life of the Muslim community in Bengal was marked by some distinctive features. The Muslim inhabitants of Bengal were divided into at least four sections on a racial basis: the Saiyads, the Mughals, the Pathans and the natives of Bengal. The new converts from Hinduism were known by the name of *Gaysal*. Here as elsewhere there were several clans among the Pathans, e.g. Subali, Nehali, Pani, Kudani, Huni, etc. Certain professions were monopolized by the Muslims. Each of these professions had apparently assumed the character of something like a caste. There were among these the cake-seller (*pithari*), the fish-seller (*kabari*), the paper-maker (*kagaji*), the cloth-dryer (*rangrej*), the "*hajam*" or barber whose special job was circumcision of children, the "*kasai*" or butcher who sold beef, the tailor, the weaver and so on. An interesting sub-caste was the "*Golas*," i.e. Muslims who had been disgraced for their non-observance of fast and ritual prayer.

The Muslim aristocrats and officers lived in a grand style and almost made a cult of display. Wherever they went, they were constantly attended by a numerous retinue of servants—slaves, both black and brown, guards, lackeys, valets and the like. The governors and high officers would be followed even on a short journey by a magnificent train of elephants, horses, cavaliers and infantrymen displaying colourful streamers and liveries and carrying for the convenience of the noble master parasols, goblets and even bath-tubs. The richest had in their service servants with specialised functions, e.g. wood-cutters, water-carriers, palanquin-bearers, etc. When they went out on longer journeys in their luxurious palanquins, or ox-drawn carriages, they were surrounded by music-makers playing on flutes and tambourines while guards, cooks, valets and slaves carried "arms, banderoles, victuals, tents and all that is necessary for the convenience of the voyage."

The Mughal grandees, while serving out their term of office in this outlying province, constructed bungalows and "lofty mansions" with bamboos or the wood of betel-nut trees in their places of sojourn. Some of these structures were even three-storied. But in remote villages an officer might condescend to live in a mud-house with thatched roof. Generally they tried to live as much after the grand style which was their usual habit as the circumstances permitted. So even in God-forsaken corners of the country their houses had "*hammams*" or bathrooms, a rare luxury in Bengal. . . .

The Muslims generally shaved their heads and kept beards. The well-to-do among them put on long *cabayas* "made of the finest cotton cloths, silk stuffs, or gold and silver and of all the costliest things." . . . A silken shoulder sash was used while going out and the court dress was made "nearly all of brocade." The Mullas, however, were very modestly dressed, "all in white from head to foot" even when attending court. In the hours of relaxation, the rich too would be dressed simply in a *lungi*, an underwear, a belt and a turban. The Muslim ladies put on "a big piece of very fine cotton cloth round their body, beginning at the waist" and coming down to the ankles. Drawers of light stuff were also worn. Another piece of cloth and occasionally also a shoulder sash were used to cover the upper part of the body; but the ladies, we are told, generally preferred while at home to go about barebodied down to the waist. Ornaments were used in profusion and there were some whose arms were "adorned therewith up to the elbow." While going out, they covered their face with a silken veil.

Washed Ashore

Frans Jansz van der Heiden and Willem Kunst

In the sixteenth and seventeenth centuries CE Europeans began to frequent the coastal waters of Bangladesh. They were merchants, pirates, and mercenaries, attracted by the riches and opportunities of the region. Some of them left behind descriptions of their adventures and encounters. Here is an example from 1661. In that year four Dutch ships left Java, Indonesia, for a journey to the Dutch settlement of Hooghly in Bengal. Two made it to Hooghly, and the other two were shipwrecked, one near the Andaman Islands and the other near Chittagong in eastern Bengal. This ship, named the Terschelling, *ran aground in a storm and forty men perished. Twenty-seven others managed to survive three weeks of deprivation as they searched for people on uninhabited islands, until they reached the island of Sondvip. They wrote an account of how the local people received them, their journey to Dhaka, and their induction into the army that the Mughal governor, Mir Jumla, had amassed to attack the king of Assam.*

We reached the mainland at about 2 P.M. The Blacks took us to the house of the village chief. . . . After we had stood around talking to each other for some time, the chief himself showed up and said through the interpreter: "Welcome here, men!" . . . Then large mats were spread in front of his door; he sat down and all of us took our seats around him. . . . While we were sitting there, an eunuch [*cappater*] arrived with an order from the wives of the chief; they were eager to see some of the youngest Dutchmen. So the chief told Jeroen, Arnhout, and Willem Kunst to go with the eunuch. When we came to a large gate, he let us enter, and when we did, it was almost as if we were in the Old Men's Hostel in Amsterdam because it was laid out in the same way. In the middle there was a large courtyard and surrounding it small houses. We looked around a little and then a bevy of the chief's wives joined us. There we stood, like dry sticks among a host of luxuriant trees. Some caught us by the nose, others stroked our cheeks, and a few ripped open our shirts and moved their hands over our chests. I think they

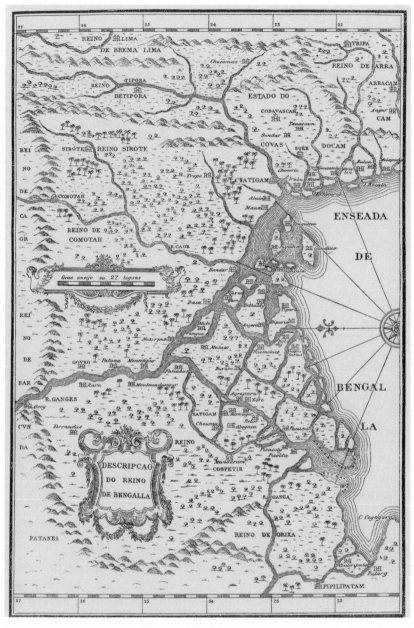

The earliest European map of Bengal, by João-Baptista de Lavanha, showing the island of Sondvip (Sundiva) and the city of Dhaka (Dacca), c. 1550. In this map north is shown on the left-hand side. Map by João de Barros, from *Ásia de João de Barros: Dos feitosque os portugueses fizeram no descobrimento e conquista dos mares e terras do Oriente, Vol 4 (Quartadécada)* (Lisbon, 1777–88), tome II, 451.

did this so that they could later say that they had felt the naked bodies of Dutchmen. . . .

The next day was market day. The village chief and we were sitting in a roadside house as people went to market, so everybody passed us with their wares. The chief exchanged our silver coins for small cowries [*hoorentjes*] because these were more useful than our silver. When we saw something we wanted, we nudged the chief and made him understand that we wished to buy it. He gestured to the market-goers and gave them so many of our cowries as he thought fit; he did this so that they would not cheat us. When the market was over, we had bought up almost all the goods that had been brought there. . . .

After five days in the village of Sondiep, we said goodbye to the village chief and thanked him for his benevolence. He was a Bengali [Bengaelder], and a very good man (there are many good people among the Bengalis and Moors) and had shown us exceptional generosity when we first arrived there from the sea. . . . He showed great compassion and sorrow at the misfortune and disaster that we had suffered. He showed us a final kindness by providing what we might need on the way. As we parted he told us through his Portuguese interpreter that he could not send us more directly to our Dutch compatriots than by sending us to Dhaka. . . . After saying a final goodbye, we settled in the boats with the Blacks and traveled to a village called Anam. From there we would travel to the town of Bhulua [Boelwa; in 1668 this town would be renamed Noakhali] and from there to Dhaka. . . .

At two hours from Bhulua, a guard put us ashore and took us to the town. He told us to wait outside the guard post while he presented our papers to the prince, for a prince resides in this town. Black Portuguese were living opposite the guard post and we asked them if they had any food for us—and they gave us milk, rice, a pot, fire, and wood to cook the food ourselves. It was almost ready when the guard returned to take us to his prince. There was no time to eat the food there but we could not leave it behind either, so we took the hot pot with rice gruel and carried it in turns through the town till we reached the prince's court; and there we set upon the food. . . . We were brought into a beautiful hall [and] there we were served a very rich dish, biryani (*brensie*). The guards told us that it was never prepared better for kings and princes than for us at that time. The prince of Bhulua probably had ordered his people to do so because he privileges whoever is known to be a Christian over his own people.

We were given this rich dish daily and as a result we quickly regained our flesh. But gradually the heaviness began to bother us and we longed for lighter fare that we could digest more easily. Biryani is very oily and filling. It is prepared, without water, from fine white rice, a whole goose or two chickens, and many cloves, mace, fine white sugar, cinnamon or cassia leaves, saffron, and many other spices. All these are braised together in butter, and in this way the goose and chickens are cooked in the rice till they are well done. This dish was so filling that ultimately it began to upset us; in the end we would have been happier eating just dry rice with salted fish. . . .

In this court the Moors and Bengalis delegated everything to the Black Portuguese, who then informed others. They were also respected more than any others. Even those Moors who carried golden daggers had to show them humility. This puzzled us because these people were merely Black Portuguese. Whoever carries a Christian name is considered an accomplished soldier there. . . .

After having stayed six days, we were put on boats to take us straight to Dhaka. The prince provided us with bodyguards, both Moors and Portuguese, and a good galley. In this way we arrived in Dhaka, two hundred miles inland. A Portuguese went ahead to our lodge [the Dutch factory at Dhaka], to announce our arrival to the chief. With him came a Dutchman who was dressed from head to toe like a Moor, which we thought very odd, and we assumed that he was circumcised, even though it was only common among Englishmen in that country. A palanquin with four Blacks also appeared to carry our bookkeeper, who was ill. Then all of us went to the lodge. In the absence of our chief, Zantvoort, who was in Hooghly [the headquarters of the Dutch East India Company in Bengal], the second in command received us very cordially and we told him about our shipwrecking, our terrible starvation, and all our other adventures. We also learned that the other ship *Wezop* [that had sailed with us from Batavia] had ended up in the Andaman Islands with six chests of money, and more than forty men were killed by cannibals. . . .

As we were about to leave Dhaka for Hooghly [to board a Dutch ship], we received letters from the nawab, the commander of the great Mughal [Mir Jumla, the governor of Bengal under Emperor Aurangzeb], ordering us to join the army immediately, so, reluctantly, we had to abandon our journey to Hooghly. . . .

Wherever the nawab went [with his army], he set fire to everything. He had countless warships and two galliots, and a huge following of traders on water and land. . . . He had beautiful cavalry and excellent light and heavy artillery, Dutch, English, and Portuguese. The nawab himself was an old man [in 1661 Mir Jumla was seventy years old] who had been making war since his youth, and during his lifetime he had conquered many strong cities and large lands for the Mughal (who receives tribute from nineteen kingdoms). . . .

After taking our leave from the lodge, twenty-five of us (for our book-keeper had died and was buried in Dhaka) boarded a large boat. Our skipper took a small boat together with the Moors, the guards and the pilots who would take us to the army. We were taken further inland, past many villages, towns, and fine-looking fields. But hardly one out of twenty houses was inhabited because the Mughal's army takes along all who can follow, even merchants.

After traveling for a full month, by boat and on foot, we moored at a fishing village. Here we hired light boats to move faster. . . . These are good-natured people, neither greedy nor deceitful, and not thievish either, although easily given to using bad language, especially when in a hurry. But they hardly ever swear and never by the devil. They make an oath by pronouncing God's name and biting their forefinger as proof of their sincerity, because they would rather die than take God's name in vain.

After five days we met one of the nawab's warships, manned by four Englishmen and many Moors and Portuguese, as well as two of the men from our wrecked ship, Adriaen Raes from Middelburg and Klaes Lambertsz from Waveren, who had been on a tiny raft that reached a reef and then the mainland, and were inducted into the nawab's army. . . . Both of them came with us. At a city called Rangamati we left the boats behind and traveled on foot to the army, only two miles from there. Having arrived there, we were brought to the nawab's tent. Here we encountered a Dutch surgeon, Gelmert Vosburg, whom our people had lent to the nawab two years earlier and who already understood the Moorish language well. After we had waited in front of the tent for some time, the nawab ordered us inside; we showed him our respect and stood in a half circle. He saw that our guardsman had but one arm and asked through his interpreter how he lost the other. When our guardsman replied, through the interpreter, "by a cannonball," the nawab hit his breast with his hand. Then he had a pot of strong "elephant arrack" brought in, specially distilled for his elephants, as well as a large wooden dish of oranges. . . . No drink ever affected us as this one from the nawab—but then, in this country arrack for human consumption is far less potently distilled than that for war elephants, who drink it as humans would.

When we were half drunk with the arrack, we began to speak freely in front of the nawab, who asked us to stay for six months, after which he would send us back to our people. We agreed willy-nilly and he promised us booty from all enemies, whether Portuguese, Black, or White: fifty rupees per head, equivalent to twenty-five *rijxdaelders* [Dutch currency], and a hundred rupees for any person we captured alive. . . .

This army that was gathered to attack the king of Assam was, according to reliable people, about 800,000 men strong on water and land. . . . The nawab came out of his tent, just put his hand lightly on his horse, and was already on its back; many people were astonished at such agility in an old man like him. Some men on elephants ride in front of him, blowing trumpets to announce his arrival and beating huge drums that make tremendous sound. A group of war elephants follows, each elephant with two big cannons and a gunner in a square howdah and, on the neck, a mahout (*karnak*) who leads the elephant with a hook.

Behind the nawab follow the slaves—White Russians—on horseback and the cavalry. Then the great infantry, soldiers armed with muskets, pikes, small artillery, spears and shields, hewers, and bows and arrows. Then follow the big war elephants, and numerous camels, each with one cannon and a gunner on its back. The elephants and camels are well trained for war; one of the elephants had trampled and destroyed an entire fortress all by itself. Then come thousands of camels who carry the cavalry's baggage, and many different traders and artisans, and after them thousands of harlots on horseback or on camels. Big merchants bring up the rear, with many commodities on horses and camels.

Translated from Dutch by Willem van Schendel.

Origin of the Sak in Bangladesh

Headman of Baishari

The Sak (or Thet, Thek, or Chak) live in the southernmost part of Bangladesh, near Nakhyongchhari in the Chittagong Hill Tracts. They are one of a dozen distinct ethnic groups in this region. Their language, Sak, is severely endangered. It is related to Kachin and other languages spoken in northern Burma, China, and northeast India. In 1959 the headman of one of their villages, Baishari, told this story of the Sak's origin to the French anthropologist Lucien Bernot.

We come from Arakan. Our ancestors lived there near the Koladan River and a mountain named Sakiunton. One day an enemy king offered our Sak king a young girl—he planned to use this girl to entrap our king. After receiving this girl, our king decided to marry her and threw a grand party that lasted for seven days. Everybody, including the king and his ministers, got very drunk; the common people were also drunk, and the Sak king was captured.

Not everybody knew about this. Four ministers who wanted to meet with their king could not do so; for several days they searched for him in vain, and they decided that he must have been abducted. Therefore these four ministers decided to go away, to leave with their families. One of them, named Twen za gru man, came this way together with his family and other Sak who had decided to follow him. They were split into two groups, one walking a half-day journey behind the other. On the way the group in front and the one behind both stopped for lunch. The second group cooked crabs. The crabs turned red. Thinking they had not cooked them sufficiently, they cooked them some more and stayed longer in that place. Ahead, their companions of the other group were on the move again after having finished the meal they had cooked at their rest place. They had cut numerous banana leaves to use as plates. But the stem of the particular species of banana plant from which they cut the leaves is able to grow new ones very rapidly— several centimeters in a few hours after the leaves have been cut off. When the travellers in the second group arrived—not aware of this characteristic

Magical depiction inscribed on a bamboo amulet, Chittagong Hill Tracts, c. 1880.
From Emil Riebeck, *Hügelstämme von Chittagong: Ergebnisse einer Reise im Jahre 1882*
(Berlin: Verlag von A. Asher & Co., 1885).

of those banana plants—they were disheartened at the thought that the others were far ahead. So they decided to settle right there. This happened in the area where they are still living today. . . . Those who left first were the Chakma, those who stayed here are we, the Sak. . . . The "ma" in "Chakma" is a Burmese word meaning "being false, mistaken," and so on; in other words, the Chakma are merely fake Sak.

Translated from French by Willem van Schendel.

Mahua and Naderchand Fall in Love

Dvija Kanai

For centuries people in rural Bangladesh have sung and performed ballads and dramas about love, changing fortune, and human frailty. These compositions were transmitted orally, and as a result many have not survived. Among those that have, however, is an extraordinary collection from the district of Mymensingh in northern Bangladesh. We owe the collection's survival to remarkable teamwork in the 1910s between Chandra Kumar De (a Mymensingh village compiler) and Dinesh Chandra Sen (a lecturer in Bengali language and literature at the University of Calcutta). Together they published four volumes of ballads and dramas (1923–32), creating an instant interest in Bengali folk literature.

Below is a fragment of the drama "Mahua." The author is thought to be Dvija Kanai, a seventeenth-century Namasudra (member of a substantial agrarian caste that bore the stigma of untouchability) from the region. He composed the poem and also organized a group of players to put it on stage. For a long time, "Mahua" was very popular in Mymensingh, but local orthodox upper-caste Hindus increasingly condemned its emphasis on the romance of love as corrupting the morals of young women. Low-caste and Muslim peasants continued to sing "Mahua," however, and two inhabitants of Mashka village, Shek Asak Ali and Umar Chandra De, were able to provide the major portions of the drama. Mashka village is in the Netrokona area, in which the story is situated.

This is the tale of love between Mahua, a beautiful girl brought up by itinerant performers, and Naderchand, a handsome young Brahmin lord. In the fragment below, Mahua and her troupe have just arrived in Naderchand's town. He hears about her beauty and commissions the group to perform at his palace. When Mahua executes her acrobatic act, the thunderbolt of love strikes both of them. This is the beginning of their flirtatious courtship.

One day Naderchand was passing that way. It was evening and the lamps were newly lighted in the houses by the wayside. Mahua was returning home, having shown her dancing in town. He met her all alone and said

Mahua dances for Naderchand. The performer in this choreo-
graphed version of the poem—staged in Dhaka in 1962—is
Shaheda Ahmed. From "Mahua Dance Performance," *Contemporary Arts in Pakistan* 3:1 (1962). Used by permission of the Heritage
Archives of Bangladesh History, Rajshahi.

softly, "Will you wait a little to hear me, O maiden? When the moonbeams
gently spread in the eastern horizon and the sun fades in the west, may I
tomorrow at such an hour expect you at the river-ghat [landing stairs] all
alone? If the pitcher in your arms proves too heavy after it is filled with water, I will be there, dear maiden, to help you in lifting it up."

With the pitcher of water she went to the riverside in the evening. Naderchand was already there waiting for her.

NADERCHAND: You are so intent on filling your pitcher with water, do you
recollect, dear maiden, what I told you yesterday?

MAHUA: But, O Prince, O stranger, not a word do I recollect of what, you say, you have told me.

NADERCHAND: So young, so fresh, and yet so forgetful! It is only one night since I told you.

MAHUA: But you are a stranger, Prince, I feel greatly embarrassed in talking with you.

NADERCHAND: You have pushed the pitcher into the water, maiden, and gentle ripples have arisen. How beautiful you look! Smile on me, maiden, and speak to me. There is none here to see us. Who is your father and who your mother? Where did you use to be, maiden, before you came to our town?

MAHUA: I have no parents, Prince, no, nor any brother to call my own. I am like a weed turned adrift in the stream. Ill-starred am I, O Prince, I have become a gipsy living among the gipsies. With the fire in my heart I am inwardly consumed. There is none here to feel for me—to whom I may open my heart! You have a beautiful wife, O Prince, and happy are you at your home with her.

NADERCHAND: Hard is your heart like stone, O fair maiden, your words are untrue. I have no wife, I am still unmarried. Hard is your heart and hard is the heart of your parents! They have not yet given you a mate. You are allowing your youth to pass in vain.

MAHUA: Hard is your heart and hard the heart of your parents! No bride have they given you though you are a grown man, O stranger.

NADERCHAND: True, dear girl, my heart is hard and hard is the heart of my parents, but I assure you if I could win one like you, I would not remain hard but become a tender husband.

MAHUA (AFFECTING TO BE ANGRY): You are a shameless youth to say so. Your words are insulting. Get a pitcher and tie it round your neck and drown yourself in the river.

NADERCHAND: Gladly do I take your sentence, fair maiden. Be the stream and I will drown myself in it.

Translated from Bengali by Dinesh Chandra Sen.

The Path That Leads to You

Modon Baul

This song by the composer Modon Baul, from the eighteenth-century CE, *represents a long-term current in the culture of Bangladesh, which has become more prominent over time and remains significant today. Indeed, in recent times musicians in the Baul tradition have become global representatives of authentic South Asian spirituality. They give concerts all over the world. The title* Baul *translates as* mad, *but members of this group see themselves primarily as seekers or followers of the path of unorthodoxy. Baul songs are part of a devotional tradition, Vaishnavism, that reaches back to the fourteenth century* CE. *This tradition acknowledges the dual existence of the human soul and the divine and incessantly seeks to overcome this duality by love expressed through music and song. In true Baul fashion, Modon addresses God directly and rejects all formal ritual in his quest for union with God.*

> The path that leads to you is cluttered with temples and mosques.
> O Lord! I have heard your call but cannot proceed:
> Hindu and Muslim teachers block my way . . .
> There are many locks to your door: the Puranas, the Koran, and
> recitations.
> Alas Lord! What a terrible torment this is, cries Modon in despair!

Translated from Bengali by Shamsuzzaman Khan and Willem van Schendel.

III

Colonial Encounters

This part deals with a period of Bangladesh's history (1757–1947) that professional historians have studied with intense interest. Rather than summarizing their debates (some of which are referenced in "Suggestions for Further Reading"), we bring this turbulent period to life through the eyes of some participants. We focus on how colonial rule gave rise to a wide variety of encounters and accommodations, some fiercely antagonistic and others affectionate and benign. We meet an eighteenth-century Scot struggling to understand a local chieftain, a woman becoming literate at the beginning of the nineteenth century, peasants resisting the cruelty of European entrepreneurs, a poet inventing a new literary form, and a boy negotiating the cultural intricacies of Dhaka city. We see how new religious movements and anticolonial agitation emerged and how wartime policies in the 1940s caused an immense famine. We also learn how cultural identities, notably religious ones, gradually turned into political categories. The part concludes with an analysis of an amazing and fateful twist at the very end of colonial rule—a sudden turn toward support for the idea of Pakistan, an imagined homeland for South Asia's Muslims. A collection of color illustrations includes images from this period.

A Tax Rebellion in Rangpur

Ratiram Das

In 1757, after winning the Battle of Polashi (Plassey), the British East India Company formally took control of the Bengal Delta. It took the company decades, however, to establish effective control of the countryside and to adjust the system of land taxation to serve colonial interests. They made terrible misjudgments, most notoriously in the case of the devastating famine of 1770, which carried millions of inhabitants to their graves. Overtaxing continued, resulting in pervasive rural resistance and migration.

In 1783 peasants in Rangpur (northern Bangladesh) rose in rebellion. They tried to put an end to the oppression of revenue farmers, people whom the East India Company had given a license to collect taxes on its behalf. One of the peasants' targets was Debi Singh, a particularly ruthless character. At first the government tried to suppress the rebellion, but later it sought to pacify the rebels by canceling Debi Singh's license and reducing the tax demand.

Local composers created songs about the rebellion that were passed on for generations. Most of these are now lost but one survived because it was written down in the early twentieth century. The composer was Ratiram Das, a member of the Rajbangshi community, who lived in the village of Itakumari, a center of the revolt. Here it is in a prose translation.

In Rangpur, Fatehpur was a big "chakla" (revenue district) and king Rajarai lived there all alone. A deeply religious man, Rajarai was given to charities and many Brahmins were gifted land. The plots of land that he gave away to Brahmins and physicians, or consecrated to gods, cannot be measured. One can name Manthana, Bamandanga and others in the Fatehpur division. Fatehpur's stock is high, because the gifts were bestowed on loyal Brahmins.

During the time of the East India Company, Debi Singh was the "Raja"; he had a dozen associates. As one looks, so one dresses or deports oneself. Because of the sins of the king, the country faced famine. People died, leaving money under their pillows. The amount of taxes to be taken from subjects was never determined; from the people they exacted as much as they could—but still wanted more. All they did was to demand more and more, and due to inhuman torture there rose a wail of agony. Even the honourable zamindar [landlord] was denied his honour; people of all classes cried in despair. Passengers on palanquins were assaulted by the "paiks" [armed men]—and everything was rendered futile by Debi Singh's oppression. Women could not move about their backyards; they were forcibly taken away by Debi Singh's men. Raja Debi Singh himself became the incarnation of "Koli" [untruth]. The subjects were utterly sick of his misrule.

Sivchandra Roy was Rajarai's son: everybody praised him as equal to Siva. He had a palace at Itakumari, massive and neatly laid, which had numerous rooms, doors and yards. No other building could stand comparison to it; the lounge with the altar of the goddess Chandi had a high ceiling; the twin-roofed room had low eaves. One never found a west-facing lounge elsewhere—one adjoining room could be seen from the other.

There were paiks, bailiffs, guards, clerks and ministers without number. Joydurga Choudhurani, the ruling lady of Manthana, was praised by all for her sagacity and forceful personality. All that Sivchandra did was on her counsel—and the whole world was firmly convinced of her wisdom.

When the country was perishing of famine, Debi Singh, the arch villain, was busy plundering the people. Their misery touched the heart of Sivchandra, who, at the command of Joydurga, made a move. He went down to the court of Debi Singh and narrated the story of the people's suffering. Debi Singh, the Rajput, was as black as a ghost in appearance, could put "Mahishasur" in the shade. On hearing this, his angry eyes turned red; "Who is here, who is here" shouted he. Sivchandra was put behind the bars, his feet in iron-fetters. Later, when his dewan [minister] learned all this, he had Sivchandra freed and brought to Itakumari—on paying a lot of money. Sivchandra was the pride of the Baidya family; he could not bear Debi Singh's oppression any longer. He wrote letters to all zamindars in Rangpur asking them to come over, he sent out an open letter to all the people of his area as well as to those outside it.

With all the zamindars arriving at Sivchandra's palace, Itakumari was filled with elephants, horses and soldiers. Also arrived the ruler of Pirgachha, Joydurga Devi. One by one, they were all seated in the Conference Hall adjoining the temple. The raiyats [tenants] kept standing, hands folded and tears rolling down their chests. They had neither food to eat nor clothes to wear; through starvation they were reduced to bones, covered only by a skin.

Sivchandra stood up with folded hands to speak; as he spoke he wept in anger. Pointing out the subjects to the zamindars, he said: "How could you eat without a thought for the sufferings of these people? Too often there were floods when the waters came down from the north, in which all the paddy was destroyed. I spent a good deal of time, labour and money to have the mouth of Caroah dyked. The subjects perish for the sins of the king. There is no water for irrigation; the paddy in the field is scorched down, and there is nothing left at home. Every year, we have a famine. There is no straw on the roof, no rice in the stores. The mother goes away, the father disappears, so does the wife—and without caring for anybody go away the son and the daughter. I went down to reason with the vicious Raja Debi Singh, but his slaves put fetters on my feet. Look at the condition of the subjects, dear zamindars, and do whatever you deem proper."

Nobody uttered a word; all heads were bowed low. Sivchandra Roy lost his temper and spoke again: "Since the Rajput robber is a scoundrel, you should all drive him out."

At this stage Mother Joydurga flared up: "Are you not men—aren't you strong? Though I am born a woman, I can seize him and cut him to pieces with a sword. Nobody would be required to do anything, everything will be done by the subjects. But we shall never bow down."

Sivchandra spoke, trembling with anger, like a charging hooded king-cobra. Sivchandra Nandy said: "Listen, my subjects. You provide the king's food, his riches. Go out to Rangpur in your thousands, plunder Debi Singh's palace and pull it down. Get him, bring him here along with his henchmen, and I will, with my own hands, cut his ears off."

At Sivchandra's command all the people took heart and rushed together in their thousands. They took sticks, spears, sickles, choppers; nobody remained to look after the children. On their shoulders, they carried a balance of load and the yoke. They were made beggars—so they ran like savages.

From all directions the people converged on Rangpur. The gentle folk came—only to watch the fun. The men threw brickbats and stones, which kept falling with thud from all directions. In the fusillade of stones, some suffered broken bones and Debi Singh's palace was reduced to a heap of bricks. He escaped through the backdoor; with him fled those twelve associates. Debi Singh got away with a wrapper on his body. Some say he went to Murshidabad, some say he fled to Dacca [Dhaka].

The Lord entrusted the English with the kingdom—and justice was done by the East India Company. The Englishmen held a court and a trial; one by one Debi Singh's associates were put in prison. Let it be known well that I live in the same village of Itakumari where Sivchandra was the king.

Translated from Bengali by Amiya Bose.

Making Sense of Hill People

Francis Buchanan

In 1798 the Scottish medical doctor Francis Buchanan received an assignment from the East India Company in Calcutta. He was to survey areas in what is now south-eastern Bangladesh, according to the report, "in order to look out for the places most proper for the cultivation of spices." His task included surveying territories beyond British control, notably the Chittagong Hill Tracts—which would not be annexed until 1860. Buchanan's detailed travel account is the first we have for this region, and because Buchanan was uncommonly observant, his account is a very valuable source of new information. This is Buchanan's first survey; he would go on to do many more in other parts of British India.

In this fragment we find him in the southern Chittagong Hill Tracts, near the Matamuhuri River and the settlement of Lama. He is clearly out of his depth, encountering people whose political systems, religious beliefs, customs, and languages confuse him. And yet, he tries vigorously to make sense of this new world, reporting on his observations and his discussions with the Mru and the Marma, two of many ethnic groups inhabiting these hills.

12th April [1798]. In the morning I set out to visit a Mo-roo [Mru] *joom* [field]. Proceeding east through the valley of Manicpour, at its head I came to woods, and a path leading through a narrow valley surrounded by low hills. The soil both of valley and hills is good. I then came to the riverside, where there is very fine scenery, with high steep hills descending on each side to the edge of the water. The river however is not rapid, and its bed is sand. Going up a little farther I observed on the opposite hills some Mo-roo-sa [Mru], who were burning the wood to clear a *joom*. On calling to them I was answered by King-dai, the man with whom I yesterday conversed. He directed me to go up a little farther, and there to cross the river. Having done so, and ascended a steep hill, which two years ago had been a *joom*, I walked on a little, and came to the village, where I was joined by King-dai. The village consisted of about twenty houses forming one straight lane, the two rows of which were distant about 10 feet. The buildings were exactly like those of the Joomea Mugs, or Kiaung-sa [Marma]. The under part is enclosed, and serves to secure the hogs, and poultry, of which these people have abundance. I went up to the house of my acquaintance King-dai by a notched stick, from which I landed on a platform. This, like that at Aung-ghio-se's [a local Marma chief], led to two apartments: the one belonging to the women, and also serving for a store house; the other serving for a hall. In this we sat down on the floor. There was no furniture in the room except a drum, and a little box full of earth placed in a corner, and serving for a hearth. Bamboos split, and laid open into a kind of plank, were used both for making the floor and Walls, and answer very well in a hot climate. The house was clean.

King-dai, whom I suspected to be the head-man of the village, utterly denied his being a great man, and said, that he was a *ryot* [tenant] or farmer belonging to Lay-Klang, who lived at a great distance. I had before detected him in endeavouring to conceal the truth, and I believe that he now was lying, being afraid, that I wanted to bring him into trouble. He was indeed very anxious to know what brought me to the village, and his suspicion was evidently increased by my saying that I was induced solely by curiosity. Soon after my arrival we were joined by eight or ten stout young men, who were desirous of partaking in the conversation. They smoked out of long pipes like those in use among the Chinese. The mistress of the house attended to give the guests tobacco and fire. The old people and children kept at a distance. Both sexes are thick and squat, and have tolerable features of the Chinese kind.

The men wear their hair tied up in a knot, which projects over the forehead. In their ears they have large circular flat rings of metal. At this season they use no clothing, but a narrow blue sash, which they pass round the haunches, and between the legs. In cold weather, or in high dress, they throw round their shoulders a piece of cotton cloth chequered red[,] blue and white, something like the highland plaid.

The women, who are a great deal too plump to be handsome, tie their hair behind. Our young landlady had cylindrical hollow silver ear-rings, about four inches long, and one in diameter, which she wore after the Burma fashion. Round her neck she had a string of coral beads, and on one of her arms a thick white metal ring. Her only clothing was a piece of blue cloth about a foot wide, and just so long as to meet at the ends round her haunches, where its upper edge was secured by a number of strings of white beads bound round her like a sash. The two ends of this cloth just meeting at one of her haunches, showed at every step almost the whole outside of her left thigh. The other women were dressed in a similar manner, but not quite so fine. In full dress the women also wear a chequered cloth round their shoulders.

These people seem to have abundance of provisions. Hogs, goats, fowls, fish, snakes, and lizards, form their common animal food. Hogs and fowls they have in plenty: but they say, that the tigers have taken away all their goats. The tigers they venture to attack with their short spears: but they do not eat such as they kill. The Bengalese, they say, falsely attribute to them, the eating of cats and dogs. This is done by a tribe only named Paung-sa, some of whom are in this neighbourhood under a *rua-sa* [leader] called Lay-sing. In their *jooms* they cultivate rice, cotton, a kind of cucumber, arum or *kutchee*, tobacco, and several other vegetables. They sell the cotton, and buy all the cloth they use. They make a kind of fermented liquor, which they call arack. It is also prepared by the Kiaung-sa, Rakain [Arakanese], and Raj-bunsee [Barua], in the following manner. The root of a shrub, which the Mo-roo-sa name *toa*, and the Bengalese call *moolee*, is bruised and from it is extracted a farinaceous substance, which with the addition of a little rice-flour is made into cakes like biscuit. These cakes also are named *toa*, and *moolee*, and may be kept for a long time. When arack is to be made, some of the *toa* cake is mixed with entire rice, and wet with water. This wet mixture by standing one day ferments, and forms a mass by the Moroo-sa called *yoo*. More water is then added to the *yoo*, and the fermentation is allowed to go on for three days. The liquor is then decanted, and boiled, when it is fit for use. The grains are given to hogs, and make them very fat. I think it probable that the Portuguese first showed the inhabitants how to distill this arack, and that the original name of the fermented liquor has now passed amongst us to that which has been distilled.

By no questions, that occurred to me, could I discover, that these people have any ideas of God, of spirits, or of a state of future existence. They said, that they did not pray, that they never saw, nor heard the spirits of the dead, and that they knew nothing of [Buddha] or *Nat*, but heard the Bengalese and Rakain talk of such things. Their dead they commonly keep in the house three days, during which time they feast, and make a great noise with drums. They then burn the body. If the deceased has been a person of note, they open the belly, and put in some drugs, by which means they can preserve the body for nine days. In King-dai's house, near where the drum hung, I observed stuck into the wall some bones and feathers, which I suspected to have been done with some superstitious view.

While I remained at this village Aung-ghio-se with all his family, and attendants, male and female passed by in procession carrying bamboos adorned with flowers. A sword of state was carried behind the chief. King-dai said, that they were going to pray at a place in the neighbourhood.

Soon after returning to my tent I was visited by Aung-ghio-se, who presented me with a fat pig. He said, that the procession, I saw, was an annual visit to the Mroo, made in order to keep up a friendly correspondence with that people. . . .

Aung-ghio-se says, that Lay-kray is the name, by which he knows the Mroo chief on the south side of the river, and that Lay-sing, and his people the Paung-sa, are exactly the same people with the other Mroo: the appellation Paung-sa arising from some circumstance in the payment of the revenue. He also says, that King-dai deceived me, when he alledged that he did not eat cats, and dogs: for among the Mroo this practice is universal. Altho' some of the richer Mroo take two wives, Aung-ghio-se says, that one is by the greater part considered as enough. The lover, when he wishes to marry, makes a present to the parents of some knives, bills, swords, or other iron work, or, if a very rich man, of a cow. If the offer is accepted, the mother delivers up the girl, who is conducted home with dancing and feasting, and without any further ceremony she is considered as married. The *Rua-sas* commonly settle disputes: but the different villages frequently fight with each other. When a man dies his property is divided equally among his children: but if the father of the deceased is living, he takes all, and gives the grandchildren only what he pleases. The wife is also entitled to a share of her husband's effects, when he dies. The Tiperah and Mroung, Aung-ghio-se says, dress alike, and speak the same language. From some circumstance in collecting the revenue these Mroung are frequently called Wa-the Mroo. From some similar circumstance the Mroo proper are called Lay Mroo.

In my evening walk I went north across the plain, and then turned west down the bank of the River. Manicpour consists of two parts: the largest on the north, the smallest on the south side of the river. The greater part of it is so high, as to lodge little water during the rainy season, some parts of it are even so high as to be unfit for the cultivation of rice. The river formerly ran by the foot of the northern hills, and there the land is still very low. The hills surrounding this valley contain much good soil, and are well watered. I have seen no place, during my journey, more likely to answer for the cultivation of spices.

Rhinos among the Ruins

A. Magon de Clos-Doré

Today the ruins of the old city of Gaur straddle the border between Bangladesh and India. Carefully restored and properly maintained by the archaeological services of two states, the ruined buildings and city walls are surrounded by rice fields and densely populated villages. Gaur is a tourist attraction that does not inspire any fear. Things were very different in the early nineteenth century, as revealed by this fragment from a travelogue published in 1822. Then the ruins were covered in, according to the travelogue, "thick bamboo and tamarind forests that made access almost impossible"; they were the domain of wild animals. Clearly this had once been a great city but very little was known about it at the time. The author of the travelogue observed: "Everywhere the ground is covered with huge broken pillars and fragments of architecture that do not belong to any known order." It took an adventurer, or a fool, to enter this wilderness. What is striking about this text—apart from the contrast it presents with the domesticated Gaur of today—is the richness of the natural environment. In a matter of hours the human intruders met with six different species of large mammals (three of which they shot) and several species of birds. And the most dangerous of these is not the tiger that attacks them but the rhinoceros that lurks in the undergrowth.

The entire surrounding country is a dreadful wilderness that travelers fear to enter. There have been several attempts to penetrate the forests that cover Gaur these days but they have met with little success. Europeans contemplating this trip have been dissuaded by the stories of exertions and dangers told by the fearless ones who have visited. I say "Europeans" because Gaur is a cursed place for Hindus and Muslims. In their imagination it is terrorized by evil spirits such as *dives, guls,* and *affrits.* . . .

The sun had just come up and its rays had not yet driven away the morning fog, which is always thick along the banks of the Ganges, when we started out for the ruins. . . . Captain W— went ahead on his big elephant, a servant sitting next to him in the *hodar* [howdah, sedan chair] with the charged firearms. I followed right behind; my much smaller mount did not inspire much confidence in its old *cornac* [elephant driver], who would show great sangfroid throughout the expedition. After we had crossed some rough terrain and passed through huge bushes, we found that the bamboo forest in front of us was so dense that we could hardly see objects ten feet away. Our elephants made a horrific noise as they pushed aside bamboos more than forty feet high and as thick as your wrist and snapped them like reeds.

Despite these obstacles we were making progress, and even merrily so, because no danger had presented itself, until my companion's elephant roared to announce that he had smelled a ferocious animal. I could not see Captain W— anymore but he shouted for me to be on my guard and soon the sound of a gunshot made me hurry toward him. He told me that a wild buffalo had just attacked him and that he had fired a bullet of more than two ounces from his carbine; the animal must have fallen near us. A moment later we heard it struggle violently in the forest.

Meanwhile our elephants were trumpeting oddly and mine moved back a few times, frightened by the smell of tigers and panthers that assemble in these places. The stench was so strong that even we could smell it as if we were in a zoo. Lost in this bamboo forest, we were suffocated by the heat and our situation was hardly pleasant or reassuring. I often saw little black bears running ahead of us and we also had a howling hyena following us. Impudently it came right near W—, who put it down with a single shot. His elephant then grabbed it with its trunk and threw it up like a stone, more than twenty feet above its head.

I saw peacocks and jungle fowl fly in all directions, but it was not the right time to enjoy the wildlife. We passed through a large group of ruins, and several fairly well-preserved pillars made it possible for me to step down and look at them from close range. As I was busy pulling away creepers covering a grayish stone on which there were still some visible figures, my driver told me to remount posthaste to come to W—'s rescue. Several gunshots and his elephant's roars told me in which direction to go. I arrived just as he had warded off an attack by a big striped tiger that, injured and enraged by the first bullet, had attacked him twice. He then told me we should not dream of carrying out our plan but rather retreat—and even that was not without danger.

"I do not fear the tigers much," he said, "but I just saw a rhinoceros, which is capable of disemboweling my elephant."

He was still speaking when the tiger showed up once more. My little elephant was so distressed by the sight that it panicked and was about to crush me by moving back among the bamboos. For a few moments no means of control could overcome its fear. Luckily my brave driver was able to reassure it by hitting it over the ears, threatening it, and praying.

"Be brave, little one," he cried, "show heart and don't bring dishonor on yourself as a coward." The animal seemed to understand this harangue and returned, with hanging head, to its big companion, which had kept its composure. It kept its trunk rolled up below its tusks, ready to hit the tiger with it if it dared to get close. It had already made the tiger fly through the air in this way, and if it could put a foot on the wild animal it would smother it in an instant. But the blasted tiger had not lost any of its agility, despite being fairly seriously injured, and therefore did not give the elephant a chance to trample it. For a moment I saw the tiger crouching on its belly, half hidden behind long grass, but a bullet hit it and made it disappear forever from our view.

We began to return, with effort and continually apprehensive about being charged by the rhinos. More than once we could hear them mooing fairly close by, but ultimately we overcame our fear and returned to the open countryside in a state that is hard to describe. We were covered in sweat and dust, and the thorns and bamboos had reduced our clothes to shreds. We arrived like that in our camp, where our servants were cutting up a deer that one of them had just killed. In our absence they had been more successful hunters than we had been, for they presented us with several peafowl, jungle fowl, and partridges. The countryside was full of wildlife, they said, but the downside was that there were tiger and buffalo tracks everywhere.

After having spent some more time near Gaur, without daring to go back to its ruins, we left with no regrets and returned to a less savage area.

Translated from French by Willem van Schendel.

A Woman Teaches Herself to Read

Rashsundari Debi

Rashsundari Debi (c. 1809–99) was a housewife who made literary history. She was the first Bengali woman to write a full-length autobiography, and her story is probably the first autobiography in the Bengali language. Rashsundari Debi was an unlikely trailblazer. Born into an upper-caste Hindu landlord family in Pabna (western Bangladesh), she received no education. In her circles women remained illiterate partly because of a belief that a woman who was educated courted disaster in the form of early widowhood. Rashsundari Debi was married at the age of twelve to a landlord from Faridpur, gave birth to twelve children, and lived the conventional life of a well-to-do rural matron running a large household.

And yet she was exceptional in two respects. She transgressed the rule barring women from reading and writing, and she felt the need to disclose her life in print. Soon after she was widowed at the age of fifty-nine, she completed the first version of Amar Jiban *(My life); a final version was published in 1897 when she was eighty-eight. The book explores a new genre, the telling of one's own life. Rashsundari Debi frames her story in two ways. On the one hand, she shows how God's mercy and benevolence have directed her life; on the other, she demonstrates how she tried to shape her own life despite social restrictions and intense fear of family disapproval. The pièce de résistance is her secret struggle to master the art of reading around 1835, at the age of twenty-six, and much later the art of writing. She places this against the background of a major cultural encounter in nineteenth-century Bengal. Christian missionaries' attempts to introduce female education ignited a spirited debate between reformist and orthodox Bengalis, which, toward the end of Rashsundari Debi's life, had resulted in increasing opportunities for girls to become literate. Rashsundari Debi offers her life story as a public testimony of the odds against women's education in her own generation.*

I was immersed in a life of labour, I hardly knew how time went by. Little by little, a desire took shape in my mind and I came to be possessed by a single wish: I will learn to read, and I will read a sacred text. I began to resent my own thoughts. "What is wrong with me? Women do not read, how will I do it, and why does this bother me so!" I didn't know what to do. It isn't as if all our ways were evil those days, but this certainly was. Everyone got together to deprive women of education. It must be said that women of those times were most unfortunate, they were hardly any better than beasts of burden. However, it is useless to reproach others about this—that was what fate had decreed for me. Really, how cross those old housewives would be if they saw a woman with as much as a piece of paper in her hands. So, how was I to learn anything? But my heart would not accept this, it was forever yearning. I began to ponder: as a child I had learnt something at that school at home from the other students who used to recite the letters loudly. Would I remember any of that? Slowly, with great effort, I managed to recall the thirty four letters, the vowels and the spellings. That, again, was something that I could recite but not write. What was I to do? Truly, if no one teaches you, you can't learn a thing. Moreover, I was a woman, and a married one at that. I'd die if someone was to rebuke me. Nor was I supposed to talk to others, so my fears kept me nearly mute. I prayed all the time: "Lord of this world! If you teach me yourself, I shall certainly learn. Who else will teach me if you don't?" These thoughts were always with me. Many days passed thus.

Then I had a dream: I was reading the manuscript of *Chaitanya Bhagabat*.[1] When I woke up, an unearthly joy possessed my body and heart. I kept closing my eyes even when I was fully awake, I kept going back to the memory of the dream. It was as if I had been given a priceless jewel. As my body and mind filled with delight, I began to wonder: "Isn't it strange? I have never seen this book before, I wouldn't even recognise it. Yet I was reading it in my dreams. I can read nothing at all, let alone something like this, it is impossible. Even then, I am blessed that I was at least able to read it in my dream. Since I am always praying to God to teach me to read, he has allowed me to do so in my dream, for he never actually did teach me. This is, indeed, a great blessing, thank the Lord for blessing my birth, for fulfilling my deepest desire." I was so happy.

I began to think, "This house has many books, maybe *Chaitanya Bhagabat* is also there." But what difference could that make to me? I didn't know how to read, I couldn't even identify the book. So I resumed my prayers: "Lord of the poor! Lead me to the book that I saw in my dream. You have to do this, who else can bring *Chaitanya Bhagabat* to me?" Thus I spoke to the Great Lord.

What a miraculous proof I had of the wonderful mercy of the Compassionate One! As I was brooding, he heard my wish and he set about granting it immediately. My eldest son was eight years old at the time. As I sat cooking in the kitchen, I heard *karta*[2] say to him: "Bepin, I have left my *Chaitanya*

Bhagabat here. When I ask for it, bring it in." He left the book there and went away.

I heard all this from the kitchen with great delight. I rushed over to look at the book. Thanking the Lord for listening to my prayer, I opened it and felt it all over. Manuscripts were very different from the printed books of these days. They used to be pressed between wooden slats which were colourfully illuminated. Since I didn't read at all, I memorised the illumination in order to identify the book.

When the book had been taken inside, I secretly took out a page and hid it carefully. It was a job hiding it, for nobody must find it in my hands. That would lead to severe rebukes and I would never be able to put up with that. It was not at all easy to do something that is forbidden and then to face the consequences. Times were very different then, and I was an exceptionally nervous person. Such days! One was entirely in bondage and my fears were great. That page was a headache. Where could I hide it that nobody would come across it? Eventually, I decided that it must be a place where I would always be present but which nobody else visited much. What else could it be but the kitchen? I hid it under the hearth. But there was never any time to look at it. I finished cooking very late in the night. After that was over, the children started waking up, one after the other. And then it was pandemonium! One says, "Ma, I need to pee," another says, "Ma, I am hungry," and yet another says, "Ma, take me on your lap," while someone else wakes up and starts bawling. I had to look after them all. After that it got even later, I couldn't fight off sleep any more, there was no time to study the page. I could see no way out of it. How can one learn without a teacher? I could silently say a few letters to myself, but I could not write them. It is impossible to master the word without knowing how to write. I saw no way of reading that page, however hard I thought about it. Moreover, the fear of exposure was always there.

Helplessly, I prayed to the Lord: "Great Lord, do help me to read this, who else is there to teach me?" Thus I prayed all the time but I would also despair at times. Even if someone did teach me the letters, where was the time to pursue that? Why cherish an impossible dream? At other times, I would hope again. Since the Great Lord himself has planted this hope in me, he will not thwart it. So I held on to the page. Even though I hardly had the time to glance at it, I would occasionally keep it in my left hand while I was cooking, and sometimes I would steal a look at it from under the veil. The letters, however, remained inscrutable.

My eldest son was practising his letters on palm leaves at that time. I hid one of them as well. At times, I went over that, trying to match letters from that page with the letters that I remembered. I also tried to match the words with those that I would hear in the course of my days. But after a quick look at them, I would hide them under the hearth once more. I spent quite a bit of time in this fashion.

Ah, what a sad thing it was! Such misery, only because one was a woman! We were in any case imprisoned like thieves, and on top of that, reading was yet another crime. It is good to see women having an easier time of it now. Even if someone has a daughter these days, he educates her carefully. We suffered so much just to learn to read. Whatever little I learnt was entirely because God was kind to me.

The man who was my master was a good person. But it is most difficult to abandon the custom of the land. That is why I suffered so. However, why dwell on past misfortunes! Those days, people were convinced that it is sinful to educate women. Why blame them alone, even now there are those who go up in smoke at the thought. It is useless to blame them either. Time is a priceless treasure. Those times and these are so different, if we compare them, we won't be able to count the changes that have happened. If people from those times were to see the ways of today, they would die of grief and horror. Actually, we happily accept whatever the Great Lord decrees at a particular time. Women would then wear coarse clothes, heavy ornaments, an armful of conch-shell bangles, their foreheads would be smeared with vermillion paste. It didn't seem so bad then. We ourselves didn't dress quite like that, but even so, I shudder to think of what we had to wear then.

Anyway, the Great Lord had taken care of me all that while; I was happy and contented. I can only say that whatever he does is providential. As a child, I had been made to sit in that schoolroom, and that now helped me a lot. I could match the letters I remembered with those on the palm leaf and on the page. I read to myself, in silence. All day, I would try to go through this in my mind. With tremendous care and effort and over a long stretch of time, I learnt somehow to limp and stammer across *Chaitanya Bhagabat*. Those days, we did not see printed letters, the handwritten letters on the manuscripts were immensely difficult to read. My reading was so painfully acquired! Even after such effort, I didn't know how to write. It takes a lot to be able to write—paper, pen, ink, inkpot. I would need to spread them all around me and then sit down to write. I was a woman, and on top of that, a married one. They are not meant to read and write. The authorities have decreed that this is a cardinal sin for women. How could I have tried to write in that situation? I was so scared of rebukes. So I killed my desire for writing and I would only read—and that, too, in secret. Even that had so far been beyond my wildest dreams. It is almost an impossible achievement; it was possible in my case only because the Great Lord himself guided me with his own hands. The fact that I could read at last was enough for me, I didn't think of writing.

Translated from Bengali by Tanika Sarkar.

Notes

1. A sixteenth-century hagiography of the famous Bengali saint Chaitanya (born c. 1486 CE).
2. "The master," i.e., her husband.

What Is Lalon's Faith?

Fakir Lalon Shah

Born in 1774 in the district of Kushtia (western Bangladesh), Fakir Lalon Shah—or Lalon Fakir—became a great mystic, philosopher, and composer. His numerous songs stand in a tradition that seems untouched by the colonial changes taking place at the time. This is perhaps the very reason that today they still provide inspiration to many in Bangladesh and beyond: they have the status of icons of Bengali authenticity. Every year in the town of Kushtia a huge festival is held in honor of Lalon, drawing tens of thousands of devotees and lovers of Lalon-giti (Lalon songs). Like his near contemporary, Modon Baul (see part II), Lalon stood in the devotional tradition of Vaisnavism, and his works became emblems of the Baul community and its nonconformist spiritual musicians. Celebrating freedom of body and soul, rejecting social and religious distinctions, and seeking union with the divine, Lalon's powerful and enigmatic voice continues to rally against narrow-mindedness and all kinds of orthodoxy.

I.
Everyone wonders, "What's Lalon's faith?"
Lalon says, "I've never 'seen' the face
of Faith with these eyes of mine!"

Circumcision marks a Muslim man,
what then marks a Muslim woman?
A Brahmin I recognize by the holy thread;
how do I recognize a Brahmin woman?

Everyone wonders, "What's Lalon's faith?"

Some wear a garland and some the *tasbi* [prayer beads],
that's what marks the Faiths apart.
But what marks them apart when
one is born or at the time of death?

Everyone wonders, "What's Lalon's faith?"

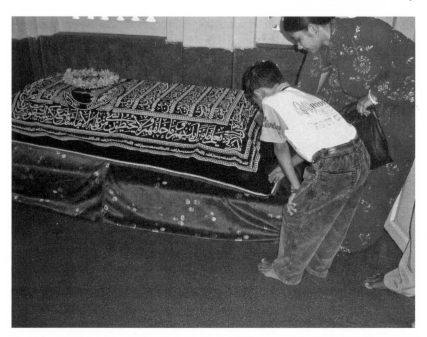

Devotees at Fakir Lalon Shah's shrine in Kushtia. Photograph by Willem van Schendel, 2006.

The whole world talks about Faith,
everyone displaying their pride!
Lalon says, "My Faith has capsized
in this Market of Desire . . . "

Everyone wonders, "What's Lalon's faith?"

2.
The unknown Bird in the cage . . .
how does it fly in and out?
Catch it, I would, if I could . . .
and put my mind's chains on its feet.

There are eight rooms with nine doors,
with lattice-work in between.
On top of that, there's a central yard
and a hall of mirrors.

The unknown Bird in the cage . . .
how does it fly in and out?

The Bird wouldn't behave so,
had it not been for my ill luck.
It has broken through its Cage
and flown away somewhere . . .

The unknown Bird in the cage . . .
how does it fly in and out?

O Mind, you have lived with high hopes,
but your Cage is made of raw bamboo.
One day this Cage (too) will fall and break.
Lalon says, "The door's ajar, the Bird's flown!"

The unknown Bird in the cage . . .
how does it fly in and out?

Translated from Bengali by Sudipto Chatterjee.

Blue Devil

George Dowdeswell, Bhobonath Joardar, Panju Mulla, and Maibulla

The British became rulers of Bengal in 1757 and they departed in 1947. In the two intervening centuries, they benefited from their colony mainly by collecting taxes, producing agricultural commodities for export, and marketing British industrial goods. In the process, the economy of the colony was transformed. In what would later become Bangladesh, a series of new cash crops were introduced. Indigo was among the first and most valuable. Indigo plants yield the best natural blue dye, and the British were keen to promote its production. They were very successful: by the early 1800s India had emerged as the world's largest exporter of indigo, a position it would hold for a century. Then another cash crop, jute, came to the fore.

Peasants cultivated indigo and delivered the crop to indigo factories that dotted the countryside. Most managers and owners of these factories were Europeans, and they soon gained a reputation for oppressing the peasantry. Often violent confrontations took place between factory staff, peasants, and landlords, as well as among competing indigo entrepreneurs. Many cultivators hated the crop, which brought them less income than rice, but they were forced to grow indigo. They called indigo the "blue devil." At times the colonial government felt obliged to intervene, for example in 1810 (this is apparent in the circular letter from the government to all district magistrates).

In the late 1850s, peasant anger erupted into widespread rebellion all over Bengal. In the wake of this rebellion (sometimes referred to as the Blue Mutiny), a government commission of inquiry was formed. It heard evidence from numerous witnesses, half of them cultivators. In the piece "Testimonies before the Indigo Commission," the voices of Bhobonath Joardar, Panju Mulla, and Maibulla express some of their grievances.

(Circular)

TO THE MAGISTRATES

SIR,

The attention of Government has recently been attracted in a particular manner to abuses and oppressions committed by Europeans, who are established as Indigo Planters in different parts of the Country; numerous as these abuses and oppressions have latterly been, the Right honourable the Governor General in Council is still willing to hope that this imputation does not attach to the character of the Indigo Planters, generally considered as a body or class of people. The facts, however, which have recently been established against some individuals of that class before the Magistrates and the Supreme Court of Judicature, are of so flagrant a nature, that the Governor General in Council considers it an act of indispensable public duty, to adopt such measures as appear to him, under existing circumstances, best calculated to prevent the repetition of offenses equally injurious to the English character, and to the peace and happiness of our native subjects.

2. The Offences to which the following Remarks refer, and which have been established, beyond all doubt or dispute, against individual Indigo Planters, may be reduced to the following heads:

   1st. Acts of violence, which although they amount not in the legal sense of the word to murder, have occasioned the death of natives.
   2nd. The illegal detention of the natives in confinement, especially in stocks, with a view to the recovery of balances, alleged to be due from them, or for other causes.
   3rd. Assembling, in a tumultuary manner, the people attached to their respective factories and others, and engaging in violent affrays with other Indigo Planters.
   4th. Illicit infliction of punishment, by means of a rattan or otherwise, on the cultivators or other natives.

3. You must of course be sensible, that it is your bounden duty to bring every act of violence, of the above nature, to the knowledge of the Government, and under the cognizance of the Supreme Court of Judicature. In order however to prevent, as far as depends on the Executive Government, the repetition of any offence of that nature, the Governor General in Council desires, that you will particularly attend to the following Instructions:

First—You will take the necessary measures to ascertain, without loss of time, whether any of the Indigo Planters resident in the district under your charge, keep stocks at their factories, and if so, you will require them immediately to destroy the stocks; should any hesitation occur on the part of the Indigo Planters in complying with this requisition, you will report the circumstance to Government, when the Governor General in Council will order such person to quit the district, and repair to the Presidency.

Second—Without encouraging vexatious and litigious complaints, we will exert yourself to prevent the practice, which government has reason to believe is too prevalent on the part of the Indigo Planters, of inflicting illegal corporal punishment on the ryots [tenants] and others; whenever cases of this nature occur, which may not appear to be of so aggravated a nature as to form the ground of a criminal prosecution in the Supreme Court of Judicature, you will report the facts to Government, in order that his Lordship in Council may take into his consideration the propriety of withdrawing the licence which the offender may have obtained for residing in the interior of the country.

Third—As opportunities may arise, of personal communication with the Indigo Planters, you will endeavour to impress on their minds, the firm determination which the Governor General in Council has adopted, not only uniformly to prosecute all offences of the above description, which can properly be brought under the cognizance of the Supreme Court; but likewise to exercise to the utmost extent the powers possessed by the Governor General in Council, of preventing the residence of any European in the interior of the country, who shall not conform to the spirit of the present resolutions of Government.

Fourth—Should it occur to you, that any other measures can be adopted, calculated for the attainment of the important objects above noticed, you are desired to submit your sentiments on the subject, to Government.

	I am, &c.
Council Chamber,	(Signed) Geo. Dowdeswell,
The 13th July 1810.	Secr. To Govt. Judl. Dept.

Testimonies before the Indigo Commission

1. Evidence given by Sri Bhobonath Joardar (inhabitant of Tarai, Hardi Police Office, Nuddea District [now: Chuadanga District]); examined on oath (9 July 1860).

The veranda of the planter's house at the Amjhupi indigo factory (Meherpur district). Photograph by Willem van Schendel, 2006.

Q: Have you sown any indigo this year?

A: This year, in the month of *Aswin* and *Kartik* [September–November], the factory people made me sow indigo, i.e., they sent for my servants, five in number, and two pairs of bullocks, and made them sow seven beegahs and a half [one hectare]. I had nobody to complain to. Mr. Tripp [the indigo planter] is judge, magistrate, collector, and everything.

Q: Did you never receive any advances from the factory?

A: No, I never did. I can't say what they have written in the books, because the pen and ink and paper all belong to them. Last year I delivered 10 or 11 bundles of plant to the factory. My grandfather sowed for the factory. My grandfather used to sow willingly. In those days they used to get cash, but since the factory has the *ijaras* [leases] and *putnis* [estate rights] we get nothing.

Q: Did your father sow indigo willingly?

A: I never saw my father sow at all. I have myself sown for 10 or 12 years.

Q: In the first year of those 10 did you get no advances?

A: I was laid hold of and taken to the factory, and told, as I was a well-to-do man, I must sow. The factory had then got the *putni*. It had the lease previously. It was in the Bengali year 1258 [1851 CE]. I did not get any cash advances. They simply told me to sow.

Q: Then the first year, when you took your plant to the factory, did you get nothing?

A: Not a thing.

2. Evidence given by Panju Mulla (inhabitant of Arpara, Hardi Police Office, Nuddea District [now: Chuadanga District]); at present a resident in the Kishnagar Gaol, called in; and examined on oath (14 July 1860).
Witness deposed as follows:

I could not sow on account of the injustice. I had sown in the previous *Baisakh* [April]. I understood that there was an order of Government that those who had not entered into an agreement [with the indigo factory] need not sow, and as I had always sown by compulsion, I would not sow any more.

Q: Would not it have been better for you to sow this year, instead of going to prison?

A: No, I would rather be killed with bullets and have my throat cut, than sow indigo.

3. Evidence given by Maibulla, inhabitant of Lakhandi (Jenaida Police Office, Jessore District [now: Jhenaidah District]), called in; and examined on oath (14 July 1860).

Q: Have you sown indigo this year?

A: Yes, I have sown it in *Kartik* [October], not in *Baisakh* [April]. There are no sowings in *Baisakh*. Since that, my children have been constantly told to weed and pick the ground, so that they have no time to cultivate our rice lands. . . .

Q: Has the Sahib *[Mr. Oman, the indigo planter] ever beaten you, or ever treated you unkindly?*

A: Yes; last year I was beaten with a piece of leather by the *Sahib* himself. I had complained about the *dewan* [steward], because I was obliged to sell the clothes of my daughter to satisfy him; I then complained to the

Sahib, and then to Mr. Meares, of Sinduri [Mr. Oman's boss]. He took up the case, did justice, and dismissed the *dewan*. Mr. Oman, in anger, beat me for this, and I thought it no use to complain to Mr. Meares again. . . .

Q: *Have you any thing else to state?*

A: The *Sahib* insists on our working in the [indigo beating] vats; we are Mussulmans; and if we do this we cannot get our daughters married.

Fundamentalist Reform and the Rural Response

Rafiuddin Ahmed

For Muslims in Bengal, the nineteenth century brought enormous spiritual chal-
lenges. Their religious practices and beliefs, inherited from previous generations,
came under attack as preachers spread across the land with the aim of "Islamiz-
ing" the local Muslims. These campaigns rejected as heresies most of what Bengali
Muslims practiced and deemed these to be incompatible with the true principles of
Islam. Instead, the preachers emphasized the need for Muslims in Bengal to conform
to a pan-Islamic identity and to connect more decisively with the Muslim world
beyond their region. This implied that Islam in Bengal should distance itself from
the regional popular culture, now seen as un-Islamic or even anti-Islamic. These
movements saw themselves as purification campaigns, aimed at purging contami-
nating elements from Islam in Bengal. At the same time, these reform campaigns
highlighted how landlords, European indigo entrepreneurs, and the British gov-
ernment oppressed the poor. Consequently, they drew most of their support from
the peasantry. In a classic study of these reform movements and how rural Mus-
lims responded to them, Rafiuddin Ahmed explains the effects of this momentous
encounter.

Muslims in Bengal experienced a profound change in their religious ideology and social mores during the latter half of the nineteenth century. These
changes, crucial to the emergence of a new sense of identity, were largely
induced by a series of reform movements. The *Tariqah-i-Muhammadiya* and
the *Faraizi* were two of the earliest and most prominent among these. The
Tariqah movement, erroneously called Indian *Wahhabism*, belonged to the
tradition of the Waliullahi School of Delhi and was, to all intents and purposes, an extension of the *jihad* [holy war] movement launched by Shah
Sayyid Ahmad (1786–1831) of Rae Bareli in northern India. It was organized
and propagated in Bengal primarily at the initiative of the well-known Patna
caliphs, Maulanas Inayet Ali (1794–1858) and Wilayet Ali (1791–1835). Inayet

Ali did extensive missionary work in the rural districts of Bengal, covering a large tract in middle Bengal, including the districts of 24-Parganahs, Jessore, Faridpur, Pabna, Rajshahi, Malda and Bogra, and his efforts were largely responsible for the great enthusiasm created in that area for the *jihad* campaigns in [northwest India]. Maulana Keramat Ali (1800–1874), who later seceded from the original movement and founded his own, called the *Taiyuni*, also did extensive missionary work in the districts of Noakhali, Dacca [Dhaka], Mymensingh, Faridpur and Barisal, and contributed largely to the success of the movement at the early stage. . . .

The *Faraizi* movement was typically an indigenous movement and was inseparably connected with the socio-economic life of the rural Muslim. In matters of law and speculative theology, it professed to belong to the school of Abu Hanifah, one of the four authoritative commentators on the *Koran*. Their principal point of difference with the general body of *Sunnis* consisted in their rejection of traditional customs and recognition of the *Koran* as the total spiritual guide. It was a fundamentalist movement involving the poorer sections of agrarian society, and it was its particular emphasis on economic and agrarian questions that primarily distinguished it from the Waliullahi tradition of Delhi. Founded by Haji Shariatullah (1781–1840) of Faridpur (in eastern Bengal)—who had been on a pilgrimage to the sacred cities of Islam at a time when the *Wahhabi* movement had stirred the imagination of the Muslims in Arabia—the movement spread with "extraordinary rapidity" in the rice-swamp districts of eastern Bengal. Shariatullah's son and successor, Dudu Miyan (1819–1862), successfully utilized the antagonism of the Muslim peasantry towards the predominantly Hindu landlords and the European indigo-planters, proclaimed the equality of man, and pursued a vigorous campaign of missionary propaganda to win over the traditionalist Muslims to his side. He partitioned the whole of eastern Bengal into circles and appointed a *khalifa*, or agent, to each, whose duties were to keep the sect together, make proselytes and collect contributions for the furtherance of the objects of the association. His determined efforts bore him immense success and, before he died in 1862, he succeeded in turning a moderate missionary association into a well-organized brotherhood, with definite social, economic, as well as religious programmes. The movement under Dudu Miyan spread all over eastern Bengal. Particularly in the districts of Faridpur, Backergunj, Jessore, Tipperah, Dacca, Mymensingh, Pabna and Noakhali, it won numerous adherents. The movement, however, started to decline after his death when it passed to less energetic hands and failed to counter the mass movement launched by Maulana Keramat

Riverside scene in rural East Bengal in the 1860s. Anonymous photographer. Image © The British Library Board, Photo 124/(60). Used by permission.

Ali, who by now had embarked on an independent campaign of missionary propaganda.

Evidently, the *Faraizi* movement and the *Tariqah-i-Muhammadiya* were two totally separate movements with distinct organizations and principles of their own. But it is highly probable that both these organizations co-operated closely with each other at a certain time, especially during the *ji-had* campaigns. However, it seems unlikely that the *Faraizis* at any stage got merged with the wider *Wahhabi* movement. . . . That the *Faraizi* movement maintained its separate existence until very late in the nineteenth century is evident from the numerous religious confrontations between the two, and activities organized under their separate auspices. The two movements had, however, certain essential similarities in their objectives, for both were reformist-revivalist movements. They both intended to purge the Muslim society of its age-long un-Islamic beliefs and practices and, at the same time, both were determined to defend Islam against all outside intervention. The *Tariqah* movement was undoubtedly more openly involved in politi-

cal struggles than the *Faraizi*, but the latter's open espousal of the cause of
the oppressed peasantry ultimately involved it in much wider conflicts. The
political distinction between the two was in consequence greatly blurred, at
least in the eyes of the anti-reformists and the British government. . . .

From a historical point of view, the reform movement represented essentially the response of the *ulema* [scholars in Islamic jurisprudence] to the loss
of their old world—gone with the decline of Muslim power in India—which
they sought to regain by a return to the primitive purity of Islam. . . .

In many districts of lower Bengal, the organizers of *jihad* set up compact
organizations in rural areas, which systematically levied men and money
and forwarded them by regular stages to the *jihad* camps in the [northwest-
ern] Frontier. *Kafelahs* (bands) of men marched regularly to the Frontier
from Bengal and they actively participated in the holy war. . . . There can be
little doubt that the *Tariqah* movement was more directly involved in the *jihad* than the *Faraizis*. . . . Unlike the *Tariqah* movement, the *Faraizis* did not
come out openly in support of the *jihad* at the beginning, nor did its socio-
economic programmes, designed to safeguard the interests of its members,
involve it in an *open* conflict with the British government at this stage. Their
dislike of British rule was however nothing secret. Their suspension of the
congregational prayers of *Jumah* (Friday prayers) and *Id* [the main Muslim
festival], indicating that Bengal was *dar-ul-harb* [an abode of war] under the
British, were a clear indication of this antagonism. Moreover, there was a
general feeling at that time that the real object of the *Faraizis* was the expul-
sion of the alien rulers and the restoration of Muslim power. The movement
later clashed directly with the government when the British intervened in
favour of the landlords to suppress peasant uprisings led by the *Faraizis*. . . .

The socio-economic programmes of the reform movements were so designed as to draw support principally from the poorer sections of the community. . . . In general, the Muslim landowners were as scared as the Hindu
landlords of the activities of the reformists. The latter's intentions menaced
both equally. The *Faraizi* threat of expropriation of the landlords was directed against all alike and the Muslim landowners had no special reason
to feel safe just because they happened to be Muslims. No wonder that they
tried various measures to stem the rising tide of the reform movements,
even by inciting the traditionalist *mullahs* [rural Islamic scholars] to issue
fatwas [religious decisions] against the reformists, denouncing the latter's
activities as un-Islamic. . . .

The millennial prospects of rent-free lands were apparently not enough
to induce any significant section of the impoverished peasantry to join hands
with the neo-revolutionaries. The number of actual "conversions" remained

small. There was considerable tension in many places, particularly in the districts of lower Bengal, over the activities of the reformist preachers and agents, and, consequently, a tendency to exaggerate their real strength. . . . The "reformed" Muslims were often concentrated in particular pockets in a district, such as Chandpur in Tipperah, Munshigunj in Dacca, Madaripur in Faridpur, and Bagerhat in Khulna (then under Jessore), and it is unlikely that their numbers were greater than a mere fraction of the total Muslim population in the province [of Bengal] as a whole. In any case, a massive switchover of allegiance from the traditional to the reformed doctrines on the part of the rural population may be altogether ruled out.

The reform movements thus achieved great fame not so much for their success in enlisting the active support of the common people, but primarily because they awakened in the oppressed peasantry a consciousness of social injustice and economic oppression, and thus threatened the *status quo* in the rural society, affecting not only the wealthy landlords or moneylenders but even the petty *mullahs*. Yet their active supporters remained small in number, and, as the century progressed, became fewer and fewer.

Wage Holy War—or Leave!

Moulvi Mirza Jan Rahman

In the early nineteenth century a number of movements sought to "purify" the religious practices of Muslims in British India. Several became important in Bengal: the Faraizi movement, the Tariqah-i-Muhammadiyah movement, and the Taiyuni movement. Although they shared some similarities with each other, and with the Wahhabi movement of Arabia, the three differed in their doctrinal tenets, and these were the stuff of many heated public theological debates (baha) across the Bengal countryside.

A major bone of contention was the issue of British rule in the country. The proponents of the Faraizi and Tariqah movements held that British India was an "abode of war" (dar-ul-harb) because it was ruled by unbelievers, while those who supported the Taiyuni movement declared it an "abode of security" (dar-ul-aman) where Muslims could practice their religion without interference. Declaring that a country is abode of war implies the legitimacy of waging holy war against that country's rulers. In the 1860s the British attempted to suppress the Tariqah movement because of its campaign against them. The movement, founded by Sayyid Ahmad Shahid (1786–1831) in north India around 1818, was active in different parts of the colony. Its followers in Bengal sometimes called themselves Muhammadis but the British routinely, but mistakenly, labeled them Indian Wahhabis.

In one of many police raids on supporters, books were confiscated. One was a book in Bengali verse published from Dhaka, titled Tattva *(Spiritual principles). J. O'Kinealy, the British official who reported it to his superiors, described it as follows: "I do not think I have ever seen a more mischievous book; outside it seems to be only a compilation of decisions on religious forms and it is only by reading it through that the real intention of the compiler appears. It is the more dangerous, as it is written (in Bengalee), so that any Bengalee Mussalman can understand it."[1] Here are some excerpts from the book.*

Every person is bound to obey the Imam. Whoever does not do so and cannot believe in him, according to the [Muslim] Law such a person should be killed. Here the Muslim Law is not in force. What more shall I say . . .

a) Sayyid Ahmad is the great Imam and obedience to him is the way to salvation. Whoever takes any other path will be destroyed. Many say they are Imams and go about the country saying that from the power of [their] prayer the world is ruled. Their hearts are set upon honour and comfort. When the Imam made preparation, he became desirous to carry on a holy war (*jihad*).

b) He [Sayyid Ahmad] conquered for his followers. True men came to the front and offered up their property and lived in his service. Moulvi Abdul Hai and Moulvi Ismail, friends of God, were killed.

c) These were brave men and so also were those who served under them. [At that time] the liars made great excuses and did not go to the fight. Some ran away and were ever afterwards known as worldly people. They call themselves subordinates of the Imam as long as they can go about as saints and teachers; but are not to be found when a holy war is being carried on. Do the faithful depart from the land of his enemies (*hijrat*)? Such people are spoken of in the Koran and are known by the following signs:

1. They are enemies of tradition (*sunnat*).
2. They prohibit *hijrat* and *jihad*.
3. They are pleased with the country of the unbelievers (*kafir*).

These are the signs of the faithful:

1. They follow tradition heart and soul.
2. They are always dissatisfied to remain in the country of the unbelievers and continue beating the drum of faith.
3. They do not care for the riches, etc., of this world.

Moulvi Ismael and Mahomed Morad are with God, having performed *hijrat* and *jihad*. Moulvi Ansul and Moulvi Ahmed Ali became saints through *jihad*. Whoever served under these men, does not desire to live in the land of unbelievers and are now ready to devote life and property to. . . .

d) Whoever prohibits *hijrat* and *jihad* is an enemy of God. In those countries in which the unbeliever is powerful, there the Law of Mohammad cannot have full force. Hence, God has ordered that all Muslims must unite and fight against the unbeliever. Those who cannot answer to the call to join in a holy war should leave their country and go to some country where Muslims are the rulers. All the learned men have decided that the faithful should leave this country. Whoever forbids you to do so is the slave of his own heart. Whoever returns from the country of Islam after having left this country, leaves his faith behind him, and if he does not leave this country again, his prayers are in vain—and should he die here, he is a heretic. I pray that God may take me to some country in which the faithful dwell.

Translated from Bengali by J. O'Kinealy.

Note

1. Moulvi Mirza Jan Rahman and Haji Budaruddeen, *Tattva* (Dhaka: Dacca Vernacular Press, 1223 BE [1815–16 CE]).

Brahmos: Rebels against Tradition

David Kopf

In the colonial period the encounter between European and South Asian ideas intensified. This led to religious reform movements among Muslims as well as Hindus. One influential group of rebels against Hindu tradition emerged among the intelligentsia and became known as the Brahmo Samaj. Members espoused social reform—notably Western education, equality for women, and widow remarriage—and sought to introduce political liberalism. Over several decades they spearheaded a range of very prominent social, political, and religious movements in Bengal. Their ideas were not, however, accepted easily. On the contrary, Brahmos met with considerable resistance from their families and community leaders who saw the movement as a serious threat to the social order and Hindu values. This was especially true outside Calcutta, which was the stronghold of the Brahmo Samaj. In eastern Bengal Brahmos faced social ostracism and persecution, as detailed in this excerpt from David Kopf's study of the Brahmo Samaj.

The new identity through Brahmoism divided the most respected families, even those that had valued Western education. The case of the famous Chattopadhyay family of Vikrampur [Dhaka district] provides an excellent illustration of how families were split as a result of the new Brahmo consciousness and intrusion. The Chattopadhyays were Kulin Brahmans, whose oppression of women was a primary target of East Bengali Brahmo reformers. Naba Kanta, the eldest son, was evidently won over to Brahmoism and converted personally by Keshub Sen [a visionary leader] during a visit by the latter to Dacca [Dhaka] in 1869. The father, Kali Kanta, who was a pleader in the Dacca court, immediately dispossessed his son and founded the local society called Dharma Rakhini Sabha against Brahmo reformers.

The persecution of Brahmos seems to have been extreme in East Bengal. Buikunthanath Ghose, who was directly influenced by Brahmo ideas in 1868, while a student at the Mymensingh Government High School, has in his autobiography reported vividly on the persecution of himself and other young Brahmos. In December 1869, Bijoy Krishna of Calcutta came to

Brahmo women in Mymensingh in the 1920s. Note their distinctive dress. Brahmo women wore their saris with the pleats at the back instead of in front, the standard style. Anonymous photographer. Courtesy of Meghna Guhathakurta.

Mymensingh to open the new Brahmo mandir [temple], and it was at that ceremony that Ghose and other young men took the oath as Brahmos. The usual persecution followed: his mother threatened suicide, while his father imprisoned him at the family home in their native village. Ghose managed to escape to Calcutta, but when he returned he was continually harassed and beaten, his property burned or otherwise destroyed. Ghose also relates an interesting experience in Tangail. After a Brahmo prayer hall was consecrated by a Brahmo missionary, the villagers came secretly at night, desecrated the building, and stole the benches. Before leaving, they urinated and defecated in the prayer hall. The sweeper who agreed to clean it all up for the Brahmos was promptly excommunicated by the villagers, and several nights later his house was burned to the ground. . . .

When Krishna Kumar [Mitra] [a boy from Mymensingh] openly declared his Brahmoism, he was persecuted, and when his family supported his convictions, they were excommunicated. In 1870, Dacca College admitted him with a scholarship that paid ten rupees a month. But shortly thereafter, an uncongenial atmosphere drove him to Presidency College in Calcutta. As a student there, he experienced a new type of persecution. He was jeered at by the West Bengal boys for being a rustic "Bangal" from the East. "Students from Calcutta used to torment us," he himself wrote later on,[1] an experience reminiscent of others in Calcutta experienced by Bipin Chandra Pal, Prafulla Chandra Ray, and Nirad Chaudhuri—all from East Bengal.

The explosive impact of Brahmoism in the 1860s cannot be minimized. And always it was the young who responded favorably to Brahmo ideas and acted defiantly against established norms and practices. One event in the important nineteenth-century river port of Barisal is significant, as it is typical of what was happening everywhere. Durga Mohun Das, a Brahmo youth of Barisal fired up by the ideal of female emancipation, married off his widowed stepmother to a local medical practitioner. It was a love marriage. What were the consequences? Sivanath Sastri has written that "the doctor's clients deserted him and he had to give up his practice. About Durga Mohun, men threw dust at him and abused him on the streets. Dirty stories were told about his stepmother. The Hindus would never hear the name of Durga Mohun uttered, but spit on the ground as a mark of their abhorrence."

In Mymensingh in 1870, a solemn ritual was held in the Brahmo mandir in which six high-caste young men removed their sacred threads and placed them on the pulpit as "a mark of public renunciation of caste."[2] The Hindu forces went on a rampage and cut off all services to Brahmo families.

Not a single house-servant came forward to offer himself to the Brahmo community.

The evidence is clear: adolescence and young adulthood for the bhadralok [cultured elite] progressives was in a great majority of cases—where evidence is available—full of storm and stress. The formation of a new identity in the young between tradition and modernity, between Bengali cultural values and the challenging values of the West, was hardly ever a smooth transition and was never afforded the luxury, by the irate orthodox, of becoming compartmentalized. The humiliation of persecution polarized differences with their antagonists. Perhaps it was different elsewhere in India, but in Bengal the facts are plain enough.

Notes

1. K. K. Mitra, *Krishna Kumar Mitrer Atma Charit* (Calcutta: Bashanti Chakraborty, 1937), 58, 64–65, 103.
2. S. Sastri, *History of the Brahmo Samaj* (Calcutta: R. Chatterjee, 1911), II, 350.

Worshipping with Cannabis

Abhilas Chandra Mukherji

The enormous turmoil that the nineteenth century bought to Bengal's society found expression in the flourishing of many new religious forms. Some have been studied in great detail (for example, the Brahmo and Faraizi movements), but many others remain little known. And yet they were often of considerable concern to contemporary observers, especially colonial bureaucrats in charge of law and order and tax collection. Their memoranda, reports, and other documentation reveal how they tried to make sense of the social changes around them.

The report here was written by Abhilas Chandra Mukherji, the second inspector of excise in Bengal, as part of a government study into the use and effects of cannabis in India, and was published in 1894. It describes the creation of Trinath Worship (or Trinath Mela) in 1867 and its very rapid spread across rural Bengal. Today Trinath melas [fairs] are still being organized in Bangladesh. An earlier observer, James Wise (Notes on the Races, Castes and Trades of Eastern Bengal, 1883), had been struck by the fact that the new Trinath Worship "is attracting crowds of uneducated and credulous Chandals, Kaibarttas and Tiyars throughout Eastern Bengal. . . . It is difficult to account for such a creed unless we believe that the Brahmanical hold on the people is relaxing, and that the masses blindly accept any worship which recognises the equality and brotherhood of all classes of mankind."

Mukherji's concise report is at pains to provide factual information based on primary source material. In this way, he provides a good example of dispassionate bureaucratic understanding of an ecstatic new cult using taxable intoxicants.

On the Origin and History of Trinath Worship in Eastern Bengal.

Date of origin. In 1867 Babu Ananda Chandra Kali or Kailai, of Dhamrai, a village in thana [police zone] Sabhar of the Dacca [Dhaka] district, first started the worship at the house of his father-in-law at Fattehpur in the Atia pargana of the Mymensingh district (sub-division Tangail).

Antecedents of the originator. Dhamrai is an important village in the Dacca district noted for its car festival, which is annually held in honor of a local idol named *Madhab Thakur,* and which is witnessed by a large gathering of people. Ananda Chandra received education at the Dacca Normal School. After leaving school he served for some time as a pundit (schoolmaster), and then entered the Police Department, but was there only a short time. He is a Barendra Brahman and belongs to a respectable family. He learnt to smoke ganja when he was only a boy. His present age is 60 years. He has the reputation of being a versifier. He smokes two pice [1/64th of a rupee] worth of ganja [marijuana] every day. He married at Fattehpur in the Mymensingh district. There he introduced Trinath worship 27 years ago. A *panchali* (poem) reciting the praises and exploits of Trinath was first published at Dacca in 1871 and the first edition (1,000 copies) was sold in a few months.

The circumstances under which the worship was first started. Ananda Chandra Kali was at the time living in the house of his father-in-law. He was thinking of introducing the worship of a common god, who might be worshipped by all classes, rich and poor, Brahman and Chandal, and by all creeds, Saktas, Baishnavas, and Shaivas, and the idea occurred to him of having the present worship at which ordinary and inexpensive things, such as ganja, oil, and betel-leaf, were alone to be used. Trinath (from Sanskrit *Tri,* three, and *Nath,* lord) is represented to be Brahma, Bishnu and Shiva, the Hindu Trinity in one. Being a ganja-smoker himself, Ananda Kali may have also thought that by introducing the worship he would be able to save the ganja-smokers from disrepute, as then ganja could be consumed in the name of a god and under colour of doing a religious or pious act.

Religious aspect of the worship. The following translation of the Introduction to the *Trinath Mela* [Fair] *Panchali* gives some idea of the subject:

> The universe consists of the earth, the heaven, and the nether world, and Trinath is the lord of these three worlds. There was an incarnation of God in the form of Gour (Chaitanya), who delivered the sinners by preaching the name of Hari, but the Lord was not satisfied with this, and became concerned for the created, and soon he became incarnate again. Brahma, Bishnu and Shiva, gods in three forms, manifested themselves in one form. The one God, the Lord of the universe, seeing the miseries of mankind, came to their deliverance. Ananda (Ananda Chandra Kali, the originator) declares that the true and sincere worshippers of Trinath are sure to obtain salvation. Brahma, Bishnu, and Shiva met together and expressed their desire to come to this world in one form to receive worship.

He is a truly pious man who worships Trinath, and blessings are showered on the worshipper. The worship should be made in a form in which the rich and the poor may equally join and may perform it easily. Only three things, each worth one pice, are required for this *puja* (form of worship). The things which please all must be selected. The offering should consist of *siddhi* (ganja), *pan* (betel-leaf), and oil, each worth one pice.

The votaries should assemble at night and worship with flowers. The ganja should be washed in the manner in which people wash ganja for smoking. The worshipper must fill three *chillums* [clay pipes] with equal quantities of ganja, observing due awe and reverence. When all the worshippers are assembled the lamp should be lit with three wicks, and the praises of Trinath should be sung. As long as the wicks burn, the god should be worshipped and his praises chanted. The god should be reverentially bowed to at the close of the puja. When the reading of the *Panchali* is finished, those that will not show respect to the *Prasad* (the offering which has been accepted by the god), *i.e. chillum* of ganja, shall be consigned to eternal hell, and the sincere worshippers shall go to heaven.

How the worship spread. Ananda Kali commenced the puja with the aid of some ganja-smokers in the village of Fattehpur. A large number of people consume ganja in the Dacca and Mymensingh districts, and the worship soon became popular. In fact, it spread like wildfire from one village to another among the ganja-smokers. Those that were not in the habit of consuming ganja also followed their example. The following circumstances assisted the spread of the worship:

I. The puja is open to all classes from Brahmans to Chandals and to the rich and poor. Caste does not stand in its way, and it may be performed almost every day and in all seasons.

II. The puja is a *Majasik Puja* (made in pursuance of a vow on the fulfilment of the object desired). People have been led to believe that Trinath possesses the power of healing the sick and fulfilling desires, and that those who neglect his worship meet with disgrace, while those who observe it attain success in life. There are several stories in the Panchali narrated in illustration of this statement. It is also popularly believed that in the house where Trinath is worshipped cold, fever, and headache do not appear.

III. This is a cheap form of worship. The puja can be performed by even the poorest, only three pice being required.

IV. Ganja can be consumed by all in the name of a god, and the practice cannot be looked down upon, because it is done under certain forms of religious ceremonies. It is also popularly believed that those who mock the worshippers of Trinath shall be ruined and shall be the victims of misfortune.

The worship prevails not only among the poor, but also among the well-to-do. The latter often entertain their friends after the puja. Women do not take any active part in the worship, but they often listen to the reading of the *Panchali*.

The worship is more or less general in the following districts: (1) Dacca, (2) Mymensingh, (3) Faridpur, (4) Backergunge, (5) Noakhali, (6) Tippera, (7) Chittagong, (8) Bogra, (9) Sylhet, and (10) Pabna (Serajganj side). The worship is on the decline. It is almost dying out among the educated *bhodrolokes*, but among the masses it still exists.

I have attained the above facts from Dr. Chandra Sekher Kali (brother of the originator, Ananda Chandra Kali) and many other respectable persons, and also from personal inquiries in the Dacca, Chittagong and Rajshahi divisions.

Blue Dakini. Illustration in a Pala manuscript, eleventh to twelfth centuries.
Used by permission of the Varendra Research Museum, Rajshahi.

Since the beginning of recorded history, powerful female deities have been very
prominent in Bengali culture. Even today great goddesses are widely venerated in
Bangladesh, for example the Hindu deities Durga and Kali and the Muslim deities
Olabibi and Bonbibi. This image shows a blue dakini, female embodiment of enlightened mental energy, in a Buddhist manuscript from the Pala period.

Two sides of a *tanka*, a silver coin from the Sonargaon mint, fourteenth century, from the Fitzwilliam Museum, CM.25–1916. Photograph © Fitzwilliam Museum, University of Cambridge. Used by permission.

When Bangladesh became an independent country, it chose to name its currency *taka*—a historical reference to coins like the one above. This tanka was minted in Sonargaon in 1346–47. At that time Sonargaon was the capital of an independent kingdom ruled by Sultan Fakhruddin Mubarak Shah and covering most of what is now eastern Bangladesh. Although the word *tanka* could refer specifically to such silver coins, its meaning was not restricted to this. For centuries people in the Bengal delta have used it as the most common general term for *money*.

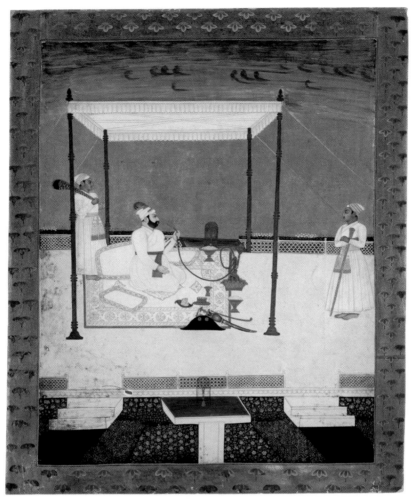

A nobleman, probably Husain Quli Khan, the deputy governor of Dhaka, c. 1750–54.
Image © Victoria and Albert Museum, London. Used by permission.

In the early eighteenth century, the rulers of Bengal moved the capital from Dhaka
to Murshidabad (which is now in West Bengal, India). They left the deputy governor
of Dhaka in charge of what we would now consider eastern Bangladesh, from the
Garo Hills in the north to Chittagong in the south. As this portrait demonstrates,
the deputy governor lived in grand courtly style. In this formal painting we see him
leisurely smoking a water pipe, seated on an elegant canopied terrace. He is attended
by servants with a peacock-feather flyswatter and a staff.

Procession in Dhaka city. Watercolor by Alam Musavvir, c. 1820. Used by permission of the Bangladesh National Museum, Dhaka.

Around 1820 Alam Musavvir, a local artist, made a series of watercolors depicting the large processions in the streets of Dhaka during Muharram and Eid, major festivals of Shia and Sunni Islam. Today these artworks are prime historical sources. They show what the city streets and buildings looked like, how the people of Dhaka dressed, and how they expressed religious and joyous sentiments. In wonderful detail we see palaces, mosques, a church, and many thatched huts in the distinctive curved-roof style of the region. Musavvir even shows us the animals of Dhaka: crows, herons, camels, and horses. But it is the people of Dhaka who take center stage. Richly dressed gentlemen are seen giving alms to beggars, and uniformed soldiers march together with musicians playing cymbals, drums, and wind instruments. Some Europeans and Africans are in the crowds who are being amused by dancers, snake charmers, wrestlers, and street vendors. In this fine example we see men and women observing the parade of carpet-decked elephants.

Chittagong: A Marriage. Painting by James George, 1821–22. Image © Victoria and Albert Museum, London. Used by permission.

For Europeans in the early nineteenth century, Bengal was full of exotic scenery and customs. In an age before photography, many took to drawing or making watercolors to capture the adventure of being in this unfamiliar world—as souvenirs for themselves or to send to friends and relatives back home. This festive dance is from a series of watercolors titled Indian Scenery, which was made by a military man while he was stationed in Chittagong.

Three women. Anonymous photographer, early 1860s. Image © The British Library Board, Photo 124/(35). Used by permission.

This impressive portrait of three women—possibly a mother and her daughters—is part of a collection of groups and individuals from across eastern Bengal. Such portraits of types became popular in the nineteenth century as the colonial government, as well as the budding science of ethnology, sought to collect systematic information about the diverse races, customs, and occupations in British India.

A Koch-Mandai man with a thick-bladed agricultural knife. Anonymous photographer, 1860. Image © The British Library Board, Photo 124/(4). Used by permission.

The plains of Bangladesh have long been inhabited by a large variety of ethnic groups. Over time, many adopted Bengali ways while others remained distinct. The man in this photograph belonged to the Koch-Mandai, a group living in the Bhowal forest tract just north of Dhaka city.

Stained-glass window in Bangladesh's Northern National Palace (Uttor Gono Bhobon) in Nator. Photograph by Willem van Schendel, 2006.

In 1897 an earthquake destroyed the palace of the Dighapatia family of Nator. The family had established themselves as feudal lords in northern Bengal not long before the British took power. During the colonial period, the Dighapatias were successful in reinventing themselves as major *zamindars* (landlords and tax collectors for the British) and they continued to prosper. Thus they were able to rebuild their palace in turn-of-the-century grandeur. This is one of the windows, proudly showing the family's heraldic emblem.

The family fortunes reversed when the zamindari system was dismantled shortly after the British left. The palace was taken over by the state. Since 1972, successive presidents of Bangladesh have used it as the Northern National Palace.

Hill or Plough Cultivation?

John Beames

In his outspoken and humorous memoirs, John Beames describes the life of a colonial district official in British India. In this excerpt he gives an account of government development policy in the Chittagong Hill Tracts in 1878 and how it went haywire. The plan—to make hill cultivators give up their form of swidden agriculture (jhum) for plough cultivation—originated with the Forest Department. The lieutenant-governor of Bengal adopted it and ordered Beames and his colleagues to carry it out, against their better judgment. It is with glee that Beames describes how the hill people (to whom he refers as Mughs) effectively thwarted this attempt to "develop" them by apparently embracing the scheme. In following generations development experts would try to implement the same policies over and over again, meeting with the same local coping strategies.

We were engaged on a very difficult, in fact an almost impossible, task with these Mughs. The tangled maze of hills in which they live is densely wooded and contains a great deal of valuable timber. It had been placed under the charge of the Forest Department. A department of any kind in India always assumes that the world exists solely for the use of itself, and considers that anything that interferes with the working of the department ought to be removed. It was undoubtedly true that the Mughs and other hill tribes used their native forests very wastefully. Their system of agriculture, called *jhūm*, consists in setting the forest on fire and burning down a whole hillside. In the space so cleared they sow their crops, the rich virgin soil bears abundantly, and the ashes of the burnt forest are excellent manure. They continue to cultivate the same spot for a few years when they find its fertility decreases, whereupon they go away and burn down a fresh place. In former times the incessant wars between the tribes kept down the population, and they were not numerous enough seriously to affect the growth of the forest. Trees grew again in the deserted *"jhūm,"* and by the time—perhaps forty years—people wanted to burn that particular hillside again there was a thick growth of trees and jungle on it. But when the Pax Britannica was extended to those wilds and intertribal warfare ceased, the population increased so much that if not checked they would soon have burnt every bit of forest off the hills.

Dr. Schlich, the Head of the Forest Department, calmly proposed that the whole Mugh and Chakma population should be removed from their native hills! He did not say where they were to go to. He merely said, in the true departmental spirit, "These people destroy the trees, therefore let them be sent away." Of course, the district officers and the Commissioner strongly opposed this view. The Commissioner [my predecessor, not me] even went so far as to say that if trees and Mughs could not live together, he thought it would do less harm if the trees were removed, which caused Dr Schlich to foam at the mouth and utter bad words. Finally some wise man observed that it was not so much the Mughs themselves as their practice of *jhūming* that did harm, and he suggested that they should be taught to till the soil by ploughing like the Bengalis. In the *jhūm* method no plough is used; they make holes in the ground with a sharp stick burnt hard at the end, and drop the seed in. No Mugh was ever known to use the plough. Sir Ashley Eden [the Lieutenant-Governor of Bengal], however, caught at this suggestion and we were ordered to induce or compel the Mughs to give up their *jhūms* and take to ploughed fields instead. With his usual bullying injustice, he intimated that if we did not succeed he should consider that it was because we did not try, or because we were incompetent idiots. So of course we had to try to do what we knew beforehand would be utterly impossible.

The Mughs declared that it was a well-known fact that if they took to ploughing their race would die out. Their women were particularly vehement on this point, more so even than the men. They are by nature an extremely cheerful race, very idle, careless and merry, but on this point they grew stern, sulky and melancholy. There seems to be something congenial to their light-hearted, easy-going nature in their method of cultivation. Burning down a whole hillside, dibbling in some seed almost anyhow in the ground, and then sitting smoking and laughing till the crop grows and ripens is a proceeding that somehow seems made for them and they for it. It is altogether a different thing from the laborious ploughing of the soil, harrowing, sowing, weeding, watering and all the rest of it which occupies the melancholy quarrelsome, anxious Bengali. These children of nature will not even reap their own crops. Every year the steamers of the British India Company carry from Bengal to Chittagong, Akyab and Rangoon thousands of Bengali labourers, who go to earn good wages for two or three months by cutting and garnering the crops, while the lazy Mugh proprietors sit in their verandas smoking their long, rank cheroots and cutting jokes at the hard-working Bengalis, And now we were ordered to turn the Mughs into ploughers and reapers!

The way we did it was this. Among the Mughs live a curious people called Chakmàs who, though Mongolian by origin and Buddhist by religion, have adopted many customs and ceremonies from Hinduism and Islam. They have a Raja. In my time the Raja bore the Hindu name of Harishchandra, but his father had a Mahomedan name. They are not so averse to the plough as the pure Mughs, so we found a flattish piece of land in the Chakma Territory which we hired, and then let it out to some Mughs who nobly sacrificed themselves for the good of their race (being also handsomely paid for so doing), and undertook to plough it and raise a crop of rice from it. But we represented to the Government that ploughing, like all other arts, requires to be learnt, so we got permission to engage a few Bengalis to teach the Mughs. When I visited the spot with Gordon, we found the Bengalis laboriously ploughing and sowing in the swampy land, and the Mughs, whom they were supposed to be teaching, sitting happily on a rising ground with their backs to the Bengalis, smoking and joking together! When we called them they came forward quite cheerfully and, in answer to our questions, said, "Oh yes! We are learning very well. It is very easy. We quite understand. Soon we shall be able to hold the plough ourselves." But I never heard of the experiment getting beyond this. It afforded, however, material for a good long paragraph in our annual report, and that was all that apparently was wanted. We had done as we were told, we had started the experiment, and must leave it to time to prove whether it would be successful or not. So long as I was in the Chittagong Division, it got no further than Bengalis ploughing and Mughs looking on and cracking jokes.

The Postmaster

Rabindranath Tagore

Rabindranath Tagore (1861–1941), the towering figure of colonial Bengali high cul-
ture, was a poet, novelist, painter, and musician who remains supremely signifi-
cant today. His cultural standing is indicated by the fact that in 1972 it was a Tagore
song, "Amar Shonar Bangla" ("My Golden Bengal"), that independent Bangladesh
chose as its national anthem. Tagore, born into one of colonial Bengal's leading
families whose wealth originated from entrepreneurship and landlordism, used his
privileges to become a stellar cultural innovator. In the 1890s he spent a period as
manager of his family's landed estates in Kushtia (western Bangladesh). There he
worked on creating a new form in Bengali literature, the short story, a genre that
was also a vogue in Europe and America at the time.

"The Postmaster" ("Postmastar") is among his most celebrated works of short
fiction. It appeared in a weekly magazine in 1891 and explores the psychology of
belonging, dependence, and separation. It can be read as a comment on the complex
encounter that developed between colonial West and East Bengal. West Bengal con-
tained Calcutta [now Kolkata], the capital of British India. It became the center of
the self-important bhodrolok *(respectable) elite whose political and cultural power*
was firmly based on economic power over the East Bengal peasantry. East Bengal—
which deurbanized under colonial rule—became the elites' exploited, disdained,
romanticized, and ultimately ignored hinterland. In "The Postmaster" it is a job in
the colonial administration that brings a "Calcutta boy" to an East Bengal village
where he is "a fish out of water."

For his first job, the postmaster came to the village of Ulapur. It was a very
humble village. There was an indigo-factory near by, and the British manager had with much effort established a new post office.

The postmaster was a Calcutta boy—he was a fish out of water in a village like this. His office was in a dark thatched hut; there was a pond next
to it, scummed over with weeds, and jungle all around. The indigo agents
and employees had hardly any spare time, and were not suitable company
for an educated man. Or rather, his Calcutta background made him a bad

mixer—in an unfamiliar place he was either arrogant or ill-at-ease. So there was not much contact between him and the residents in the area.

But he had very little work to do. Sometimes he tried to write poems. The bliss of spending one's life watching the leaves trembling in the trees or the clouds in the sky—that was what the poems expressed. God knew, however, that if a genie out of an Arab tale had come and cut down all the leafy trees overnight, made a road, and blocked out the sky with rows of tall buildings, this half-dead, well-bred young man would have come alive again.

The postmaster's salary was meagre. He had to cook for himself, and an orphaned village-girl did housework for him in return for a little food. Her name was Ratan, and she was about twelve or thirteen. It seemed unlikely that she would get married. In the evenings, when smoke curled up from the village cowsheds, crickets grated in the bushes, a band of intoxicated Baul singers in a far village sang raucously to drums and cymbals, and even a poet if seated alone on a dark verandah might have shuddered a little at the trembling leaves, the postmaster would go inside, light a dim lamp in a corner of the room and call for Ratan. Ratan would be waiting at the door for this, but she did not come at the first call—she would call back, "What is it, Dadababu, what do you want?"

"What are you doing?" the postmaster would say.

"I must go and light the kitchen fire—"

"You can do your kitchen work later. Get my hookah ready for me."

Soon Ratan came in, puffing out her cheeks as she blew on the bowl of the hookah. Taking it from her, the postmaster would say abruptly, "So, Ratan, do you remember your mother?" She had lots to tell him: some things she remembered, others she did not. Her father loved her more than her mother did—she remembered him a little. He used to come home in the evening after working hard all day, and one or two evenings were clearly etched in her memory. As she talked, Ratan edged nearer to the postmaster, and would end up sitting on the ground at his feet. She remembered her little brother: one distant day, during the rainy season, they had stood on the edge of a small pond and played at catching fish with sticks broken off trees—this memory was far more vividly fixed in her mind than many more important things. Sometimes these conversations went on late into the night, and the postmaster then felt too sleepy to cook. There would be some vegetable curry left over from midday, and Ratan would quickly light the fire and cook some chapati: they made their supper out of that.

Occasionally, sitting on a low wooden office-stool in a corner of his large hut, the postmaster would speak of his family—his younger brother, mother and elder sister—all those for whom his heart ached, alone and exiled as he was. He told this illiterate young girl things which were often in his mind but which he would never have dreamt of divulging to the indigo employees—and it seemed quite natural to do so. Eventually Ratan referred to the postmaster's family—his mother, sister and brother—as if they were her own. She even formed affectionate imaginary pictures of them in her mind.

It was a fine afternoon in the rainy season. The breeze was softly warm; there was a smell of sunshine on wet grass and leaves. Earth's breath—hot with fatigue—seemed to brush against the skin. A persistent bird cried out monotonously somewhere, making repeated and pathetic appeals at Nature's midday durbar. The postmaster had hardly any work: truly the only things to look at were the smooth, shiny, rain-washed leaves quivering, the layers of sun-whitened, broken-up clouds left over from the rain. He watched, and felt how it would be to have a close companion here, a human object for the heart's most intimate affections. Gradually it seemed that the bird was saying precisely this, again and again; that in the afternoon shade and solitude the same meaning was in the rustle of the leaves. Few would believe or imagine that a poorly paid sub-postmaster in a small village could have such feelings in the deep, idle stillness of the afternoon.

Sighing heavily, the postmaster called for Ratan. Ratan was at that moment stretched out under a guava tree, eating unripe guavas. At the sound of her master's call she got up at once and ran to him.

"Yes, Dadababu, you called?" she said, breathlessly.

"I'm going to teach you to read, a little bit each day," said the postmaster. He taught her daily at midday from then on, starting with the vowels but quickly progressing to the consonants and conjuncts.

During the month of Śrāban, the rain was continuous. Ditches, pits and channels filled to overflowing with water. The croaking of frogs and the patter of rain went on day and night. It was virtually impossible to get about on foot—one had to go to market by boat. One day it rained torrentially from dawn. The postmaster's pupil waited for a long time at the door, but when the usual call failed to come, she quietly entered the room, with her bundle of books. She saw the postmaster lying on his bed: thinking that he was resting, she began to tip-toe out again. Suddenly she heard him call her. She turned round and quickly went up to him saying, "Weren't you asleep, Dadababu?"

"I don't feel well," said the postmaster painfully. "Have a look—feel my forehead."

He felt in need of comfort, ill and miserable as he was, in this isolated place, the rain pouring down. He remembered the touch on his forehead of soft hands, conch-shell bangles. He wished his mother or sister were sitting here next to him, soothing his illness and loneliness with feminine tenderness. And his longings did not stay unfulfilled. The young girl Ratan was a young girl no longer. From that moment on she took on the role of a mother, calling the doctor, giving him pills at the right time, staying awake at his bedside all night long, cooking him convalescent meals, and saying a hundred times, "Are you feeling a bit better, Dadababu?"

Many days later, the postmaster got up from his bed, thin and weak. He had decided that enough was enough: somehow he would have to leave. He wrote at once to his head office in Calcutta, applying for a transfer because of the unhealthiness of the place.

Released from nursing the postmaster, Ratan once again took up her normal place outside his door. But his call did not come for her as before. Sometimes she would peep in and see the postmaster sitting distractedly on his stool or lying on his bed. While she sat expecting his summons, he was anxiously awaiting a reply to his application. She sat outside the door going over her old lessons numerous times. She was terrified that if he suddenly summoned her again one day, the conjunct consonants would all be muddled up in her mind. Eventually, after several weeks, his call came again one evening. With eager heart, Ratan rushed into the room. "Did you call, Dadababu?" she asked.

"I'm leaving tomorrow, Ratan," said the postmaster.

"Where are you going, Dadababu?"

"I'm going home."

"When are you coming back?"

"I shan't come back again."

Ratan did not question him further. The postmaster himself told her that he had applied for a transfer, but his application had been rejected; so he was resigning from his post and returning home. For several minutes, neither of them spoke. The lamp flickered weakly; through a hole in the crumbling thatched roof, rain-water steadily dripped on to an earthenware dish. Ratan then went slowly out to the kitchen to make some chapati. She made them with none of her usual energy. No doubt her thoughts distracted her. When the postmaster had had his meal, she suddenly asked, "Dadababu, will you take me home with you?"

The Selaidaha manor stands on the banks of the Ganges in Kushtia. Here Rabindra-nath Tagore managed the family estates and wrote "The Postmaster" in 1891. Today it is a museum. Photograph by Willem van Schendel, 2006.

"How could I do that!" said the postmaster, laughing. He saw no need to explain to the girl why the idea was impossible.

All night long, whether dreaming or awake, Ratan felt the postmaster's laugh ringing in her ears. "How could I do that!" When he rose at dawn, the postmaster saw that his bath-water had been put out ready for him (he bathed according to his Calcutta habit, in water brought in a bucket). Ratan had not been able to bring herself to ask him what time he would be leav-ing; she had carried the bath-water up from the river late at night, in case he needed it early in the morning. As soon as he finished his bath, the post-master called her. She entered the room softly and looked at him once with-out speaking, ready for her orders. "Ratan," he said, "I'll tell the man who replaces me that he should look after you as I have; you mustn't worry just because I'm going."

No doubt this remark was inspired by kind and generous feelings, but who can fathom the feelings of a woman? Ratan had meekly suffered many scoldings from her master, but these kindly words were more than she could bear. The passion in her heart exploded, and she cried, "No, no, you mustn't say anything to anyone—I don't want to stay here." The postmaster was taken aback: he had never seen Ratan behave like that before.

A new postmaster came. After handing over his charge to him, the resigning postmaster got ready to leave. Before going, he called Ratan and said, "Ratan, I've never been able to pay you anything. Today before I go I want to give you something, to last you for a few days." Except for the little that he needed for the journey, he took out all the salary that was in his pocket. But Ratan sank to the ground and clung to his feet, saying, "I beg you, Dadababu, I beg you—don't give me any money. Please, no one need bother about me." Then she fled, running.

The departing postmaster sighed, picked up his carpet-bag, put his umbrella over his shoulder, and, with a coolie carrying his blue-and-white-striped tin trunk on his head, slowly made his way towards the boat.

When he was on the boat and it had set sail, when the swollen flood-waters of the river started to heave like the Earth's brimming tears, the postmaster felt a huge anguish: the image of a simple young village-girl's grief-stricken face seemed to speak a great inarticulate universal sorrow. He felt a sharp desire to go back: should he not fetch that orphaned girl, whom the world had abandoned? But the wind was filling the sails by then, the swollen river was flowing fiercely, the village had been left behind, the riverside burning-ground was in view. Detached by the current of the river, he reflected philosophically that in life there are many separations, many deaths. What point was there in going back? Who belonged to whom in this world?

But Ratan had no such philosophy to console her. All she could do was wander near the post office, weeping copiously. Maybe a faint hope lingered in her mind that Dadababu might return; and this was enough to tie her to the spot, prevent her from going far. O poor, unthinking human heart! Error will not go away, logic and reason are slow to penetrate. We cling with both arms to false hope, refusing to believe the weightiest proofs against it, embracing it with all our strength. In the end it escapes, ripping our veins and draining our heart's blood; until, regaining consciousness, we rush to fall into snares of delusion all over again.

Translated from Bengali by William Radice.

Sultana's Dream

Rokeya Sakhawat Hossain

In 1905 a woman from a well-off family in Rangpur (northern Bangladesh) created a satirical story about Ladyland, a society where "ladies rule over the country and control all social matters, while gentlemen are kept in the Mardanas [men's quarters] to mind babies, to cook and to do all sorts of domestic work." This humorous inversion of gender roles made Rokeya Sakhawat Hossain (1880–1932)—or Begum Rokeya, as she is often called—instantly famous. Today she is widely claimed as one of the pioneers of South Asia's women's movement. Remarkably, Begum Rokeya wrote her story in English, the language of colonial rule and the educated elite, at a time when English education was hardly available to women in Bengal. This challenge was all the more remarkable as she had received no formal education but was taught by her brother and her husband.

One evening I was lounging in an easy chair in my bedroom and thinking lazily of the condition of Indian womanhood. I am not sure whether I dozed off or not. But, as far as I remember, I was wide-awake. I saw the moonlit sky sparkling with thousands of diamond-like stars, very distinctly.

All on a sudden a lady stood before me; how she came in, I do not know. I took her for my friend, Sister Sara.

"Good morning," said Sister Sara. I smiled inwardly as I knew it was not morning, but starry night. However, I replied to her, saying, "How do you do?"

"I am all right, thank you. Will you please come out and have a look at our garden?"

I looked again at the moon through the open window, and thought there was no harm in going out at that time. The men-servants outside were fast asleep just then, and I could have a pleasant walk with Sister Sara.

I used to have my walks with Sister Sara, when we were at Darjeeling. Many a time did we walk hand in hand and talk light-heartedly in the botanical gardens there. I fancied, Sister Sara had probably come to take me to some such garden and I readily accepted her offer and went out with her.

When walking I found to my surprise that it was a fine morning. The town was fully awake and the streets alive with bustling crowds. I was feeling very shy, thinking I was walking in the street in broad daylight, but there was not a single man visible.

Some of the passers-by made jokes at me. Though I could not understand their language, yet I felt sure they were joking. I asked my friend, "What do they say?"

"The women say that you look very mannish."

"Mannish?" said I, "What do they mean by that?"

"They mean that you are shy and timid like men."

"Shy and timid like men?" It was really a joke. I became very nervous, when I found that my companion was not Sister Sara, but a stranger. Oh, what a fool had I been to mistake this lady for my dear old friend, Sister Sara.

She felt my fingers tremble in her hand, as we were walking hand in hand.

"What is the matter, dear?" she said affectionately. "I feel somewhat awkward," I said in a rather apologizing tone, "as being a purdahnishin [a woman in purdah, or seclusion] woman I am not accustomed to walking about unveiled."

"You need not be afraid of coming across a man here. This is Ladyland, free from sin and harm. Virtue herself reigns here."

By and by I was enjoying the scenery. Really it was very grand. I mistook a patch of green grass for a velvet cushion. Feeling as if I were walking on a soft carpet, I looked down and found the path covered with moss and flowers.

"How nice it is," said I.

"Do you like it?" asked Sister Sara. (I continued calling her "Sister Sara," and she kept calling me by my name.)

"Yes, very much; but I do not like to tread on the tender and sweet flowers."

"Never mind, dear Sultana; your treading will not harm them; they are street flowers."

"The whole place looks like a garden," said I admiringly. "You have arranged every plant so skilfully."

"Your Calcutta could become a nicer garden than this if only your countrymen wanted to make it so."

"They would think it useless to give so much attention to horticulture, while they have so many other things to do."

"They could not find a better excuse," said she with smile.

I became very curious to know where the men were. I met more than a hundred women while walking there, but not a single man.

"Where are the men?" I asked her.

"In their proper places, where they ought to be."

"Pray let me know what you mean by 'their proper places.'"

"O, I see my mistake, you cannot know our customs, as you were never here before. We shut our men indoors."

"Just as we are kept in the zenana [women's quarters]?"

"Exactly so."

"How funny," I burst into a laugh. Sister Sara laughed too.

"But dear Sultana, how unfair it is to shut in the harmless women and let loose the men."

"Why? It is not safe for us to come out of the zenana, as we are naturally weak."

"Yes, it is not safe so long as there are men about the streets, nor is it so when a wild animal enters a marketplace."

"Of course not."

"Suppose, some lunatics escape from the asylum and begin to do all sorts of mischief to men, horses and other creatures; in that case what will your countrymen do?"

"They will try to capture them and put them back into their asylum."

"Thank you! And you do not think it wise to keep sane people inside an asylum and let loose the insane?"

"Of course not!" said I laughing lightly.

"As a matter of fact, in your country this very thing is done! Men, who do or at least are capable of doing no end of mischief, are let loose and the innocent women, shut up in the zenana! How can you trust those untrained men out of doors?"

"We have no hand or voice in the management of our social affairs. In India man is lord and master, he has taken to himself all powers and privileges and shut up the women in the zenana."

"Why do you allow yourselves to be shut up?"

"Because it cannot be helped as they are stronger than women."

"A lion is stronger than a man, but it does not enable him to dominate the human race. You have neglected the duty you owe to yourselves and you have lost your natural rights by shutting your eyes to your own interests."

"But my dear Sister Sara, if we do everything by ourselves, what will the men do then?"

"They should not do anything, excuse me; they are fit for nothing. Only catch them and put them into the zenana."

"But would it be very easy to catch and put them inside the four walls?" said I. "And even if this were done, would all their business—political and commercial—also go with them into the zenana?"

Sister Sara made no reply. She only smiled sweetly. Perhaps she thought it useless to argue with one who was no better than a frog in a well.

By this time we reached Sister Sara's house. It was situated in a beautiful heart-shaped garden. It was a bungalow with a corrugated iron roof. It was cooler and nicer than any of our rich buildings. I cannot describe how neat and how nicely furnished and how tastefully decorated it was.

We sat side by side. She brought out of the parlour a piece of embroidery work and began putting on a fresh design.

"Do you know knitting and needle work?"

"Yes; we have nothing else to do in our zenana."

"But we do not trust our zenana members with embroidery!" she said laughing, "as a man has not patience enough to pass thread through a needlehole even!"

"Have you done all this work yourself?" I asked her pointing to the various pieces of embroidered teapoy cloths.

"Yes."

"How can you find time to do all these? You have to do the office work as well? Have you not?"

"Yes. I do not stick to the laboratory all day long. I finish my work in two hours."

"In two hours! How do you manage? In our land the officers—magistrates, for instance—work seven hours daily."

"I have seen some of them doing their work. Do you think they work all the seven hours?"

"Certainly they do!"

"No, dear Sultana, they do not. They dawdle away their time in smoking. Some smoke two or three choroots during the office time. They talk much about their work, but do little. Suppose one choroot takes half an hour to burn off, and a man smokes twelve choroots daily; then you see, he wastes six hours every day in sheer smoking."

We talked on various subjects, and I learned that they were not subject to any kind of epidemic disease, nor did they suffer from mosquito bites as we do. I was very much astonished to hear that in Ladyland no one died in youth except by rare accident.

"Will you care to see our kitchen?" she asked me.

"With pleasure," said I, and we went to see it. Of course the men had been asked to clear off when I was going there. The kitchen was situated in a beautiful vegetable garden. Every creeper, every tomato plant was itself an ornament. I found no smoke, nor any chimney either in the kitchen—it was clean and bright; the windows were decorated with flower gardens. There was no sign of coal or fire.

"How do you cook?" I asked.

"With solar heat," she said, at the same time showing me the pipe, through which passed the concentrated sunlight and heat. And she cooked something then and there to show me the process.

"How did you manage to gather and store up the sun-heat?" I asked her in amazement.

"Let me tell you a little of our past history then. Thirty years ago, when our present Queen was thirteen years old, she inherited the throne. She was Queen in name only, the Prime Minister really ruling the country.

"Our good Queen liked science very much. She circulated an order that all the women in her country should be educated. Accordingly a number of girls' schools were founded and supported by the government. Education was spread far and wide among women. And early marriage also was stopped. No woman was to be allowed to marry before she was twenty-one. I must tell you that, before this change we had been kept in strict purdah."

"How the tables are turned," I interposed with a laugh.

"But the seclusion is the same," she said. "In a few years we had separate universities, where no men were admitted.

"In the capital, where our Queen lives, there are two universities. One of these invented a wonderful balloon, to which they attached a number of pipes. By means of this captive balloon which they managed to keep afloat above the cloud-land, they could draw as much water from the atmosphere as they pleased. As the water was incessantly being drawn by the university people no cloud gathered and the ingenious Lady Principal stopped rain and storms thereby."

"Really! Now I understand why there is no mud here!" said I. But I could not understand how it was possible to accumulate water in the pipes. She explained to me how it was done, but I was unable to understand her, as my scientific knowledge was very limited. However, she went on, "When the other university came to know of this, they became exceedingly jealous and tried to do something more extraordinary still. They invented an instrument by which they could collect as much sun-heat as they wanted. And they kept the heat stored up to be distributed among others as required.

"While the women were engaged in scientific research, the men of this country were busy increasing their military power. When they came to know that the female universities were able to draw water from the atmosphere and collect heat from the sun, they only laughed at the members of the universities and called the whole thing 'a sentimental nightmare!'"

"Your achievements are very wonderful indeed! But tell me, how you managed to put the men of your country into the zenana. Did you entrap them first?"

"No."

"It is not likely that they would surrender their free and open air life of their own accord and confine themselves within the four walls of the zenana! They must have been overpowered."

"Yes, they have been!"

"By whom? By some lady-warriors, I suppose?"

"No, not by arms."

"Yes, it cannot be so. Men's arms are stronger than women's. Then?"

"By brain."

"Even their brains are bigger and heavier than women's. Are they not?"

"Yes, but what of that? An elephant also has got a bigger and heavier brain than a man has. Yet man can enchain elephants and employ them, according to their own wishes."

"Well said, but tell me please, how it all actually happened. I am dying to know it!"

"Women's brains are somewhat quicker than men's. Ten years ago, when the military officers called our scientific discoveries 'a sentimental nightmare,' some of the young ladies wanted to say something in reply to those remarks. But both the Lady Principals restrained them and said, they should reply not by word, but by deed, if ever they got the opportunity. And they had not long to wait for that opportunity."

"How marvelous!" I heartily clapped my hands. "And now the proud gentlemen are dreaming sentimental dreams themselves."

"Soon afterwards certain persons came from a neighbouring country and took shelter in ours. They were in trouble having committed some political offense. The king who cared more for power than for good government asked our kind-hearted Queen to hand them over to his officers. She refused, as it was against her principle to turn out refugees. For this refusal the king declared war against our country.

"Our military officers sprang to their feet at once and marched out to meet the enemy. The enemy however, was too strong for them. Our soldiers fought bravely, no doubt. But in spite of all their bravery the foreign army advanced step by step to invade our country.

"Nearly all the men had gone out to fight; even a boy of sixteen was not left home. Most of our warriors were killed, the rest driven back and the enemy came within twenty-five miles of the capital.

"A meeting of a number of wise ladies was held at the Queen's palace to advise as to what should be done to save the land. Some proposed to fight like soldiers; others objected and said that women were not trained to fight with swords and guns, nor were they accustomed to fighting with any weapons. A third party regretfully remarked that they were hopelessly weak of body.

"'If you cannot save your country for lack of physical strength,' said the Queen, 'try to do so by brain power.'

"There was a dead silence for a few minutes. Her Royal Highness said again, 'I must commit suicide if the land and my honour are lost.'

"Then the Lady Principal of the second university (who had collected sun-heat), who had been silently thinking during the consultation, re-marked that they were all but lost, and there was little hope left for them. There was, however, one plan which she would like to try, and this would be her first and last efforts; if she failed in this, there would be nothing left but to commit suicide. All present solemnly vowed that they would never allow themselves to be enslaved, no matter what happened.

"The Queen thanked them heartily, and asked the Lady Principal to try her plan. The Lady Principal rose again and said, 'before we go out the men must enter the zenanas. I make this prayer for the sake of purdah.' 'Yes, of course,' replied Her Royal Highness.

"On the following day the Queen called upon all men to retire into ze-nanas for the sake of honour and liberty. Wounded and tired as they were, they took that order rather for a boon! They bowed low and entered the ze-nanas without uttering a single word of protest. They were sure that there was no hope for this country at all.

"Then the Lady Principal with her two thousand students marched to the battle field, and arriving there directed all the rays of the concentrated sunlight and heat towards the enemy.

"The heat and light were too much for them to bear. They all ran away panic-stricken, not knowing in their bewilderment how to counteract that scorching heat. When they fled away leaving their guns and other ammuni-tions of war, they were burnt down by means of the same sun-heat. Since then no one has tried to invade our country any more."

"And since then your countrymen never tried to come out of the zenana?"

"Yes, they wanted to be free. Some of the police commissioners and dis-trict magistrates sent word to the Queen to the effect that the military officers certainly deserved to be imprisoned for their failure; but they never neglected their duty and therefore they should not be punished and they prayed to be restored to their respective offices.

"Her Royal Highness sent them a circular letter intimating to them that if their services should ever be needed they would be sent for, and that in the meanwhile they should remain where they were. Now that they are accustomed to the purdah system and have ceased to grumble at their seclusion, we call the system 'Mardana' instead of 'zenana.'"

"But how do you manage," I asked Sister Sara, "to do without the police or magistrates in case of theft or murder?"

"Since the 'Mardana' system has been established, there has been no more crime or sin; therefore we do not require a policeman to find out a culprit, nor do we want a magistrate to try a criminal case."

"That is very good, indeed. I suppose if there was any dishonest person, you could very easily chastise her. As you gained a decisive victory without shedding a single drop of blood, you could drive off crime and criminals too without much difficulty!"

"Now, dear Sultana, will you sit here or come to my parlour?" she asked me.

"Your kitchen is not inferior to a queen's boudoir!" I replied with a pleasant smile, "but we must leave it now; for the gentlemen may be cursing me for keeping them away from their duties in the kitchen so long." We both laughed heartily.

"How my friends at home will be amused and amazed, when I go back and tell them that in the far-off Ladyland, ladies rule over the country and control all social matters, while gentlemen are kept in the Mardanas to mind babies, to cook and to do all sorts of domestic work; and that cooking is so easy a thing that it is simply a pleasure to cook!"

"Yes, tell them about all that you see here."

"Please let me know, how you carry on land cultivation and how you plough the land and do other hard manual work."

"Our fields are tilled by means of electricity, which supplies motive power for other hard work as well, and we employ it for our aerial conveyances too. We have no rail road nor any paved streets here."

"Therefore neither street nor railway accidents occur here," said I. "Do not you ever suffer from want of rainwater?" I asked.

"Never since the 'water balloon' has been set up. You see the big balloon and pipes attached thereto. By their aid we can draw as much rainwater as we require. Nor do we ever suffer from flood or thunderstorms. We are all very busy making nature yield as much as she can. We do not find time to

quarrel with one another as we never sit idle. Our noble Queen is exceedingly fond of botany; it is her ambition to convert the whole country into
one grand garden."

"The idea is excellent. What is your chief food?"

"Fruits."

"How do you keep your country cool in hot weather? We regard the
rainfall in summer as a blessing from heaven."

"When the heat becomes unbearable, we sprinkle the ground with plentiful showers drawn from the artificial fountains. And in cold weather we
keep our room warm with sun-heat."

She showed me her bathroom, the roof of which was removable. She
could enjoy a shower bath whenever she liked, by simply removing the roof
(which was like the lid of a box) and turning on the tap of the shower pipe.

"You are a lucky people!" ejaculated I. "You know no want. What is your
religion, may I ask?"

"Our religion is based on Love and Truth. It is our religious duty to love
one another and to be absolutely truthful. If any person lies, she or he is.
. . . "

"Punished with death?"

"No, not with death. We do not take pleasure in killing a creature of
God, especially a human being. The liar is asked to leave this land for good
and never to come to it again."

"Is an offender never forgiven?"

"Yes, if that person repents sincerely."

"Are you not allowed to see any man, except your own relations?"

"No one except sacred relations."

"Our circle of sacred relations is very limited; even first cousins are not
sacred."

"But ours is very large; a distant cousin is as sacred as a brother."

"That is very good. I see purity itself reigns over your land. I should like
to see the good Queen, who is so sagacious and far-sighted and who has
made all these rules."

"All right," said Sister Sara.

Then she screwed a couple of seats onto a square piece of plank. To this
plank she attached two smooth and well-polished balls. When I asked her
what the balls were for, she said they were hydrogen balls and they were
used to overcome the force of gravity. The balls were of different capaci-
ties to be used according to the different weights desired to be overcome.
She then fastened to the air-car two wing-like blades, which, she said, were
worked by electricity. After we were comfortably seated she touched a knob

and the blades began to whirl, moving faster and faster every moment. At first we were raised to the height of about six or seven feet and then off we flew. And before I could realize that we had commenced moving, we reached the garden of the Queen.

My friend lowered the air-car by reversing the action of the machine, and when the car touched the ground the machine was stopped and we got out.

I had seen from the air-car the Queen walking on a garden path with her little daughter (who was four years old) and her maids of honour.

"Halloo! You here!" cried the Queen addressing Sister Sara. I was introduced to Her Royal Highness and was received by her cordially without any ceremony.

I was very much delighted to make her acquaintance. In the course of the conversation I had with her, the Queen told me that she had no objection to permitting her subjects to trade with other countries. "But," she continued, "no trade was possible with countries where the women were kept in the zenanas and so unable to come and trade with us. Men, we find, are rather of lower morals and so we do not like dealing with them. We do not covet other people's land, we do not fight for a piece of diamond though it may be a thousand-fold brighter than the Koh-i-Noor, nor do we grudge a ruler his Peacock Throne. We dive deep into the ocean of knowledge and try to find out the precious gems, which nature has kept in store for us. We enjoy nature's gifts as much as we can."

After taking leave of the Queen, I visited the famous universities, and was shown some of their manufactories, laboratories and observatories.

After visiting the above places of interest we got again into the air-car, but as soon as it began moving, I somehow slipped down and the fall startled me out of my dream. And on opening my eyes, I found myself in my own bedroom still lounging in the easy-chair!

The Other Bank of the River

Nirad C. Chaudhuri

In one of South Asia's best-known autobiographies, Nirad Chaudhuri (1897–1999) painted a wonderfully evocative portrait of Kishorganj, the small town in north-eastern Bangladesh where he grew up. Chaudhuri was a captivating writer, but he became a controversial figure because of his admiration for the British and his criticism of nationalism. He dedicated his autobiography, The Autobiography of an Unknown Indian *(1951), to "the memory of the British Empire in India, which conferred subjecthood upon us, but withheld citizenship: to which yet every one of us threw out the challenge: 'Civis Britannicus sum' (I am a British citizen) because all that was good and living within us was made, shaped and quickened by the same British rule." Although this dedication was removed from reprints of the book, in later life Chaudhuri considered himself an Englishman in spirit.*

The autobiography provides the reader with a vivid sense of middle-class family life and the social distinctions in a colonial town at the beginning of the twentieth century, seen through the eyes of a clever and introspective young boy. In this brief excerpt, he speaks of his reasons for looking down on the other bank of the river— and of his intense embarrassment at being confronted with some of its inhabitants.

The town of Kishorganj was divided into two nearly equal halves by the river. But we did not think equally well of both. Actually, we were openly contemptuous of the *other bank.* This was not egoism, a tribute of vanity to our own presence on *this* bank, but an indication of the spirit of the age of our boyhood, which was vastly different from the spirit of the present or contemporary age. The bazaars and all the important shops were on the other bank, which meant that it had the formidable backing of economics. Yet we could afford to look down upon it on the strength of religious, cultural, political, and aesthetic considerations. The temple of the goddess Kali, the most important Muslim prayer hall in the town, the Idgah where the annual Id prayers were said, the prayer hall of the Brahmos or reformed monotheistic Hindus, were all on our bank. So were the schools, the cricket ground, the public library, the government dispensary, and the hospital.

And so were the courts, the treasury, the police station, the post office, and the dak bungalow. Above all, we had not spoilt our river front. The road running along the river on our side had been kept as a sort of strand. But on the other bank there were, except for a small section, houses on the riparian side of the road. It goes to the credit of our crude childish aesthetic sense that we condemned this turning of the back on the river as a mark of stupidity, and the presence of the sanitary conveniences of these houses on the river we loathed as an abomination.

Another fact which prejudiced us against the other bank was the location there of the prostitute quarters, which was a concentrated collection of some thirty or forty small huts, enclosed on all sides, like our inner house, by a high screen. Although the servants, the shopkeepers, and other small fry seemed to take much interest in this part of the town, we hated the very sight of the screen, and we hated still more the simpering women whom at times we saw sailing out from behind the barrier. We felt indignant when they invaded our bank on a certain day in the week in order to go to the police station to register themselves, or at all events to comply with some formality of which we had no very clear idea. One day I rather overdid the horror. Standing with a number of playmates on the road I suddenly saw a group of these woman coming. I at once put my hands over my eyes and then, not satisfied with that, ran into a hut to keep myself hidden until the group had passed by. We, the boys, whether brothers, cousins, or playfellows, never discussed these women amongst ourselves. Whatever intercommunication we had on this subject took place through the inaudible language of look and expression. But my conduct on that day proved too much for the normal decorousness of my companions. They at first looked embarrassed, and then ragged me as Lakshman, the brother of Rama of the Hindu epic, the *Ramayana*, who is supposed never to have cast his eyes on the face, or any other part of the body except the feet, of his sister-in-law, Sita, although he had to attend her constantly.

"The Muhammadan Community"

A. K. Fazlul Huq

In the early twentieth century, Muslims emerged as a political category for the first time. In 1905, amid widespread agitation, Bengal was divided administratively, and most of what is now Bangladesh became part of the new province of Eastern Bengal and Assam. This is sometimes referred to as the first partition of Bengal. By the time the new province was abolished and Bengal reunited in 1911, the political land-scape of Bengal had been transformed. Now politicians spoke largely to religious constituencies. As political identities, Hindu and Muslim took on new substance, and these were the identities that would dominate South Asian politics from then on. A. K. Fazlul Huq (1873–1962) emerged as one of the most vocal leaders of what was now thought of as the "Muhammadan community." He became a member of the new Bengal Legislative Council and introduced a combative style to demand Muslim rights that made him famous and soon earned him the sobriquet Sher-e-Bangla (Tiger of Bengal). In his maiden speech in 1913, excerpted here, he attacked discrimination of Muslims in education.

My Lord, if human memory is short, official memory is very much shorter, and I am not surprised that within the twelve months that have elapsed since the annulment of the partition, officials have managed to forget their special obligations to the Muhammadan community. Only the other day, the Hon'ble Mr. Kuchler seemed to be somewhat impatient of criticism on the subject of Muhammadan education, and he actually complained that Muhammadan leaders are slow to acknowledge the help and assistance which Government has all along given to Muhammadans in the matter of education. If the remark had been made previous to the 12th of December 1911, I would have considered it necessary to attempt a justification of our attitude in agitating for increased privileges, and for a wider recognition of the claims of our community on the resources of the State in educational matters. But I do not think that, after the memorable date officials can expect that Muhammadan will consent to talk of their grievances with bated breath, or continue to brood over their lot in silent d[e]spair. I would only remind the officials that they are in honour bound to render adequate compensations to the Muhammadan community for all the [grievous] wrong inflicted on them by the unceremonious annulment of the partition. My Lord, it seems to me that officials make a very fundamental mistake with regard to the claims of Muhammadans on the Government, where it be the question of State [patronage], grant of political rights or privileges or expenditure from provincial revenues for promoting Muhammadan education or other matters of special interest to the community. We are often told that we have got our share, and we should not complain. But those who say so seem to forget that we claim not only our share, but also a substantial excess throughout. Our share we claim as our indefeasible right, and the excess we claim by way of compensation for the wrong done to us by the annulment of the partition. This is the view of the general Muhammadan public, and if the officials will not meet the demands in full there is certain to be discontent in the community. Whether the discontent would be worth the consideration of the Government is a different question. The situation is no doubt an embar[r]assing one, but has been deliberately created by the officials themselves, and they must be prepared to face it bravely.

My Lord, in the despatch of August 25th the Government of India pledged itself to see that the Muhammadan interest would not be affected by the change brought about by the annulment of the partition. More than eighteen months have elapsed since then, and it is time to see how far the solemn promises have been fulfilled. When His Excellency the Viceroy visited Dacca [Dhaka] shortly after the Durbar announcements [announcement that King-Emperor George V would hold Court in Delhi in 1911], every one expected that His Excellency will be able to announce something particularly gratifying to the Muhammadan community. We got the announcement about the Dacca University, but I must confess that it fell far short of our expectations. I do not wish to belittle the importance of the Dacca University, as a factor in priventing [*sic*] a set-back in the educational advancement of Eastern Bengal, or the incalculable advantages of a residential University in the centre of that large Muhammadan population. But I wish to protest against the theory that the University is meant to benefit Muhammadans alone, or that it can be regarded as a definite step towards a conciliation of Muhammadan feelings. The Viceroy has distinctly said that the University is, as it should be, for the benefit of Hindus and Muhammadans alike. Its area of operations has been curtailed, out of deference to the apprehensions of the Hindu community [lest] it would lead to a revival of the effects of the partition. Even the proposed Muhammadan College and the establishment of a faculty of Islamic Studies in connectin [*sic*] with the

University, cannot be credited to any particular desire to favour the Muhammadan community. For more than half a century, Government has maintained a purely Hindu College at Calcutta, with all its elaborate staff and necessary equipments and the Muhammadan College at Dacca would only be a tardy recognition of the long neglected claims of the Muhammadan community. . . .

My Lord—I regret that I have not got sufficient time at my disposal to discuss the statements made by the Hon'ble Mr. Kuehler the other day regarding the Muhammadan education. It is a remarkable instance of the self-glorification in which Indian officials too often indulge in order to impress the public with their activities in the performance of their duties. Beyond a few thousand rupees spent on Muktabs [Muslim primary schools] and middle Madrasahs, and on the training of Muhammadan teachers, together with a few conferences for the improvement of the Madrasahs, leading to no practical result, I do not think any thing definite has been pointed out as having been accomplished in furtherance of the cause of Muhammadan education. . . .

I wish to take this opportunity of commenting on a mistake which officials generally commit in calculating the share of the Muhammadan community in allotments in the matter of education. It is argued that the true basis of calculation is not the numerical strength of our community, but the very small fraction of it that attend educational institutions. I protest against this method of dwarfing Muhammadan claims, both because it is unjust and unfair. If Muhammadan boys are in such a minority in educational institutions it is due to a system of education which has been utterly unsuited to the requirements of the community, and which the authorities themselves permitted to continue in the face of protests. And now to make this minority a basis for the calculation of educational grants is to penalise the Muhammadan community for a state of things for which the officials themselves have been primarily responsible and which has been brought about by causes over which the Muhammadan have had no control.

An Elder Brother's Duty

Md. Bosharot Ali

The colonial period saw the beginning of an encounter that remains unresolved today: the logic of kinship being challenged by the logic of bureaucratic rule and impersonal law. Kinship was, and continues to be, extremely important in Bangladesh. It is the dominant ideology that structures social relationships. Not only are your family members usually the most important individuals in your life but a large family also gives you security and protection. Kinship is the grammar of everyday life beyond the family as well. By addressing nonrelatives with kinship terms, you can easily include them in family-like networks and regulate your behavior with one another. In this way familial relations of hierarchy, respect, and closeness permeate many social relationships, including the bureaucracy, law, the state, and the market. The wife of your husband's boss is your apa *(elder sister), your local politician your* chacha *(father's younger brother), and so on.*

Being high up in the kinship system brings many advantages but also definite duties. The text here provides an example. It is from an unusual source, a recently discovered diary that Md. Bosharot Ali, a well-off villager in Comilla (then Tipperah) district, kept from 1923 to 1943. The diary is full of observations about everyday life and provides an uncommon perspective on the period. As the eldest of four brothers, Bosharot Ali was responsible for running the family, and this was often an onerous task. He wrote the excerpts below mostly in English, but some were originally in Bengali. They deal with a three-year period in which he was trying to get his youngest brother, Zulfu Miah (Zulfikar Ali), established in life. This meant, first of all, finding him a bride, which was not easy because Zulfu apparently had a physical problem. Parents of prospective brides would consent only if Zulfu's family spent extra money. After two years of negotiations with one family, Bosharot Ali finally managed to get Zulfu married in 1926. Now came the next step: he had to set him up in business. Tragically, Zulfu died within months of his marriage.

Monday 3 Ashar 1330 BE *[Bengali Era, the local calendar] (18 June 1923).* My brothers—none can have so good brothers. They are very obedient to me. They obey my orders to the point. Their wives also obey me very much.

The wife of Shuju Miah is somewhat nervous. The wife of my brother Sharu Miah is after my liking. But she always kept herself aloof from us as she lives with my brother in towns where he serves.

Saturday 26 Srabon (11 August). Went to Comilla by 1.28 PM train to know about the information of marriage of Zulfu Miah and returned home at 10 PM.

Monday 15 Boishakh 1331 BE (28 April 1924) [in Bengali]. Haji Abdul Gofur Miah received a packet of clothes sent by post from Calcutta by young Zulfu Miah. Four *dhotis* [loincloths] and one shirt piece. Momtaz [a brother] wants to have two dhotis, leaving mother and me one each, and the shirt piece.

Thursday 25 Boishakh (8 May). We cannot settle marriage of Zulfu Miah, though we are trying in many. Soon we have to do anything for it. . . .

Saturday 10 Srabon (26 July). My father-in-law called me in the morning. I went to see him. He told me not to marry Zulfu Miah with A. Samad's daughter as his daughter is blind of one eye. People say she is blind but in reality she is not so. I was much willing to make the connection. . . . Zulfu Miah has gone to Comilla in 1.30 PM train today. He is going there for an interview with the Magistrate for an appointment in the Collectorate where [several] posts have fallen vacant.

Sunday 11 Srabon (27 July). Father is willing to marry Zulfu with the d/o [daughter of] A. Samad Miah but father-in-law not agreed to this. . . .

Friday 23 Srabon (8 August). After candle light I and father went to my father-in-law to consult with him for the marriage of Zulfu Miah. After much [talk] he advised us to propose the marriage of Fatahabad, the daughter of Sadu Miah. He himself will go there to consulting with them tomorrow morning. . . .

Saturday 24 Srabon (9 August). My father-in-law went to Fatahabad for consulting for the marriage of Zulfu Miah's with d/o Sadu Miah s/o [son of] late Joynal Hossain. We tried many places for the marriage at last we come to this place. We were in the opinion of marrying him in a respectable & well connected and promising family but as there is some difficulties in his appearance so everyone disagrees. . . .

Monday 13 Poush 1332 BE (28 December 1925). In the morning of this day came to Shibpur but in the evening went Fatahabad with Jamiruddin Munshi of Shibpur. There we remained for the night. Saw Sadu Miah son of late Joynal Hosain, talked with him for the marriage of Zulfu Miah. The father of the bride, i.e. Sadu Miah want[s] a loan of Rs. 400/- [400 rupees] to me not directly but indirectly on condition to repay the sum in two instalments in Assin [September–October] next without interest. Aziz Bhai agreed to give them the money on their granting a bond to him. But they are not willing to give & sign any bonds. They want money . . . but I don't like to grant him so large a sum without any bond. The ornaments & clothes as usual.

Sunday 16 Phalgun (28 February 1926). Went to Fatahabad for marrying Zulfu Miah with 18/19 men. Reached at 7 PM.

Tuesday 18 Phalgun (2 March) [in Bengali]. Wedding travel expenses:

1. Tamna's mother's trip back and forth
2. Bringing Telufa
3. Two persons from Alombari
4. Bringing Kulsum's mother
5. From Kapitola:
   - 10 persons for the wedding at Fatahabad
   - 6 persons from Araiutha
   - 2 persons from Agborani

[In English] Rs. 20/- will be paid all together & 12 pieces of cloths may be given to them.

Friday 3 Boishakh 1333 BE (16 April 1926) [in Bengali]. Today at 8 or 9 AM young Zulfu Miah set out for Brahmanbaria. We have sent him there to trade in paddy and rice. He started the business with Abdul Kader Munshi. We gave him a capital of Rs.200/-. That munshi and his brother took the money by means of a hand note dated 13 Chaitra [27 March].

Bengali fragments translated by Willem van Schendel.

Women's Hunger for Education

Shudha Mazumdar

A century after Rashsundari Debi taught herself how to read and write (see "A Woman Teaches Herself How to Read" in this part), upper-caste women in rural East Bengal were better educated but still hungering for more, as Shudha Mazumdar describes in the following text.

The wife of a colonial official, Mazumdar spent her life in provincial towns all over Bengal. In 1926 her husband was posted to Manikganj, a town in Dhaka district. He said he was much dismayed at "another East Bengal posting . . . after distant Chittagong." By train, steamer, country boat, and palanquin, it took them a night and two days to reach Manikganj from Calcutta. Ten years earlier, in another district town, Mazumdar had joined the Mahila Samiti (Women's Society), an organization of, according to her, "women of gentle birth," to help them overcome the loneliness of their secluded lives. Gradually, its social functions had broadened to include giving support to women in improving themselves and placing their demands in front of men with power. As she followed her husband to his different postings it became her mission to set up new branches of the Women's Society. Manikganj was no exception.

I found the local ladies here most friendly and receptive to the idea of establishing a *Mahila Samiti*. We met periodically and exchanged cooking recipes and designs for needlework, held musical evenings, and subscribed to a monthly journal for circulation amongst members. This women's association became so popular that the leading lady of another village became interested and invited us to hold a meeting at her home. Since this was during the rainy reason, the function had to be after dusk, to allow *purdah* [secluded] women to travel without being seen. My husband was also wanted there for some work so we would go together. I looked forward to this new experience of visiting a remote village during the rainy season and was thankful for the clear skies that afternoon.

Our host had sent his personal boat, a huge ungainly vessel, with a multicoloured patchwork sail that made it look quite gay and inviting. The setting sun tinged the waters with a vivid orange and rose as we glided past the Law Court buildings, the Boys' School and the "mart." Nosing its way through masses of mauve water hyacinths the boat gained in speed as the boatmen silently plied their oars. Slowly the skies darkened and night fell and it was pitch dark except for the flickering flame in our hurricane lantern. The stillness of the night was broken only by the lapping of the waters as the boat cleaved its way through shallow water and plants, and I wondered how the boatmen could make out where to go.

Losing count of time, we sailed in silence till at last lights could be discerned in the far distance. Shadowy figures moved forward and by blazing gaslights our boat was tethered. It was a pleasant surprise to step out before a brick building with massive pillars and lime washed walls, as the homes I had visited before had mud walls, with roofs of corrugated iron. The periodical tornadoes that devastated this part of East Bengal made it convenient to live in these hutments that had a chance of escaping the velocity of the gale and even if swept away, were less expensive to reconstruct than brick and mortar buildings. These were thrifty and conservative people and neither University degrees nor prosperity seemed to change their taste in housing.

We were warmly welcomed on landing. My husband remained with the men while I followed some small girls up a narrow flight of stairs to a large hall lighted for the occasion with rented gaslights. There was a large gathering of women and children of all ages sitting on the gaily woven cotton carpet and I was made to sit on a high back chair draped with gold-embroidered crimson velvet and garlanded with fragrant flowers. A welcome song was sung by a group of pretty young girls and then the widowed mother of our host stood up to read her address. It was remarkably well written and delivered with dignity and ease. Speaking on behalf of those assembled, the speaker emphasized the importance of women's education in this part of the world. They had learnt with pride and joy of the attainments of their foreign and Indian sisters and regretted their own educational inadequacies. They wanted education to make themselves real helpmates of their husbands, to help them rear strong and healthy children, and to give widows and other poor women a way of earning their own livelihood. She concluded with the oft-quoted lines, "Until the women of Bharata [India] awaken, Bharata will never awake!"

Then a very old lady rose, adjusted her *sari*, peered through her steel framed spectacles, and in a quavering voice welcomed me to their village. This once prosperous town was now sadly stricken by poverty and disease. Notable men had been born here, she said, naming a few well-known public figures, but alas, they had forgotten their humble birthplace. If these men would take a little interest in their village, it would flourish. "Our needs are many," she continued, "But the first thing we want is education. We must have knowledge for only this can give us the power to break our fetters of ignorance and superstition and then the women of India will be able to regain the honoured position that was theirs in the golden days of the Vedic age."

The next speaker was a bright teenage daughter of the house. Eager to learn all that the modern world offered, she was convinced the deterioration of Bengal was closely related to the backwardness of her daughters. Education to equip them for service in the home and perhaps later in spheres beyond the home was badly needed. With ease and conviction she deplored the meagre facilities offered in the village and implored me to exert my influence to improve the Girls' School, which she had left long before.

I was moved and impressed. Here were minds different from the fiercely conservative ones I had met in West Bengal. Yet all these women were from orthodox homes. I don't remember what I said in reply, but they had enjoyed voicing their thoughts to sympathetic ears. After the farewell song we moved to the narrow veranda. Here we had a good view of the magic lantern show held below in the courtyard. Requested by our *Mahila Samiti*, the Publicity Department at Calcutta had sent an officer to give a talk on health and hygiene and exhibit suitable slides. It dwelt on the heart-rending toll of infant mortality with hints on mothercraft and how to avoid malaria and cholera. A large crowd had gathered to witness all this and I was thankful that our luck held and no rain spoiled the show.

The Field of the Embroidered Quilt

Jasim Uddin

The book-length poem Nokshi Kanthar Math *(The Field of the Embroidered Quilt) is considered one of the masterpieces of Bengali literature. Jasim Uddin (1903–76) evokes the mood and beauty of the Bangladesh countryside with unparalleled ease and simplicity. It is for this reason that he is often referred to as the country's Polli Kobi (Rural Poet). He was born in Faridpur district and became an avid collector of folklore, and he was also successful as a songwriter and radio personality. His literary style differed markedly from that of the Calcutta literati—his inspiration was emphatically rural and East Bengali, and his poetry echoed the rhythms of the region's folk songs. Generations of children in both East and West Bengal have read his poems in their school textbooks, which may partly explain his wide appeal.*

These are the opening lines—in English and Bengali—of his most famous poem, written in 1929. The "embroidered quilt" of the title refers to the delicately decorated folk textiles of Bengal that almost disappeared but staged a comeback in the 1980s as a symbol of Bangladeshi authenticity.

> My Love's house and mine are parted by a river;
> I want to fly, but God has given me no wings.
> (Shepherd's song)

A village here, a village there,
And a broad field in between
A page to read all written over
With crops and rice so green
This village beneath the tall trees
Plays at hide-and-seek.
Here and there the peasants' huts
Among the shadows peep
That village lies closely bound together
By the blackened-eyelash gloom
All-enfolding shade enhancing
The charm of the cottage home.

বন্ধুর বাড়ি আমার বাড়ি মধ্যে ক্ষীর নদী,
উইড়া যাওয়ার সাধ ছিল, পাঙ্খা দেয় নাই বিধি।
- রাখালী গান

এই এক গাঁও, ওই এক গাঁও – মধ্যে ধু ধু মাঠ,
ধান কাউনের লিখন লিখি করছে নিতুই পাঠ।
এ-গাঁও যেন ফাঁকা ফাঁকা, হেথায় হোথায় গাছ;
গেঁয়ো চাষীর ঘরগুলি সব দাঁড়ায় তারি পাছ।
ও-গাঁয় যেন জমাট বেঁধে কনের কাজল-কায়া,
ঘরগুলিরে জড়িয়ে ধরে বাড়ায় ঘরের মায়া।

এ-গাঁও চেয়ে ও-গাঁর দিকে, ও-গাঁও এ-গাঁর পানে,
কতদিন যে কাটবে এমন, কেইবা তাহা জানে!
মাঝখানেতে জলীর বিলে জ্বলে কাজল-জলা।
বক্ষে তাহার জল-কুমুদী মেলছে শতদলা।
এ-গাঁর ও-গাঁর দুধার হতে পথ দুখানি এসে,
জলীর বিলের জলে তারা পদ্ম ভাসায় হেসে!

This village looks to that,
And that one looks to this;
Who knows how many days will pass
Just like this?
Between them lies the Joli Lake,
Her waters sparkling jet;
The thousand-petalled lily opens,
Upon her bosom set.
From that village to this
Two separate paths entwine;
While in the waters of Joli Lake
Two lilies, floating, smile.

Translated from Bengali by E. M. Milford.

Terror for the Nation

Anonymous

In December 1931 two schoolgirls appeared at the office of Mr. Stevens, the district magistrate of Comilla (Tippera). They were Suniti Chowdhury (fourteen) and Santi Ghose (fifteen), and they carried a petition to start a swimming competition at their school. An orderly ushered them in. The girls handed the petition to Stevens, drew automatic pistols, and assassinated him.

These girls were members of a militant nationalist organization, Jugantar (New Era), which used murder as a political technique to dislodge British colonial rule. In February 1932, Chowdhury and Ghose appeared in a Calcutta court for their sen-

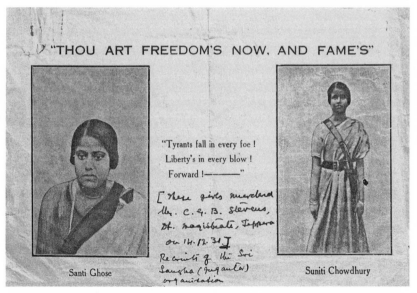

Anticolonial flyer celebrating the girl assassins Ghose and Chowdhury, 1932. The handwritten note was added by Sir Charles Tegart of the Calcutta police. One-page flyer, "Thou Art Freedom's Now, and Fame's," from the Lady Tegart Collection, 04076/4.21. Photograph © Tegart Collection, Centre of South Asian Studies, Cambridge University. Used by permission.

tences. Time *magazine reported: "In bright colored saris, with flowers in their hair, they listened unmoved as they were sentenced to transportation for life [life-long banishment] from Bengal Presidency. Said they lightly: 'It is better to die than live in a horse's stable.'"* [1] *A few days after the verdict the intelligence branch of police in the district of Rajshahi discovered this flyer extolling the two teenagers as heroines of nationalism.*

Note

1. "India: I and My Government," *Time* magazine, 8 February 1932, http://www.time.com/time/magazine/article/0,9171,743094,00.html#ixzzosIy6rgci.

The Cultural Mix of Old Dhaka

Syed Najmuddin Hashim

In these boyhood memories, Syed Najmuddin Hashim (1925–99) evokes the cultural richness of life in the oldest part of Dhaka. As he marvels at the city at dawn and moves effortlessly from one religious and cultural sphere to the next, he lovingly depicts the multifaceted lifestyle of late-colonial Dhaka that would be a thing of the past by the time he reached his twenties.

It was 1935 or '36 when I was a boy of ten, clad in shorts and [the company] Bata's ubiquitous "Naughty Boy" shoes, wandering around in the half-dusk of the first light in wide-eyed wonder in the Armanitola park, flanked on one side by the magnificent carved teak wood portal of "Roy House," the town family mansion of a Hindu lawyer and landlord and, on the other side, by the magical "Picture Show House" with its huge hoardings displaying one of the earliest sci-fi movie heroes, Flash Gordon, and the Indian *Stunt Queen* Nadia, miraculously blown up to many times their life size by untutored painters, perched precariously on rickety scaffoldings! Nestling slightly behind the cinema house was another huge ebony wooden door studded with iron spikes, which used to be locked night and day with massive chain and a padlock of truly Gargantuan proportions!

Suddenly early one morning, wonder of wonders, it was Open Sesame and out of a postern gate stepped a short stature person with a flowing snowy white beard, clad in black priest's raiment. I had barely reached there, having carefully skirted the forbidden red-light area of Zinda Bahar, carefully averting my gaze and curiosity away from the young gay girls in their clinging wet sarees as they wended their way back from a dip in the river at Badamatali Ghat, past the bakery where one could smell *Bakarkhani*, *Sukha* and *Nim-Sukha* unleavened bread being baked in earthen ovens, the unique *Amriti* sweetmeat being fried in clarified butter on the boil in big iron pans over wood fire in Akali Shaha's shop, over the humpbacked Baburbazar bridge lined with shops selling ball-shaped hand-made washing soap and kneaded fragrant tobacco for the *Farshi* and *Daba* hubble-bubble [water pipe], then very much in vogue. The *Batti-walah* in singlet, blue government-issue shorts, a dirty *Dopalli* cloth cap of his own rakishly tilted and a portable bamboo step ladder on his frail shoulder, was still shuffling forward, putting out the kerosene street lamps, and the first *Gharri-wallas* were urging on their emaciated horses and clanking carriages towards Badamatali, Wise and Sadar ferry ghats in search of their first fare of the day.

The priest showed me round my first Armenian church and the nearby graveyard where I recall the headstones of a unique latticed stonework with carved flowers and clinging vine called *Khachkar*, each different in workmanship from the other. To a willing teenage boy the old priest, standing in front of the eighteenth-century church, related the story of the Great Flood, Noah's unaccounted preference for the Armenian language on his first landfall, how Christianity came to Armenia in the fourth century, half a millennium before it was introduced to *Kiev-Rus* and long before it was introduced elsewhere in the Russian Empire, how the Armenian-Gregorian Church followed the Monophysites who believed, unlike the Catholic and Georgian and Russian Orthodox Churches[,] that Jesus had only one nature—the divine—and not two.

I put up a weak protest because my schooling was at two Catholic schools at the other end of the town in the Lakshmi Bazar area, the *St. Francis Xavier's* Convent and the *St. George's* High English (H.E. for short) School.

I still miss the English countryside expanse and pervasive friendliness of our convent, the twin trees, bare and gnarled, which blossomed overnight with white "wood-rose," Mother Superior of the stern visage, the friendly Sisters who glided noiselessly like apparitions down the cool corridors, even the flock of overfed geese, who chased us with their long stretching snake-like necks and raucous screams if we strayed too near their preserve. . . . I still remember my friends of those early years, Leslie Lazarus, a Jew, and the only other boy in a girl's convent, who was getting me into endless scrapes. Later in the boy's school I had another Jewish friend, Moses Levy. I have been to the Levy house in a narrow, over-crowded lane predominantly inhabited by the Hindu low-caste Basak weavers and goldsmiths, off the arterial Nawabpur road. I still remember his mother, old and ague-ridden, forever reciting in sonorous Hebrew (the only language except Yiddish she seemed to know) from the Talmud and Torah, which she kept wrapped in velvet covers in a little wall recess fitted with an enamelled iconostasis of the Prophet Moses and the Burning Bush. She used to feed me with lovely multi-coloured home-made cookies on the occasion of seemingly interminable Jewish festivals. I still recall the unending love and the ineffable sadness in her coal black eyes. To my questions, interpreted by my friend, she replied: "Sad we are, we suffer purgatory, because for our own inequities we have suffered banishment and dispersal by the command by our stern and unforgiving Lord Jehovah!" . . . The same settled melancholy I beheld in the eyes of the old Armenian priest in that half-light, bowed down with the burden of his nation's history, standing pensively before a tombstone.

Walking down memory lane, I always identify Old Dhaka with these two figures—the old woman praying in an unknown tongue before guttering candles, which barely kept at bay the enveloping gloom, and the ancient priest keeping his lonely vigil in an Armenian township among an uncomprehending Moslem people. It seems that all through life I have carried deep within me something of their pain and alienation.

Messages of Equality and Love

Kazi Nazrul Islam

Kazi Nazrul Islam (1899–1976)—Bangladesh's official national poet—was a powerful voice against bigotry and conventionalism. The iconoclasm of his ideas and the originality of his compositions caused a transformation of twentieth-century Bengali poetry and music. Nazrul was a prolific writer, composer, playwright, and journalist as well as an accomplished performer. Public appearances in addition to gramophone recordings, radio appearances (from the late 1920s on), and films (from the 1930s on) made him famous all over Bengal. Today Nozrul giti *(Nazrul songs) are a distinct and very popular genre.*

The British authorities considered Nazrul's political stridency a threat and jailed him for his political poems. In 1942 illness robbed him of his voice and memory— and for many years his life continued in silence. He was showered with awards, and he died in 1976 and was buried with state honor on Dhaka University Campus. His works focus on freedom, revolution, and love. Here are two examples of his songs. Rather than focusing on political themes, these songs face colonialism in cultural terms, celebrating indigenous traditions. The first expresses a yearning for spiritual inclusiveness; the second explores the anguish of love.

Spread your message once more, O Hazrat![1]
From the heavens, your message of equality.
I cannot bear this cruel bloodbath anymore
This strife within humanity.

O Hazrat, tell those who love you, your *umma*,[2]
He who loves mankind, loves all creation
He who loves mankind knows your creation.

Out of your generosity
Faith was brought to half the world
Yet without heeding that
We listen vacantly to words in the Koran and Hadith.

Ignoring your instructions
We suffer our time in Tribhuvan[3]
Neglecting those who need us
Meaninglessly we declare that we believe.

Spread your message once more, O Hazrat!
From the heavens, your message of equality.

The lightning strikes the dense sky
Drenched clouds pour rhythmically.
Sitting alone by the window
She waits . . . her heart forlorn, full of desire.

The easterly winds blow, frogs call out
She sets out for a tryst, seeking someone.
The night appears in desolate isolation.

Translated from Bengali by Meghna Guhathakurta.

Notes

1. The Prophet Muhammad.
2. Community of believers.
3. The three worlds—the universe according to Hindu traditions.

The Great Famine Strikes the Land

Tushar Kanti Ghosh and others

In 1943 Bengal was hit by a huge famine that would cause the death of more than three million people. Known as the Famine of '50 (after the Bengali year 1350, when it began), it led to epidemics, distress migration, family breakdowns, and widespread impoverishment among survivors. This reprehensible calamity was a classic example of a manmade disaster. It was the result of many different factors, most of them directly related to World War II. Japan had invaded neighboring Burma in 1942, and fear spread that Bengal would be next. People started hoarding food, rice from Burma could not be imported, and rice exports from Bengal to other parts of India increased. Food prices went up. On top of this, the colonial authorities sought to thwart any Japanese advance by a "denial policy": removing from coastal provinces all "excess" rice as well as all boats capable of carrying ten passengers or more. The authorities also fueled inflation by printing money to fund their wartime expenses. Rice stocks were moved from the countryside to the center of government control, Calcutta. There distribution schemes ensured that urban social unrest was minimized. In this overwrought atmosphere, traders resorted to speculative food hoarding, which increased prices well beyond the purchasing power of agricultural laborers, fisher folk, artisans, and peasants on small farms, who had to buy rice in the market. These rural groups became the main victims of the catastrophe, which lasted more than two years. Private organizations set up gruel kitchens. These saved many lives but could not be more than a drop in the ocean of human suffering. Tushar Kanti Ghosh, a newspaper editor, collected witness accounts of the horrors and published these in a book titled The Bengal Tragedy. *Some of these accounts are anonymous, others are not.*

At one of the [gruel] kitchens in Faridpur I noticed a man lapping up food like a dog. I saw abandoned children in the last stages of emaciation; men and women who had been without food for so long that they could now be fed only under strict medical supervision. Dead bodies were being daily picked up and also those who had fallen by the wayside through sheer exhaustion. A man after vainly wandering for food collapsed on the door-

Famine victims, by Zainul Abedin, 1943. Used by permission of Bangladesh National Museum.

steps of the Collector's [highest district official] court room. As the body was being removed, a woman huddled in a corner pushed out a bundle and cried: "Take that also." It was her dead child. At a kitchen, a woman had been walking every day more than a dozen miles to and from her home to take gruel to her sick and famished husband—[report by] *Sir Jagdish Parshad.*

A shocking incident of jackals devouring a starving man has been reported from Barodi Union, in the Narayanganj sub-division. It is stated that recently a famished fisherman, who was reduced to skin and bone, came from the interior and took gruel in the free kitchen of the Union. Thereafter he lay down nearby for rest. In the morning he was found with a portion of his body devoured by jackals, but he was still alive. Later, he died.

"Deaths owing to the food shortage are occurring daily in large numbers in the Chandpur Area," writes a special representative of [the newspaper] *Amrita Bazar Patrika*, who has been investigating conditions there. He adds that owing to the fuel shortage these bodies are being given mass burial. Sometimes bodies are also thrown into the river.

A report from Bera in Pabna District states that the high cost of funeral rites is compelling people to throw dead bodies into the river. Six or seven deaths from cholera and small-pox, it adds, have been occurring there daily.

Pakistan as a Peasant Utopia

Taj ul-Islam Hashmi

The final phase of colonial rule witnessed a most remarkable and rapid political development. Until then rural politics had been largely class based, and communists and other activists had been successful in pitting tenants against landholders in a series of uprisings. Even as these were continuing in the 1940s, a new political alliance emerged as large numbers of peasants suddenly swung their support behind upper-class Muslim leaders. To the peasants, an independent Pakistan now appeared to be their best ticket to emancipation because it would rid them of their (largely Hindu) landlords. Here the historian Taj ul-Islam Hashmi explains the murky complexity of interests that gave rise to this unforeseen alliance.

With the emergence of western educated leaders in the arena of the politics of the peasants, transcending the boundaries of villages and communities, the rural-based upper peasant leaders and the rural elites, including the *ulama* [Muslim theologians], emerged as a political force to play an important role in moulding the subsequent politics of the region. The Namasudra [a large community in East Bengal who bore the stigma of untouchability] and other non-Muslim peasants had their indigenous leaders too, who had close links with urban Hindu as well as Muslim *bhadralok* [educated elite] leaders, to champion their cause. The leadership, however, did not emerge out of the blue. Under the changed socio-economic and political circumstances, which precipitated a significant shift in the attitude of the government towards the *bhadralok* and non-*bhadralok* classes, both the urban leaders and their rural followers needed each other more than ever before.

Most peasants believed that, being illiterate and poor, they were incapable of leading their movements against the exacting landlords and moneylenders without the help of educated outsiders. . . . The leaders, both urban and rural based, on the other hand, needed not only peasant votes after the extensions of the franchise in 1919 and 1935, but also peasant support to fight their enemies, the rival elites or the government. The various divisive measures of the government, including the granting of separate electorates [for Muslims and Hindus] and the promises of radical anti-*zamindar* [land-lord] and anti-moneylender legislation, brought the Muslim masses closer to the Muslim aristocracy and middle classes whose interests conflicted with those of the Hindu *zamindars*, moneylenders and *bhadralok* classes. The urban-based Muslim *ashraf* [Urdu-speaking elite]—the Nawabs, Khwajas, Ispahanis, Suhrawardys and Adamjees—wanted a foothold in the *mofussil* [rural areas] to fight their politico-economic rivals, and established common ground with the *jotedars* [intermediary land holders], *ulama* and other elements of the budding Muslim middle classes from peasant backgrounds by laying increasing stress on the themes of the "common enemy" and "Islam in danger." . . .

In short, the marriage of convenience between the *ashraf* and the *jotedar*-occupancy *ryot* [tenant] categories was the determining factor in mobilizing the lower peasantry on communal lines throughout the region. The rich peasants thought that they had better socio-economic and political prospects in collaboration with the *ashraf*, who had wealth and influence to fight the powerful high-caste *zamindars, mahajans* [moneylenders] and *bhadralok*, the common enemies of the *ashraf, ulama, jotedars* and the lower peasantry. After the Tenancy Amendment Act of 1938, which further weakened the power and position of the *zamindars*, the *jotedars* and occupancy *ryots* emerged as powerful classes in the countryside. This worked as a catalyst in disestablishing the *zamindars* and Hindu *bhadralok* as dominant classes in the region. The recommendations of the Land Revenue Commission in 1940 in favour of the abolition of the *zamindari* system further emboldened the upper peasantry to challenge the legitimacy of the *zamindari* system. The absence of any parallel piece of legislation to strengthen the position of the lower peasantry left it at the mercy of the rich peasants and non-peasant leaders long after 1947. The *ashraf* . . . leaders' false promises, including the Bargadars [sharecroppers] Bill of early 1947, which the Muslim League government of Bengal never intended to enact into law, were mere carrots.

IV

Partition and Pakistan

In 1947 the British left and the colony of British India was partitioned. Most of the Bengal Delta joined the new state of Pakistan. Partition was a sudden event. It turned out to be an unprecedented social, economic, demographic, and cultural calamity that continues to reverberate strongly in contemporary Bangladesh—as it does in India and Pakistan. The first six texts in this part explore the experience of partition: the demarcation of the new territory, emotions of hope and despair during the first days, migration across the new border, the creation of a new political party, and lingering anger over, in Taslima Nasrin's words, "the man-made filth of religion, barbed wire," that divided what was once whole.

The part then examines how a new society took shape in East Pakistan. Several texts give details about the main issue of the period: why attempts to create a Pakistani nation soon faltered and a regional counterelite emerged to express economic, political, and cultural grievances. The economic disparities between East and West Pakistan became more glaring and the religious (Islamic) identity that had mobilized people against British colonial rule turned out to be insufficient to keep the Pakistani nation united. In East Pakistan a linguistic (Bengali) nation began to replace the idea of Pakistan. This is why Rounaq Jahan, in her contribution, speaks of a vernacular elite. As members of this regional elite distanced themselves from the Pakistan nation-building project, they imagined an East Pakistan that would be autonomous within a federal union. When this turned out to be a chimera, they began to dream of an independent Bangladesh.

Although this major drama shaped the lives of many people in East Pakistan in countless ways, much more was going on in the period between 1947 and 1971. This part captures some of these other developments and experiences as well. Among them is the search for postcolonial modernity, both at the level of individual East Pakistanis and at that of the state. Popular advertisements sought to persuade consumers to adopt modern lifestyles, and the state ordered a daringly avant-garde architectural design. Foreign

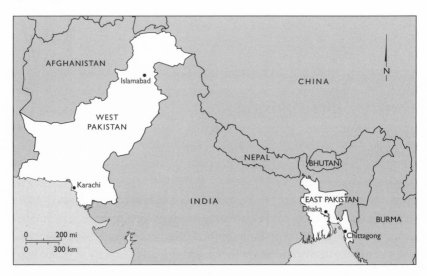

Map of Pakistan from 1947–1971.

development aid brought other forms of modernity—for example a huge hydroelectric project in the Chittagong Hill Tracts—as well as continuities. Foreign development experts replaced British bureaucrats, but these new-comers inherited much of the elite lifestyle of their predecessors, as revealed by the short piece on how to deal with servants.

The part concludes with five texts highlighting East Pakistan in the 1960s. One contribution shows how the shockwaves of partition continued to uproot non-Muslim inhabitants, and another presents an influential thesis on rural social organization. The final texts illustrate the unraveling of the state of Pakistan, from the 1965 war between India and Pakistan to the increasingly vocal demands for representation, a federal state, and, ulti-mately, national independence.

Creating an International Border

Cyril Radcliffe

The Report of the Bengal Boundary Commission *(1947) determined the partition of Bengal. Its bland administrative language belies both the high political drama of which it was the capstone and the awesome distress that it initiated. The report fashioned an oddly shaped territory that would first be called East Bengal (1947–56), then East Pakistan (1956–71), and, after the Bangladesh Liberation War in 1971, Bangladesh. According to the report, the colonial authorities had ordered the commission "to demarcate the boundaries of the two parts of Bengal on the basis of ascertaining contiguous areas of Muslims and non-Muslims." It also had been told to divide the district of Sylhet (then a part of Assam rather than Bengal) on the same principles.*

The commission was not unanimous; its members disagreed on many points, so the chairman, Cyril Radcliffe, made the decisions: "In the absence of any reconciliation on all main questions affecting the drawing of the boundary itself, my colleagues assented to the view at the close of our discussions that I had no alternative but to proceed to give my own decision." The Radcliffe awards, as they became known, created an international border that continues to be hotly disputed in many places. There are numerous border conflicts between India and Bangladesh, and hundreds of people are killed and wounded there every year.

A) Report of the Bengal Boundary Commission

1. A line shall be drawn along the boundary between the Thana [subdistrict administrative unit, literally "police station"] of Phansidewa in the District of Darjeeling and the Thana Tetulia in the District of Jalpaiguri from the point where that boundary meets the Province of Bihar and then along the boundary between the Thanas of Tetulia and Rajganj; the Thanas of Pachagar and Rajganj, and the Thanas of Pachagar and Jalpaiguri, and shall then continue along the northern corner of the Thana Debiganj to the boundary of the State of Cooch-Behar. The District of Darjeeling and so much of the District of Jalpaiguri as lies north of this line shall belong to West Bengal,

but the Thana of Patgram and any other portion of Jalpaiguri District which lies to the east or south shall belong to East Bengal.

2. A line shall then be drawn from the point where the boundary between the Thanas of Haripur and Raiganj in the District of Dinajpur meets the border of the Province of Bihar to the point where the boundary between the Districts of 24 Parganas and Khulna meets the Bay of Bengal. This line shall follow the course indicated in the following paragraphs. So much of the Province of Bengal as lies to the west of it shall belong to West Bengal. Subject to what has been provided in paragraph 1 above with regard to the Districts of Darjeeling and Jalpaiguri, the remainder of the Province of Bengal shall belong to East Bengal.

3. The line shall run along the boundary between the following Thanas: Haripur and Raiganj; Haripur and Hemtabad; Ranisankail and Hemtabad; Pirganj and Hemtabad; Pirganj and Kaliganj; Bochaganj and Kaliganj; Biral and Kaliganj; Biral and Kushmundi; Biral and Gangarampur; Dinajpur and Gangarampur; Dinajpur and Kumarganj; Chirirbandar and Kumarganj; Phulbari and Kumarganj; Phulbari and Balurghat. It shall terminate at the point where the boundary between Phulbari and Balurghat meets the north-south line of the Bengal-Assam Railway in the eastern corner of the Thana of Balurghat. The line shall turn down the western edge of the railway lands belonging to that railway and follow that edge until it meets the boundary between the Thanas of Balurghat and Panchbibi.

4. From that point the line shall run along the boundary between the following Thanas: Balurghat and Panchbibi; Balurghat and Joypurhat; Balurghat and Dhamairhat; Tapan and Dhamairhat; Tapan and Pathnitala; Tapan and Porsha; Bamangola and Porsha; Habibpur and Porsha; Habibpur and Gomastapur; Habibpur and Bholahat; Malda and Bholahat; English Bazar and Bholahat; English Bazar and Shibganj; Kaliachak and Shibganj; to the point where the boundary between the two last mentioned thanas meets the boundary between the districts of Malda and Murshidabad on the river Ganges.

5. The line shall then turn south-east down the River Ganges along the boundary between the Districts of Malda and Murshidabad; Rajshahi and Murshidabad; Rajshahi and Nadia; to the point in the north-western corner of the District of Nadia where the channel of the River Mathabhanga takes off from the River Ganges. The District boundaries, and not the actual course of the River Ganges, shall constitute the boundary between East and West Bengal.

6. From the point on the River Ganges where the channel of the river Mathabhanga takes off the line shall run along that channel to the northern-

most point where it meets the boundary between the Thanas of Daulatpur and Karimpur. The middle line of the main channel shall constitute the actual boundary.

7. From this point the boundary between East and West Bengal shall run along the boundaries between the Thanas of Daulatpur and Karimpur; Gangani and Karimpur; Meherpur and Karimpur; Meherpur and Tehatta; Meherpur and Chapra; Damurhuda and Chapra; Damurhuda and Krishnaganj; Chuadanga and Krishnaganj; Jibannagar and Krishnaganj; Jibannagar and Hanskhali; Meheshpur and Hanskhali; Meheshpur and Ranaghat; Meheshpur and Bongaon; Jhikargacha and Bongaon; Sarsa and Bongaon; Sarsa and Gaighata; Gaighata and Kalarao; to the point where the boundary between those thanas meets the boundary between the districts of Khulna and 24 Parganas.

8. The line shall then run southwards along the boundary between the Districts of Khulna and 24 Parganas, to the point where that boundary meets the Bay of Bengal.

NEW DELHI; *The 12th August, 1947.* Cyril RADCLIFFE

B) Report of the Bengal Boundary Commission (Sylhet District)

A line shall be drawn from the point where the boundary between the Thanas of Patharkandi and Kulaura meets the frontier of Tripura State and shall run north along the boundary between those Thanas, then along the boundary between the Thanas of Patharkandi and Barlekha, then along the boundary between the Thanas of Karimganj and Barlekha, and then along the boundary between the Thanas of Karimganj and Beani Bazar to the point where that boundary meets the River Kusiyara. The line shall then turn to the east taking the River Kusiyara as the boundary and run to the point where that river meets the boundary between the Districts of Sylhet and Cachar. The centre line of the main stream or channel shall constitute the boundary. So much of the District of Sylhet as lies to the west and north of this line shall be detached from the Province of Assam and transferred to the Province of East Bengal. No other part of the Province of Assam shall be transferred.

NEW DELHI; *The 13th August, 1947.* Cyril RADCLIFFE

Joy, Hope and Fear at Independence

Ahmed Kamal

August 1947 was a moment of great excitement in East Bengal: 190 years of British colonial rule came to an end as independent Pakistan was born. Today that excitement is rarely recalled because most Bangladeshis now think of the Pakistan period as a dark one. For them, independence came in 1971, when Pakistan shrank to its western wing and the eastern wing became Bangladesh. But for those who lived in 1947, Independence Day was a stunning event. Suddenly a long-cherished dream had come true: the foreign rulers were departing and the future was full of opportunities.

It was also a fraught moment because East Bengal gained independence as part of a new homeland for South Asian Muslims. Those who had fought for the idea of Pakistan were overjoyed because independence meant the emancipation of Bengali Muslims from Hindu domination—from now on Muslims would be masters of their own fate. Millions of other Muslims—and some non-Muslims—who had not supported the movement for Pakistan were still pleased with the creation of the new country. But there were many who were deeply unhappy. Some were Muslims who had wanted a unified Bengal. Others were Hindu landlords and professionals, Christians, Buddhists, and other non-Muslims who wondered whether there was any future for them in a Muslim homeland (and, if so, whether they would be second-class citizens). In this excerpt, the historian Ahmed Kamal brings to life the emotions that were unleashed on this fateful day. He also shows that contrasting feelings did not necessarily follow religious lines. Educated urbanites often had very different expectations than peasants. While the former dreamed of grasping the helm and controlling the state, many of the latter imagined the demise of the state itself.

At midnight of 14 August 1947, the eastern part of the Indian province of Bengal was partitioned and became what was later known as East Pakistan. Muslims all over East Bengal welcomed the birth of the new nation with the *azan* (call to prayer). Tajuddin Ahmed, a young Muslim nationalist during the late 40's, mentioned in his diary that people all over the Muslim areas of

Dhaka, which earned for itself the distinction of being the provincial capital of East Pakistan, were found busy, day and night, in erecting gates and decorating the city for Independence Day celebrations. Public and private buildings were illuminated at night and fireworks dazzled the sky. Crowds of "holiday makers" thronged the streets, "some riding trucks and some even on elephants." The highlight of the day, according to a *Statesman* report [in the issue of August 15, 1947, of this newspaper], was a procession by Hindus and Muslims, which converged on Victoria Park, where speeches were made by leaders of all important political parties.

The celebration was not confined to Dhaka. In the town of Barisal, victory gates were erected and musical soirees were organised. The distinguished historian Tapan Roy Chowdhury recollects nearly half a century after the event that in Barisal at 12 midnight all the steamers, steam launches, [and] motor boats anchored in the river *Kirtonkhola* blared out the birth of the new nation; the riverine town reverberated with sky-rending shouts of "Quaid-e-Azam zindabad" [Long live Jinnah], "Pakistan zindabad" [Long live Pakistan].[1] The day was observed with a public meeting in Sylhet where the siren on 14 August [at] midnight announced that the district had ceased to be a part of the Indian province of Assam. Batches of Muslims paraded the streets in procession. Provash Chandra Lahiry, a prominent District Congress leader, recollects that "every face of the vast population" that gathered at Rajshahi, a north Bengal town, showed "signs of radiant glow of fulfillment of a long cherished desire of winning freedom."[2] Even the tribal population of the border districts of East Pakistan were apparently "inspired and joyous" on achieving political freedom from the Raj. A communist activist and writer observed that "like the others they too were overwhelmed with joy" at the imminent prospect of independence.[3] On 15 August, meetings and processions were organized in Durgapur, Haluaghat, Nalitabari and Bhatpur in Mymensingh district by tribal leaders. They expressed their solidarity with the new nation state. . . .

A sudden sense of defeat, frustration and betrayal gripped the minds of the upper-caste Hindus of Eastern Bengal as soon as Pakistan was created. One Hindu leader expressed his disenchantment in the following manner: "Hindus never wanted Pakistan. Pakistan has been thrust upon their unwilling heads."[4] . . . In some places the reactions of the Hindu professionals were so bitter that they plundered government property before leaving the country. Ajoy Bhattacharya mentions that the caste Hindus employees of Sylhet hospital plundered the hospital's property and then crossed over to India.[5] The Hindu clerks and prisoners of Munshiganj sub-jail were reported to have declined their quota of "extra ration" granted to mark the celebration of Independence Day.[6] The leading class in the society of East Pakistan, constituted by the upper-caste Hindus, had turned overnight into political paupers. . . . However, many caste Hindus belonging to various strains of radical politics in East Bengal decided to stay on and contribute to the political life of East Pakistan. Troilokyanath Chakrabarty, one such Hindu, writes: "I decided that I would not leave the country. I should stay on in Pakistan. By sharing the happiness and sufferings of the people of Pakistan I would stay on. This country, East Bengal, is my country . . . why should I have to leave this country?"[7] . . .

Independence was also widely perceived as an occasion for the abolition of police and state institutions associated with the Raj. "Now that Pakistan has been achieved, should there still be police, courts and Kutcheries [offices], soldiers and sentries, Jails and lockups?" Ataur Rahman Khan, a district level Muslim League leader was asked by an elderly villager.

Khan replied, "Why not? How could you protect the State without these institutions?"

With a sigh the bewildered old man said, "then what kind of Pakistan [have we got]? Change the name please. You will name it Pakistan [yet] allow sins and corruption to exist."[8]

To the old man, the colonial institutions of the State, especially the police and the judiciary, were at odds with his notion of independence.

Notes

1. Hedayet Hussain Murshed, *Altaf Mahmud* (Dhaka, 1982), 7. Also see Tapan Roy Chowdhury, *Romonthon Athaba Bhimrati Prapter Parocharit Charcha* (Calcutta, 1993), 98.

2. Provash Chandra Lahiry, *India Partitioned and Minorities in Pakistan* (Calcutta, 1964), 1.

3. Satyen Sen, *Bangladesher Krisaker Sangram* (Dhaka, 1964), 57.

4. Letter from S. Bhattacharya, President Hindu Sevak Sangha, Sylhet, on 7 October 1947, Home Political Bundle, National Archives of Bangladesh, Dhaka.

5. Ajoy Bhattacharya, *Nankar Bidroho* (Dhaka, n.d.), Vol. II, 147.

6. Jail Bundle, B Proceedings, February 1956, Nos. 1–18, National Archives of Bangladesh, Dhaka.

7. Sri Troilokyonath Chakrabarty (Maharaj), *Jele Trish Bachar O Pak Bharater Swadhinata Sangram* (Mymensingh, 1968), 361.

8. Ataur Rahman Khan, *Sairacharer Dash Bachar* (Dhaka, 1974), 45.

Where Is the Border?

Indian and Pakistani Officials

The newly independent states of India and Pakistan were faced with a huge task: to delineate the outlines of their territories. Where exactly was the new international border? How would they demarcate it? Officials who had been colleagues only yesterday now represented sovereign states that stood in an uneasy relationship to one another. Together they had to inscribe a line of some four thousand kilometers in the landscape of the Bengal Delta. Despite a complete absence of experience in this field, Indian and Pakistani officials were able to sort out most problems. But not all: to this day India and Bangladesh quarrel over the precise location of several stretches of the border and over the ownership of dozens of bits of territory. Unpublished official records show that officials in the border districts often had to feel their way toward a solution. They would meet, go on fact-finding missions, and present joint reports to their respective governments.

In the first example, some officials were unable to locate the border because rivers often change course in an active delta. In 1950 a survey team had settled the provisional border along a small canal, but by 1953 the border had disappeared, which led to local disputes. This prompted a second visit by the highest-ranking officials in charge of the border districts. Here is an excerpt from their report.

The second example shows that even where the border had been established, its location was often difficult to discern. In the early 1950s a paramilitary force known as Ansars guarded Pakistan's side of the border. This report describes how an Ansar patrol party found itself on the wrong side of the border.

1.

District Magistrate, Mushidabad [India], District Magistrate, Rajshahi [East Pakistan] and the Superintendent of Police, Rajshahi, visited Char Nawshera on 7.6.53 for inspection of the disputed area to ascertain the ad hoc boundary fixed in 1950. Since 1950 topography of the locality seems to have undergone a considerable change. The middle point of a *nullah* [*nala*, a small canal] was made ad hoc boundary and it was agreed upon that two chains

In a marshy field in Banglabandh (the country's northernmost point) a pillar marks the border with India, seen in the background. Photograph by Willem van Schendel, 2000.

[forty meters] on either side were to be kept uncultivated by the tenants. It seemed that the condition could not be enforced. The *nullah* itself has now become the subject matter for dispute. On the spot the Indian nationals urged that the *nullah* existed to the north and they sought to point out the alleged course of the *nullah* but no sure trace of the *nullah* could be found in the locality in that direction. To the further south of the aforesaid *nullah* the Pakistani nationals pointed out a track to which the *nullah* was said to have passed[,] taking bends at places. The traces of a *nullah* were more vivid [in] that direction though with breaks at certain points. From the conflicting and confusing version it was not possible to take any agreed decision about the ad hoc boundary of 1950. It seemed that the Khash Mahal [Public Land] department of both the dominions [India and Pakistan] settled *khash* [public] lands after the fixation of the ad hoc boundary of 1950 to their respective tenants. It is therefore decided that the Khash Mahal staff of both the dominions would survey the area and plot out the lands on an agreed map to ascertain whether any encroachment has been made in granting settlement of *khash* lands.

2.

I made the enquiry at Barashashi [Dinajpur district, East Pakistan] and near about area from our own men as well as from the members of the public.

It was revealed that on 19.11.51 one constable and four Ansars with rifles and ammunition were deputed for patrolling the border towards the village Amarkhana side. Most of these men excepting one Ansar were new in that border outpost and had joined only a few days back. Just at sunset it is confirmed that they reached the village Amarkhana where they took signature of a local Muslim. After that the patrol party left the village to resume their patrol. By the time the local Muslim who had signed finished his "Maghrib" prayers he heard some shouts coming from the side to which the patrol party had gone. The border lies within a short distance of this village.

The men of the patrol party could not make out the boundary clearly and strayed into the Indian Territory by mistake in village Chilahati. On reaching near the house of one Jadab Burman, who was originally a resident in Pakistan and who has now shifted to India, they enquired from a boy who was looking after some cattle whether the area was in Pakistan. The boy kept quiet but meanwhile Jadab with a few others, who were present in his compound, came out and on recognising the patrol party of Pakistan caught hold of c/1199 Kandu Mia and Ansar Kasiruddin and uttered that they had come to India and they should be arrested and beaten. The constable and the Ansar finding themselves in Indian Territory lost their nerves and instead of putting up resistance and instead of firing tried to run away somehow or the other.

Ansar Azizuddin was one who was farthest away from the party and therefore could manage to escape with his rifle and ammunition. Others had to lose their rifles and some ammunition and somehow extricated themselves and ran away. Ansar Dasiruddin, however, could not escape and was arrested by the villagers.

When the constable and the three Ansars returned to the border outpost they did not give out the true story because they feared that they would be taken to task for going into India. The villagers in Pakistan had not seen the actual incident and hence all of them were thinking that, perhaps, the Pakistan patrol party was forcibly taken away from within our border. None of them could think that our men could commit the mistake of going into India. . . . I could find the whole story because a good deal of time had elapsed and by that time some of our villagers had come to know this story from Indians living on the other side.

Teenage Migrant

Hasan Azizul Huq

The partition of 1947 upset the lives of millions. Among them were many migrants who trekked across the new border to settle in their country of choice—as well as refugees who fled to safety. Much has been written about the hundreds of thousands who crossed from East Pakistan to India. By contrast, historians have largely ignored the fate of the hundreds of thousands who went the other way, from India to East Pakistan.

For all these migrants, the border created unanticipated puzzles of identity and citizenship. For example, after partition many schools and colleges were separated from their traditional student catchment areas. Despite the imposition of an international border, people continued to send their children to schools in what was now a foreign country. Take Hasan Azizul Huq, son of a well-established family in rural Burdwan (India) who completed high school in 1954.

And then I came to East Pakistan. Why? I think you can only say for personal or family reasons[;] . . . the reason for my moving here was almost accidental. My sister's husband taught English at [a college in East Pakistan] right after Partition when you did not have passports or visas. People cannot look very far into the future and he considered it one and the same country. . . . They wrote: "Let him come stay with us." That is why I came. Had the letter arrived one week later, I probably would already have entered Burdwan Raj College—I do not think I would have come then. And really, when I came to East Pakistan, I had no thought at all of staying here. There was no reason to do so. Because we had a huge family . . . the land produced enough. So why go? Why leave? . . . And let me be clear, after 1947 the Muslims of that area did not experience any real trouble. Our family was an influential family.

[So I took an Indian passport, went over to East Pakistan, and studied up to the MA degree at Rajshahi University. During these years, I visited my home three times a year.] Then, after getting my degree, I went back home [to India]. . . . My deepest wish was to become a teacher so I became a teacher at the village high school. I taught there for three months. Then I got into trouble. The school inspector asked:

"Where did this young man come from?"

"He graduated from Rajshahi University."

"So what about his citizenship? It can't be Indian. . . . How can you teach at the school, since you're not an Indian?"

"But I have an Indian passport! Are there any rules that a degree from Rajshahi University is not recognised in India?"

"No, that is not the problem."

"So then you don't have any grounds for objection." But still, after three months, I had to leave that job.

[Shortly afterwards I got a job at a college in Rajshahi and settled there. Together with my sister and another brother, I persuaded my parents to join us in East Pakistan. None of my uncles or cousins came.] And I'll tell you that some of them were at one time very keen supporters of Pakistan, and were part of the struggle for Pakistan[,] . . . but it never entered their heads that they might leave their homes to *live* in Pakistan.

Interview by Md. Mahbubar Rahman; translated from Bengali by Willem van Schendel.

Establishing the Communist Party of Pakistan

Moni Singh

Beginning in the 1920s, Communists were active in underground organizations and social movements in Bengal. Their activities were illegal until 1942, when the Communist Party of India was allowed. After the British left and the colony was divided between Pakistan and India, many political parties faced a dilemma: should they also break in two? At first the Communist Party of India, which had a strong base in East Pakistan, refused to do so. But at a congress in Calcutta in 1948 the delegates from Pakistan realized that they had no choice but to form a separate party. Moni Singh (or Moni Singha, 1901–90), one of the initiators, tells the story in his memoirs, titled Life Struggle. *By 1948 Singh already had a long record of organizing workers and peasants, from a successful textile workers' strike in Calcutta in 1928 to the Tanka (or Hajong) movement against sharecropper oppression in his native Mymensingh in the 1930s and 1940s. During the colonial period he had spent time in jail for his political activities; shortly after that the Pakistan government would outlaw the new party and Moni Singh would find himself in hiding and in jail again.*

The Second Congress of the Communist Party of India took place on 22 February 1948, a few months after the partition of India and Pakistan. This congress was held under a big tarpaulin in Mohammed Ali Park in Calcutta. After the withdrawal of the British and the division of the subcontinent into two nation-states, India and Pakistan, all the major political parties, like [Indian National] Congress, Muslim League, and the Communist Party retained their All India character. That is why in the All India Congress, comrades from Pakistan were also present. Delegates came from all over India and Pakistan. About 919 were elected representatives; out of these 632 came as delegates. In accordance with the All India structure of the party that was adopted during colonial times, 125 people came as delegates from East Pakistan. At that time, total membership of the party in All India was ninety thousand. Twelve thousand came from East Pakistan. Only five members participated from West Pakistan. From the parties of other like-minded countries, there were Lautissier and Tomović, from Yugoslavia; Lawrence Sharkey, from Australia; and Than Tun, from Burma. He gave a very rousing speech. He said: "It is through armed struggle only that we will attain Liberation, and that is the way we are going now." The keynote address of this congress was presented by B. T. Ranadive. The main trend of the congress was to evaluate the past activities and decide on future strategy. Ranadive said in his speech:

> So far we have been taking a reformist path. We dovetailed with bourgeois interests. We could not take an independent stance in the movement on the issue of freedom. As a result, the reactionary forces of Congress and Muslim League through a forged alliance ushered in a so-called Independence. This is not real independence, it is false! (*Eeye jhuta azadi hai!*). Just as in a postwar situation, there is still grounds for revolution. That is why we must continue our struggle against the bourgeoisie. Strikes, mass rallies, demonstrations, and armed struggles must be used to challenge this false sense of freedom. Democratic revolution in India has been delayed, but proletarian revolution has been successful in the world. Thus two kinds of revolution have been threaded into one. India has entered the socialist revolutionary stage. The proletariat and semiproletariat must lead the revolution. So far, under the leadership of P. C. Joshi, we have been following the reformist line. That is why the party has failed to fulfill its vanguard role. We must follow the path to oust bourgeois power.

Those of us who remained in Pakistan thought of ourselves as citizens of a separate state. Hence we had to think of establishing our party in the context of Pakistan. It was mentioned earlier that in the post-1947 period the Communist Party, like most other parties, still constituted itself in an All India framework. Later these parties formed themselves separately in the context of two different states. We too had not previously thought of separately constituting our party. But now we thought that our activities were going to differ in the context of each nation. Because Pakistan was a separate nation, we were going to have a different work agenda there, geared to different problems. That is why all the participants who came from Pakistan gathered together on 6 March to form the Communist Party of Pakistan.

The Central Committee consisted of nine members. They were Sajjad Zahir, Ata Mohammed, Jamaluddin Bukhari, Ibrahim (labor leader), Khoka Roy, Nepal Nag, Krishna Binod Roy, Mansur Habib, and Moni Singh. The politburo consisted of Sajjad Zahir, Khoka Roy, and Krishna Binod Roy.

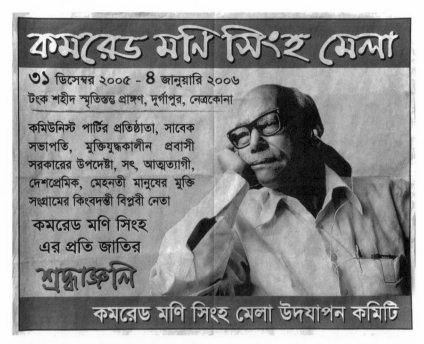

Poster for the Comrade Moni Singh Fair (2005–6), organized in Durgapur (northern Bangladesh) where Singh had led the communist-inspired Tanka movement in the 1930s and 1940s. Used by permission of the Heritage Archives of Bangladesh History, Rajshahi.

Mansur Habib was a resident of West Bengal. Later he shifted to East Bengal. After that he was arrested and held in jail in Rajshahi. In 1950, when prisoners were fired upon, he was injured. He later returned to India and became Speaker of the West Bengal Legislative Assembly, and more recently he was nominated as a minister. Krishna Binod Roy was also arrested and he too left for India.

Just after the Calcutta congress, the governments of both India and Pakistan started mass arrests and repression of Communist Party leaders. Therefore, in Pakistan the leaders of the Communist Party had to go underground.

The Pakistan Communist Party had mechanically adopted Ranadive's strategy, a strategy that declared democratic revolution and socialist revolution to be one. This was a technically wrong strategy. These were two different stages of revolution. According to Leninist thought, one came after the other. But Ranadive had combined them into one. Indian conditions were not ready for such a situation. The adoption of this wrong strategy by the party in Pakistan had fearful repercussions for the Communist movement later on.

An Incident. After the formation of Pakistan, the Communist Party would never have gone underground willingly. It was only in the face of continuous state repression that they had to take such measures. The Central Committee office of Dhaka district was located on Court House Street. In addition a residential hostel of the Dhaka district organization was located in Koltabazaar. On 12 March 1948, during the language movement [protest against the imposition of Urdu as national language of Pakistan], hooligans from the Muslim League attacked the hostel and trashed the place. On 10 March Ronesh Dasgupta and Dhoroni Roy had been arrested. When the people who had been arrested for taking part in the language movement were freed, Ronesh Dasgupta was also due to be set free but was later denied release. But when those in the language movement, especially Sheikh Mujibur Rahman, pressured the government, both Ronesh Dasgupta and Dhoroni Roy were released on 15 March. In June of that year the women members of the party called a mass rally. Police and hooligans of the Muslim League attacked the rally. About eleven women cadres, including Nibedita Nag, were arrested.

The party decided to hold a large rally in Coronation Park on 30 June 1948 and started a big campaign around it. Munir Chowdhury (later martyred in 1971) was to chair the meeting. The main speakers were Sardar Fazlul Karim and Ronesh Dasgupta. Fazlul Karim spoke about local problems and the party agenda. Ronesh Dasgupta talked of the international scenario and imperialist designs. There were about a thousand people present. At that time, Shah Azizur Rahman [a Muslim League politician] and his cronies arrived on the scene. No sooner had Fazlul Karim spoken, or Shah Aziz started passing notes full of questions to the speaker. From time to time he [Shah Aziz] began to create disruptions by shouting during the speeches. Ronesh Dasgupta in his speech also spoke of the necessity to withdraw from the commonwealth. When Shah Aziz created a disturbance, Munir Chowdhury quickly brought the meeting to an end. Shah Aziz and his cronies vehemently protested against this and demanded to be heard. As soon as the supporters of the Communist Party had departed, Shah Aziz captured the floor and started shouting abuse at the party.

After the Coronation Park meeting about a thousand people surrounded the office on Court House Street and attacked it. This resulted in a half-hour-long fight between party cadres and attackers. About twenty young supporters were present in the office, in addition to Binoy Basu, Amula Sen, Ronesh Dasgupta, Munir Chowdhury, and Sarder Fazlul Karim. Through their heroic efforts, they were able to defend the party office from being invaded by the outsiders. The party was not yet banned, it is true, but through continuous harassment, the party's activities were curbed. On 7 July Ronesh Dasgupta and Dhoroni Roy were again arrested. From then on the party decided to stop all overt activities and go underground with its activities. State repression against the party was the sole reason for this decision.

Translated from Bengali by Meghna Guhathakurta.

Broken Bengal

Taslima Nasrin

The partitioning of Bengal into West Bengal (now in India) and East Bengal (first renamed East Pakistan, now Bangladesh) created a historical and cultural trauma of the first order. It continues to be hugely significant in both Bangladesh and India, where people often refer to it in daily conversation. Partition still has a direct impact on millions of personal lives as well as on national politics, economic relations, and the arts. In the early years, when East Bengal had just become part of Pakistan, there was widespread elation and a strong sense of new opportunities. But over time the negative aspects became far more dominant, and partition came to be seen as a terrible mistake that could not be undone. This poem by Taslima Nasrin evokes the nostalgia, outrage, and lasting sense of loss that many inhabitants of Bangladesh share.

There was a land watered and fruitful
People of that land used to swing on festive days
Just as the golden paddy swung in breeze,
There was a land which held happy fairs
Merging the smell of soil in soil
When autumn clouds held fairs in the sky.
There was a land of mangoes, jackfruits
Where one could get soaked to the skin
Returning home in rain then faintly tremble,
Or bask in the sun after the fog cleared.
There was a land—yours, mine, our forefathers'?
Some suddenly halved this land of love into two.
They who did it wrenched the stem of the dream
Which danced like the upper end of the gourd,
Dream of the people.
They shook violently the roots of the land
And people were flung about who knows where,
None kept account of who perished who survived.

Residents of Bikrampur landed on Gariahata crossing
Some came to Phultali from Burdwan,
Some fled to Howrah from Jessore,
From Netrokona to Ranaghat,
From Murshidabad to Mymensingh.
The outcome was inevitable,
As when you release a wild bull in a flower garden.
Two parts of the land stretch out their thirsty hands
Towards each other. And in between the hands
Stands the man-made filth of religion, barbed wire.

Translated from Bengali; translator not acknowledged.

The Pakistan Experiment
and the Language Issue

Willem van Schendel

The partition of 1947 created two new independent states, India and Pakistan. The eastern part of Bengal joined Pakistan. Pakistan was a highly ambitious experiment in twentieth-century state making. And yet, from the beginning the state was beset with enormous challenges. This excerpt from a recent survey history of Bangladesh explains how these challenges worked out in East Pakistan and why political struggles soon crystallized around the issue of the Bengali language. This historical background is indispensable to understand the intense emotions surrounding the national language in Bangladesh today.

Under its new name—East Pakistan[1]—the Bengal delta now joined a unique experiment in state making. There were three reasons why Pakistan was a very special state. First, it was founded upon religious nationalism. Religion was supposed to cement a new national identity, something that had not been tried before—the only other modern example of a religiously based nation-state being Israel, which was founded a year later than Pakistan. Second, Pakistan was a state administering two discrete territories, separated from each other by about 1,500 km of Indian terrain. West Pakistan was by far the larger of these two wings but East Pakistan was more densely populated. In fact, most Pakistani citizens lived in East Pakistan: the first population census in 1951 revealed that Pakistan had seventy-eight million inhabitants, of whom forty-four million (55 per cent) lived in East Pakistan.

These two factors combined with a third: Pakistan did not become heir to any of the colony's central state institutions. India, on the other hand, inherited the capital New Delhi as well as most of the civil bureaucracy, armed forces and police. The bulk of the colony's resources and industries, and its major port cities of Mumbai (Bombay) and Kolkata (Calcutta), also went to India. By contrast, Pakistan inherited largely raw-material producing regions. Whereas the new rulers of India supplanted the British in the old centre of colonial power, the new rulers of Pakistan had a much harder time to establish themselves. In other words, Pakistan was uniquely experimental: no other post-colonial state combined the loss of its administrative hub, the need to govern two unconnected territories, and the ambition to found a national identity on a religious one.

In the eastern "wing" of the country the situation was especially difficult. In August 1947, "the new East Pakistan government was hastily housed in a College for Girls [Eden College in Dhaka], with a large number of improvised bamboo sheds added to it for greater accommodation. On partition, East Pakistan received only one member of the former Indian Civil Service [the elitist corps of colonial bureaucrats, the 'steel frame' that had kept the colony together] who belonged to that region. Six others were hastily promoted from the Provincial Civil Service."[2] As a result, the civil service of East Pakistan was largely non-local and decision-making was in the hands of officials with little knowledge of East Pakistan's needs. An official publication described the predicament of the administrators in heroic terms: "For the many directorates there was no accommodation at all and these were sent to outlying districts. One Minister sat in a boat on the Buriganga river, disposing of files and transacting official business. Hundreds of officers chummed together in ramshackle tenements. Even camps were a luxury and bamboo constructions sprang up to provide shelters for officials and staff who were used to comfortable Calcutta flats and rooms."[3]

The General Officer Commanding (East Bengal), who arrived in January 1948, later reminisced: "The provincial government . . . was newly formed and poorly staffed. But worse still, it was politically weak and unstable. There was no army. All we had in East Pakistan at the time of Independence were two infantry battalions [one with three and one with only two companies]. We had very poor accommodation: at Headquarters there was no table, no chair, no stationery . . . we had virtually nothing at all; not even any maps of East Pakistan."[4]

These initial uncertainties and the artificial nature of Pakistan's unity fuelled the desire for a strong, centralised state. The ruling party, the Muslim League, benefited from the prevailing mood in Pakistan, which was one of euphoria. Having attained a sovereign homeland, Muslims could now safeguard their political, religious and cultural rights and they could complete their economic emancipation. But it did not take long for them to realise that the road ahead was anything but smooth: the two elements that most Pakistanis shared—an Islamic identity and a fear of India—proved insufficient to keep them united. Immediately fights broke out over the equitable distribution of resources, both material and symbolic. Only three months after independence a first serious crack in the edifice of Pakistan appeared over the question of the national language. It was the initial portent of enormous tensions over how the new state should be organised. These strains would gradually spoil the prospect of building a Pakistani nation. Right from the beginning, they took the form of a confrontation between Pakistan's two wings over issues such as language, autonomy, food security and economic policy. In the unfolding drama of Pakistani politics, the Bengal delta would play the role of the disenfranchised sibling clamouring consistently and unsuccessfully for rights withheld. Throughout the twenty-four years of the Pakistan experiment, the country's various rulers shared two nightmares: to be humiliated by India and to see control of the state pass democratically to East Pakistan. The latter fear would be their undoing. It animated an extraordinary political obstinacy that would, in the end, lead them to wage war on the majority of Pakistan's citizens. This strategy blew up in their faces, resulted in their utter humiliation by India, and left them no other choice but to separate themselves from East Pakistan and hang on to what was left of their power in Pakistan's western wing.

In 1947 the new Pakistani elite faced the difficult task of welding its citizens into a united Pakistani nation. Immediately the question came up in what language Pakistan's state business should be conducted. The Pakistan Educational Conference of November 1947 proposed Urdu as the national language, a suggestion that was opposed by representatives from East Pakistan. A few months later an East Pakistan member of the Constituent Assembly tabled an amendment to allow the Bengali language to be used in the Assembly alongside Urdu. He was sharply rebutted by the prime minister, Liaquat Ali Khan, who averred: "Pakistan has been created because of the demand of a hundred million Muslims in this subcontinent and the language of a hundred million Muslims is Urdu . . . It is necessary for a nation to have one language and that language can only be Urdu and no other language."[5]

This was quite an extraordinary statement in view of the fact that Pakistanis spoke dozens of languages and that Urdu was spoken by only 3 per cent of them. Bengali was very clearly the principal language of the country: it was spoken by 56 per cent of all Pakistanis. So why was the prime minister so adamant about Urdu?

The language issue stood for a more general cultural and political divide within the fledgling state. Muslim politicians in Bengal had imagined Pakistan differently from their counterparts in Northern India. The Bengalis had dreamed of a land free from the economic domination of Hindus and they imagined a leading role for themselves as representatives of the majority of

Pakistani citizens. North Indian Muslim politicians, on the other hand, had pictured themselves as the natural leaders of Pakistan because they considered themselves to be the guardians of the Muslim renaissance movement in South Asia and, therefore, arbiters of the future of all Muslims. They insisted that their vision of Pakistan should rightfully take precedence.

From the beginning, the "North Indian" view dominated the institutions of state. There were two regional groups that endorsed it. The first became known as the *Muhajirs* (= migrants). They were largely members of Urdu-speaking intellectual and trading elites from North India who moved to Pakistan's cities in their hundreds of thousands and immediately exerted an influence on politics and social life that was way out of proportion to their numbers. What made them unusual immigrants was that many of them expected the local population to adapt to them rather than the other way around. They took hold of almost all higher positions in the administration and the executive power. Most of these immigrants settled in West Pakistan but over 100,000 Muhajirs made their new homes in East Pakistan. The second regional group was Muslims from Punjab. They were heavily over-represented in the armed forces, manned the state administration and controlled valuable irrigated land. The Punjabis progressively outflanked the Muhajirs to become the hegemonic power in Pakistan. This was symbolised in 1959 by the transferral of the capital from Karachi (Pakistan's prime Muhajir city) to the Punjab garrison town of Rawalpindi, and from there to newly constructed Islamabad a decade later.

The Bengali political elite took exception to the North Indian view of Pakistan's future. The country's new rulers, concentrated in West Pakistan, used Islam as the political idiom to justify their actions and this caught the Bengalis in a quandary: their protests were easily dismissed as un- or anti-Islamic. This was no mere tactical ploy on the part of West Pakistani politicians. There was a widespread perception in West Pakistan that Bengali Muslims were not only socially inferior but also lesser Muslims because they did not adhere to many of the cultural practices that North Indians considered properly Islamic. The message from West Pakistan was that however passionately Bengalis might think of themselves as Muslims, they fell short of the mark and they could not be fully-fledged Pakistanis unless they shed much of their Bengaliness. In this climate the dilemma for politicians from East Pakistan was that they needed constantly to underline their Islamic *bona fides* and at the same time defend a regional interest.

The language issue became the focal point of this conflict because imposing Urdu was part of a mission to "Islamise" East Pakistan. Many in West Pakistan knew very little about the Bengali language but thought of it as in need of "purification" from Hindu influences. To them the Bengali script (evolved from Sanskrit), the Sanskritic vocabulary of Bengali and the dominance of Hindus in the Bengali literary pantheon were all irksome. The Bengali Muslims' obvious attachment to their language and literature was puzzling, and their rejection of Urdu rather suspect.

When students in East Pakistan came to know about the plan to make Urdu the national language, they held meetings and demonstrations and then formed the first Language Action Committee in December 1947. Things came to a head in March 1948 when general strikes were observed in East Pakistan's towns and the movement's leaders were arrested and injured. Mohammad Ali Jinnah, Governor-General of Pakistan at the time, visited Dhaka a few days later. Addressing a large audience, he stated that the Bengali language could be used in East Pakistan, "but let me make it clear to you that the state language of Pakistan is going to be Urdu and no other language. Anyone who tries to mislead you is really the enemy of Pakistan. Without one state language, no nation can remain tied up solidly together and function. Look at the history of other countries. Therefore, so far as the state language is concerned, Pakistan's language shall be Urdu. But as I have said, it will come in time."[6]

This uncompromising attitude led to rapid disillusionment with the Muslim League government amongst East Pakistani intellectuals, civil servants, politicians and students. This was not just a matter of regional pride, cultural identity and democratic principles but also a reflection of frustrated career ambitions. Urdu-speaking candidates were preferred for jobs in the state bureaucracy and, in East Pakistan, this excluded almost all locals (fewer than 1 per cent spoke Urdu as a second language) and favoured North Indian immigrants.

The Language Movement, or Bhasha Andolon, gave rise to a new type of politician in East Pakistan: the Bengali-speaking student agitator. Throughout the Pakistan period students at schools, colleges and universities often played a decisive role in turning political grievances into popular resistance and forcing the Pakistan state to change its policies. The most critical event of the Language Movement, and a pivotal moment for the Pakistan experiment, occurred in early 1952. There was a growing sense of deprivation and disappointment in East Pakistan and a feeling was spreading that a new form of colonial rule had replaced British imperialism. The Language Movement, which had declined after 1948, reignited when the new prime minister of Pakistan, Khwaja Nazimuddin, came to Dhaka and addressed a large crowd at a central green. When he pronounced that the people of East Pakistan could decide what would be the provincial language but only Urdu would

21 February 1952: students are gathering on the Dhaka University campus to defy the government's ban on demonstrations in favor of the Bengali language. Used by permission of the Heritage Archives of Bangladesh History, Rajshahi.

be Pakistan's state language, he received a very angry reaction. Students responded with the slogan "We demand Bengali as a national language!" (*rastrabhasa bangla chai!*). Dhaka University went on strike and a number of organisations called a protest meeting, chaired by Maulana Abdul Hamid Khan Bhashani. Bhashani was a long-term supporter of the idea of Pakistan who had broken with the Muslim League in 1949 to form a new party, the Awami [People's] Muslim League. The meeting sharply denounced the decision to make Urdu the state language and also rejected a government plan to introduce Arabic script to write Bengali. It decided to call a general strike (*hartal*) and demonstrations throughout East Pakistan on 21 February 1952.

The government imposed a ban on these demonstrations in Dhaka and although some organisers hesitated to violate it, many students were determined to persevere. Thousands of boys and girls from schools and colleges all over Dhaka assembled on the campus of Dhaka University together with university students. They then started marching and shouting slogans. As soon as they passed the campus gates armed policemen baton-charged them. The students retaliated by throwing bricks, upon which the police used tear gas and then fired into the crowd. Many were injured and five people, including a nine-year-old boy, were killed. Over the next few days more demonstrations, killings and arrests occurred, and a memorial was hastily erected on the spot where the first killings had taken place.

This memorial was removed by the authorities and recreated several times before it was replaced by a concrete monument, the Martyrs' Memorial or Shohid Minar (*śahīd minār*), in 1962. Today this monument continues to be a focal point of national identity politics and there are martyrs' memorials in every delta town. The twenty-first of February (*Ekushe*) became a key national holiday and in 1999, following a proposal by the Bangladesh government, UNICEF created International Mother Language Day, celebrated annually on 21 February.

The events of 1952 were critically important, and not just because the Pakistani armed forces had turned murderously violent against fellow Pakistanis demonstrating for their rights, thus exposing the brutal nature of the state's leadership. This had happened before, e.g., in July 1948 when the army put down a police revolt in Dhaka. What made 1952 a defining moment was that it marked a sharp psychological rupture. For many in the Bengal delta, it signified the shattering of the dream of Pakistan and the beginning of a new political project, still hazy and fully supported by only a few: the search for a secular alternative to the communal idiom of Pakistan politics and for an autonomy that the delta had last experienced in pre-Mughal times.

Notes

1. Initially, the eastern wing of Pakistan was known officially as "East Bengal." It became "East Pakistan" in 1956.

2. A. M. K. Maswani, *Subversion in East Pakistan* (Lahore: Amir Publications, 1979), 84–85.

3. *Five Years of Pakistan (August 1947–August 1952)* (Karachi: Pakistan Publications, 1952), 243.

4. Muhammad Ayub Khan, *Friends Not Masters* (London: Oxford University Press, 1967), 22.

5. Hasan Zaheer, *The Separation of East Pakistan: The Rise and Realization of Muslim Bengali Nationalism* (Karachi: Oxford University Press, and Dhaka: University Press Limited, 1994), 21.

6. Z. H. Zaidi (ed.-in-chief), *Jinnah Papers: Pakistan—Struggling for Survival, 1 January–30 September 1948*, Vol. VII, Quaid-i-Azam Papers Project, Government of Pakistan (Karachi: Oxford University Press, 2003).

A Vernacular Elite

Rounaq Jahan

The political scientist Rounaq Jahan's influential text, Pakistan: Failure in National Integration, *published in 1972, was the first to analyze the Pakistan period by pointing to the democratic deficit in the Bengal Delta. She demonstrates that it was the Pakistani state elite's fear of democratic political institutions and the resulting exclusion of Bengalis from national policymaking that explains the breakup of Pakistan. The collapse of Pakistan was not something that was rooted in developments just before the war of 1971 but went back to its early days. Jahan outlines a crucial process in East Pakistan: the rapid emergence of a new group between 1947 and 1954 that would act as a regional counterelite to the national power holders of Pakistan. She introduces the term* vernacular elite *to describe the group.*

From the viewpoint of east-west integration, the most crucial development during the first decade [1947–57] was the rise of a vernacular elite in East Pakistan. Unlike the ruling elite at the center or in West Pakistan, which changed little over the years, the Bengali elite changed a great deal during this period. At the time of independence, the ruling elite in East Bengal, like the central ruling elite, was "national" and "nonvernacular," or bilingual. The Bengali Muslims entered the modern age at a relatively late stage. Before independence their leaders generally were landlords or Calcutta-based urban cosmopolitans who were either nonvernacular or bilingual. But in the year following independence, preexisting factional groups and new social forces gave rise to a Bengali counterelite which was mostly "vernacular" and regional. During its struggle for supremacy (1947–54), the vernacular elite developed its own separate political party and platform and a distinct linguistic nationalism. The election of 1954 marked the loss of power of the old ruling elite. The ascent of the vernacular elite to power within the relatively short period of seven years was due partly to preexisting factional opposition to the "national" elite and partly to the inept policies followed by that elite and its allies in the center.

Origins of the vernacular elite. The vernacular elite drew its strength from various groups and organizations. At the initial stage, Muslim League factions opposed to the ruling faction played a key role. Prior to independence, the Muslim League was divided into three major factions: the Dacca [Dhaka], or Nazimuddin, faction; the Fazlul Huq faction; and the Suhrawardy faction. The Dacca faction, led by men like Khawaja Nazimuddin and Akram Khan, was an essentially traditional, conservative faction that represented the landed interests. Its leadership was nonvernacular and had little popular support in the countryside. The Suhrawardy faction was mostly modernist and urban-based, primarily in Calcutta. Many of the members, including Suhrawardy himself, were nonvernacular. Their main strength lay in their organizational capability and in their hold over the mobilized urban literati groups, especially the students. The Fazlul Huq faction was vernacular and rural-based. It was organizationally weak but had mass support because it championed popular socioeconomic causes like the abolition of landlordism and the settlement of rural debt, as well as specifically Muslim causes.

Both the Huq and Suhrawardy factions fell out with the central Muslim League hierarchy, one of the reasons being their disagreement over the issue of Bengal's political autonomy. After partition, the Nazimuddin faction came to power in East Pakistan with the help of the central Muslim League hierarchy. Thus the early power elite in the east wing was essentially nonvernacular, organizationally weak, and opposed by the Huq and Suhrawardy factions. A few of the prominent supporters of these factions were accommodated by the ruling elite; but the majority, including Fazlul Huq and Suhrawardy themselves, remained outside the government. The inability of the ruling elite to incorporate these dissatisfied factions spurred the quick rise of the vernacular counterelite. The opposition factions, coupled with Maulana Bhasani's group, which had its main strength in Assam and Sylhet, laid the foundation of a separate political party and platform. Unlike the other leaders, Bhasani believed in nonconstitutional methods and civil disobedience, and he was the only Pakistani leader who sought a rural base. His belief in socialism and anti-imperialism made him a catalyst for leftist forces in East Pakistan.

In addition to these Muslim League factions, the Congress and Communist parties helped shape the ideology and organization of the Bengali counterelite. At the time of partition, Congress was the only official opposition party in East Bengal and hence bore the main burden of criticizing the policies of the ruling elite. Congress, for example, undertook the championship of the Bengali language and principles of secularism. The Communists

Women educators pose after a cultural performance at the Maniza Rahman Girls'
School in Gandaria, Old Dhaka in 1954. Anonymous photographer. Courtesy of
Meghna Guhathakurta.

also had considerable impact. After independence, the Communists at first
adopted the policy of working for an immediate revolution, and organized
a peasant movement. The quick suppression of the revolutionary movement, and a change in the policy of Cominform, led the Communists to
work in other, non-Communist front organizations. They worked in the
Youth League, East Pakistan Students Union (EPSU), Ganatantri Dal, and
the Awami League—organizations from which the vernacular elite drew
substantial support. The Communists also aided the vernacular elite in the
1952 language movement and the election of 1954.

It was, however, the student organizations that proved to be the vernacular elite's major source of strength. Students continued their pre-
independence tradition of political activism, and provided leadership and
support for the various political movements undertaken by the vernacular elite. After independence, the enrollment of Muslim students increased
steadily. The majority of them went to vernacular language schools, and
they were an ever-expanding base of support for the vernacular elite.

East and West Pakistan: Economic Divergence

Rehman Sobhan

Pakistani policymakers saw themselves as champions of modernization, but the development regime that they created widened the gap between rich and poor and between the country's two wings, fueling mass discontent in East Pakistan. The East Pakistani elite began to demand that regional disparities be recognized and remedied. One strong voice was that of Rehman Sobhan, a young economist who would develop the idea of regional economic autonomy by means of a "two-economy policy." The economy of each wing—West Pakistan and East Pakistan—should be treated as completely separate, and an appropriate policy should be devised for each. This demand would become the cornerstone of the influential Six Point Programme of 1966, but in this piece from 1962, economic federalism is not yet in the cards. Instead Sobhan goes to great lengths to demonstrate the growing regional disparity and the need for an immediate, drastic change of development policy in favor of East Pakistan.

The factor which distinguishes Pakistan from other similarly placed underdeveloped economies is the fact that its two major component regions, East and West Pakistan, are separated by 1,000 miles of foreign territory. About 55% of the nation's population is located in the East and 45% in the West. Hence, the facts of geography are at the center of Pakistan's problems. Furthermore, given the uncertain political relations with the intervening country, India, the principal means of communication is by sea, which is a distance of several thousand miles. Of course, there is a well-developed air network, but this is only for passenger services and a small volume of air cargo, which in value constitutes about 1% of total inter-area trade. Overland rail traffic exists, but is virtually negligible at present.

Apart from the problems caused by separation is the fact that natural conditions in the two parts of the country are also quite disparate. East Pakistan is essentially a monsoon region with an abundance of water. However, the land-labor ratio is very low, with a population density of about 930 per square mile. West Pakistan is largely arid with scant rainfall, heavily dependent on an irrigation economy. It has a much bigger land area, which gives it a population density of 140 per square mile. However, some of the land is desert or otherwise uncultivable. Furthermore, the West is faced with an acute problem of water-logging and salinity which is threatening to contract further its productive area. A heavy investment program to counteract this is already being drawn up.

These elementary facts of geography are, of course, known to most informed people, and one simply reiterates them as a background to the subsequent discussion of some of the economic implications of this separation. The most important feature of the Pakistani economy is the low mobility between the two regions. This is a direct result of the problem of distance. Over the last 14 years, very few people have moved from one region to another as settlers. A small number of East Pakistani farmers were settled in Sind under the Thal Development Authority, a big land reclamation scheme, but this has not been repeated on any significant scale. There is a certain amount of movement by government servants and business executives from East Pakistan to the national capital, first in Karachi and now in Rawalpindi. Businessmen were mostly located in Karachi. However, these together constitute a negligible number. The reverse flow is not much greater. West Pakistani businessmen and technicians have moved across, albeit temporarily, to fill the gap in technical and commercial expertise in the East Pakistani economy, but in aggregate, labor mobility is very restricted and shows no likelihood of increasing.

Apart from the problem of distance, which makes mobility an expensive and difficult proposition, cultural differences must also be considered. Differences in language, diet, and general customs make social integration difficult though perhaps not impossible. Religion is of course a unifying factor and may in some cases exercise a substantial influence on behalf of integration, but it is not certain how far this can counteract economic differences and cultural diversity in other respects.

These factors in themselves may not have special significance. Cultural homogeneity is not always present in a modern political society. However, these problems have really provided the leaven for the central issue, the economic disparity between the Eastern and Western sectors of the nation. In this context the term disparity is used to mean differences in levels of development and the manifestation of this in differences in the average standard of living between the two regions. The indices of this disparity are provided by regional per capita income figures. In 1960, the East Pakistani per capita income was estimated at Rs. 213 while the figure in West Pakistan was approximately Rs. 305, a difference of nearly one-third. It should be mentioned that national income accounting in Pakistan is still in its infancy; hence, regional income estimates are little more than imaginative guesses. However, these figures, inaccurate though they may be, give a modest indication of the problem. An index of available commodities provides another useful indicator of disparity. The following tables, which are somewhat more reliable than the per capita income figures, give evidence of the existence of disparity and show how this has been gradually widening (Table I). Table II shows absolute figures for the availability of commodities on a per capita basis.

In conclusion the following points emerge. Pakistan is a geographical peculiarity with its two sectors separated by 1,000 miles. There is relatively little labor mobility between the sectors. East Pakistan has lagged behind in the race for economic development and today has a lower aggregate and per capita income than West Pakistan, even though it has 55% of the total population. This disparity has been perpetuated by both the First Five Year Plan (1955–60) and the Second Five Year Plan (1960–65). There are certain built-in forces in the economy emanating from the laws of cumulative causation which are further aggravating the imbalance. It is now fully realized that this imbalance has serious economic, social and political consequences. The Government of Pakistan has placed on record its desire to remove disparity. This can be done by accelerating the rate of investment in East Pakistan. At the same time, technical and foreign aid and foreign exchange will

*Table I. Regional Income Estimates**

	QUANTITY INDICES		PER CAPITA INDICES	
YEAR	WEST PAKISTAN	EAST PAKISTAN	WEST PAKISTAN	EAST PAKISTAN
1951–52	100	100	100	100
1952–53	103	105	101	103
1953–54	112	120	107	115
1954–55	123	111	115	105
1955–56	126	98	114	91
1956–57	133	127	118	116
1957–58	143	122	124	109
1958–59	147	110	125	96

* S. U. Khan, "A Measure of Economic Growth in East and West Pakistan," *Pakistan Development Review* (Autumn 1961).

Table II. Per Capita Availability of Specified Commodities*

COMMODITY	UNIT	1951–52 WEST PAKISTAN	1951–52 EAST PAKISTAN	1959–60 WEST PAKISTAN	1959–60 EAST PAKISTAN
Wheat	Oz. per day	9.9	0.1	10.0	0.4
Rice	Oz. per day	1.4	14.7	1.7	16.0
Other cereals	Oz. per day	4.4	0.1	3.5	0.1
Pulses	Oz. per day	0.2	0.5	0.2	0.3
Raw sugar	Lbs. per annum	32.7	15.7	50.3	13.3
Refined sugar	Lbs. per annum	8.0	2.7	6.5	2.6
Tea	Lbs. per annum	0.5	0.1	1.0	0.1
Salt	Lbs. per annum	17.0	11.6	10.0	11.3
Cigarettes	Nos. per annum	76.0	5.0	183.0	33.0
Tobacco	Lbs. per annum	1.8	2.5	1.7	1.8
Fish	Lbs. per annum	2.4	3.9	3.5	9.3
Rapeseeds	Lbs. per annum	7.8	7.6	8.2	7.1
Cloth	Yards per annum	1.4	1.7	9.0	3.0
Paper	Lbs. per annum	0.5	0.2	1.4	0.3
Matches	Nos. per annum	10.0	7.0	16.0	13.0
Coal	Lbs. per annum	87.0	46.0	66.0	28.0
Kerosene	Gallons per annum	0.5	0.5	0.9	0.6
Petroleum	Gallons per annum	1.0	0.1	1.3	0.1
Electricity	Kwh. per annum	8.6	0.5	28.8	1.6

* S. U. Khan, "A Measure of Economic Growth in East and West Pakistan," *Pakistan Development Review* (Autumn 1961).

have to be made available in East Pakistan to ensure implementation of the proposed plans. This will have to be markedly different from past policies where about 80% of all aids and loans went to West Pakistan as did the major part of exchange from national exports. This was true in spite of the fact that East Pakistan earned 60–70% of Pakistan's foreign exchange, mainly from her exports of raw and manufactured jute.

There is no reason why these objectives should not be attained providing there is full recognition of the nature of the problem and a continuous commitment to its removal. In many respects, the problem of Pakistan economic development is truly unique. In addition to the conventional problems of under-development, it has special ones derived from its particular geographic and cultural divisions.

Modern Lifestyles

Anonymous

Pakistan was a case of state formation before nation building. In August 1947 Pakistan came into existence as a homeland for South Asia's Muslims, but what did it mean to be a "Pakistani"? This was a particularly vexed question in eastern Bengal, which had long taken its cultural cues from the elite in Calcutta, now beyond reach in India. What mix of identities—Bengali, Muslim, "modern"—would emerge to forge a satisfactory Pakistaniness in the eastern wing of Pakistan? Here millions of people were not Muslims, many were not Bengalis, and modernist and conservative Muslims had very different ideas about the future nation. It was never going to be easy.

PAKISTAN ZINDABAD!

.

To be a worthy Citizen of a Modern state

READ MORE AND MORE BOOKS

.

For Books worth reading please contact

FRANKLIN PUBLICATIONS, INC.
29, Purana Paltan, Dacca-2.
OR
Book Promotion & Distribution Centre
Franklin Publications, Inc.
67/A, Purana Paltan, Dacca-2.

Gram: FRANDAC   Phone: 4608

"Pakistan Zindabad!" (Long live Pakistan!). An advertisement in the Independence Day issue of a Dhaka newspaper, *Morning News*, 14 August 1959. Used by permission of the Heritage Archives of Bangladesh History, Rajshahi.

"For the most modern [*adhunikotom*] furniture, visit Modern Furniture Ltd., the biggest furniture manufacturer of the eastern wing." Advertisement in the women's magazine *Begom*, 27 July 1969. Used by permission of the Heritage Archives of Bangladesh History, Rajshahi.

There was a general sense that Pakistaniness would not develop automatically but had to be nurtured. The nation had to be fashioned by teaching people how to be proper Pakistanis, or, as the book advertisement here puts it, "how to be a worthy Citizen of a Modern state."

Worthy citizens should be modern consumers. Advertisements in popular magazines attempted to communicate modern lifestyles to potential customers. They frequently employed the words adhunik and modarn (both mean modern) to introduce products that were seen as indispensable additions to contemporary life. The furniture ad here uses both.

After independence, East Pakistanis were exposed to new ideas about the family and sexuality, notably through foreign-funded family-planning campaigns. Responsible citizens should procreate in moderation and they had at their disposal a host of modern ways to curb fertility. The family-planning ad here addresses the reader in typically didactic style.

"Did you know? There are more than ten different methods of family planning. You can choose any of the following from your nearest family-planning clinic: plastic coil, condom, foam tablet, Durafoam, contraceptive pill, sponge, jelly/cream, Emko, pessary, operation for men or women, etc." Advertisement in the women's magazine *Begom*, 27 July 1969. Used by permission of the Heritage Archives of Bangladesh History, Rajshahi.

Architectural Masterpiece in Dhaka

Andrée Iffrig

In 1959, in a gesture to appease East Pakistani resentment, the Pakistan government decided to create a "second capital" in Dhaka. Islamabad, the new ultramodern national capital, was located in West Pakistan. Now a complex of striking government buildings and residences for top politicians and high officials was to emerge on the outskirts of Dhaka. The centerpiece was the second seat of the Pakistan Parliament—the idea was that parliamentary sessions could alternate between the country's wings.

The American architect Louis Kahn (1901–74) was commissioned and he created a grand plan. Construction started in 1964, but by the time it was completed, Pakistan had disintegrated. Today the main building is known as Jatiya Sangsad Bhaban—the seat of Bangladesh's National Parliament.

In the flood plains of Bangladesh lies an architectural masterpiece that would be a jewel anywhere in the world. It seems especially luminous in a poor country like Bangladesh. The design was architect Louis Kahn's last opportunity to explore a timeless form of architecture that marries the modern and traditional.

The capital buildings of Dhaka represent the justice system, government and prayer life of the country, founded in 1971 as a parliamentary democracy. Kahn worked on the 900-acre site in the decade before his death. The commission permitted Kahn to design at a large scale, incorporating his ideas about monumentality and spirituality in architecture.

Finished in 1982 in spite of war and instability, the National Assembly Complex or Sher-E-Bangla Nagar as it is called, is a vision of the new country. Like the medieval cathedral which was conceived as a microcosm of heaven on earth, and the great Buddhist stupas, replicas of the universe which symbolize man's journey to enlightenment, Kahn's design is about an ideal community which is just, governed wisely and at one with the universe.

The National Parliament Building in Dhaka. Photograph by Willem van Schendel, 2002.

Monumental Design with Traditional Materials and Technologies.

The approach to the capital complex in Dhaka is a study in contrasts. Poverty is endemic in Dhaka, but having once crossed the densely inhabited city, the visitor to the National Assembly Complex finds herself in parkland looking across a man-made lake to the assembly site. The country has a history of political unrest, but at Sher-E-Bangla Nagar, Kahn designed a shimmering stretch of water that reflects the complex's buildings and creates an aura of peacefulness.

Earlier in his career, in projects like the Trenton Boathouse in New Jersey, and the Yale Art Gallery extension, Kahn had experimented with monumental forms and simple construction materials, such as brick and concrete. His goal was to realize contemporary buildings with a universal quality. For the national assembly project, he deployed a red brick produced by local craftsmen. Indigenous technologies were used to build the various parts of the complex, from the assembly hall to the mosque.

As a complement to this local knowledge, the scale of the building is humane. Kahn believed that architecture was the thoughtful making of places, and pedestrians making their way through the complex experience his solicitude. Elevated interior streets are crafted in local materials, and artfully placed windows ensure comfort for building occupants in a hot climate.

Form and Light in the Service of Democracy.

Drama and monumentality go hand-in-hand at Sher-E-Bangla Nagar. Kahn was a master at designing with light. In the assembly hall, which accommodates 300 delegates, he used natural light to transform the space and engage the senses. The space is lit from above by an octagonal opening with an umbrella-like ceiling suspended within the aperture. As the sun moves overhead during the day, the quality of the light shifts and changes.

Kahn was a mystic whose intention for the parliament buildings was to produce an ideal expression of a new democracy using perfect forms: the circle, half-circle, square and triangle. In his lifetime, his design philosophy was misunderstood by most of his peers in the International Style of architecture, yet his vision for an ideal community continues to inspire and hold tremendous power. Sher-E-Bangla Nagar is the ultimate combination of form and intention. It has no modern architectural peer.

Lake Kaptai

Shilabrata Tangchangya and Nripati Ranjan Tripura

One of East Pakistan's initial problems was a scarcity of power. Pakistan's plan-
ners scored a great success when they persuaded foreign aid givers to finance a huge
hydroelectric project in the Chittagong Hill Tracts. The project brought thousands
of Bengali workers from the plains and engineers from North America and Europe
to this non-Bengali area. By 1961 a dam had been constructed across the Karnaphuli
River at a village named Kaptai. It was widely celebrated as a triumph of moder-
nity. But before its powerhouse could begin producing electricity for faraway cit-
ies and industries, the immense (650 square kilometers) and weirdly shaped Kaptai
Lake had to fill up. The lake submerged many villages and forests and 40 percent of
the arable land in the Chittagong Hill Tracts. Displacing about a hundred thousand
people and devastating wildlife, it was a typical example of top-down development.

Those who were displaced—such as Shilabrata Tangchangya and Nripati Ran-
jan Tripura—remember the construction of the Kaptai dam not as a triumph of
development but as the Boro Porong (Great Exodus). One of them, Raja Tridiv Roy,
recalled in his memoirs, titled The Departed Melody, *that it was "grotesque and*
monstrously iniquitous. . . . We had no guns so we wept in silence, in humiliation
and in anger." Meanwhile, the electricity generated by the Kaptai project reached
the cities in the plains but not the villages of the Chittagong Hill Tracts.

Shilabrata Tangchangya: "I still hear the booming sounds of the dam gate
closing that continued throughout the night. By the morning, the water
had reached our doorsteps. We set free our cows and goats, hens and ducks,
and then began the rush with the affected people to take their rice, paddy,
furniture and whatever else possible to the nearby hills. Then, many people
started clearing the jungles on the hills to build shelters. Though every possible belonging was taken to the hill top, many still went to their houses to
spend the night. But many of them had to rush out of their houses at dead
of night when the swelling waters touched them while they slept. We just
helplessly watched our beloved homes going under the water. This dam has
turned us into paupers."

A part of Lake Kaptai, seen from the village of Shubalong. Photograph by Willem van Schendel, 2003.

Nripati Ranjan Tripura: "What's the use now talking about the dam? It took from us all that we had. . . . We lived in Kellamura village. It was not very far from Rangamati town. Our village was situated on relatively higher land compared to many other villages of the locality. But the water did not spare us. Our village was also devoured. We first took shelter on an adjacent hill. The hill was not affected by the inundation in the first year. The water came up to the base of the hill and stopped. During that time it looked like an island. But gradually, in the following months, the sides of the hill began to erode as the waves hit them. It completely went under water in the second year. We had no choice but to move."

What Do I Pay My Cook?

Ellura and Robert Winters, and others

The British era had come to a close, but some things remained the same. Expatriate experts replaced British officials. Their lifestyles were very similar. Here is an excerpt from a guide for U.S. State Department personnel spending time in the city of Chittagong. Written in 1954 by Americans who had lived there, it was largely concerned with a core issue in an expat's life, in the 1950s as well as in the twenty-first century: servants. Why you must have them, how to handle them, and what to pay them.

Servants provide one of the most delightful phases of life in the Orient as well as one of the most exasperating. To maintain "face" in the community it is essential for all Europeans to have servants, and all native families that can possibly afford them have at least two or three. Servants are not only a mark of social rank, but save their employers from being robbed by everyone and the newcomers from making many "blunderbusts." . . .

Pay for Servants.

Be sure to check with European families regarding the monthly wages they are paying. Nothing causes more friction in a compound or apartment building than for one family to pay higher wages than the others. Here each type of servant has a minimum wage that he will accept. A poor mali [gardener] is paid about the same as a good one, and an inexperienced cook or bearer [house servant] expects about the same pay as one with many years of experience. There is little idea of pay raise based on efficiency or years of service.

Those servants who can speak English do rate a higher pay, and there is a social prestige for the servants who work for European or American families. Most of these have more training in cleanliness, efficiency, western ways of cooking and housekeeping, and therefore are paid at a higher rate than servants of even the wealthy native families. Gifts of money or new clothes are expected by the servants on Eid Day—the most important of Muslim festivals, June 21—and at Christmas. The usual rate of servant's wages is as follows:

Bearer	70 to 90 rupees per month.
Cook	65 to 85 rupees per month.
Sweeper	40 to 55 rupees per month.
Ayah [nurse]	70 to 90 rupees per month.
Durwan [night watchman]	70 to 90 rupees per month.
Dhobi [laundryman]	15 to 20 rupees person per month (not including cook, nor bearer).
Mali	50 to 65 rupees per month, paid by FOA [Foreign Operations Administration].
Driver	90 rupees per month, paid by Government of Pakistan for the official jeeps.

The Garo Exodus of 1964

Ellen Bal

The partition of Bengal broke up an old region and created many unanticipated long-term effects that are still only partly understood. This case study of the Garos shows some of these effects. The Garos (or Mandis) are an ethnic group in northern Bangladesh and adjacent Meghalaya (India) who speak languages that are unrelated to Bengali and who are largely Christian. As partition approached, they tried to have their area included in India rather than in Pakistan, the prospective homeland for South Asia's Muslims. They used the administrative status of their area as their argument. In 1936 the five northern thanas, or administrative units, of Mymensingh district (now Bangladesh) had been designated a Partially Excluded Area and put under the direct control of the governor of Bengal. The Garos' appeal failed, however, and soon afterward they found the partition border running right through their homeland. Thus began a process of "minoritization" among the Garos who lived in Pakistan: they had to accept minority status in the new state and felt increasingly exposed and unprotected. Land encroachment, arrivals of Muslim refugees from faraway communal disturbances in India, and lack of security produced not only cross-border flight but also legal marginalization (under the Enemy Property Ordinance) and a vigorous rethinking of community boundaries. Such minoritization and rethinking have continued after the birth of the state of Bangladesh. The Garos of Bangladesh are just one of many groups among whom partition lives on as a daily reality—as an ongoing process of losing control and strategizing to cope. The historian Ellen Bal analyzes the process.

On the eve of Partition, the PEA [Partially Excluded Area] came to play a central role in the attempts of a number of politically-active lowland Garos, the self-styled A'chik Shongho [Garo Association], to have their "homeland" included in India. They wanted, in the words of former A'chik Shongho general secretary Arun Gagra, "that our PEA should be amalgamated with Assam [India]. We didn't want to remain in Pakistan because we have most social similarity with the hill people."[1] The A'chik Shongho members raised money to send a "Garo delegation" to Calcutta to meet members of the Partition Boundary Commission—but only lowland Garos took part. Monendra, one of its members, recalls: "We sent our demands to the commissioner of the Division Committee. Radcliffe was in charge of this area. He was in Calcutta, so we went there to meet the committee . . . There was a lawyer who dealt with the objections about the Partition. We met him and he listened very carefully. He tried his best but did not manage to settle the matter. Radcliffe said that this was a very small area without a special boundary, so it was not possible to attach the area to India."[2]

The story is confirmed by an unpublished report of members of the Boundary Commission. Two of its Muslim members wrote: "A claim has been made on behalf of a minor non-Muslim organization that the non-Muslim portion of the Partially Excluded Areas located on the northern side of Mymensingh district in East Bengal should be excluded from East Bengal and added to the Garo Hills area of Assam. The main ground for this claim is that this area is inhabited by tribes who have not much in common with the residents of the remaining part of East Bengal, but have racial, social, and economic ties with the tribes inhabiting the Garo Hills."[3]

But the bid failed. On 15 August 1947, the Garos of Bengal became citizens of the newly established Dominion of Pakistan. The Boundary Commission had found no reason to take the Garo claim into consideration. Nevertheless, their territorial link with the PEA continued to play a vital role in the self-perception of the Garos.

According to the 1951 census, only some 40,000 Garos lived within the borders of East Pakistan. Documentation about the Mymensingh border during the first months after Partition is scarce, and only a few elderly Garos have any clear recollections of the period. Yet it seems that, compared to other parts of the Bengal borderland, this area remained relatively undisturbed for some years to come.

Slowly, however, the Garos were confronted with the fact that they had become a tiny minority in an overwhelmingly Muslim, Bengali-dominated society. At the same time, the cosy relationship between the Christian missionaries and the state was severed. While the missionaries had been in a relatively influential position earlier, they now were confronted with a suspicious state—despite their efforts to demonstrate a pro-Pakistan attitude. In 1952, three criminal cases were filed against foreign Catholic missionaries in Haluaghat and Durgapur accusing them of forcing Muslim converts (Garos) to return to Christianity.

Although the sparse data (occasional interview fragments, missionary documents, and administrative notes) suggest that the situation in the border area remained comparatively calm, life never returned to what it had been before Partition. Fear and insecurity became a constant factor in the lives of Bengal's Garos. An elder Garo informant told us that "after the Partition we knew that it would become difficult for non-Muslim people to live in East Pakistan. The leaders of the Muslim League spoke openly that everyone in East Pakistan had to become Muslim, or leave the country."

At the beginning of 1964, northern Mymensingh witnessed a sudden influx of Bengali refugees from Assam, followed by Bengalis from other parts of Mymensingh (such as Gafargaon, Kishorganj, Trisal, and Nandail). Although the inflow had begun in 1963, it increased dramatically in early 1964 when India and East Pakistan witnessed new outbursts of communal violence. In the wake of these riots, East Pakistan took in more than a million Muslim refugees from the Indian states of West Bengal, Tripura, and Assam.

The arrival of Bengali newcomers coincided with thievery and intimidation of the local non-Muslim population and with illegal settlements on their lands. Rumours rapidly spread throughout the border area that more Bengalis would come to rape and kill. Within one month, almost all the Garos from the border area had fled (with the exception of the people from Durgapur thana). Haluaghat thana, where I conducted most of my field research, was seriously affected by the disturbances. Villagers' stories tell of an influx of Muslim Bengali refugees from India; the arrival of landless Muslim Bengalis from other places in East Pakistan; illegal occupations; illegal settlements on the land of local non-Muslim people; robbery; the spread of rumours; and intimidation (with a strong communal flavour) by the newly-arrived Bengalis, local Bengalis, and representatives of the state (East Pakistan Rifles, paramilitary Ansars, and police).

When news reached the villagers that the East Pakistan Rifles (EPR) had been shooting at the Garos fleeing across the border, the villagers gathered on the Catholic mission compound and decided to leave. Within one day, on 5 February 1964, almost all the Garos left—leaving behind the Muslim Bengalis. A Garo informant recounted the events of the day: "The next day, we found all surrounding houses and villages occupied by [Bengali] refugees. Not a single house was left unoccupied. The same day, Bengalis from Trisal, Nandail, Kishorganj, and Gafargaon arrived by buses and trucks. I don't know how they got the news so quickly. The whole day they continued to arrive."

In India, the Garo refugees were housed in camps. Conditions were bad. Many people fell ill and died. Local Garos encouraged the refugees to stay, and both missionaries and the Indian government took steps to rehabilitate them and provided financial support. Nevertheless, many did not want to

Garo refugees from East Pakistan in the Garo Hills (India), 1964. Used by permission of the International Institute of Social History, Amsterdam, Image BG B31/779.

stay in India. After two or three months, people started, slowly and hesitantly, to return. The newsletter "Chronicles of Biroidakuni Mission" reported: "there is a state of restlessness very noticeable in those who have returned to stay and in those who went back to the hills. They seem to be going in circles."[4] Our informants provided several reasons for this behaviour. They wanted to escape the dire conditions in the camps but many also wanted to return to the place they considered home: "It was our motherland, and we had lands here. That is why we came back."

Garos refer to the 1963–64 events as a conscious attempt by the Pakistan government, in the words of one informant, "to drive the tribals out of this area." "After the eviction of the Hajongs (in 1950) they now wanted to kick out the Garos." Another Garo contended that the government had been behind the lootings and suppression of the Garos and other minorities in the border area. Available documents support the suggestion that state agencies, such as the East Pakistan Rifles, the paramilitary Ansar, and the police played an active role in the suppression and intimidation of the Garos and that the leniency of the central government allowed the situation to escalate. For example, after a visit to the border area, the Archbishop of Dhaka wrote in his yearly Easter message in March 1964: "I was aware of the danger long ago, and I warned the Government of what was likely to happen if strict measures were not taken to stop these injustices. Unfortunately, my warnings were not heeded. I have spent a great deal of time during these months in the border area, trying to keep our people from going away. You would not believe that such things could happen in such a short time."[5]

Remarkably in light of these atrocities, the Pakistan government finally invited the Garos to return—literally called on them to do so through loudspeakers installed on the border. This sudden change in state attitude was probably caused by international pressure. On other levels, however, a more aggressive state attitude towards the non-Muslim population of northern Mymensingh developed after 1964. For example the "Enemy Property Ordinance" ruled that the property of Indian nationals and East Pakistanis residing in India was forfeit to the Pakistan government. People who had their lands declared "Enemy Property" were forced to spend a great deal of money on court cases. Meanwhile lands belonging to non-returnees were occupied by Bengalis, whether illegally or under the ordinance. It has been argued that the law was strategically (mis)used against all non-Muslim inhabitants of East Pakistan (and later of Bangladesh).

After 1965, foreign missionaries were no longer allowed to work in the border area. In practice, this meant that particularly the Garos of Mymensingh (living in a borderland) lost their support. Contemporary Garos often point to 1964 as the turning point between good and bad times, between the days when they were left to themselves and the days of Bengali Muslim domination. Only then did all the Garos put aside their differences and come to realise that they were one and the same people. An informant recalled: "In 1964, the Mandi [i.e., Garo] people got in trouble for the first time. These problems were the same for all groups and everyone had to flee to India. During those days, all Mandis became united. They realised that they were the same people. Since then they have not cared about who is an Atong or a Megam. Before that, we maintained no relationships with Megam and Atong."

Notes

1. Personal interview with Arun Gagra by Suborno Chisim and Ellen Bal.
2. Personal interview with Monendra by Suborno Chisim and Ellen Bal.
3. Mr. Justice A. S. M. Akram and Mr. Justice S. A. Rahman, "Report of Muslim Members," 28 July 1947, in "Reports of Members of the Boundary Commission," India Office Library Collections, British Library, London, U.K.
4. "Chronicles of Biroidakuni Mission" (5 July, 25 Oct., and 10–30 Nov. 1964).
5. "Archbishop's Easter Message," *Protibeshi*, 11 (29 Mar. 1964), 3. See also "Chronicles of Biroidakuni Mission" (28 Jan. 1964).

Elusive Villages

Peter J. Bertocci

In the 1960s social scientists began to study East Pakistan society. Among them was the anthropologist Peter Bertocci whose fieldwork focused on rural communities in Comilla district. In this deltaic, flood-prone environment there were no nucleated villages but rather "a pattern of settlement which is in effect socially random, in which scattered, sometimes clustered, groupings of homesteads are produced," according to Bertocci. This random settlement pattern translated into a distinct rural social organization without central village authority. Bertocci launched the idea of "elusive villages," setting off an intense debate about the specificity of rural communities in the Bengal Delta. This debate was especially significant because, at the time, anthropologists of South Asia used the village as their basic unit of study. Could rural settlements in East Pakistan actually be called villages?

Neither of the communities [of Hajipur and Tinpara] had any formal centralization of authority at the "village" level; that is, no single headman in either case. Rather there are within each village several recognized leaders or "influentials" known as *sardars* who are members of (*sardari*) lineages which usually exceed their neighbors in land ownership and homestead population. . . . The sardars . . . have formally recognized, although not always necessarily obeyed, authority over the homesteads comprising their respective groups. As there is no centralization of village authority, local affairs are when necessary formally regulated on a kind of ad hoc basis by the sardars when, for example, a conflict must be settled. . . . The formalized unity among member households in such groups is reflected in the term by which they are known, *reyai*, a word of apparently Arabic origin meaning "protégés; those who are under the domain of others." . . .

[Reyais form] part of a multi-reyai grouping known locally as *samaj*, a word whose generic meaning is "society," but which is also translatable in various specific contexts as "association" (a functionally specific "society"). The sardars of the various reyais which comprise the samaj are members of a kind of "Council of Elders" whose jurisdiction in local affairs extends over an area much wider than that of the reyais in which each individual sardar holds sway. . . . Its manifest function is largely one of social control [but] its latent function is to channel political relations between the prestigious sardars and the groups they represent when those relations are thrown into open conflict. . . .

[W]ith respect to political relations, especially as regards the resolution of conflict, the village (*gram*), where it consists . . . of several reyais, is afforded no formal recognition. . . . [T]he village cannot be seen, as peasant villages elsewhere have often been described, as a territorially bounded residential social system. Rather it is at best an intervening level of social organization.

Effects of the India-Pakistan War of 1965

Badruddin Umar

In 1965 Pakistan and India fought a seventeen-day war that had important conse-quences in East Pakistan. The war was fought on the western front—on the border of India and West Pakistan—with much popular support in East Pakistan. But the Pakistani armed forces left East Pakistan largely undefended, and an attack there by India could not have been warded off. Realizing this after the war, East Paki-stanis became intensely resentful toward Pakistan's military government, headed by Ayub Khan. They understood that they had to take care of their own military and economic security. This fueled the dream of a federated state that would give East Pakistan almost complete control over its resources. The Awami League's Six-Point Programme was the outcome of this process. Here is an account by one of Bangladesh's most prominent political analysts.

The second India-Pakistan war happened at a time of increasing political and industrial unrest in the whole of Pakistan, particularly in East Pakistan. There is hardly any doubt that this war was a very calculated step by the government to achieve a number of objectives. It hoped to divert the atten-tion of the people away from their domestic problems and struggles and arouse a kind of "nationalist" frenzy and inspire the people to rally around the government of Ayub Khan.

Before full-scale war broke out between India and Pakistan in Septem-ber 1965, Pakistan suddenly attacked an Indian military post at the Gulf of Kutch and occupied it, without facing any resistance. It was, in fact, an unprotected post and it, therefore, did not need any great military feat to occupy. But it led the Pakistan government and their armed farces to un-derestimate the military capabilities of India with the memory of India's humiliation in the 1962 India-China War.

They thus decided that by infiltrating para-military forces called *"Muja-hids"* into Kashmir and then by making a direct attack, they would be able to quickly occupy Kashmir. This began on 1 September 1965, and India re-taliated with a full-scale counterattack on 6 September, crossing the inter-national border into Sialkot in East Punjab.

A bitter fight ensued, resulting in great losses for both sides, and within a few days the Indian army reached the outskirts of Lahore. The Secretary General of the United Nations, U Thant, made an appeal to both Ayub Khan and the Indian Prime Minister, Lal Bahadur Shastri, to end hostilities, but neither was prepared to listen. Finally, on 20 September 1965 the UN Security Council called for a cease-fire, and following that the Soviet Prime Minister, Alexei Kosygin, offered to mediate between the two parties. Ayub sought the advice of U.S. President Johnson who advised him to accept the mediation offer. Ayub and Shastri met in Tashkent in the Soviet Union, for talks to end the war and for the restoration of peace through the mediation of Kosygin. Finally a peace agreement called the "Tashkent Declaration" was signed on 10 January 1966. Soon after signing the declaration, Lal Bahadur Shastri, the Indian Prime Minister, died of a massive heart attack in Tashkent and Indira Gandhi became the Prime Minister of India on 19 January 1966.

The Indo-Pakistan war created hysteria among large sections of people in both parts of Pakistan and there was an unprecedented rise in anti-Indian feeling. Thousands of people began to join the voluntary Civil Defence Forces for training. Within a few days of the war their numbers rose to two million in East Pakistan and three and a half million in West Pakistan. India did not attack East Pakistan, but the fear of such an attack led the people to join the *Ansar-Mujahid* forces to be able to resist any possible attack.

So during the period of the war, Ayub's objective of diverting the attention of the people from other vital areas of interest was largely successful, and taking advantage of this situation the Pakistan Government declared an Emergency and promulgated a Defence Act, repressing all democratic movements. A strict ban was imposed on strikes and a large number of progressive political persons were arrested.

The gains for the Ayub Government from the Indo-Pakistan war were very short-lived in both parts of Pakistan, though in different ways. In West Pakistan the Punjabis were humiliated because the Indian army had occupied parts of their province and had even reached within a few miles of Lahore, which would surely have been occupied by them if the cease-fire had not been declared by the UN Security Council. It also raised doubts about the capabilities of the Pakistani Armed Forces. Secondly, there were others who strongly opposed the Tashkent Peace Agreement because it clearly showed that Pakistan had not gained anything by launching the war against India in the name of liberating Kashmir and they were in favour of continuing the war. There were huge anti-government demonstrations in Lahore and Multan. Even Ayub's hand-picked Foreign Minister, Zulfikar Ali Bhutto, felt humiliated and offended by the Agreement because in the specially convened session of the UN, he had declared, obviously in line with the thinking of Ayub Khan, that Pakistan would fight for a thousand years in order to liberate Kashmir from Indian occupation.

After the Tashkent Declaration, differences between Ayub and Zulfikar Ali Bhutto became so bitter and open that Bhutto had to resign from the government. He was arrested almost immediately and those opposed to the Tashkent Declaration began to rally round him, and opposition to the Ayub regime began to emerge on a large scale in West Pakistan. It became the turning point in the political career of Ayub Khan.

In East Pakistan the gains of the government were lost in a different way. After the war hysteria subsided, the people began to realize that East Pakistan had been in an indefensible position during the seventeen-day Pakistani war. The only reason it was not occupied by India was because India did not want to open a second front. But had they made the attack, East Pakistan had no way of defending its borders with India and it would have been a walkover. Thus the anti-Indian war hysteria, which bolstered Ayub's position during the war, was eventually turned against him when the people realized that they had been left defenceless against the enemy whom they had been prepared to resist so strongly. It was, therefore, no surprise that after the end of the 1965 India-Pakistan War, the question of East Pakistan's share of defence expenditures, recruitment of East Pakistanis to the armed forces in much larger numbers and other questions relating to defence appeared prominently in public discussions and in criticisms by the opposition of the government. During the war, the Awami League had been silent and refrained from making any official statement on the war. But within two weeks the Working Committee of the Awami League, through a resolution, demanded that the defence system in East Pakistan would have to be strengthened.

Anti-American feelings rose high during the war and continued even afterwards, because the US and its allies were deemed to have supported India. The September war was preceded by months of acrimonious exchanges between the governments of Pakistan and India and by border skirmishes. A war situation was thus created before the actual battle took place. On 10 May 1965 the Soviet Union, which was much closer to India than to Pakistan, declared that it would not side with India if war broke out between the two countries. China, which was a very close ally of Pakistan since the 1962 Indo-China war, declared on 5 September before the Indian army crossed the international border and attacked Sialkot, that it would support Pakistan against the aggressors. The government of Sukarno in Indonesia also declared its support for Pakistan. Thus it appeared that in the India-Pakistan war, India was supported by the US and its allies, whereas Pakistan was supported by socialist and other anti-imperialist countries, while the Soviet Union maintained a neutral position.

Owing to this international polarization various nationalist, socialist and progressive elements were vociferous in their criticism of the US, but the Awami League, as has been mentioned earlier, refrained from making any anti-American statement or making any statement whatsoever on the war situation. But it is quite interesting to note that an Awami League leader of some importance made a bitter statement against the US and Pakistan's military alliances with the Western powers led by the United States. During a debate on foreign policy in the National Assembly on November 1965, A. H. M. Quamruzzaman said, "We have seen what America has done during 17-day war with India. We should be courageous enough to get out of CENTO [Central Treaty Organization] and SEATO [South East Asia Treaty Organization] and have pacts with communist China or Russia or with any other country. We must have boldness. If we sail in two boats, we are definitely going to sink."[1] It is not only interesting but also quite surprising that a leader of the Awami League, who had so far remained a staunch ally of the US and a strong defender of CENTO and SEATO, should speak in such terms against the US and the military pacts. This statement was quite out of step with the official position of Awami League, but it was significant that it reflected the anti-US feeling of a very large section of the people.

But whatever was said by Quamruzzaman in the National Assembly, it had nothing to do with the actual Awami League party line regarding international alliances, and his exhortation for showing courage and boldness did not make anybody more courageous, including the president of the Awami League, Sheikh Mujibur Rahman.

However, Sheikh Mujibur Rahman, realizing the depth of the feeling of the people against the central government for its gross negligence of the defence of East Pakistan, and against the ever-expanding disparity between the two parts of the country which appeared in very bold relief after the war, the Awami League began to concentrate its efforts on strengthening the demand for regional autonomy for East Pakistan, which was formulated in very clear terms in the Awami League's 6-point programme.

Note

1. Rangalal Sen, *Political Elites in Bangladesh* (Dhaka: University Press Limited, 1986), 207.

Six Points towards a Federation

Awami League

In 1965 Pakistan and India fought a short war during which East Pakistan was practically undefended because the Pakistani armed forces were amassed in West Pakistan. As we saw in the previous entry, this led to great indignation in East Pakistan, where many were already disgruntled because of the economic disparities and what was increasingly felt to be internal colonialism of West Pakistan over East Pakistan.

The party that grabbed the political opportunity was the Awami League. A group of advisors of Sheikh Mujibur Rahman drew up a charter of demands that aimed to turn Pakistan into a federated state with far-reaching autonomy for the two wings. When Mujib—as Sheikh Mujibur Rahman was popularly known— presented this Six-Point Programme to a national political convention in early 1966, the West Pakistani politicians were shocked and rejected it as separatist. The Awami League adopted it, however, and started a campaign to have the six points implemented. The Six-Point Programme proved to be a great political asset. It filled many East Pakistanis with enthusiasm and hope for the future. The military rulers of Pakistan, on the other hand, saw it as a serious challenge and a threat to the country's unity.

1. The Constitution should provide for a Federation of Pakistan in its true sense on the basis of the Lahore Resolution, and the parliamentary form of government based on the supremacy of a directly elected Legislature on the basis of universal adult franchise.
2. The Federal Government should deal with only two subjects: Defense and Foreign Affairs, and all other residuary subjects will be vested in the federating states.
3. Two separate but freely convertible currencies for the two Wings should be introduced, or, if this is not feasible, there should be one currency for the whole country but effective constitutional provisions should be introduced to stop the flight of capital from East to West

Pakistan. Furthermore a separate Banking Reserve should be established, and separate fiscal and monetary policy be adopted for East Pakistan.

4. The power of taxation and revenue collection shall be vested in the federating units and the federal centre will have no such power. The Federation will be entitled to a share in the state taxes to meet its expenditures.

5. There should be two separate accounts for the foreign exchange earnings of the two Wings; the foreign exchange requirements of the federal government should be met by the two Wings separately, or in a ratio to be fixed; indigenous products should move free of duty between the two Wings, and the Constitution should empower the units to establish trade links with foreign countries.

6. East Pakistan should have a separate militia or paramilitary force.

This Time the Struggle Is for Our Independence!

Sheikh Mujibur Rahman

The political elite of Pakistan did not call the first national parliamentary elections until 1970—twenty-three years after the country was born. This came about in the wake of countrywide demonstrations in 1968 and 1969, which impelled the military regime to topple its leader, Ayub Khan, and replace him with the general Yahya Khan. The new military leader decided to seek the voters' verdict.

The election results were stunning and unexpected. They revealed the profound divisions between the two wings. In East Pakistan, the Awami League won by a landslide; in West Pakistan the major party to emerge was the Pakistan People's Party (PPP). The Awami League alone captured 53 percent of the seats in the National Assembly (167 out of a total of 313 seats) and thus the constitutional right to form the new government. This was anathema to West Pakistan's political leaders, headed by Zulfikar Ali Bhutto of the PPP, and they maneuvered for months to avoid the creation of a Pakistan government headed by the leader of the Awami League, Sheikh Mujibur Rahman.

Widespread violence erupted in East Pakistan when Yahya Khan postponed, and then canceled, the opening session of the new parliament (in Dhaka). Most Bengalis felt that there was no longer any hope for them in Pakistan—even a federated one as demanded in the Six Points Programme of 1966—and they began hoisting flags of a future independent Bangladesh. Sheikh Mujib Rahman came under intense pressure from two sides. Leftist politicians and activists in East Pakistan demanded that he declare independence right away, while Pakistan's military leaders flew in troops to make sure that he would abstain from such a pronouncement. In this extremely precarious situation, the Awami League called a huge public meeting at the Ramna Race Course Maidan in Dhaka on 7 March 1971. Here Sheikh Mujibur Rahman delivered this speech, which tried to steer a strategic middle course by launching a nonviolent movement of noncooperation while also declaring: "The struggle this time is for emancipation! The struggle this time is for independence!" Less than three weeks later the Pakistan Army cracked down on East Pakistan, igniting the Bangladesh Liberation War, also known as the War of Independence or the 1971 War.

I have come before you today with a heavy heart. All of you know how hard we have tried. But it is a matter of sadness that the streets of Dhaka, Chittagong, Khulna, Rangpur and Rajshahi are today being spattered with the blood of my brothers, and the cry we hear from the Bengali people is a cry for freedom, a cry for survival, a cry for our rights.

You are the ones who brought about an Awami League victory so you could see a constitutional government restored. The hope was that the elected representatives of the people, sitting in the National Assembly, would formulate a constitution that would assure that people of their economic, political and cultural emancipation.

But now, with great sadness in my heart, I look back on the past 23 years of our history and see nothing but a history of shedding the blood of the Bengali people. Ours has been a history of continual lamentation, repeated bloodshed and innocent tears.

We gave our blood in 1952. We won a mandate in 1954. But we were still not allowed to take up the reins of this country. In 1958, Ayub Khan clamped Martial Law on our people and enslaved us for the next 10 years. In 1966, during the Six-Point Movement of the masses, many were the young men and women whose lives were stilled by government bullets.

After the downfall of Ayub, Mr. Yahya Khan took over with the promise that he would restore constitutional rule, that he would restore democracy and return power to the people. We agreed. But you all know of the events that took place after that. I ask you, are we the ones to blame?

As you know, I have been in contact with President Yahya Khan. As leader of the majority party in the National Assembly, I asked him to set February 15 as the day for its opening session. He did not accede to the request I made as leader of the majority party. Instead, he went along with the delay requested by the minority leader Mr. Bhutto and announced that the Assembly would be convened on the 3rd of March.

We accepted that, and agreed to join the deliberations. I even went to the extent of saying that we, despite our majority, would still listen to any sound ideas from the minority, even if it were a lone voice. I committed myself to support anything that would bolster the restoration of a constitutional government.

When Mr. Bhutto came to Dhaka, we met. We talked. He left, saying that the doors to negotiation were still open. Maulana Noorani and Maulana Mufti were among those West Pakistan parliamentarians who visited

Dhaka and talked with me about an agreement on a constitutional framework. I made it clear that I could not agree to any deviation from the Six Points. That right rested with the people. Come, I said, let us sit down and resolve matters.

But Bhutto's retort was that he would not allow himself to become hostage on two fronts. He predicted that if any West Pakistani members of Parliament were to come to Dhaka, the Assembly would be turned into a slaughterhouse. He added that if anyone were to participate in such a session, a countrywide agitation would be launched from Peshawar to Karachi and that every business would be shut down in protest.

I assured him that the Assembly would be convened and despite the dire threats, West Pakistani leaders did come down to Dhaka. But suddenly, on March 1, the session was cancelled. There was an immediate outcry against this move by the people. I called for a *hartal* [general strike] as a peaceful form of protest and the masses readily took to the streets in response.

And what did we get as a response? He turned his guns on my helpless people, a people with no arms to defend themselves. These were the same arms that had been purchased with our own money to protect us from external enemies. But it is my own people who are being fired upon today. In the past, too, each time we, the numerically larger segment of Pakistan's population, tried to assert our rights and control our destiny, they conspired against us and pounced upon us. I have asked them this before: How can you make your own brothers the target of your bullets?

Now Yahya Khan says that I had agreed to a Round Table Conference on the 10th. Let me point out that is not true. I had said, Mr. Yahya Khan, you are the President of this country. Come to Dhaka, come and see how our poor Bengali people have been mown down by your bullets, how the laps of our mothers and sisters have been robbed and left empty and bereft, how my helpless people have been slaughtered. Come, I said, come and see for yourself and then be the judge and decide. That is what I told him.

Earlier, I had told him there would be no Round Table Conference. What Round Table Conference? Whose Round Table Conference? You expect me to sit at a Round Table Conference with the very same people who have emptied the laps of my mothers and my sisters?

On the 3rd, at the Paltan, I called for a non-cooperation movement and the shutdown of offices, courts and revenue collection. You gave me full support. Then suddenly, without consulting me or even informing us, he met with one individual for five hours and then made a speech in which he placed all the blame on me, laid all the fault at the door of the Bengali people! Bhutto created the deadlock, yet the Bengalis are the ones facing the

"Ebar Shadhinotar Songgram: Mujib" (This time the struggle is for independence! Mujib). Headline in the newspaper *Shongbad*, 8 March 1971. Used by permission of the Heritage Archives of Bangladesh History, Rajshahi.

bullets! We face their guns, yet it is our fault. We are the ones being bitten by their bullets—and it's still our fault!

So, the struggle this time is our struggle for emancipation! This time the struggle is for our freedom! Brothers, they have now called the Assembly to commence on March 25, with the streets not yet dry of the blood of my brothers. You have called the Assembly, but you must first agree to meet my demands. Martial Law must be withdrawn; the soldiers must return to their barracks; the murderers of my people must be redressed. And power must be handed over to the elected representatives of the people. Only then will we consider if we can take part in the National Assembly or not. Before these demands are met, there can be no question of our participating in this session of the Assembly. That is one right not given to me as part of my mandate from the masses. As I told them earlier, Mujibur Rahman refuses to walk to the Assembly trading upon the fresh stains of his brothers' blood!

Do you, my brothers, have complete faith in me? Let me tell you that the Prime Ministership is not what I seek. What I want is justice, the rights of the people of this land. They tempted me with the Prime Ministership but they failed to buy me over. Nor did they succeed in hanging me on the gallows, for you rescued me with your blood from the so-called conspiracy case. That day, right here at this racecourse, I had pledged to you that I would pay for this blood debt with my own blood. Do you remember? I am ready today to fulfill that promise!

I now declare the closure of all the courts, offices, and educational institutions for an indefinite period of time. No one will report to their offices—that is my instruction to you. So that the poor are not inconvenienced, rickshaws, trains and other transport will ply normally—except for serving any needs of the armed forces. If the army does not respect this, I shall not be responsible for the consequences. The Secretariat, Supreme Court, High Court, Judge's Courts, and government and semi-government offices shall remain shut. Banks may open only for two hours daily, for business transactions. But no money shall be transmitted from East to West Pakistan. The Bengali people must stay calm during these times. Telegraph and telephone communications will be confined within Bangladesh.

The people of this land are facing elimination, so be on guard. If need be, we will bring everything to a total standstill. Collect your salaries on time. If the salaries are held up, if a single bullet is fired upon us henceforth, if the murder of my people does not cease, I call upon you to turn every home into a fortress against their onslaught. Use whatever you can put your hands on to confront this enemy. Every last road must be blocked. We will deprive them of food, we will deprive them of water. Even if I am not around to give you the orders, and if my associates are also not to be found, I ask you to continue your movement unabated.

I say to them again, you are my brothers, return now to the barracks where you belong and no one will bear any hostility toward you. Only do not attempt to aim any more bullets at our hearts: It will not do any good! And the seventy million people of this land will not be cowed down by you or accept suppression any more. The Bengali people have learned how to die for a cause and you will not be able to bring them under your yoke of suppression!

To assist the families of the martyred and the injured, the Awami League has set up committees that will do all they can. Please donate whatever you can. Also, employers must give full pay to the workers who participated in the seven days of *hartal* or were not able to work because of curfews.

To all government employees, I say that my directives must be followed. I had better not see any of you attending your offices. From today, until this land has been freed, no taxes will be paid to the government any more. As of now, they stop. Leave everything to me. I know how to organize a movement. But be very careful. Keep in mind that the enemy has infiltrated our ranks to engage in the work of provocateurs. Whether Bengali or non-Bengali, Hindu or Muslim, all are our brothers and it is our responsibility to ensure their safety. I also ask you to stop listening to radio, television and the press if these media do not report news of our movement.

To them, I say: You are our brothers. I beseech your to not turn this country into a living hell. Will you not have to show your faces and confront your conscience some day? If we can peaceably settle our differences there is still hope that we can co-exist as brothers. Otherwise there is no hope. If you choose the other path, we may never come to face one another again. For now, I have just one thing to ask of you: Give up any thoughts of enslaving this country under military rule again!

I ask my people to immediately set up committees under the leadership of the Awami League to carry on our struggle in every neighborhood, village, union and subdivision of this land. You must prepare yourselves now with what little you have for the struggle ahead. Since we have given blood, we will give more of it. But, Inshallah, we will free the people of this land!

This time the struggle is for our freedom! This time the struggle is for independence! Be ready. We cannot afford to lose our momentum. Keep the movement and the struggle alive because if we fall back they will come down hard upon us. Be disciplined. No nation's movement can be victorious without discipline.

Joy Bangla! [Victory to Bangladesh!]

V

War and Independence

The Liberation War of 1971—or Muktijuddho, as it is called in Bengali—is the single most important episode in the history of independent Bangladesh. Given the war's foundational nature, its ethos is almost sacrosanct today. Even so, debates and controversies around the Bangladeshi Declaration of Independence of 1971 have been used to polarize mainstream politics. This part serves as a reminder of some of the basic texts on which the country's independence is based, and it presents the Liberation War as a people's war with many sides to the story.

War affects a society on many levels. It is a time when the day-to-day activities of a community are often suspended—and men and women find themselves taking up roles they would not normally play. This is especially so in a people's war like the Liberation War in Bangladesh, when students became soldiers and women became breadwinners. At the same time, war brings losses all around: loss of lives, loss of property, and even loss of identity. It affects different sections of the population in different ways. Violence also assumes different forms: genocide, sexual slavery, religious repression, and revenge killing.

There is as yet no official history of the war, just an official fifteen-volume collection of documents, *Bangladesher Swadhinota Juddho: Dolilpottro.* In the absence of an analytical narrative, it is the emotive content of the war that has been most apparent. In the independent nation of Bangladesh, the war has been ensconced in a nationalist narrative that essentially conflates the history of the Liberation War with the history of Bengali nationalism. Usually, the Liberation War is said to have its roots in a day in 1952. On 21 February that year the demand that Bengali become a state language of Pakistan resulted in the martyrdom of five young Bengali students. Several decades later, at the suggestion of the Bangladesh government, UNESCO (United Nations Educational, Scientific and Cultural Organization) declared 21 February to be International Mother Language Day. In 1966 Bengali linguistic nationalism found a political platform in the Awami League's six-point

The National Monument for the Martyrs of the Liberation War (Jatiyo Smriti Soudho) is located at Savar in the center of the country. Photograph by Willem van Schendel, 2006.

program for autonomy that was launched by the Awami League, a major political party, and snowballed into the demand for full independence as repression and atrocities by the Pakistan regime increased.

This part contains documents and texts from the time of armed conflict between the Pakistan regime and the Bangladesh Freedom Fighters (Mukti Bahini) as well as later reflections. It opens with the declaration of independence that Sheikh Mujibur Rahman, the leader of the Awami League, issued on 25–26 March 1971. This declaration was a direct response to the Pakistan Army's crackdown on Dhaka, code-named Operation SEARCHLIGHT. The next day a short radio announcement was broadcast from a makeshift transmitter. The third text is the proclamation of the government in exile of the newly independent country of Bangladesh. These texts set the scene for the nine-month war between the Freedom Fighters—in the final stages joined in frontal combat by the Indian Army—and the Pakistani forces.

Four texts present evidence of the brutality and repression that Pakistani armed forces inflicted on the unarmed public in the opening phase of the war. Two of these texts are from the Pakistan side, one is a victim's memoir, and one is a telegram from the U.S. consul in Dhaka. The next two texts touch on the impact on family life and wartime sexual exploitation, and they are followed by a text on the fate of non-Bengali citizens in the Chittagong Hill Tracts. An oath of allegiance and a diploma given to East Pakistanis fighting on the side of the Pakistan Army complete this section of the part.

With millions of people flowing across the border to become refugees in India, the war had repercussions beyond East Pakistan/Bangladesh. This is illustrated by the next contribution, a concerned Indian civil rights activist's call to his counterparts in Pakistan to take action against the killing of unarmed civilians by Pakistani forces. Expatriates inside Bangladesh were also witness to the events that evolved, as an American missionary's memoir attests.

The day of surrender was one of mixed responses. Both the joy of victory and sadness at the terrible human costs of war are represented here. A Freedom Fighter's diary and a headmistress's eyewitness account of a college that was turned into a concentration camp bring out these conflicting emotions. The next entry focuses on the Urdu-speaking "Biharis," most of whom would, by the war's end, declare themselves to be "stranded Pakistanis." A sobering analysis follows on how high expectations of a quick postwar recovery were dashed when the party in power failed to translate these expectations into reality.

The Declaration of Independence

(25–26 March 1971)

Sheikh Mujibur Rahman

During the night of 25–26 March 1971, Pakistani troops started their crackdown on Dhaka to suppress what they thought of as a provincial insurrection. They moved quickly to secure strategic buildings and traffic nodes and to destroy symbols of Bengali nationalism. They met with strong opposition, notably from the paramilitary East Pakistan Rifles (EPR) and the police, both largely Bengali.

One of their targets was Sheikh Mujibur Rahman, the leader of the Awami League and Pakistan's prime minister in waiting. Just before he was arrested, he wrote a brief declaration of independence. It began with the words: "Today Bangladesh is a sovereign and independent country."

The Bangladesh Liberation War had begun.

Today Bangladesh is a sovereign and independent country. On Thursday night, West Pakistani armed forces suddenly attacked the police barracks at Razarbagh and the EPR headquarters at Pilkhana in Dhaka. Many innocent and unarmed [people] have been killed in Dhaka city and other places of Bangladesh. Violent clashes between EPR and police, on the one hand, and the armed forces of Pakistan, on the other, are going on. The Bengalis are fighting the enemy with great courage for an independent Bangladesh. May Allah aid us in our fight for freedom. *Joy Bangla* [Victory to Bangladesh]!

A Radio Message from Kalurghat
(27 March 1971)

Ziaur Rahman

On 27 March 1971, the independence of Bangladesh was broadcast from a make-shift radio transmitter in Kalurghat, Chittagong, in the southeast. The speaker was Ziaur Rahman. He was a major who had just defected from the Pakistani armed forces. His short statement did not reach many—the transmitter had little power—but nonetheless it was noteworthy.

Much later this broadcast gained unforeseen political importance in Bangladesh. In 1975 Ziaur Rahman came to power in an armed coup d'état and he ruled the country for six years. As part of the personality cult that developed around him, the claim was put forward that he, rather than Sheikh Mujibur Rahman, should be recognized as the proclaimer of the country's independence. This became a core topic of partisan politics between the two parties that continue to dominate the political scene in Bangladesh, the Awami League (tracing its roots to Sheikh Mujibur Rahman) and the Bangladesh Nationalist Party (created by Ziaur Rahman).

Major Zia, Provisional Commander-in-Chief of the Bangladesh Liberation Army, hereby proclaims, on behalf of Sheikh Mujibur Rahman, the independence of Bangladesh.

I also declare, we have already framed a sovereign, legal Government under Sheikh Mujibur Rahman, which pledges to function as per law and the constitution. The new democratic Government is committed to a policy of non-alignment in international relations. It will seek friendship with all nations and strive for international peace. I appeal to all Governments to mobilize public opinion in their respective countries against the brutal genocide in Bangladesh.

The Government under Sheikh Mujibur Rahman is the sovereign legal Government of Bangladesh and is entitled to recognition from all democratic nations of the world.

Mujibnagar: Proclaiming
a New Country (17 April 1971)

The Elected Representatives of
the People of Bangladesh

Three weeks after the outbreak of the Bangladesh Liberation War, a group of people gathered at a mango orchard in the border village of Baidyanathtala, not far from the western town of Meherpur. Among them were members of Parliament who had been elected a few months previously. After the war broke out, they had fled to India where they formed a government in exile. Now, under Indian military protection, they briefly recrossed the border to proclaim themselves the government of a new country, Bangladesh. They read the proclamation here, thereby declaring themselves to be the legitimate government of the territory that the world still referred to as East Pakistan. Shortly afterward, the village was renamed Mujibnagar (Mujib Town), after Sheikh Mujibur Rahman, the leader who at that time was being held in a jail in West Pakistan.

Mujibnagar, Bangladesh
Dated 10th day of April, 1971.

Whereas free elections were held in Bangladesh from 7th December, 1970 to 17th January, 1971, to elect representatives for the purpose of framing a Constitution,

AND

Whereas at these elections the people of Bangladesh elected 167 out of 169 representatives belonging to the Awami League,

AND

Whereas General Yahya Khan summoned the elected representatives of the people to meet on the 3rd March, 1971, for the purpose of framing a Constitution,

AND

Whereas the Assembly so summoned was arbitrarily and illegally postponed for indefinite period,

AND

Whereas instead of fulfilling their promise and while still conferring with the representatives of the people of Bangladesh, Pakistan authorities declared an unjust and treacherous war,

AND

Whereas in the facts and circumstances of such treacherous conduct Bangabandhu [Friend of Bengal] Sheikh Mujibur Rahman, the undisputed leader of the 75 million people of Bangladesh, in due fulfillment of the legitimate right of self-determination of the people of Bangladesh, duly made a declaration of independence at Dacca [Dhaka] on March 26, 1971, and urged the people of Bangladesh to defend the honour and integrity of Bangladesh,

AND

Whereas in the conduct of a ruthless and savage war the Pakistani authorities committed and are still continuously committing numerous acts of genocide and unprecedented tortures, amongst others on the civilian and unarmed people of Bangladesh,

AND

Whereas the Pakistan Government by levying an unjust war and committing genocide and by other repressive measures made it impossible for the elected representatives of the people of Bangladesh to meet and frame a Constitution, and give to themselves a Government,

AND

Whereas the people of Bangladesh by their heroism, bravery and revolutionary fervour have established effective control over the territories of Bangladesh,

We, the elected representatives of the people of Bangladesh, as honourbound by the mandate given to us by the people of Bangladesh whose will is supreme, duly constituted ourselves into a Constituent Assembly, and

having held mutual consultations, and

in order to ensure for the people of Bangladesh equality, human dignity and social justice, declare and constitute Bangladesh to be a sovereign Peoples' Republic and thereby confirm the declaration of independence already made by Bangabandhu Sheikh Mujibur Rahman, and do hereby affirm and resolve that till such time as a Constitution is framed, Bangabandhu Sheikh

The acting president Syed Nazrul Islam addresses the meeting during which Bangladesh was officially proclaimed, 17 April 1971. From *Shadhinota Shonggrame Bangali*, 3rd ed., edited by Aftab Ahmed (Dhaka: Borna-ShagorProkashoni, 1998), 96. Used by permission of Aftab Ahmed.

Mujibur Rahman shall be the President of the Republic and that Syed Nazrul Islam shall be the Vice President of the Republic, and

that the President shall be the Supreme Commander of all the Armed Forces of the Republic,

shall exercise all the Executive and Legislative powers of the Republic including the power to grant pardon,

shall have the power to appoint a Prime Minister and such other Ministers as he considers necessary,

shall have the power to levy taxes and expend monies,

shall have the power to summon and adjourn the Constituent Assembly, and

do all other things that may be necessary to give to the people of Bangladesh an orderly and just Government,

We, the elected representatives of the people of Bangladesh, do further resolve that in the event of there being no President or the President being unable to enter upon his office or being unable to exercise his powers and duties, due to any reason whatsoever, the Vice-President shall have and exercise all the powers, duties and responsibilities herein conferred on the President,

We further resolve that we undertake to observe and give effect to all duties and obligations that devolve upon us as a member of the family of nations and under the Charter of United Nations,

We further resolve that this proclamation of independence shall be deemed to have come into effect from the 26th day of March, 1971.

We further resolve that in order to give effect to this instrument we appoint Prof. Yusuf Ali our duly Constituted Potentiary and to give to the President and the Vice-President oaths of office.

Translator not identified.

Operation Searchlight

Siddiq Salik

Until recently, most available testimonies of the Bangladesh Liberation War (1971) presented the perspective of the victim rather than the oppressor. In recent times, however, Pakistani generals and other army men have been publishing autobiographies. Here is one of the earliest testimonies of the Pakistani military crackdown on the night of 25 March 1971. Siddiq Salik, a junior officer in the Pakistan Army during that time, provides an eyewitness account of Operation Searchlight, the military operation that was the beginning of what he described as a "bloody holocaust."

Major-General Khadim Hussain was brooding over the possible outcome of political talks on 25 March when his green telephone rang at about 11 A.M. Lieutenant-General Tikka Khan was on the line. He said, "Khadim, it is tonight."

It created no excitement for Khadim. He was already waiting for the fall of the hammer. The President's decision coincided with the second anniversary of his assumption of power. General Khadim passed the word to his staff for implementation. The lower the news travelled, the greater the sensation it created. I saw some junior officers hustling about mustering some extra recoilless rifles, getting additional ammunition issued, a defective mortar sight replaced. The tank crew, brought from Rangpur (29 Cavalry) a few days earlier, hurried with their task to oil six rusty M-24s for use at night. They were enough to make a noise on the Dacca [Dhaka] streets.

The general staff of Headquarters 14 Division rang up all the out-station garrisons to inform them of H-hour. They devised a private code for passing the message. All garrisons were to act simultaneously. The fateful hour was set at 260100 hours—1 A.M. 26 March. It was calculated that by then the President would have landed safely in Karachi.

The plan for operation SEARCHLIGHT visualized the setting up of two headquarters. Major-General Farman, with 57 Brigade under Brigadier Arbab, was responsible for operations in Dacca city and its suburbs while Major-General Khadim was to look after the rest of the province. In addition, Lieutenant-General Tikka Khan and his staff were to spend the night at the Martial Law Headquarters in the Second Capital to watch the progress of action in and outside Dacca.

A few days earlier, General Yahya had sent Major-General Iftikhar Janjua and Major-General A. O. Mitha to Dacca as possible replacements for Khadim and Farman in case they refused to "crack down." After all, they had formed General Yakub's team until very recently and might still share his ideas. General Hamid had even gone to the extent of questioning Khadim's and Farman's wives to assess their husbands' views on the subject. Both the generals, however, assured Hamid that they would faithfully carry out the orders.

Junior officers like me started collecting at Headquarters, Martial Law Administrator, Zone "B" (Second Capital) at about 10 P.M. They laid out sofas and easy chairs on the lawn and made arrangements for tea and coffee to last the night. I had no specific job to perform except "to be available." A jeep fitted with a wireless set was parked next to this "outdoor operations room." The city, wrapped in starlight, was in deep slumber. The night was as pleasant as a spring night in Dacca could be. The setting was perfect for anything but a bloody holocaust.

Besides the armed forces, another class of people was active that night. They were the Awami League leaders and their private army of Bengali soldiers, policemen, ex-servicemen, students and party volunteers. They were in communication with Mujib [Sheikh Mujibur Rahman], Colonel Osmani and other important Bengali officers. They were preparing for the toughest resistance. In Dacca, they erected innumerable road blocks to obstruct the march of troops to the city.

The wireless set fitted in the jeep groaned for the first time at about 11:30 P.M. The local commander (Dacca) asked permission to advance the H-hour because "the other side" was hectically preparing for resistance. Everybody looked at his watch. The President was still half way between Colombo (Sri Lanka) and Karachi. General Tikka gave the decision. "Tell Bobby (Arbab) to hold on as long as he can."

At the given hour, Brigadier Arbab's brigade was to act as follows:

- 13 Frontier Force was to stay in Dacca cantonment as reserve and defend the cantonment, if necessary.
- 43 Light Anti-Aircraft (LAA) Regiment, deployed at the airport in an anti-aircraft role since the banning of overflights by India, was to look after the airport area.

- 22 Baluch, already in East Pakistan Rifles Lines at Pilkhana, was to disarm approximately 5,000 E.P.R. personnel and seize their wireless exchange.
- 32 Punjab was to disarm 1,000 "highly motivated" policemen, a prime possible source of armed manpower for the Awami League at Rajarbagh Police Lines.
- 18 Punjab was to fan out in the Nawabpur area and the old city where many Hindu houses were said to have been converted into armouries.
- Field Regiment was to control the Second Capital and the adjoining Bihari localities (Mohammadpur, Mirpur).
- A composite force consisting of one company each of 18 Punjab, 22 Baluch and 32 Punjab, was to "flush" the University Campus, particularly Iqbal Hall and Jagannath Hall which were reported to be the strong points of the Awami League rebels.
- A platoon of Special Group (Commandos) was to raid Mujib's house and capture him alive.
- A skeleton squadron of M-25 tanks was to make an appearance before first light, mainly as a show of force. They could fire for effect if required.

These troops, in their respective areas, were to guard the key points, break resistance (if offered) and arrest the listed political leaders from their residences.

The troops were to be in their target areas before 1 A.M. but some of them, anticipating delay on the way, had started moving from the cantonment at about 11.30 P.M. Those who were already in the city to guard the radio and television stations, telephone exchange, power house and State Bank etc., had also taken their posts much before the H-hour.

The first column from the cantonment met resistance at Farm Gate, about one kilometre from the cantonment. The column was halted by a huge tree trunk freshly felled across the road. The side gaps were covered with the hulks of old cars and a disabled steam-roller. On the city side of the barricade stood several hundred Awami Leaguers shouting *Joi Bangla* [Victory to Bangladesh] slogans. I heard their spirited shouts while standing on the verandah of General Tikka's headquarters. Soon some rifle shots mingled with the *Joi Bangla* slogans. A little later, a burst of fire from an automatic weapon shrilled through the air. Thereafter, it was a mixed affair of firing and fiery slogans, punctuated with the occasional chatter of a light machine gun. Fifteen minutes later the noise began to subside and the slogans started dying down. Apparently, the weapons had triumphed. The army column moved on to the city.

Thus the action had started before schedule. There was no point now in sticking to the prescribed H-hour. The gates of hell had been cast open. When the first shot had been fired, the voice of Sheikh Mujibur Rahman came faintly through on a wavelength close to that of the official Pakistan Radio. In what must have been, and sounded like, a pre-recorded message, the Sheikh proclaimed East Pakistan to be the People's Republic of Bangladesh. The full text of the proclamation is published in *Bangladesh Documents* released by the Indian Foreign Ministry. It said, "This may be my last message. From today Bangladesh is independent. I call upon the people of Bangladesh, wherever you are and with whatever you have, to resist the army of occupation to the last. Your fight must go on until the last soldier of the occupation army is expelled from the soil of Bangladesh and final victory is achieved."

I didn't hear this broadcast. I only heard the big bang of the rocket launcher fired by the commandos to remove a barrier blocking their way to Mujib's house. Lieutenant-Colonel Z. A. Khan, the commanding officer, and Major Bilal, the company commander, themselves had accompanied the raiding platoon.

As the commandos approached Mujib's house, they drew fire from the armed guard posted at his gate. The guards were quickly neutralized. Then up raced the fifty tough soldiers [to] climb the four-foot high compound wall. They announced their arrival in the courtyard by firing a stengun burst and shouted for Mujib to come out. But there was no response. Scrambling across the verandah and up the stairs, they finally discovered the door to Mujib's bedroom. It was locked from outside. A bullet pierced the hanging metal, and it dangled down. Whereupon Mujib readily emerged, offering himself for arrest. He seemed to be waiting for it. The raiding party rounded up everybody in the house and brought them to the Second Capital in army jeeps. Minutes later, Major Jaffar, Brigade Major of 57 Brigade, was on the wireless. I could hear his crisp voice saying "BIG BIRD IN THE CAGE . . . OTHERS NOT IN THEIR NESTS . . . OVER."

As soon as the message ended, I saw the big bird in a white shirt being driven in an army jeep to the cantonment for safe custody. Somebody asked General Tikka if he would like him to be produced before him. He said firmly, "I don't want to see his face."

Mujib's domestic servants were released immediately after identification while he himself was lodged in the Adamjee School for the night. Next day, he was shifted to Flag Staff House from where he was flown to Karachi three days later. Subsequently, when complications arose about the "final disposal" of Mujib (such as international pressure for his release), I asked my friend Major Bilal why he had not finished him off in the heat of action. He said, "General Mitha had personally ordered me to capture him alive."

While Mujib rested in the Adamjee School, the city of Dacca was in the throes of a civil war. I watched the harrowing sight from the verandah for four hours. The prominent feature of this gory night was the flames shooting to the sky. At times, mournful clouds of smoke accompanied the blaze but soon they were overwhelmed by the flaming fire trying to lick at the stars. The light of the moon and the glow of the stars paled before this manmade furnace. The tallest columns of smoke and fire emerged from the university campus, although some other parts of the city, such as the premises of the daily *People*, had no small share in these macabre fireworks.

At about 2 A.M. the wireless set in the jeep again drew our attention. I was ordered to receive the call. The Captain on the other end of the line said that he was facing a lot of resistance from Iqbal Hall and Jagannath Hall. Meanwhile, a senior staff officer snatched the hand-set from me and shouted into the mouth-piece, "How long will you take to neutralize the target? . . . Four hours! Nonsense . . . What weapons have you got? Rocket launcher, recoilless rifles, mortars and . . . O.K., use all of them and ensure complete capture of the area in two hours."

The university building was conquered by 4 A.M. but the ideology of Bengali nationalism preached there over the years would take much longer to subdue. Perhaps ideas are unconquerable.

In the rest of the city, the troops had accomplished their tasks including disarming the police at Rajar Bagh and the East Pakistan Rifles at Pilkhana. In other parts of the city they had only fired a sniping shot here and a burst there to create terror. They did not enter houses, except those mentioned in the operational plan (to arrest the political leaders), or those used by rebels as sanctuaries.

Before first light on 26 March, the troops reported completion of their mission. General Tikka Khan left his sofa at about 5 A.M. and went into his office for a while. When he reappeared cleaning his glasses with a handkerchief and surveying the area, he said, "Oh, not a soul there!" Standing on the verandah, I heard his soliloquy and looked around for confirmation. I saw only a stray dog, with its tail tucked between its hind legs, stealing its way towards the city. After day-break, [Zulfikar Ali] Bhutto was collected from his hotel room and escorted to Dacca airport by the Army. Before boarding the plane, he made a general remark of appreciation for the Army action on the previous night and said to his chief escort, Brigadier Arbab,

"Thank God, Pakistan has been saved." He repeated this statement on his arrival at Karachi. When Bhutto was making this optimistic remark, I was surveying mass graves in the university area where I found three pits of five to fifteen metres diameter each. They were filled with fresh earth. But no officer was prepared to disclose the exact number of casualties. I started going round the buildings, particularly lqbal Hall and Jagannath Hall which, I had thought from a distance, had been razed to the ground during the action. Iqbal Hall had apparently been hit by only two, and Jagannath Hall by four rockets. The rooms were mostly charred but intact. A few dozen half-burnt rifles and stray papers were still smouldering. The damage was very grave—but not enough to match the horrible picture I had conjured up on the verandah of General Tikka's headquarters. The foreign press fancied several thousand deaths (in the university area) while army officers placed the figure at around a hundred. Officially, only forty deaths were admitted.

From the university area, I drove on the principal roads of Dacca city and saw odd corpses lying on the footpaths or near the corner of a winding street. There were no mountains of bodies, as was alleged later. However, I experienced a strange and ominous sensation. I do not know what it signified but I could not bear it for long. I drove on to a different area.

In the old city, I saw some streets still barricaded but there was no one to man the road blocks. Everybody had shrunk to the sanctuary of his house. On one street corner, however, I saw a shadow, like a displaced soul, quickly lapsing into a side lane. After a round of the city, I went to Dhanmandi where I visited Mujib's house. It was totally deserted. From the scattered things, it appeared that it had been thoroughly searched. I did not find anything memorable except an overturned life-size portrait of Rabindranath Tagore. The frame was cracked in several places, but the image was intact.

The outer gate of the house, too, had lost its valuable decoration. During Mujib's rule they had fixed a brass replica of a Bangladesh map and had added six stars to represent the Awami League's Six Points. But now only the black iron bars of the gate, with holes for the metal fixtures, were there. The glory that had quickly dawned, had quickly disappeared.

I hurried back to the cantonment for lunch. I found the atmosphere very different there. The tragedy in the city had eased the nerves of defence personnel and their dependents. They felt that the storm after a long lull had finally blown past leaving the horizon clear. The officers chatted in the officer's mess with a visible air of relaxation. Peeling an orange, Captain Chaudhry said, "The Bengalis have been sorted out well and proper—at least for a generation." Major Malik added, "Yes, they only know the language of force. Their history says so."

I Was Just a Kid Then

Odhir Chandra Dey

Operation SEARCHLIGHT—*the Pakistan Army's genocidal crackdown on Pakistani citizens who were Bengali—made many victims. Here we experience it through the eyes of a seven-year-old, caught up in the carnage. He describes the cold-blooded murder of his family, targeted simply because his father, Modhushudon Dey, was the owner of a restaurant (popularly known as Modhur Canteen) on the campus of Dhaka University. Student leaders used to gather in Modhur Canteen for political discussions.*

In Pakistan, Operation SEARCHLIGHT *was later widely defended as necessary to quell the Bengali rebellion that was instigated by outsiders, notably Indian infiltrators. The government of Pakistan has yet to recognize that the unconscionable atrocities it committed, from 25 March 1971 onward, constituted crimes against humanity. Many Bangladeshis feel strongly that relations between Pakistan and Bangladesh can never be close until such recognition is voiced unreservedly.*

I was just a kid then, 7 years only, but the trauma of 25 March 1971 still haunts me. . . . I woke up from my slumber with a sudden shock at about 11.30 P.M., hearing heavy gunfire and ammunition. My parents, my brother and his wife, and my siblings all woke up. They moved the curtain a little and peeped out to see what was happening. I joined them and watched Jagannath Hall in high flames and saw that people were screaming for rescue, "Help! Help!" We spent the ghastly night in great anxiety. By dawn the Pakistani military had cordoned the whole area. G. C. Dev, the philosophy professor of Dhaka University and the provost of Jagannath Hall, probably was their first target. We watched a few soldiers dragging his body out from his residence. He was soaked in blood and seemed to be dead. Even the abbot of the Shiva Bari temple was not spared. The soldiers looked for young men in every building and brought them out. They aligned them on an open space and whimsically let them go after a while.

Our quarter was between Jagannath Hall and "Shiva Bari." After the brutal devastation of both places, I saw them marching towards our building.

Now it was our turn. My father, leaning on the chair in the corridor, was saying his usual prayer. He asked my mother for a cup of tea. She, out of fear, limped her way to the kitchen to prepare it. All of a sudden the "Pak *hanadar*" [raiders] started to kick the door terribly and ordered us to open it with abusive words in Urdu. The heavy blows on the door interrupted my father's prayer and baffled him. He could not understand whether he should open the door or not. Mother rushed to my father and muttered something. My brothers and sisters and I all started trembling in fear. When the door was about to be broken, my father opened it. As soon as he opened it, they pointed their guns to my father. As per international law, there is a rule not to kill the person who surrenders. My father might have known it. So, with a twinkle in his eyes, he surrendered by raising his hands. Even after surrendering two soldiers grasped his hands and snatched him with a sudden pull. My father was a very tall and healthy person. With the jerk he tumbled onto the corridor of the house next door. The door of the house was wide open, as the members of it had already been seized by the army.

By that time, six to seven soldiers had gotten into our house and they started destroying all our belongings. We screamed and rushed back to hide ourselves. Some of us took shelter under a cot, some of us in the toilet, and some hid inside the almira [cupboard]. Ranjit Dey, our eldest brother, fled to the third floor. Our house was on the second floor. Then the bloody brute saw my newly married *boudi* [sister-in-law, wife of Ranjit]. She started running to and fro within the house. When they were about to catch her, my sister screamed and called my brother to rescue my *boudi* from the clutch of the brute. Ranjit-*da* rushed to the spot and said, "Rina! Rina! Hold up your hands!" *Boudi*'s name was Rina. As soon as he said it, the soldiers turned back and shot him. My sister Ranu was very near to my brother. The bullet pierced my brother's chest and came out through his back, and then it hit the cheek of Ranu-*didi*. Dada (my brother) fell down on the floor at once. The floor around him was soaked with blood. After that, the military shot my *boudi*. She was pregnant then. The bullet hit her chest. I saw the dead body leaning against the wall and it seemed to me that it was not bullet but panic that was responsible for her death. Then they snatched the earrings of my *boudi* from her ears.

After that they went back to kill my father in the [flat next to ours]. My younger brothers and sisters and I were all sobbing bitterly on seeing the merciless treatment by the *hanadar bahini*. My mother got horrified seeing the bloody dead bodies of Ranjit-*da* and *boudi*. When the military aimed their gun to shoot my father, my mother ran to him and stood in front of him spreading her hands. She begged the military, "You have ruined me!

You killed my son, my daughter-in-law. Don't kill him, I beg for his life!" They did not pay any heed to her appeal, and instead ordered her to go away. They tried to drag her forcibly but failed. Lastly, out of rage, they cut both of her hands with a bayonet. Her hands got totally dispersed and were hanging just on the skin. Then they shot her. The bullet hit her throat, and her tongue got exposed. Even after she died, they shot her body several times in front of my father. Father also got shot. Both bodies were wet with blood. [W]e did not realize that my father was still alive.

My parents had eleven children and seven of us were very young. All of us were crying over the dead bodies of our family members. All of a sudden, we noticed that our father was still alive. He stood up and limped to us from the house [next door]. He wailed for long on seeing the dead bodies of Ranjit-*da* and *boudi*. Then, hugging us, he went to my mother's corpse.

The people who were responsible for our ruin appeared in front of us again with two Bengalis; one worked as a gardener in G. C. Dev's house and the other was a student. As far as we know, a driver of Dhaka University named Tota Mia who used to live on the fourth floor of our building informed the military that my father was still alive. They started dragging my father out of our house. We surrounded the military and requested them to spare our father. We kept asking, "Where are you taking my father? You killed all of us, if you take our father also, how will we lead the rest of our lives?" They were least bothered and it was a fruitless effort. They replied, "We will give back your father after a proper medical treatment." By that time Ranu (our sister) had been shot in her chest. Father requested them, "My daughter is also injured, take her also." They replied, *"Nehi! Larkiko hatao"* [Urdu: No! Keep the girl away]. A soldier kicked her. She fell down near the stairs.

We kept waiting for the arrival of our father. The military used the two Bengalis to drag the dead bodies. Although both of them were also shot by the military, they did not die. Both were Hindus. We came to know from them that the military had lied to us that day. They actually took my father to the Jagannath Hall premises and shot him with G. C. Dev Sir and Maniruzzaman Sir. It was indeed a proper medical treatment to my father! They compelled the two Bengalis to make a big hole in the ground and bury the corpses, piling them one after another. We still recall the memory of the mass burial at Jagannath Hall.

Throughout the whole day there was heavy bleeding from Ranu-*didi*'s chest. The dead bodies of my mother, *dada* and *boudi* remained at the same place where they died. We were all too young to remove the corpses. It was getting dark. So the very sight of the dead bodies was intensifying our fear.

"Mashima" (aunty), a woman from the third floor, consoled us in that crucial situation and came forward to assist us. She told us to stay with them.
By that time, the people of the house in front requested us to remove the
dead body of my mother from that area, so that their children [would] not
get scared of the horrible sight. Then we, mainly with the assistance of our
youngest sister Durga, positioned the dead body of my mother just beside
the dead bodies of *dada* and *boudi*. Then we locked our house and went to
the house on the third floor. We got our food and shelter over there. They
also tried to provide primary nursing to Ranu-*didi*, who was having difficulty to eat anything. Whatever she tried to eat was coming out through
the hole made in her chest. There had been unbelievable bleeding for a few
consecutive hours. She was trying to pull herself up to go to the toilet but
with every attempt there was excessive bleeding. She struggled for survival
throughout the whole night. On 27 March at dawn a few young men came
forward to help her. They placed her on a tin, which was wrapped up with a
mat, and took her to Dhaka Medical College Hospital, passing the big drain
beside Shiva Bari, and admitted her there. Later on they took us to the hospital. Hundreds of people took shelter in the hospital, thinking that at least
they could escape the killing. On 27 March, the curfew was withdrawn and
the army announced that the military would kill the wounded people in
the hospital. People quickly fled from the hospital. Our Balai *mama* (uncle)
and Hiralal (my father's friend) took us to Hiralal's house. Ranu was left in
the hospital. When the doctors came to know that Ranu was the daughter of "Modhu-*da*," they provided us with all kinds of necessary medication
for her. They gave her oxygen and blood, and bandaged her wound. A boy
named Bacchu (now working in a Dhaka University canteen at the fourth
floor of the Arts Building), who worked in our canteen, got the information
that Ranu's condition had improved a little. He took Ranu to our village
home at Srinagar.

We returned from Savar (from Hiralal's house) to our village after eleven
days. Ranu got her treatment in our village hospital. The bullet in her cheek
was removed by a major operation. She survived. After a few days, famine
broke out. There was no money, no food; we had to sell even the tin sheds
of our house. Even the villages were not spared the brutality of the military.
With the assistance of a few *razakars* (traitors) they entered our village. We
had to leave our house as well. We fled to India. We spent many days as refugees in camps in India. After independence we came back to our country.
We got freedom thirty-six years back but the wound caused by the Pakistani
hanadar bahini is still there in my body and soul.

A Telegram and a Phone Call

Archer Blood, Richard Nixon, and Henry Kissinger

On 28 March 1971 Archer Blood, consul general of the United States in Dhaka, sent a confidential telegram to the secretary of state in Washington, D.C. The telegram, titled "Selective Genocide," expresses horror at the recent events in Dhaka. It flew in the face of U.S. policy, which supported the Pakistan government.

The telegram did not make a dent in this policy. A fragment of a telephone conversation from the next day between the U.S. President, Richard Nixon, and his advisor, Henry Kissinger, reveals this. The United States would stand by the Pakistan government throughout the Liberation War.

Telegram from Archer Blood, 28 March 1971

1. Here in Dacca [Dhaka] we are mute and horrified witnesses to a reign of terror by the Pak military. Evidence continues to mount that the MLA [Martial Law Administration] authorities have a list of Awami League supporters whom they are systematically eliminating by seeking them out in their homes and shooting them down.

2. Among those marked for extinction in addition to A.L. [Awami League] hierarchy, are student leaders and university faculty. In this second category we have reports that Fazlur Rahman, Head of Applied Physics Department, Professor Dev, Head of Philosophy Department and a Hindu, M. Abedin, Head of Department of History, have been killed. Razzak of Political Science Department is rumored dead. Also on list are bulk of MNA's [Members of the National Assembly] Elect and number of MPA's [Members of Provincial Assembly].

3. Moreover, with support of Pak Military, non-Bengali Muslims are systematically attacking poor people's quarters and murdering Bengalis and Hindus. Streets of Dacca are aflood with Hindus and others seeking to get out of Dacca. Many Bengalis have sought refuge in homes of Americans, most of whom are extending shelter.

4. Tight[e]ning of curfew today (it is being reimposed at noon) seems designed to facilitate Pak military search and destroy operations. There is no rpt [repeat] no resistance being offered in Dacca to military.

5. Full horror of Pak military atrocities will come to light sooner or later. I, therefore, question continued advisability of present USG [U.S. government] posture of pretending to believe GoP [government of Pakistan] false assertions and denying, for understood reasons, that this office is communicating detailed account of events in East Pakistan. We should be expressing our shock, at least privately to GoP, at this wave of terror directed against their own countrymen by Pak military. I, of course, would have to be identified as source of information and presumably GoP would ask me to leave. I do not believe safety of American community would be threatened as a consequence, but our communication capability would be compromised. [Signed:] Blood.

Transcript of a telephone conversation between Richard Nixon (P)
and Henry Kissinger (K), 29 March 1971.

P[RESIDENT]: Hello.

K[ISSINGER]: Mr. President.

P: Hi Henry. You sleep well?

K: Yes, very well. It's really a very restful place out here.

P: What's new today? Got anything on the wires or anything of interest?

K: There's nothing of any great consequence Mr. President. Apparently Yahya [the President of Pakistan] has got control of East Pakistan.

P: Good. There're some times the use of power is . . .

K: The use of power against seeming odds pays off. Cause all the experts were saying that 30,000 people can't get control of 75 million. Well, this may still turn out to be true but as of this moment it seems to be quiet.

P: Well maybe things have changed. But hell, when you look over the history of nations[,] 30,000 well-disciplined people can take 75 million any time. Look what the Spanish did when they came in and took the Incas and all the rest. Look what the British did when they took India.

K: That's right.

P: To name just a few.

K: Well in those cases the people were more or less neutral. In the Inca case they expected a god to come from the West . . .

P: That sort of . . . yeah, put them out.

K: Which helped a bit.

P: That's right. But anyway I wish him well. I just . . . I mean it's better not to have it come apart than to have to come apart.

K: That's right. The long-term impact of its coming about . . . people now say that the fellow Mujib in the East is really quite moderate and for a Bengali that's right. But that's an extremely unstable situation there and the radical groups are likely to gain increasing strength.

P: This will be only one blip in the battle and then it will go on and on and on and it's like everything in the period we live in isn't it since World War II.

K: That's right, that's right.

P: Where revolution in itself, independence is a virtue which of course it never was. That wasn't true at the time of the French revolution either and it isn't any more true today. The real question is whether anybody can run the god-damn place.

K: That's right and of course the Bengalis have been extremely difficult to govern throughout their history.

P: The Indians can't govern them either.

K: No, well actually the Indians who one normally would expect to favor a breakup of Pakistan aren't so eager for this one. Because they're afraid that East Pakistan may in time, or East Bengal may in time have an attraction for West Bengal with Calcutta and also that the Chinese will gain a lot of influence here.

P: Interesting.

K: And that, I think, is a good chance.

From Counter-Insurgency to Defeat

A. A. K. Niazi

The Bangladesh Liberation War gave rise to a new literary genre: Pakistani and Indian army men writing accounts of their war experiences. One of these accounts is A. A. K. Niazi's The Betrayal of East Pakistan. *General Niazi was not just any military man: he was in charge of Pakistan's Eastern Command beginning in April 1971, which means that he directed the Pakistani armed forces in East Pakistan/ Bangladesh during the war. This text outlines his offensive deployment of troops to clear the region of all "rebels/infiltrators" by mid-May 1971. The plan was unsuccessful, and the war dragged on until the Indian Army invaded and the Pakistan Army was defeated. Niazi was forced to sign the instrument of surrender in December 1971. He then spent more than two years in an Indian prisoner-of-war camp before being allowed to return to Pakistan, a country now shrunk to what was formerly its western wing.*

When I took over the Eastern Command, the prevailing situation reminded me of Field Marshal Foch of Word War I, when he said, "My centre is giving way, my right flank is falling back, situation is excellent, I must attack." I said to myself, "My centre is breached, my flanks are turned, and I am more or less surrounded. The situation could not be better, I must attack." I did attack immediately and by the grace of Almighty Allah I had complete success in the first round of the war. I addressed two letters to all formations on maintenance of discipline and training. . . .

As mentioned above, the former East Pakistan is surrounded by Indian territory on three sides. The total frontage comes to 3,000 miles (2,500 miles land and 500 sea). The frontage is not in one line or in a semicircle as in West Pakistan, but makes more or less a complete circle which is divided into four sectors by mighty rivers. Therefore, to hold a continuous defensive line, even with gaps between defensive localities and areas, was not possible. Even Divisional defensive areas could not be organized. At most battalion, and at places Brigade, localities could be organized in Divisional defensive areas.

Dhaka, 16 December 1971: General A. A. K. Niazi (seated on the right) signs the instrument of surrender on behalf of the ninety-thousand-strong Pakistani armed forces in
Bangladesh. The Indian general Jagjit Singh Aurora is sitting next to him, while the
representative of the new Bangladesh government, the group captain A. K. Khonda-
ker, can been seen standing on the far right. From *Dhaka 1948–1971: AlokchitraSangka-
lan/An Album of Photographs*, edited by Muntassir Mamoon and Hashem Khan (Dhaka:
Mowla Brothers, 2007), 131. Anonymous photographer.

I inherited General Tikka's deployment. I wanted to evict the guerrillas
and I had two courses open to me:

a. Start pushing them towards the borders and eventually destroy them
   or push them across India. This would have taken me a long time and
   would have been expensive in men and materials. I would have been
   fighting on ground of their choosing, and their routes of reinforcement and withdrawal would remain open till the end.
b. Without caring for flanks and rear, shoot out with multiple columns
   for the borders and seal the routes of reinforcement and withdrawal.
   By our fast move and multiple thrusts we would be able to achieve
   surprise and thus create panic among the guerrillas, and the fear that

they were being isolated. Hence they were likely to leave their prepared positions and safe areas and run for India for security and safety.

I decide to adopt the second course.

General Tikka's deployment was mostly of a defensive nature. For an offensive, some changes in grouping and deployment were required, but as I wanted to achieve surprise and wrench the initiative from the enemy, speed was most essential to reach the borders quickly. So I made minimum changes, gave new tasks to formations, and told them to shoot out. I just told them to "reach the borders fastest with the maximum speed."

I issued directives which were to be carried out in the following four phases:

Phase 1: clearing of all major border towns and sealing of the routes of infiltration, exfiltration, and smuggling, and clearing Chittagong base and keeping it safe from artillery and mortar fire.

Phase 2: opening of essential river, road, and rail communications.

Phase 3: clearing of all towns in the interior and coastal areas of Mukti Bahini [Freedom Fighters].

Phase 4: combing of the whole of the province and eliminating rebels/infiltrators.

The tasks were to be completed by 15 May 1971 at the latest. It was emphasized that speed and multiple thrusts would pay dividends.

A Father's Letter to His Daughter

Ataur Rahman Khan Kaysar

In this letter to his very young daughter in Chittagong, a father tries to explain why he is missing her birthday and why there is a war going on in the country. The father, a politician from Chittagong, was on the run in the countryside, hiding from the Pakistani armed forces. His daughter, Waseka, later donated the letter for inclusion in a book of wartime correspondence.

16th July, 1971
Dearest sweet one,

This letter is meant for the day when *Inshallah* [by the Grace of God] you will have learned to read and understand. You must have stored up a lot of anger and resentment in that little heart of yours. . . . Why doesn't Daddy come to see you? Sweetie, if you only knew how unforgettable this pain is, the pain of not being able to hold you close to my heart on your birthday. What must be the reason behind not being able to come to you on this day? Why it is not possible for Daddy to hold you close to him? Perhaps you will understand when you grow up— because what seems like an injustice now won't seem like that then. The people of this country are accused of the same thing that your Daddy is charged of, for claiming their rights. Among those accused are patriotic leaders, writers, artists, novelists, journalists, all intellectuals . . . because they love this country. For the occupying forces, for the rulers, this is one of the greatest crimes that one can commit. The punishment for this crime is death. To escape this punishment, hundreds of thousands of people have fled this land. To escape that punishment, your father has had to wander from village to village, through hills and jungles. So, even if my heart breaks, Daddy cannot come and embrace you. Your dear sweet face is constantly in my heart and I kiss it so many times in my imagination. That is the only way your Daddy can get some consolation.

Sweet one, at each *waqt* of *namaj* [prayer time], I pray for you. I pray to Allah Rahman-e-Rahim [God, the Most Gracious, the Most Merciful] that he keeps Mummy and you healthy and free from danger. My dearest one, Mummy wrote to me that you have now learned to talk. You say that Daddy used to sing "Joy Bangla" (Victory to Bengal). Inshallah that day is not too far away, the day when Daddy will sing "Joy Bangla" to you again! If Daddy is not there, then Mummy will sing it to you. Mummy also wrote that if she slaps you, you threaten her that you will chase her out of the house! You know, Mummy is very stupid! She suffers a lot for us both. If you chase her out, you will see that she will come back again in no time. She won't be able to live without us.

If Mummy is sad, she can't tell anyone now. She will just cry by herself. You will hold her and console her, won't you? Lots and lots of kisses to you,

Yours,
Daddy.

Translated from Bengali by Meghna Guhathakurta.

Powdered Pepper

Shaheen Akhtar

Every war has its silences—silences that are slowly exposed by successive genera-
tions of writers and scholars. The rape and torture of Bengali women was one such
silence. The shame that accompanies such acts has been one of the foremost reasons
for the lack of openness about this aspect of the war. Therefore it is quite natural to
see the first hints emerge in works of fiction rather than nonfiction. This story by the
contemporary writer Shaheen Akhtar is titled "She Knew the Use of Powdered Pep-
per." The author translates an actual experience into a short story, thereby seeking
an understanding that was absent in the real world.

On the Silver Jubilee of the Liberation, a stone was flicked into a calm pond.
A group of researchers spread out in all directions like water hyacinths in
search of female freedom fighters. They traced one woman-warrior who
knew multiple uses of powdered pepper. In 1971, she vanquished a number
of Pakistani soldiers by flinging powdered red chilli on their eyes and noses.
The problem was that her name was not on the list of freedom fighters. Her
identity was also awkward. In the birth-hour of freedom, the *Mukti Bahini*
Commander of the Mohakhali area had included her name in the list of collaborators. On the other hand, the interviewer of the Women's Rehabilitation Centre had filled in the identity box of the form by writing *virangana*[1]
because the medical examination had revealed such damage in her reproductive organs that could only occur with a rape victim. In addition, an
Irish doctor identified her varied versions of what had happened and time-
confusion as post-rape mental disorder. Despite having these important details close at hand, the Centre's interviewer was severely confused about
her identity. Hence, at the top of the report, the sentence "She knew the
use of powdered pepper" was written in thick block-letters. Because of this,
she even managed to get a job in the spice-grinding section of the centre at
the time. A few days after that, in the deep of night, she threw powdered
pepper into the eyes of the uniformed guard of the Women's Rehabilitation Centre and ran away. The team of researchers learnt from the former

Director of the centre that her aim was as deadly as a skilled archer. As a result of which—although the guard survived—he lost his eyesight forever. Hence, the authorities did not attempt to again locate and rehabilitate such a dangerous woman. When the centre was closed down and the thousands of forms were poured into a dry tub, doused with kerosene and set on fire, her *virangana* identity was also reduced to ashes. The collaborator file had disappeared before that. Twenty-five years after Liberation, the team of researchers interviewed her again. Their report was headlined in accordance with the title of the Women's Rehabilitation Centre report. Despite the fact that the story of the powdered pepper had not seemed credible to them from the very beginning. Then they thought about it deeply and realized that if one left out the tale of the powdered pepper, with the remainder, one could not even label her a collaborator let alone a freedom fighter. And if they called her *virangana*, then that insulted the whole race of *virangana*. Then who was she? Attempting to explore all this objectively a quarter century after Liberation further muddied the issue of her identity. In this situation, the researchers felt that publishing the interview would be risky and meaningless. This story has been based upon that discarded interview. The interview has been presented exactly the way it was, including the titles. The author did not feel any desire or responsibility to invest her with any specific identity. All the author has attempted to do in this story is to break through the boundaries of human credulity, just a little bit.

This Could Even Be a Dream

Two months after March 25, my husband decided to go off to the Liberation War. I was such a fool! I grabbed his hand, fell on his feet, wept, "Take me with you, make the arrangements to take me along." He said, "Okay, I'll do it." And then he left. He disappeared. There was this abandoned house owned by someone. I had been living there for two days. Since my husband's left here, they haven't called me for meals. They're whispering. They're thinking I'm a woman of the streets. Does anyone's husband just leave them like this in an unknown house? Even if it is wartime. The man of the house woke me up in the morning to ask me, "Where did your husband go?" I said, "Who knows where he went."

"Do you have anywhere to go to?" He held the door to the street wide open as he said this to me.

I start walking the streets. I have no shoes. I have lost everything; I've been on the run for two months.

I roamed the streets without rhyme or reason. Where should I go? Where could I stay? I had nothing to eat at night. I had pins and needles in my stomach from hunger. Suddenly, there appeared a Bihari boy called Chullu. Chullu came to me and said, "Hello, Apa, you here! Do you want a job?" I don't know whether people have jobs during wartime. For the past two months I have been fleeing with my husband from one place to another. Now he has gone and left me. I said, "I do want a job, Chullu Bhai. Or else what shall I eat, where shall I live? But how can I get a job? I can't go that way. They'll kill me." That way meant Mohakhali, the part of the city that we'd left behind. I had worked at a private company there before March 25. The boy gestured towards the sun-grilled almost empty city and said, "Come with me. No one will say anything."

I'm going to Mohakhali by rickshaw with Chullu. I don't have a single penny in my pocket. I can't open my mouth and tell him, Chullu Bhai, buy me something to eat before I start at my new job. Except when I kept on looking at my bare feet and oh-ed and ah-ed, Chullu said, "Nothing to worry about, you will get everything."

Chullu sat me down in an abandoned house and went out looking for a job. There were several guards at the front and back of the house. No one else. I sniffed around the kitchen. Empty bottles of marmalade, jelly and pickles. The remnants at the bottom of coffee and Horlicks [a malted milk drink] containers had congealed into hard rock. There was nothing in the fridge except a few bottles of whisky. A huge piano beside it, with a family group photo atop. Their faces and clothes made me think that they were non-Bengalis. I felt spooked. I opened a bottle and poured half of the whisky down my throat. Absolutely raw. Then suddenly I noticed the house-guards. Although they were scattered here and there, they were guarding me in a circle. It was late afternoon. What should I do? I had to escape from there and that before evening.

When I found a guard by himself, I asked him, "Who lives in this house?" He turned his face away pretending he couldn't hear me. I had come out of the house and was walking on the lawn. My throat stung, my innards were burning inside my belly, and amid all this I was making plans to escape. There were a few rickshaws on the other side of the open iron gate; they even had some passengers. But it would be no use shouting. No one would have courage enough to stand face to face with armed guards.

They had surrounded me now and were circling me. Gradually the circle was closing in. "Look, I'm very hungry. I haven't eaten anything all day." They pursed their lips in laughter, as if what I had said was very funny. I was stubborn, "Can you tell me where I can get some food?" I looked at all of them simultaneously when I asked the question this time. Chatting and jabbering, I actually wanted to break out of their circular formation. One guard said, "Yes, yes, you'll have everything in the evening," and asked another to bring some tea. As soon as he moved away, I raced towards the street. With a tremendous roar, the five thugs ran after me.

I am running. I hold my life in my hands and run.

It was like it happens in dreams: I was running but could not move forward. At one point they surrounded me in a ring again. I stood with my face lifted toward the sky. Oh, I'd forgotten to mention, I had packets of powdered pepper with me. Not one, lots. I flipped open the packets and threw them. Once, twice, thrice . . . The skies of Mohakhali turned as red as Karbala that day. As if a blood-rain was pouring from the sky. The booming cannons of the *ferishtas* [angels] in the sky sounded at the same time. I would throw a packet, and then move away step by step. Where to? I didn't know. When I think of it now, all of this seems a dream.

Then I Wanted to Live or Die

My husband was taking the dog Pinky instead of me. Not a sound emerged from my lips in sorrow and humiliation. I stared and stared as I watched him put the chain around the dog's neck, pacing this end of the room to the other. After a long time Pinky had been bathed in hot water mixed with a little Dettol. He was looking at the clock repeatedly; Pinky was standing there wagging her tail. When the horn blows from downstairs they will leave the room and go off to the Liberation War. I couldn't stand it any more and grabbed hold of my husband's collar and tie and shook him with all my might, grinding my teeth together. A screaky sound emerges from them, "If you're not going to take me with you, then why did you marry me? Is Pinky your girlfriend or your wife? Tell me, tell me, girlfriend or wife?" He loosened the vise of my fingers from his collar and tie, "Oh brother! Here you are all worried about yourself, and here I am . . . ." He began pacing again. I ran toward him to shake him again. He shoved me onto the floor with a single push and walked out with Pinky. With all the commotion, I hadn't heard when the horn had sounded from downstairs. It was when the green jeep gunned its engine and sprayed dust as it climbed onto the main road that I saw that they were leaving. So if you're going, go. Guerilla wars, liberation wars aren't fought with dogs. Were they actually going to the Liberation War at all? As if I didn't know. It was all a con.

That man had tricked me into marriage in the very month of March 1971. Believe me, I hadn't wanted to. The people in my house said, So how long are you going to live by yourself? The way that things are? Who knows what will happen when? Tell me, can you trust a man that quickly? And then someone who owns a bitch named Pinky! So it was because of their words that I got married to this brute.

My husband left me and went off to the Liberation War or hell with Pinky. I spent the night at that abandoned house and came out on the streets while it was still dark. Back then I wanted to live or die. So I appeared at the office at 10 in the morning. The non-Bengali big boss jumped up from his chair when he saw me, *"Arre larki, tum kahase ayi?"* (Hey, you girl, where did you spring from?) The others were in uproar. Which is what happens when prey walks into a trap. "Sir, I need some money. If you could give me my salary for March." The big boss called a peon in and immediately wrote me a check. I grabbed the check from the peon's hand and clutched it in mine. Then I ran off. All the Bengali and non-Bengali employees of the office ran after me. I zig-zagged down the staircase. A single step ahead. Just as I was tearing open a packet of pepper, Chullu appeared from somewhere and blocked my path. That Bihari boy. The one I had tricked yesterday and escaped from that abandoned house.

My trance was broken when the peon entered the room. I stood up and accepted the money from his hands. It's because he is a non-Bengali that I show him this respect. Then the big boss said, "Start at your job here today. You're not going anywhere now. Have lunch with me in the afternoon. You can't stay anywhere else at night; you have to stay at my quarters." I staggered and collapsed onto the chair with the check in my hand. My head was reeling; I hadn't had anything to eat in two days. The big boss brought his lips near my ears and whispered, "You know, errm, I'm alone now. I'm living a bachelor's life. I need you . . ."

A Thousand and One Arabian Nights

There's no work at the office. All day I just stare at the air without comprehension. And I think, what I would be thinking, doing, if the war had not happened. All the people of my household, they all went every which way! Who knows where home is? Now I am part of the big boss's household. At times I am even called into the air-conditioned office of the big boss to feed paper into the typewriter. I stuff carbon paper in the typewriter. The big boss undoes the buttons of my blouse and plunges his face in my breasts, whining like a puppy. As if he has a tummy ache. Then he stuffs money in my cleavage—whatever he feels like that day, five taka or ten taka. He deducts all of it to account for my keep—food and boarding. When I return to my desk, I see not a mountain of money but of red powdered pepper.

One day after the office hours were done, the big boss said, "Commander Selim is waiting for you in a car downstairs. The Naval Commander." Naval Commander Selim! From whom no woman ever returned, no matter how pretty or how ugly. When the night was through, he would kill the girl and dump her into the Rupsha River. I was being sent to this Sultan of the Arabian Nights! I said, "Sir, I won't go. I'll stay with you. I won't ever be disobedient again, Sir. Save me." The big boss didn't agree. His family was arriving from Pakistan. He was kicking me out and purifying his household. I was being sacrificed for this purity. The middle-aged killer Commander stood holding the car door open, saying, "Come, Memsahib, come."

The car sped toward the naval jetty with a whoosh. That was my last day. Life or death would be decided that day. When we arrived in front of the level crossing, the signal barrier came down. Commander Selim stopped the car and left the motor running. The signal light turned on and off, off and on. A train had been passing for an eternity, crawling on its chest. Finally the light turned off altogether. The crossing barricade was rising upward. I opened the car door and jumped. The naval commander's car disappeared under the powdered red pepper. As I escaped, I turned and threw back packets, packets of red pepper. Once the packets were gone, I was weightless. I left as a plane leaves the runway and flies into the sky—fearless, free.

That night there was no pause to the chop-chop sounds of the slaughterhouse by the port jetty. My eyes closed as dawn neared. Countless army vehicles surrounded my quarters. They had encircled the house in a honeyed ring. It was still dark outside. There was no light in the stairwell. What if the freedom fighters lay in wait there? So no one had the courage to climb upstairs. I stood at the top of the third floor stairs and threw them a challenge. I was well turned-out, my ammunition pouch filled with red powdered pepper. That was my weapon. I would throw it on whoever climbed up those stairs. A call came from downstairs, "Come down, you bitch. You've murdered Commander Selim. You have to go down to the cantonment." I responded from atop the stairs, "Why don't you come up?" A brave *jawan* [soldier] raised his arms above his head and climbed up the stairs. When he reached the second-floor landing, he raised his face, puffed through his nostrils and sniffed the air, I lobbed a packet of powdered pepper at him, in the same way that dynamite, hand grenades are thrown. He collapsed. He rolled down the stairs into the downstairs garage. Then another one climbed up. I flung my packets. They couldn't stand the burning of the pepper and jumped into the river one by one. Where the corpses of the slaughterhouse were dumped in the night.

No One in the World Will Believe It

The country was liberated. The first few days, interrogation followed interrogation. One group left, then another group arrived. Each time the same words, "You were Commander Selim's mistress. You are a collaborator." I gave the same answer. "It takes money to buy packets of powdered pepper. If I hadn't stayed with him, where would I have gotten the money? Who would've given me the money during wartime?"

"Why your husband would have, he could've given you money."

"He was in the *Mukti Bahini*."

"No, he wasn't. We've made enquiries."

"Perhaps he couldn't make it. Every time he tried to cross the border, Pinky started barking so loudly—she's a Pakistani supporter, see—that he couldn't make it across."

"Pinky? Her name isn't in the list of collaborators."

"It isn't. Because Pinky is a bitch."

They exchanged looks. They thought I was crazy. But I wasn't crazy. I started telling them how I had flung powdered pepper like dynamite and felled the Pakistanis. They were bewildered. They couldn't figure out whether to believe me or not, whether they should continue with the interrogation.

In these 25 years I have answered whatever questions anyone has asked me. But I have never been able to open my heart. Now I am 50 years old. I've heard, at 60, even whores become innocent in the eyes of God. They can enter the community if they want. If I live for another ten years, if I did not die in 1971, I will open my heart and speak then.

Anyway, I was let go. They let me go. Besides, why shouldn't they let me go? The Indian Army had rescued me from the cantonment. They were witnesses, those men of our allied forces.

They had abducted and taken me to the cantonment. That day when several carloads of Pakistani army men had surrounded my quarters in a honeyed ring. Their accusation was that I had murdered the commander. The man was about my father's age. One day while playing cards, I had implored him, "Teach me how to shoot a pistol. I want to see whether I can." His hands had grown still in the midst of riffling through the cards. His eyelids were motionless. I was scared. "No, no. I was just kidding. Please don't be angry. Oh, it's your turn now," I shook and shook him awake. That day we didn't play cards any more. He took me to the shooting range and taught me how to shoot a pistol all afternoon. In point of fact, he wanted to die. He had aged, and he had committed so many murders and atrocities in the past few months that he couldn't sleep, day or night.

We were returning from the range to the naval camp amid the light and shadows of the evening. Commander Selim was driving; I was sitting in the seat next to him. I was playing around with the pistol in my hand; it looked rather like a toy. When we reached the level crossing the commander stopped the car but kept the engine running. The night train was entering the city then. That was my chance. I opened the car door and jumped out. I still remember, just before I jumped out, Commander Selim had extended one hand in front of him like a blind man to block the bullet.

Translated from Bengali by Shabnam Nadiya.

Note

1. Translator's Note: *Virangana*—the feminine for war heroine, the male term is *vir*—was the title used to identify the countless women who were raped by the Pakistani soldiers and Bengali collaborators during the 1971 Liberation War. Although the word is used supposedly to recognise the great sacrifice made by these women—albeit unwillingly— for the war effort, to this day there are mixed feelings regarding the usage of this term. The word has lost its original meaning and has become coloured by how society views victims of rape.

A Raja's Protection

Raja Tridiv Roy

The history of the Bangladesh Liberation War has been mostly constructed around, informed by, and equated with the history of Bengali nationalism. As a result, the role of others, such as indigenous communities, has been excluded from this history. In recent years some scholars have attempted to rectify this. In the case of the Chittagong Hill Tracts, the situation was especially complex because Raja Tridiv Roy, the chief of the Chakma Circle (one of the three subdivisions of the Chittagong Hill Tracts) and member of Parliament for the region, showed his allegiance to the Pakistani forces. The Pakistan government designated him special envoy, ambassador extraordinary, and plenipotentiary. After the war, Raja Tridiv Roy stayed back in Pakistan and continued his diplomatic career. In 2003 he was appointed as a federal minister. In his memoirs, titled The Departed Melody (Memoirs) *(2003), Raja Tridiv Roy explains the circumstances that led him to give allegiance to the Pakistani forces in 1971.*

The hillpeople were generally hoping that the Bengali rebellion would be quelled. They sympathized with East Pakistan's quest for full and maximum autonomy. What they did not support was total secession through violent means. In this they were at one with many Bengalis who wanted justice and autonomy but not secession. After all, from being an increasingly potent partner in a nation that was the third largest in Asia, after China and India, to be reduced to a tiny poverty stricken overcrowded nation smaller than Nepal in territory was obviously not every Bengali's ambition or objective. On their part, the Jummas [hill people] had their own future at stake. They were convinced that if the Awami League's struggle for Bangladesh succeeded the Hill Tracts would be thrown open to Bengalis who would grab their land and dishonour their women and turn them into slaves in their own habitat. Save for a few Muslim Leaguers, who in fear of being liquidated paid lip service to *Joi Bangia* ["Victory to Bengal," the battle cry of the Bengali Freedom Fighters], Bengalis in Rangamati were all pro-Bangladesh.

The Bengali Deputy Commissioner Taufique Imam had joined the rebels, crossed to India and held secret meetings with the Indians. He requisitioned, or rather commandeered, most government as well as private motor launches and trucks. With these he transported rations, arms and ammunition as well as Indian infiltrators down from Demag[i]ri in Mizoram to Chittagong. He was also in wireless communication with the Indians. The army at Dhaka had intercepted some of these messages but this he could not have known, not that it would have made much difference. The Deputy Commissioner's doings were more or less general knowledge in Rangamati. A few days before the army arrived in mid-April, he decamped to Sabrum in Tripura just across the Feni River opposite Ramgarh with money from the National Bank of Pakistan branches in Rangamati and Kaptai. There he helped in the refugee camps inducting, training and equipping the Mukti Bahini [Freedom Fighters] and sending them back to East Pakistan. Kumar Kokonadaksha Roy, the Awami League candidate for the Provincial North had fled to Tripura. Imam had him arrested and incarcerated there in Tripura.

The spring and New Year Festival called *Pahela Baisakh*, to us the Bizu Festival, is held every year on 12, 13 and 14 April, all over the subcontinent and Southeast Asia. However, this year, for us there were no festivities, no joyous laughter, only a sombre suspense full of impending sorrow. A day or so later, at about 4 o'clock in the afternoon, I was informed that the two seniormost government officials present at Rangamati, M. M. Ali better known as Mahadev (another of Shiva's 1008 names), a portly and kind-hearted gentleman supposedly resembling Shiva, and Monem Chowdhury, along with some Muslim League leaders sought permission to come across to the island to meet me. In normal times the ferryman just paddled the canoe and brought anyone across to the island, but these days he was under orders to bring no non-hillman to the island without prior approval.

They were about half a dozen. I met them in the drawing room and we all had tea. In those days there was no sugar available. *Gur* or molasses used to stand in for sugar. One of the Muslim Leaguers said he had contacted the army at Raozan, some miles outside Chittagong and vouched for the Bengali people's non-resistance if the army did not blast their way through to Rangamati. However, he said, the army was not prepared to believe the offer of non-resistance unless I guaranteed it personally. I could have sent representatives to meet the army; my father-in-law volunteered. It was a risk I could not allow others to take on my behalf. Firstly, the Mukti Bahini might open fire on them on the way to Raozan. Secondly, the army, made out to be worse than the hordes of Genghis Khan, who shot at sight as well as committed atrocities, might not accept anyone but me as I was the Chakma Raja as well as the elected leader of the Tracts. One of the visitors also was against sending representatives in my place as their bonafides might be in question.

Finally, it was decided we would go to the army the following day. And to ensure that the populace would honour our commitment we would first speak to the people in the two bazars of Rangamati. With Col. Hume, my brother Johnny and others including the visitors, we crossed the lake and drove to Rangamati town. In doing this we had to override the objections of the ladies at home. Fearing for our safety, they were not keen on our mission to the bazars. It was known there were still many Mukti Bahini there.

At the Reserve Bazar the two Muslim League leaders and I addressed the people. One of them described the army takeover of Chittagong town in terrifying terms, embellishing his recital with gory details. They said the army would in any case capture Rangamati sooner or later and shuddered at the prospect, real or imagined, of gross indignities if not certain death. A chorus of terror-stricken Bengalis urged me to save them by going to the army. At the Tabalchari bazar also hundreds of people shouted pro-Pakistan slogans and entreated me to face the army on their behalf. Slogans of *zindabad* (long live) for me rent the air. It was getting dark and we knew there were *muktis* [Freedom Fighters] amongst the crowd. But there was no alternative. Leadership entails responsibility. I warned them if there was any sniper fire at the army then my word would have been broken. If they, the civilian population, suffered as a consequence, I was not to be held responsible.

Early next morning, 16 April perhaps, we set off for Raozan in two jeeps and a landrover. The rebels had installed some machine-guns at Ghagra, 12 miles from Rangamati. Their position was beside the Dak Bungalow (Rest House) on the top of a steep hill overlooking the junction of the Chittagong–Rangamati and the Kaptai–Chandraghona road. We were told that this outpost had been dismantled a day or two earlier and the rebels had run off to the north. But no one could vouch for its veracity. As we meandered along the tortuous road we could have been fired upon by any lurking rebel. The hills were full of jungles and trees and we were simply sitting ducks to anyone on the roadside with a rifle. Fortunately we were neither waylaid nor fired upon and reached the road barrier at Raozan, about 30 miles from Rangamati, without misadventure. At the barrier we stared at a machine-gun pointed straight up the road at us. A *Jawan* [soldier] toting a submachinegun asked a few questions and then lifted the barrier.

A Junior Commissioned Officer received us and led us into a small building. This was the office of the Captain-in-Charge. While we waited, soldiers brought us mugs of hot sweet milky tea. Later, the Captain advised us that we had better proceed to the East Bengal Regimental Centre at Nutanpara, where the army was headquartered. It was here that I had been dined in years ago as an Honorary Captain (I was promoted to Major in 1963 on return from Washington D.C.[,] where I had gone as a delegate to the World Food Congress). At that time there had been only tin roofed barracks, and leopards roaming about the vicinity. Subsequently, all that had changed and there were many large buildings, parade grounds and all the appurtenances of a modern regimental centre. Among the young officers there at the time of my dining in were two subalterns that later rose to hold political office— Gen. Sardar Farooq S. Lodi who became Governor of Sind, and Major General Hossein Mohammad Ershad who seized power, promoted himself to Lt. General and later to President of Bangladesh. He was removed from office due to mass uprisings against him in 1990. He formed the Jatiya Party, which is the third largest political party after the Bangladesh National Party (BNP), which too was founded by a coup making general. The first of the three of course is the Awami League, but twice it lost to the BNP in the general elections.

At Nutanpara more officers interviewed us and asked probing questions. It was apparent nobody was able to take decisions here either. We were advised to go to the Circuit House in Chittagong, which was the Martial Law Headquarters. On the way we saw the ravages of war—villages destroyed, buildings broken and charred, walls demolished. At a railway crossing a derailed train with about six bogies stared at us from a grotesque angle. The town had a desolate look. Where there should have been hustle and bustle and teeming crowds now there was nothing save emptiness and silence. The only movement was that of occasional soldiers desultorily manning their beats.

At the Circuit House we met one or two senior officers but could not find out who it was that could take a decision with regard to the manner of takeover of Rangamati. Eventually Angus Hume spotted a newly arrived General from Dhaka whom he knew. He took me over and introduced me to the General. We explained the desirability of taking over Rangamati without use of force and assured him there would be no armed resistance. After some discussion he agreed to send a young naval officer named Khan to his brother Lt. Col. Z. A. Khan at Kaptai, the one detailed for the capture of Rangamati. They were two among eight siblings, some with a brilliant record of service in the various armed forces. Armed with the General's letter, Monem Chowdhury and some others went along with the naval officer to Kaptai. The rest of us returned to Rangamati having in the nick of time been able to avert needless bloodshed, horror and destruction at Rangamati and in the Hill Tracts. We later learnt that the army had decided to attack on the following day.

On the way back, at Ranirhat, 18 miles from Rangamati, a number of very frightened people asked us when the army was going to take over these areas. They said they were suffering at the hands of the *Mukti Bahini*. We told them that the army would be coming at any moment. That evening at dusk the army, in launches and speed boats[,] made a sort of miniature Normandy landing (the Allied landing in France on 6 June 1944) at Rangamati and swiftly took command of the situation.

The next morning a Major of the Special Services Group and a Captain, who was a Bengali doctor, came over to the island and told me the Colonel-in-Charge desired to see me. Col. Hume and I accompanied them. In that first interview with Col. Z. A. Khan, one of the first questions he asked me was why I had attended a peace committee meeting at Rangamati on 7 March. He showed me the minutes of the meeting too. This was surprising because I was in Dhaka on that date and told the Colonel so. The Special Services Group was extremely efficient and by and large in The Hill Tracts there was no harassment or oppression of the civilian population—hillmen as well as Bengalis. However, those that had taken up arms and had fought the army or committed murders were reportedly either summarily executed or, in some instances, sent to the Army Headquarters in Chittagong.

The hillpeople as well as Bengalis in the Tracts on the whole co-operated with the army. As the word spread in the plains districts that there was peace in the Tracts under the army and that no brutalities were permitted, many Bengalis came and took shelter in the Tracts and many of them blessed me for interceding with the army on their behalf whenever there was a question of harassment of the civil population, and spread the word that under the Raja's protection all were like infants in the lap of their mother.

A Razakar Oath and Diploma

Anonymous

As the war between the Pakistani armed forces and the Muktijoddhas (Freedom Fighters) raged on, the Pakistani regime felt the need to recruit inhabitants of East Pakistan to support it and fight on its side. The regime needed locals to show it the way, point out Freedom Fighters and their supporters from among the general Bengali populace, and defend what was then the official line: to secure the national integrity of Pakistan. Hence, the Pakistani regime created a pro-Pakistan militia and named it the Razakars (Volunteers). Here are an oath of allegiance to Pakistan and a diploma, signed by a representative of the Jamaat-e-Islami [Islamic Assembly] party, attesting to a person's training as a Razakar.

Schedule B
form of oath
Rule 16
I ...., S/O ...., Vill. ....,
P.O................, Dist .... do solemnly declare that from this moment I shall faithfully follow the injunctions of my religion, and dedicate my life to the service of my Society and Country. I shall obey and carry out all lawful orders of my superiors. I shall bear true allegience to the Constitution of Pakistan as framed by law and shall defend Pakistan, if necessary, with my life.

Signature
Oath taken in my presence this.....day of 1971

Signature
Deputy Commandant
.... Subdivision
......District

A Razakar oath. From *Ekattorer Gaibandha*, by Md. Mahbubar Rahman (Dhaka: Bangladesh Chorcha, 2005), 215. Used by permission of Md. Mahbubar Rahman.

This is to certify that ....,
S/O........................, Vill..................., P.O.............,Thana...............,
District................ is our active worker. He is true Pakistani and
dependable. He is trained Razakar. He has been issued a Rifle
No.........with ten round ammunation for self protection.

Sd/-

Incharge
Razakar & Muzahid
Jamaat-e-Islami
91/92, Siddique Bazar
Dacca

A Razakar diploma. From *Ekattorer Gaibandha*, by Md. Mahbubar Rahman (Dhaka: Bangladesh Chorcha, 2005), 215. Used by permission of Md. Mahbubar Rahman.

To the People of West Pakistan

K. K. Sinha

As throngs of people from East Pakistan fled across the border to India, especially to West Bengal, many volunteers from West Bengal and beyond came to give aid to the war refugees and help out in the mushrooming camps. K. K. Sinha, a humanist philosopher and political thinker, was among them. During one of his visits to the camps around October 1971, he and his wife were in a car accident; he succumbed to his injuries after taking his wife to the hospital. Like many, he had felt the need to wake up civil society in West Pakistan to the atrocities of the Pakistan regime and to exhort them to help the victims. His wife, Sati Sinha, wrote in the preface to his posthumously published collected writings on Bangladesh, Bangladesh Revolution for Liberation: *"The author's prayer and dream was to see Bangladesh liberated, which he could not witness due to his untimely and sad passing away. But his dream has come true. Bangladesh was liberated from the clutches and tyranny of West Pakistan and achieved full independence."*

Sinha was closely associated with many leaders of the freedom struggle, and perhaps this is why, during the heat of war on 22 June 1971, he wrote this impassioned plea to the people of West Pakistan on the leaders' behalf.

For a long time you have not heard the voice of the people of Bangla Desh[,] previously called East Pakistan. It was only during the elections in December last that you had heard the genuine voice of Bangla Desh and the results of the elections showed to you very unmistakably who represented the true feelings. Sheikh Mujibur Rahman and his Awami League polled 98% of the votes of Bangla Desh and came out as a single party with absolute majority in the National Assembly of Pakistan.

If we have committed any crime, it was this that we solidly voted for Mujibur Rahman and established a clear majority over all others. If we committed any sin, it was because we wanted real autonomy. Yes, if that is a crime, we are proud to be guilty of it.

But in that case why did those self-appointed rulers of Islamabad have the elections at all? If they were afraid of the people they should not have dared

Refugees from Bangladesh/East Pakistan in a camp in India, 1971. From *Bangla Name Desh* (Kolkata: Ananda Publishers, 1990), 62. Anonymous photographer. Used by permission of ABP Pvt. Ltd., Kolkata.

to hold an election. The results terrified them and therefore all of a sudden on the fateful day of March 25 Awami League and Mujibur Rahman and the entire people of East Bengal constituting 55% of the total population of Pakistan became "traitors." They must be killed, they must be mercilessly butchered and their women raped and their houses burnt and their property looted. They must be hounded out of the country, their blood sucked out and their bodies left floating on the rivers.

Dear Peoples of West Pakistan, by now news must have trickled to you second hand, third hand or fourth hand of what has been happening in Bangla Desh in the name of your President Yahya Khan and your Army and your own selves. Do you know the full story? No. How could you? Your radio is as truthful as the late lamented Dr. Goebbels himself. If you want to know the truth, the real truth, the whole truth come and listen to Radio Bangla Desh.

But I want you to ask one question, dear friends. Have you, the people of Pakistan, given any authority to your President and to your army to kill defenceless men, women and children, to rape women and to loot their property on a scale unprecedented in human history? Even Hitler and Mussolini did not go that far. Did *you*, the Punjabi people, the Sindhis, the Beluchis, the Frontier men, give this authority to your soldiers? Is that the way they will defend Pakistan?

I may tell you, we of Bangla Desh seek no mercy. I may add that now it is the turn of your young boys to be killed. Beginning with dozens they are now being killed in hundreds. And lest you know the real truth, the dead bodies of your sons are not being sent to you, and even the information of their death is being withheld. But how long? When the killing will leap to thousands, it will be difficult to withhold the truth anymore and only then you will begin to realise what we have been experiencing. Now your younger boys are coming to our battle-field. Fine specimen of humanity they are. They could be able engineers and doctors and administrators of their own land. And now this flower of manhood will lay on the mud of Bangla Desh and will be eaten up by vultures and stray dogs, just as our youth is being treated.

People of (West) Pakistan—there is no East Pakistan any more—you *have* a responsibility for this butchery in Bangla Desh by Yahya's men, for he is doing it in *your* name, saying he is doing it *for* you. So far as we are concerned, it is a war to the finish. We shall rest only after we have killed all and every Pakistani brute on our land. But we have no quarrel with the *People* of Pakistan. You are being fooled by your selfstyled leaders. Those days of domineering over us are dead and gone, and we *are* independent in spirit and mind. If you do not want your youths to be killed by our Liberation Army, you must exert your influence on your Government. They are operating under the authority that they say you have given them. If therefore you want a change, it is your responsibility to move in the matter effectively. How you do it is your business. But do it in *your own interest*. So far as we are concerned, we are confident that in this total war we shall spare no one who calls himself a defender of the occupation forces.

June 22, 1971.

A Missionary Family in the War

Jim McKinley

Not many people are aware that, at the onset of the Bangladesh Liberation War, a large number of expatriate development workers were residing in East Pakistan. Some had been there for years, and others were there in connection with the massive relief and development effort that came on the heels of one of the most disastrous cyclones and tidal waves ever to hit the country: at least 350,000 people had perished in November 1970. The failure of Pakistan's military government to competently deal with the disaster was widely seen as callous indifference to the fate of the victims, and this caused tremendous anger in East Pakistan. Foreign emergency aid was gratefully accepted.

The fact that so many outsiders were in East Pakistan when the military crackdown occurred in March 1971 greatly added to the internationalization of the war. Expatriates focused on the humanitarian disaster that unfolded around them. Most foreigners tried to leave as soon as they could, but an American Baptist missionary and his family decided to stay on. His lively account of the war and liberation gives an impression of their daily fears and hopes.

We knew there was no preparation we could make to help in the event of a direct hit by a bomb. But we also knew something could be done to help if a bomb fell nearby or if there was street fighting in our area.

So John Freeman assumed the responsibility for preparing the Guest House as best he could. We helped John line the outside of the back porch with anything and everything we could find. We placed the refrigerator, the deep freeze, book shelves loaded with books, and every available piece of furniture in the place we felt it offered the most protection. We also prepared for blackouts by covering the windows and vents with heavy black paper. We removed the ceiling lights and all picture frames from the walls, for we didn't want anyone to be cut by glass.

The only things left in the room where we slept were the dining tables, a desk and the foam mattresses. At night we separated the narrow dining tables and placed them along the wall, which appeared the safest. Kathy didn't want to be disturbed by any of us, so she chose to sleep under the desk. We covered the tables with the mattresses, and Cherie slept under the one nearest Kathy. Betty and Wade slept together near Kathy; Keith and I slept nearest the outside door.

The Thurmans moved downstairs and prepared their room by lining the outside wall with wooden closets. They moved a large chest near the table under which they slept. John and Howard moved into the Bennetts' house and prepared a room for themselves. Pastor Sircar came asking to move in with us since their house was even nearer the airport and there were no friends nearby; for most people had vacated that area. His family was welcomed, of course.

The evacuation continued to be delayed and this created further havoc for those preparing to leave. In some respects, it didn't help us either. One foreigner came bursting into the Guest House one day and screamed out, "You had better leave. When the Bengali fighters come into this city, they will slaughter every one left!"

I wondered what Cherie thought when she heard him. I knew his words were spoken without love for or an understanding of the Bengalis' situation. But Cherie had just gone through the difficult struggle of deciding whether or not to leave. And she knew that there were some Bengalis who knew nothing about our position and our relationship to other Bengalis. She also knew there were some who had learned to kill without thinking. They would not care what our position might have been. But Cherie's decision had not been made lightly. Many times she had considered all of this and more, too. Her reaction was anger at this gentleman for his loose talk. The statement was too inclusive for a thinking Christian young lady, so she gave little attention to what he said.

The size of our group grew rapidly. Another pastor moved into a small brick building near the Bennetts' house with his family. Since one of the Bennetts' helpers already had his family there, they soon had their area filled. One large Christian family moved into the brick building in the Guest House area. They brought all of their precious belongings as did the other families, for they knew their houses would be looted.

The guards who worked for us at night began staying full-time since they might get caught by a sudden curfew. But they also remained because they felt safer with us. It wasn't long until they had a room filled with Bengali men. The curfew, which sometimes lasted up to forty-eight hours, created real problems. The military order was to shoot on sight anyone breaking the curfew. This worked well for them. They were able to detect the movement of Bengali men easily. The slightest noise during a curfew created tenseness.

For us it primarily meant being extremely careful when we had to go outside, for military vehicles constantly passed by the Guest House. We occasionally had to go out for water, and at night we carefully checked the outside of the house to make sure no light was seen. The checking was done in complete silence. When we opened the door to go out and to enter, we turned off lights to make sure there was no shooting in our direction.

One afternoon the curfew was suddenly put into force. The service station next door was open, so the men quickly closed the doors and ran to their houses. But in their haste they left all of the lights on. Just as darkness fell, I looked out the back door. The bright lights from the service station glowed over the area. This made the station and our two houses a perfect target for the shooting planes. I called out, "Keith, come, let's see if we can get those lights out." Those who heard us knew there was no other choice. The only word was, "Be careful." We ran out the gate; and as we reached the service station, a truck load of soldiers drove up. They jumped out with their guns ready. Apparently Keith and I didn't look too dangerous.

But the situation was a little tense. They were angry, so I said, "Sir, I'll turn the lights out somehow. Just give me a minute." I threw a brick through the glass door and entered. The soldiers still had their guns drawn. They seemed to think it was a plot, but I felt it was only a mistake. I found several light switches but couldn't find the main switch, so I shoved tables under the lights that I couldn't turn off, jumped up quickly and took out the fluorescent bulbs. Keith stood nearby and held the bulbs.

There was one outside light left. After several throws with brick pieces, it crushed and the job was complete. Keith and I carried the light bulbs to the Guest House. The soldiers said nothing as we left. A few minutes later, we heard the truck drive away. I am sure they scratched their heads trying to figure out who we were. Perhaps they didn't know what we knew. The owner of that station was in prison on the military base. He had been arrested a few years earlier and accused by Pakistan of being a spy trying to overthrow the government along with Sheik Mujibur Rahman, who, as far as we knew, was still in prison in West Pakistan.

The next day during a short curfew break, I returned the tubes and told them I was the culprit who had broken their glass. No thanks were necessary, but they did thank me for helping them. Someday I hoped to meet Mr. Rahman, the owner of the service station. From the accounts I had read of the trial involving the supposed conspiracy, one of the men had stayed in a small hotel in Feni before crossing into India in their attempt to overthrow the government. That hotel was next door to our library in Feni. But that hope wasn't too strong; because from what we were hearing, no one would survive that military prison. . . .

When we all got settled into the Guest House area, our total number was forty-five—thirty Bengalis and fifteen in our missionary families. The telephone was still working. Rab Chawdhury called, speaking in an almost indistinguishable voice. I feared greatly for Rab. Following the [previous year's] tidal wave, he was the relief coordinator for our Noakhali District and some other areas. He and I talked often during the war. We knew that when the army decided to make an all-out attempt to eliminate leading Bengali government officers, he would be among those. In December of 1970, he had refused to "bow" to a West Pakistani Army major. As a result of this, the major had been transferred back to West Pakistan. If that major were back in East Pakistan now, we well knew that Rab was in trouble because of that confrontation and because he was a faithful Bengali.

Rab and I talked briefly on the phone and agreed to keep in touch daily, either by phone, by my going to his home, or by a messenger from him. Of the three Muslim gentlemen whom I admired the most, Rab was the only one with whom I could talk. Mr. Alam, the diplomat turned farmer, was, as far as we knew, still the Foreign Secretary of the Bangladesh government in exile. The professor was a collaborator with the Pakistan army. So when rumors began spreading that many Bengali government officers were being arrested, I told Betty, "If ever I fail to establish contact with Rab, I will go searching for him and will not return until I have found him or until I know he is dead." . . .

But eventually those evacuation planes came on December 12th. We watched the c-130's of the United States Air Force land quietly at Dacca [Dhaka] Airport. Before that day ended, the evacuation was complete. We didn't have all the facts, but we understood that the only American children left in Dacca were the Thurmans, Debbie Bennett, Lindy Parshall, and ours. . . . As soon as the evacuation planes departed, the war took on a new course. Full scale rocketing and bombing began. It must have been that the Indian Air Force had waited until the foreigners were out of Dacca before they turned on their real strength. The quivering earth told us that the bombs being dropped were larger.

Rumors spread that China was sending planes to aid Pakistan. So the Indian Air Force soon destroyed the runways at the airport by filling it with huge craters to make the Chinese landings impossible.

To me, it was evident—the foreigners were gone; now if necessary, the city could be blasted apart. There would be no international repercussions. This is something of the cheapness of war in Asia. The Bengalis might be blasted into shreds, and little would be said or thought just as it had been for the last nine months. Around the world there were those few who cared, but they were not the ones who could alter decisions already made.

Obviously, the attacks on Dacca were hastening the day of freedom for the Bengalis. So for this, we as a family were glad; but all principles involving the liberation of Bangladesh had been cast aside. The United States was castigating India for her involvement. But she had been strangely silent during the past nine months about the atrocities being committed by the Pakistanis against the Bengalis. If any objections had been made known, they were so silent we did not hear them.

But the United States did not say too much against Pakistan, for it was Pakistan who arranged Kissinger's secret trip to China [in July 1971,] during the time of the Freedom Movement [Bangladesh Liberation War]. Some of us who saw how Bengalis were being slaughtered in 1971 did not think too highly of Mr. Kissinger's widely acclaimed journey to Peking. In fact, I felt it was the blood of the Bengalis that paid the price of his ticket on Pakistan International Airlines.

Now, of course, China was verbally blasting away at India as if she [China] herself were too moral for any such involvement. The Tibetans and South Koreans gave a different assessment of her morality. And the other big bully, Russia, was also piously sounding off at the United Nations as if she [Russia] had been invited into Hungary in 1958 and more recently into Czechoslovakia.

We watched during the day and heard and felt during the night as Indian planes continued saturation bombing and rocketing of Pakistan military installations. Bengalis cheered as the planes struck the military targets during the day, but like us, they feared the night.

During the night following the evacuation of the foreigners, the drone of a plane's propelled engines awakened us from our light sleep. The drone increased. There was no doubt the plane was near the Guest House. Then, all of a sudden, the loudest thud we had ever heard, the greatest shaking the Guest House had ever done, frightened us terribly. Within moments another thud, louder, stronger and closer, jerked our house. By the time we had swallowed, a third, with even more force, tore its way into the earth. There was only room for one thought—the next one would get us. The fourth one made us wonder how much a building could take without a direct hit. But then a beautiful sound brought relief. The plane pulled out of its dive and seemingly touched the top of the Guest House's flat roof. It began its way back into the sky. We trembled but gave thanks that we had made it again. The next day, we discovered that the bombs had been dropped a good distance from the Guest House between us and the airport, but it had seemed to us as if it were next door. . . .

We received word that all remaining foreigners were permitted to stay at the Intercontinental Hotel which had been declared a neutral zone by the International Red Cross. However, we never discussed our going there. The Bengalis with us were not offered that privilege, so what right did we have to it? And hopefully it was apparent that we were not neutral, nor had we been since the brutal plane attack on Feni about eight months before.

A Christian friend, Shova, who was living nearer the airport than we, sent word for me to come. She was living with her three children. I visited her each day since her husband had been transferred to another city by the government. He was a doctor and subject to transfer as often as there was need. Each time Shova seemed to be doing okay; but eventually she asked me, "Mr. McKinley, is there some way you can get me and the children outside of the city? We are especially afraid at night." She continued, "And the soldiers may come at any time. Without my husband I will have trouble." I checked every possible route but there was no way to get them out of the city. We had even discussed this possibility for ourselves earlier but found that it did not seem practical. I reported to Shova the impossibility. Indian troops and Freedom Fighters were now surrounding the city.

Betty told me to invite Shova and her children to the Guest House. I did, but she said, "We will just stay here. It is our home. But come as often as you can and see about us." Shova was not the smiling teenage girl we had known when we first moved to Comilla, her home town, in 1959. But like many others, she had gained courage during the past few months. We still, however, felt a deep responsibility to her and her children.

Soon after the evacuation, foreign news broadcasts began telling of a fleet of American ships entering the Bay of Bengal or that section of the Indian Ocean. Reportedly, they were making their way toward the port city of Chittagong. We heard many rumors as to why they were coming. One was that they were going to challenge the Indian fleet in the Bay. Another was that they were going to pick up all retreating Pakistan soldiers and take them to West Pakistan so that there would be no slaughter by the advancing Indian and Freedom Fighter Forces. Actually, by this time, thousands of Pakistani soldiers had surrendered in the border areas and were being treated as prisoners of war. But the crowning reason given was that the ships were coming to evacuate the few remaining Americans in Dacca and other parts of East Pakistan so that they would not be slaughtered by the Bengalis.

This put us in a most dangerous position. The thought of the presence of American planes from aircraft carriers sent Bengali blood boiling. Who were the Americans to be evacuated? We supposed that we must be in the group. But just a few days before, we had passed by an opportunity for evacuation and were told then that this was our last opportunity. We had accepted that. We had no part in such request for evacuation. The thought of American involvement with India in the Bay of Bengal created new fears for us. But we were helpless by-standers watching and listening to the international game of war. We hoped and prayed that those ships were not really entering the Bay.

The early morning of December 14th, our telephone rang. It was a Christian friend, Sudhir Adhikary. Sudhir said, "Mr. McKinley, Rani is sick. Can some arrangement be made to take her to the hospital?" I quickly answered. "Yes, I will come immediately." But Sudhir said, "There is a curfew. How can it be done?" I replied, "I don't know, but I'm on my way." When we lived in Faridpur, Rani was a most attractive and very sweet young lady. She was now married and living about three blocks from the Guest House. Sudhir, her husband, had spoken in a troubled voice over the telephone. There was no objection from Betty and the children as I hurriedly drove out on the vacant street. I stopped a short distance away at a police road block and kept on the offensive by saying, "I'm on my way to the hospital. Will one of you accompany me?" The reply came, "Oh, no, you can make it okay." That's all I wanted, so in a few minutes I drove up to a locked gate. While the low-flying Indian planes were attacking the paramilitary base nearby, Sudhir came running out. His face, as did all our faces, revealed fear and distress. I asked, "How's Rani?" He replied, "She's coming." Rani didn't look sick—just extremely disturbed. As the planes zoomed over our heads, we hurried over to the brick wall close by. There Sudhir told the terrible story, "Last night Dr. Siddique Ahmed was taken from our apartment building. I know that I also am on the list to be taken, so can you move us to a safer place?" The answer was, "Of course, I can." A Muslim gentleman standing nearby said, "Then will you come take my family?"

We quickly loaded some of their more valuable possessions and made our way to the office of the East Pakistan Christian Council. I breathed a silent prayer for deliverance from road blocks. Sudhir and his family tried to keep out of sight as we moved rapidly. The quietness of the vacant streets felt dangerous. After unloading their things, Sudhir said, "We may have to move again if our location is discovered." I answered, "Let me know if I need to come."

A few minutes later, I was back at the same apartment house and was glad that my vehicle was a microbus because the Muslim family was large. They quickly piled in some of their possessions as I talked to Mrs. Siddique Ahmed. Mrs. Ahmed was Swedish and seemed so helpless in this land of her husband, who was a scientist. Mrs. Ahmed asked, "Do you think you could possibly find where they have taken my husband?" I could only answer, "I don't know, but I will try. Please give me his full name and address." Mrs. Ahmed wrote her husband's name on the back of a calling card. She gave me the card, and I promised to contact her as soon as I learned something. The other family wanted to join relatives on the other side of the city. There was no choice but to take them. We wound through the streets of the old city to places I had never seen. Finally, the gentleman said, "This is it." We banged on a locked gate for several minutes before someone finally peeped out and saw us.

I wished the best for my new friends and made my way to the International Red Cross Office in the Intercontinental Hotel. I passed on the information about Dr. Ahmed. The reply was, "It's been several hours; there isn't much hope of finding him alive, but we will try to contact the army to see if we can learn anything." Of course, as was now the usual, the army denied any knowledge of Dr. Ahmed. But Mrs. Ahmed learned the next morning that her husband's body had been found. The Razakars, the paramilitary unit collaborating with the army, had worked fast and brutally. Dr. Ahmed's crime, like that of many other Bengalis, was that he was educated, he was a leader and he might give trouble. The next morning Howard Teel moved Mrs. Ahmed into the hotel. She was even then making plans for returning to Sweden as a widow whose husband had been brutally slaughtered.

We no longer wondered what the occasional buses were doing passing the Guest House loaded with blindfolded men during curfew. We now knew it was the brutal Razakars hauling away their Bengali prisoners.

The long night of December 14th gnawed savagely at us. The Indian planes attacked constantly. But added to this was the roar and blasts from the Indian heavy artillery on the outskirts of Dacca. . . . The Bengali and Indian military forces had Dacca surrounded. Radio reports revealed that there were about 40,000 Pakistani soldiers well fortified in the city. General Niazi, Commander of the Pakistan forces, swore that he would fight to the last man. The American ships were splitting their way through the waters of the Indian Ocean. There were still threats from China to the north. Time was running out.

Dacca was filled with strong ten-inch walled buildings. Each floor and roofing of most of those buildings was steel reinforced concrete. Nearly every building was surrounded by strong brick walls. The city buildings provided the rugged Pakistani soldiers with the opportunity of surviving any onslaught of the Bengali and Indian ground attack for weeks, or even as a buffer to protect the soldiers. With the continuous swearing by General Niazi to fight to the last man, we expected rough days leading up to Christmas and on into the New Year. I wondered—were we emotionally and spiritually prepared for such a struggle?

We constantly listened to various short-wave radio broadcasts. We had heard the news clearly telling of the advance of the Indian and Bengali forces. Each day, we knew their distance from Dacca. On the morning of December 15th we heard, "The Indian Army has the city of Dacca surrounded. Their planes control the air. General Niazi continues to say he will fight to the last man to hold the city." Such news caused us to tremble. Though thousands had left Dacca in early December, it was estimated that possibly up to 200,000 people were still in the city with no way out. But we were also sure that since we were hearing these shortwave broadcasts, our friends around the world had the same news. Neither we nor these estimated 200,000 Bengalis were forgotten.

Though often we were so low we hardly felt like praying, we knew strong friends were praying.

During the few times of December 15th when the planes were not attacking, there was absolute silence except the bursting of shells on the periphery of the city. There weren't many smiles on our faces. That night it was rather quiet. Only the sounds from planes bombing the army areas north of the airport troubled us.

We had heard rumors that Pakistan was going to surrender, but I didn't believe the Muslim Army had reached the point when it was ready to surrender to an army dominated by Indian Hindus. From what I knew of the city, before India and the Bengalis could take it, the Pakistan army was in a position to kill two or even three of their opposition before one of their own men died.

On the early morning of December 16th, I climbed the steps leading to the flat roof of the Guest House. Only one Indian plane was in the sky. The burst of shells could be heard and smoke seen in the distance, but the city was not being attacked. It seemed that this was the calm before the storm. But thanks to God I was wrong. We were sitting in the death trap, but the radio news said, "General Niazi has been ordered to surrender his forces in East Pakistan." With that statement, there was no more East Pakistan to

Freedom Fighters, 1971. Used by permission of the Heritage Archives of Bangladesh History, Rajshahi.

anyone. Suddenly, we saw—we experienced, the birth of a giant nation—the world's eighth largest in population. Bangladesh, the nation of the Bengalis was born. And we felt like one of them.

Within an hour's time, hundreds of fully armed Pakistan soldiers came from every direction and moved north up the road by the Guest House toward the army base to surrender to the Indian Army. We had no idea that so many of them had been in hiding near us waiting for the arrival of their would-be attackers. The Pakistani soldiers' heads drooped low as they dragged their feet. For thirteen days, they had been under heavy attacks from the air. Most of them had had little sleep. They seemed hardly able to carry their rifles. From this problem, some of them received help as Bengali young men ran out into the streets and pulled at their rifles. Some of them handed the rifles to the Bengalis.

Within that same hour, the Bengali and Indian soldiers poured into the city. The first main entrance into the city was from the west down the road by our Guest House. So we were in the welcoming group. The Bengalis went wild. Everywhere we looked, there were people carrying rifles, firing them wildly into the air. Some little boys had to drag theirs, for they were too heavy to carry.

Some young men ran past the Guest House changing clothes as they ran. We knew they were the Razakars, who had collaborated with the army. They were quickly trying to change their appearance.

The police vacated the station just south of the Guest House, since some of them had been collaborators. Civilians ransacked the station carrying away pistols, rifles and other weapons as well as boxes of shells. Though we sensed a new danger, we too, were caught up in the excitement of freedom. Our children, along with Debbie Bennett, the Thurman boys and the Bengali children, stood by the gate waving wildly to the victorious soldiers as they continued to enter the city. Gloria Thurman helped Cherie and Kathy make a Bangladesh flag. We raised it on top of the Guest House. But even before that, the first flag we saw in free Bangladesh was one that Marj Bennett pulled out of hiding as soon as the surrender was announced. The children, standing by the gate, drew wild applause when the little flag was seen.

Indian soldiers stopped by the Guest House to inquire who we were and if we were okay. Bangladesh was free. That was all that counted right then.

The Diary's Final Pages

Mahbub Alam

The Bangladesh Liberation War pitted peasants, schoolchildren, students, and a handful of soldiers against the well-equipped professionals of the Pakistani armed forces. The Muktijoddha (Freedom Fighters) formed a large assemblage of guerrilla units. Many of these worked together closely, increasingly with Indian support and guidance. Other units remained largely autonomous throughout the nine-month war. Mahbubul Alam was one of these Freedom Fighters. He had left his student days for the hard life in the trenches. Throughout the war he kept a detailed personal diary that was published in book form in 1993. Here we reproduce the diary's last pages. We find Mahbubul Alam and his unit in northwestern Bangladesh, a fort-night after the Indian armed forces had invaded East Pakistan/Bangladesh to fight alongside the indigenous Mukti Bahini (Freedom Fighters). These final pages tell us how they heard about the end of the war and how intense happiness swept over them when they realized liberation had finally been achieved.

16 *December 1971 (afternoon):* It was afternoon when Captain Khaleque approached us with his familiar gait. A few soldiers accompanied him. We were lying in our bunkers, passing through a rather sluggish period. General Rao Farman Ali had been given an ultimatum to surrender. But so far no signals had come from him. On the other hand, it was all quiet on the battle front. No attacks on the part of the combined forces (the Indian troops and the Mukti Bahini), just the news that Bhatga had been occupied. Furthermore, the Indian Army had constructed a temporary bridge across the river next to the original bridge and had advanced to the ten-mile point with a convoy of tanks. A section of the Mukti Bahini was among the Indian Army's foot soldiers. Our Bablu, Motiar, and Ekramullah were with them. I asked the captain:

"Where are you off to, *dadu* [elder brother, a respectful term for an older man]?"

"Oh, just here. Come, let's go and see what's happening at the gruel kitchen. It's tough having to pass time like this."

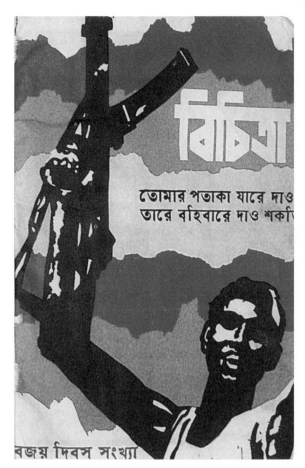

Triumphant Freedom Fighter. Depicted on the cover of the first Victory Day issue of the magazine *Bichitra*, December 1972. Used by permission of the Heritage Archives of Bangladesh History, Rajshahi.

"Okay, let's go."

And taking Pintu with us, we took off. Our walkie-talkie set had not been working for the last few days because it lacked batteries, but yesterday the batteries were replaced. I asked Pintu to take it along. You never knew when some instructions might come.

The gruel kitchen was a twenty- to twenty-five-minute walk away. It was located in a big dilapidated rice mill. All our food was cooked there. It engaged the labor of countless volunteers who took up this work with unrivaled dedication and commitment, regardless of the hostile environment and in the face of grave danger. Using traditional bamboo poles, they carried food from the kitchen to each of the bunkers and trenches on the battlefront. Many had to give their lives for this job. On the very first day that I took part in combat on the front line, I saw four such food carriers from Chaitanyapara being blown to bits by a bomb. There must have been innumerable similar stories elsewhere.

The workers in the gruel kitchen were busy preparing the evening meal. The commanding lieutenant came over to greet us. Everyone got busy finding us a place to sit. They all seemed happy with such a casual visit. The lieutenant arranged for tea and snacks. He started to talk to Captain Khaleque about some of the problems he was facing. We also exchanged news about the war in general. Finally we got ready to head back to our posts.

It was around 4 P.M. We had left Birganj and were nearing our post. Suddenly from our walkie-talkie came Captain Shahriar's voice:

"Two-four-one, two-four-one, can you hear me? Over."

I responded: "One-four-two. One-four-two. Loud and clear. Over."

"Congratulations, Mahbub! Great news! The Pakistani forces have surrendered this afternoon on the Racecourse in Dhaka! Over."

"Congratulations, Sir! This is great news! The war is over then! Independence has come at last! Over."

"Yes, boys! Spread this happy news to all the bunkers and trenches. But be in control, boys. Do not celebrate today. There is much work ahead of us. Over."

"Okay, Sir. We shall spread the word to everybody! Over."

"There are some Pakistani soldiers scattered along the Bhatga River on the Saidpur battlefront. They may surrender today. You must follow the rules of surrender. No one will be asleep tonight on the front. No celebrations tonight. You must stay alert. Tonight may be the last night of our toil. Tomorrow we celebrate. Do you understand? Over."

"Yes, Sir. Your instructions will be followed word for word. As field commander, on behalf of everyone here, I am sending you and Subsector Commander Saddruddin our heartiest congratulations. Over."

"Thanks. Over."

"Over."

As soon as our conversation was over, Captain Khaleque embraced me and burst into tears of joy! My second in command, Pintu, was also beside himself. He grabbed me first and then suddenly let go and started a revolving dance with hands in the air, shouting: "independence, independence, liberation, liberation, surrender, surrender!" And finally that undying slogan that we had all been waiting for ripped through his throat: "Joy Bangla [Victory to Bangladesh] . . . !"

The wintry evening descended on us. Mist covered us from all sides. Captain Khaleque took his soldiers and made his way back to his B-Company [army unit] outpost. Pintu and I returned to our Madhupara Company outpost. We spread the good news to every bunker, every trench. We instructed everyone about the steps that needed to be taken when the Pakistani soldiers wanted to surrender. The boys did not want to let us go. They embraced us emotionally. There was sheer joy in their eyes and faces. They were unstoppable. The sounds of celebration and slogans of "Joy Bangla" surged like waves across the battlefronts that night.

It was around 8 P.M. when we returned to our bunker underneath the bamboo grove. It was then that we witnessed a festival of flames. At first, one of the thatched roofs of a bunker was set ablaze, and then another, and so on. In seconds, the bunkers on the whole battlefront turned into flames, accompanied by shouts of sheer joy and people madly rushing helter-skelter. The news of freedom could not hold anyone down.

The whole night passed like that. Eventually dawn peeked through. It was still dark inside the bunker. I told Pintu to strike a match. I took up the notebook that I used to write my diary in. I felt an inner urge to record these special moments of freedom. I started writing. Pintu struck match after match and I kept writing! Dawn pierced through the misty shadows. The blood-red sphere of the sun emerged in the sky of an independent Bangladesh. . . .

17 December 1971: Finally dawn emerges, the first dawn in independent Bangladesh. How many times in one lifetime do you see a sunrise like this! It is washed in the blood of one million martyrs. That is perhaps why it appears redder than usual.

The time has come for us to return. The pain and suffering of the last nine months have come to an end. Soon we will go home. Families, friends, dear ones—how are they; how have they fared? Who is alive; who has died? Is it going to be a happy reunion, or a sad one? Who knows. . . .

But no, we are not dead. Some are but, like many others, I am alive and victorious in this war of independence! If Golam Gaus were alive today, or Akkas, or Motiar [fallen comrades], what harm would it be to anyone? If there is a soul, then surely their souls must be happy today, satisfied. Until this day their souls have craved revenge, but today they are fulfilled.

I shall always remember this area of Birganj. We have defended this area, and it is in this area that we first experience freedom. Now is the time for assessment. From guerrilla war to front-line combat, the experiences have been incredible. I have learned so much. Life in bunkers and trenches, hands and feet frozen, eating and living in many different conditions, and so on. And, of course, our dealing with the EPR [East Pakistan Rifles]. I got to know many people, many characters, characters who will remain ingrained in my memory forever: Khaleque, Shahdat, Mossadeq, Barek, Shafi, Doctor, Lieutenant Masud, and many others inside and outside Bangladesh. On such a day I should write about everybody, I suppose, including her. How is she, I wonder? Fine, I hope, and keep my fingers crossed.

Translated from Bengali by Meghna Guhathakurta

The Jagannath College Concentration Camp

Basanti Guhathakurta

Women's memoirs bring out special dimensions of the war, such as intricate de-
tails of everyday life and the struggle for physical and mental survival. Basanti
Guhathakurta was the headmistress of a girl's school in old Dhaka. Right at the
beginning of the war, during the crackdown of the Pakistan Army on 25 March
1971, she witnessed the execution of her husband who was a professor of English at
the University of Dhaka. Fearing for her life and that of her young daughter, she
had to go into hiding. For the full nine months of the war, she moved from house to
house and from shelter to shelter, being protected by friends and sympathizers. She
wrote about these experiences in her memoirs Ekattorer Smriti *(Memories of '71).*
Here is her description of her visit, just after the end of the war, to the campus of a
college that was reported to have been a torture center used by the Pakistan armed
forces.

It must have been either the twenty-second or twenty-third [of January 1972]
that I went to Jagannath College with Suraiya. Classes had not yet begun.
She was just going to have a look around. She taught philosophy there.

We climbed the stairs [from the ground floor] to the first floor of the old
building and wandered around the veranda. After exchanging a few words
with the guard, we were coming down when we noticed that a middle-aged
man wearing a *lungi* [sarong] and a soiled vest was following us. I suddenly
realized that he had silently followed us up from below. As we reached
the bottom of the stairs, we wondered for a while where to go from there.
Suraiya had heard of a room where people had been brought to be tortured.
They had brought a colleague's brother there. Her husband had somehow
managed to get him free.

The man asked us, "Do you want to go to that room, *apa* [sister]?" I was
thinking whether the man was a spy, or just demented. I asked, "Which
room?" He replied, "*That* room. . . . Where they used to take everyone to
be killed."

I shuddered and asked, "Who are you?" He replied, "I am the guardian

of one of your students. My daughter is Malati. She studied at your school. I
too was brought here. I don't know how I escaped."

I turned and took a good look at him. He was fair. His face, round and
broad, had such a shadow that it seemed he had put up stage makeup. Where
was Malati, I wondered? Was she no longer alive? Why was her father wandering these dark corridors? Was he crazy? Then I asked him, "Will you take
us to that room?"

Just past the college gate at the left are the principal's living quarters,
and behind the garden is a row of newly built two-storied buildings. We re-
traced our footsteps to the bottom of the staircase there. The man led us to
the room that people had come to call "the red room." We took the narrow
veranda facing south. There was no lock on the door. With one push of his
hand, he opened the door.

It was a big room, with a few benches and desks littered across it. There
was blood on the floor and on the benches, and the desks had blood splat-
tered on top. The most horrifying scene was where some hapless victim
must have been speared on a bayonet and the blood gushing from his heart
was sprayed high on the eastern walls. The walls all around bore witness to
this bloody episode, the stains appearing like sparklers in the night. In one
place the blood had trickled down the walls, onto the desks, and from there
it had clotted in a thick mass on the floor.

We could not bear to stay there much longer. A silence-filled terror struck
us. But even so, our guide, Malati's father, kept on saying, "Look, apa, this
must be where they dragged the bodies through the door on to the narrow
corridor and staircase." We saw the foot-wide brush mark of blood gradually thinning out as it reached the stairs. Our knees started to quiver.

Our guide must have had more eyewitness stories to tell us. We did not
ask him, we *could* not ask him, and the stories remained untold. A silence
enfolded us as we got into our car. The man put his palms together to say
farewell. My head was spinning, my throat parched. I tried to moisten my
mouth with my saliva. It was only on reaching Suraiya's house that I could
regain my strength with a cup of hot tea.

I never told anyone about this experience, not even my daughter. The
face of Malati's father haunted me night and day. Where was Malati? How
was she? Was she alive? Why couldn't I bring myself to ask our guide about
her, about her family? Did he come to tell me something as a guardian, as a
father? Why did I not ask him about her? Now, in March 1990, after so many
years, I am thinking I must have been mad not to do so. I must have lost
my senses.

Translated from Bengali by Meghna Guhathakurta.

Stranded Pakistanis ("Biharis")

Ben Whittaker

The tearing apart of Pakistan was particularly heart wrenching for the millions who had fled or migrated to the country after partition. Among them were many Urdu speakers from northern India. Initially they were called Muhajirs (migrants), but in East Pakistan they soon became known as Biharis, a term of reproof referring to their privileged positions and their inability to speak Bengali. Many "Biharis" were not from Bihar at all but from other parts of India. The events of 1971 were a moment of truth for them. Would they uphold the dream of a united Pakistan (and side with the Pakistan Army)? Or would they join the movement for independence?

This piece, written just after the war, shows that many "Biharis" were victimized just before the war broke out, that the Pakistani authorities actively sought to recruit and use them during the war, that many atrocities were attributed to them, and that they were demonized after the war. Driven together in camps and denied citizenship for many years, many considered themselves stranded Pakistanis and sought to be repatriated to Pakistan.

After Yahya Khan on 1 March 1971 postponed the promised National Assembly, Bengalis turned on the Biharis as Urdu-speaking targets that were readily available as symbols of the Pakistani domination. Over 300 of them were killed by extremist mobs at Chittagong in early March 1971. There were other attacks at Jessore, Khulna, Rangpur and Saidpur. A further slaughter at Mymensingh caused a large influx of Biharis into the Mirpur suburb of Dacca. The Urdu-speaking community claim that in all several thousands of their people were killed by pro-Bengali supporters of secession prior to the Pakistani army's ruthless intervention on 25 March 1971. Further reprisals against the Biharis followed when Yahya Khan arrested Sheikh Mujib and outlawed the Awami League.

For local support, the Pakistani army created an auxiliary force, the Razakars, one wing of which (Al-Shams) was mainly—but not entirely—composed of young Biharis. Some Biharis were only conscripted into this by force; others ran considerable risks to shelter Bengali friends from persecution, and some even surreptitiously helped the Mukti Bahini by night. But when civil bloodshed broke out on a large scale in 1971, there is no doubt that numbers of the Razakar Biharis seized the opportunity to take their revenge on the Bengalis, slaughtering, raping and looting alongside undisciplined Pakistanis.

The Pakistani authorities had also made a practice of appointing Biharis to replace educated Hindus in many key jobs in the administration, as well as in the railway workshops and jute mills. For its part, the Bihari community remained blind to the growing rise of the Bangladeshi movement under Sheikh Mujibur Rahman—and indeed a few of them today still appear unable to accept that Bangladesh is a permanent fact. Three million has become established as the number of people who were killed in all during the period of terror between March and December 1971. It is a situation where rumours and exaggerations, from all sides, easily take root—and continue to do so. The Pakistanis say the total was very much fewer. The true number will never be known; but it is the accepted legendary figure which continues to have an effect on Bangladeshi emotions. Even after the Pakistani army had capitulated in East Bengal, the Al-Badr massacred several hundred Bengali intellectuals in Dacca, and the Bihari community as a whole continue to be popularly blamed in particular for the deaths of these Bangladeshi martyrs.

In fact, the Al-Badr was a predominantly Bengali Razakar organisation.

On Bangladesh's independence in December 1971, most of the West Pakistani civilians here were evacuated to India, along with the defeated army. But the Biharis were left behind as castaways. Outside observers feared there would be a general massacre; but this did not take place, although several thousand of the Bihari leaders were arrested and their shops and homes were robbed and occupied. The Indian army, while it remained, protected the Biharis from reprisals as much as possible, for their safety they were grouped in the enclaves in which they are now living. Water and power were cut off from these areas, but the Biharis were too terrified to move out of them in search of food or work, for fear of being killed or held for ransom. Their former houses and shops continue to be occupied and their property looted by Bengalis whose hatred against the Biharis is repeatedly being refuelled by the nationalistic local press. The dispossessed Biharis in the camps have now sold for food almost all the belongings with which they fled.

Following the Indian army's withdrawal on 27 January 1972, a sharp struggle took place in the Bihari enclave at Mirpur. When Bangladeshi soldiers and Mukhti [Mukti Bahini, Freedom Fighters] irregulars on the night of 28/29 January carried out a search to enforce the Sheikh's order that all arms must be surrendered, they were forcibly resisted by Pakistani remnants who had taken refuge there. At least one hundred persons on each side were killed, and this incident seems to have had an important effect on the Sheikh's own attitude towards the Biharis. It had largely been the authority of the Sheikh, together with the universal respect in which he is held in Bangladesh, which had previously prevented any massive bloodbath of vengeance after the Pakistani collapse. At first the Bangabandhu [Friend of Bengal, a respectful reference to Sheikh Mujibur Rahman] had been personally well disposed towards reconciliation with the Biharis—his wife is reported to have been helped by some of them during the period of terror—and his first speech on his return in triumph to Dacca emphasised the place all peoples had in Bangladesh. But he has made little effort since then to translate this ideal into practical steps, nor to give any real public lead to encourage Bengalis to distinguish those Biharis who were collaborators of the Pakistanis from the larger number of Bihari families, including widows and children, who can have committed no crime. The words "collaborator" and "miscreant" are rapidly becoming the shorthand means of denouncing any element—including economic rivals or political opponents—whom the militant Mukti Bahini [Freedom Fighters] wish to see eliminated. Government speeches castigating "trouble-makers" and "lawless elements" are often interpreted by extremist nationalists as referring to the Biharis rather than their hooligan persecutors.

Party over State

Willem van Schendel

*Many Bangladeshis expected the postwar recovery to be quick. Now that West Paki-
stani economic exploitation had ceased, a very popular government had come to
power, and the world was extending aid to the new country, things were rapidly
going to get better. These expectations soon proved to have been too optimistic.*

After the war the institutions of state were weak and in disarray. Many senior positions in the bureaucracy and armed forces lay vacant because their
occupants had been from West Pakistan. These institutions as well as the
political parties now became arenas of factional struggle between those who
had actively supported independence from exile in India and those who had
tried to weather the storm of 1971 inside Bangladesh. The weak new state
was confronted with enormous challenges: it needed to disarm groups of
freedom fighters and establish law and order, run the newly nationalised
industries, restore the infrastructure and become a player in the international state system. Most importantly, the state had to deliver economic
development. The promise of emancipation from political domination by
Pakistan had been fulfilled; now the government would be judged on its
performance regarding its other promise: to emancipate the delta from economic exploitation, poverty and stagnation.

In a feeble state confronted with high popular expectations, the role of
a charismatic leader is crucial. [Sheikh] Mujib relied on his personal popularity and political intuition to tackle the new challenges. It was an almost
impossible balancing act and it soon became clear that he had been far more
effective as an opposition leader than he was as a statesman—fiery rhetoric
was more his style than forceful governance. He was unable to transform
his personal relationship with his followers into an established authority
structure independent of his personal qualifications. In an eerie replay of
the late 1940s and early 1950s—when the Muslim League had been unable to
switch from being the engine of the movement for Pakistan to being an effective ruling party—the early 1970s saw a steep erosion of the popularity of

the Awami League. Among the reasons were a blossoming personality cult (which reminded people of the Ayub era), the attempt to dub the state ideology "Mujibism" (*mujibbād*), charges of undue Indian influence in Bangladesh, and reports of widespread corruption and nepotism in the party. But these were not the main reason: the government squandered its popularity chiefly because it was seen to contribute to a deep malaise in the economy.

After the war many Bangladeshis, expecting a rapid recovery of the economy, were shocked to see that the living standard of the majority of the population did not improve. On the contrary, it kept on falling. Economic productivity lagged far behind the pre-war level and by 1973 agricultural and industrial production had declined to 84 and 66 per cent respectively of what they had been just before the war. The real income of agricultural and industrial labourers went down drastically. For example, the cost of living for agricultural labourers increased by 150 per cent as overall real incomes slumped to 87 per cent of what they had been in 1970.

What was going on? Partly, it was a matter of inexperience. Many top positions in the state were now occupied by politicians and bureaucrats who had been suddenly promoted from the middle ranks of a provincial government to the highest rank of a national one; they needed time to learn their jobs. Another factor was that most members of the power elite assumed that the removal of Pakistani exploitation by itself would lead to an economic resurgence, and hence they paid more attention to political, legal and diplomatic matters than to economic ones. Third, the economic circumstances had changed enormously. Gone were Pakistan's "twenty-two families" [who had dominated the national economy] and their allies, the landlords and armed forces. Instead, economic power was now in the hands of the delta's surplus farmers, small-scale entrepreneurs and industrial trade unions. Each expected that its support for the Awami League would translate into greatly expanded economic opportunities.

These dynamics exacerbated the economic muddle and prevented the new regime from developing a social agenda. Further problems arose from its failure to create a professional, politically neutral state bureaucracy that could have implemented its policies effectively. Instead, it engaged in an abundant politics of patronage that continues to plague the Bangladesh state machinery today. In independent Bangladesh, ruling-party loyalty supersedes state interest. Rulers use the state to further their party rather than the other way around.

The Awami League was plagued by internal rivalries and sought to secure its members' commitment by creating networks of patronage that colonised the state. It appointed party loyalists, often irrespective of their administrative competence, to key positions in the state bureaucracy. This dominance of party-political considerations forestalled any coherent economic policy, let alone its implementation. Awami League ideologues could not reach a consensus over the correct national and socialist development policies and, worse, despite high-minded rhetoric and much suffering during the Pakistan period and the liberation war, the Awami League "had not imbued its leaders or members with idealism to work selflessly for the reconstruction of the war-ravaged country."[1]

Awami League rule soon turned out to be a case of party over nation. Management of the nationalised enterprises was handed to inexperienced political activists, leading to a sharp drop in production and a sharp rise in managerial wealth. Similarly, import licences, distributed among Awami League protégés, became a rich source of illegal pickings, partly by means of smuggling imported goods, jute and rice to India. Thugs with connections in the Awami League became notorious for extortion and Awami League leaders used a new paramilitary force—the Rokkhi Bahini (National Security Force)—to spread fear through intimidation and torture. Mujib was aware of the "blatant abuse of power and corrupt practices of his party people"[2] but, always the party loyalist, did nothing to stop them.

Notes

1. Talukder Maniruzzaman, *The Bangladesh Revolution and Its Aftermath* (Dacca: Bangladesh Books International, 1980), 159.
2. S. A. Karim, *Sheikh Mujib: Triumph and Tragedy* (Dhaka: University Press Limited, 2005), 289.

VI

Dilemmas of Nationhood

In postindependence Bangladesh, national identity has never been stable. On the contrary, it has been the subject of many political and ideological rifts, which is why we devote an entire part to it. The two main constructions of nationhood revolve around being either Bengali or Bangladeshi, between a language-based and a religion-based national identity. This part looks at these competing notions of nationhood in Bangladesh with a third eye: to seek diversity of interpretation as well as to interrogate aspects of the current common-sense understandings of nationhood.

The texts in this part look at the disputed terrain of nationhood in Bangladesh through various lenses. The first two texts provide an overview. They approach the subject from two angles: culture and ecology. In the 1950s the cultural perspective converged on language; the third text shows how budding Bengali-language nationhood manifested itself in the creation of symbols such as the Central Shohid Minar (Martyrs' Memorial). The next text reveals the continuing relevance of these symbols; student activists who demonstrate against state violence and other injustices gravitate toward them.

But the construction of the Bangladesh nation is not merely a contest between religious and secular configurations. Added dimensions are provided by ethnicity and gender. In the 1970s an ethno-nationalist movement in the southeast of the country took up arms to fight for autonomy. It was a major regional challenge to both the linguistically conceived Bengali nation and its religiously inspired counterpart. It took more than twenty years for a peace accord to be signed by the government of Bangladesh and the representatives of this autonomy movement. This accord is a landmark, and we reproduce core excerpts here. We see a state that considers itself as unitary and presiding over one nation and yet has to find a way to accommodate regional forces and devolve power to them. The absence of consensus with regard to the accord has led to a major political fissure in the regional movement and to successive national governments falling short of full implementation of the peace accord.

A wall mosaic on a street in Dhaka shows symbols of the nation: freedom fighters with flags displaying the territory of Bangladesh, the National Martyrs' Memorial in Savar, and the national flower, the water lily. Photograph by Willem van Schendel, 2006.

The gender dimension is brought out by another text that takes its cue from the same regional movement. At the national level, both internal and external dynamics have forced the "woman question" onto the mainstream political agenda. But the disappearance of a woman activist, the organizing secretary of Hill Women's Federation, caused her personal writings and her views on gender relations within her own movement to come to light. Her diary had a major impact on ideas of nationhood and the agenda of her political associates.

Two pieces by Amena Mohsin dissect core terms of nationalist discourse in Bangladesh. The first explains how *Bangladeshi* can have two quite distinct meanings; the second explains that *secular* has very specific connotations in Bangladesh—religious tolerance rather than a separation of state and religious institutions.

Following these explanations, we include two contributions about interpreting the nation from a religious point of view. Islam is the dominant religion, and there are a variety of Islamic discourses in Bangladesh. These interact with nationalism in different and mutable ways. The contributions we include both underscore the current tensions between the international appeal of Islam and the national context in which it is practiced.

Three final entries revisit the instability of national identity that has been a hallmark of independent Bangladesh. The first explores the alternation of military and parliamentary aspirations. The second looks at the continual tinkering with the constitution of 1972 and presents the most recent, fifteenth, change. The last text is a newspaper columnist's humorous critique of a common presentation of the nation—as victim.

What Makes Us a Nation?

Abdur Razzaq

In Bangladesh the discourse on nationhood has been anything but a debate in the calm and quiet atmosphere of academia. It has been at the center of very public ideological strife, and contested amid the clamor and chaos of the streets and in the popular media. In the process, the two mainstream political parties—Awami League and Bangladesh Nationalist Party—elaborated two polarized and incompatible versions of the nation. The former presents Bengali nationalism as its ideological cornerstone, and the latter claims Bangladeshi nationalism. In the suffocating climate of political deadlock in the 1980s, Abdur Razzaq's perceptive and thoughtful treatise—part of his Muzaffar Ahmed Choudhuri memorial lecture—brought a breath of fresh air. Abdur Razzaq (1914–99) was a much-admired teacher of political science at Dhaka University; he was given the distinction of National Professor in 1975.

The nation of which we speak is about 80 million strong; God willing, it is likely to be in the year 2000 A.D. nearly 115 million. The habitat is approximately 55 thousand square miles today and we assume, will continue to be that in 2000 A.D. It is probably the most densely populated 55 thousand square miles on earth. The volume of production, processed, semi-processed and unprocessed, after necessary exercise gives us nearly the lowest per capita income in the world. These indubitable and unflattering facts have enabled international jesters to exercise their wit at the expense of Bangladesh. We have heard epithets such as "international basket case."

It is possible to make a catalogue of unflattering facts about other people and nations at other times. Even as late as the middle of the 19th century the British press did not have a very flattering view of American commercial morality. Spain in her heyday entertained a rather poor view of England. A hundred years ago Japan, or the USSR, would have been very differently described than they are today. The facts, singly or even taken in conjunction are not particularly meaningful, or at least lend themselves to very different meanings. For one thing, I do not know of any developing society, which has effected the development with a declining or stationary population. In fact, a decline in society has invariably showed itself in a stationary or declining population. No doubt, there is in a society, at least in an isolated society, a definite ratio between food production and its population, which it is dangerous to ignore. But changes in food habits—one has only to notice that changes in the pattern of food consumption in the developed western world during the past 150 years—are sometimes far more important than strenuous, nearly futile attempts at increasing the cereal quota of food production and consumption of a society. There is no doubt that misconceived and misguided policy decisions may sometimes retard desirable consummation. But the point we are trying to make is that one has to go more deeply into the obvious hard facts before these can be used as data to describe the state of the nation.

To begin with, how firm is the foundation of the nation we are considering? Nearly 75 years ago the Bengali-speaking people of the British Indian Empire, at least the vocal and vociferous section of it, vowed to unsettle a settled fact and to a large extent succeeded in unsettling it. The Bengali-speaking people were to live together ever after, presumably happily too. In 35 years' time a vocal and vociferous section of the Bengali-speaking people, albeit a minority section of the Bengali-speaking people, would have nothing to do with a future in which it did not have the right to lose itself in the great identity of an Indian nation. I do not know how well it has succeeded in its renunciatory task: of course there has always been a strand of thought developed in the sub-continent which has glorified in losing itself in a greater identity. But the majority of the Bengali-speaking people, not altogether unwilling to go it alone, outside India and Pakistan, eventually opted to merge itself in the new nation state of Pakistan, but not without reservation. The reservation resulted in the Language Movement [to make the Bengali language a state language of Pakistan], the end product of which is the new nation state of Bangladesh.

Of the developing or underdeveloped states of the world[,] Bangladesh is probably the most homogeneous. Even among the developed nations there are not many ... which are as fortunate. In speaking of the state of my nation I intend to count all my blessings, major and minor. And this homogeneity is not a minor blessing. Important as the fact of homogeneity is, I believe what is far more important is the use we make of the fact of homogeneity. To this aspect of the question I shall revert later. When I speak of homogeneity I do not have in mind only the rather elusive ethnicity of the people. The Bengali-speaking people of the subcontinent is the residuary legatee of hordes of people coming principally from Northwest and Northeast India. There are also descendants of those who came from across the seas. The result is an interesting but ethnically difficult to define identity, not very different from the situation obtaining elsewhere in the world. The institutional framework bears traces of experience in distant lands in other times. The ideas which can be traced in the everyday practices of the people are again common to many people, [and] by now very different from this Bengali-speaking nation. The cultural heritage in art and architecture, in music or in poetry, is peculiar to the land and its people, but the family resemblance to similar ventures elsewhere is unmistakable.

The manner in which a people dresses itself, houses itself or dresses its food, or conducts its ceremonials, or lays down what it believes to be rule of etiquette is peculiar to itself but not uninfluenced by practices and ideas obtaining elsewhere in other places in the world in similar fields. The sub-continent can be the subject of a mapmaking venture in which a large number of maps will result[,] depicting the various arts, music or painting; styles of housing or organizing its villages; dressing themselves or dressing their food—not one of which will be exactly coterminous with another, yet each containing what is peculiar to itself and distinct from others in the sub-continent.

The most abiding product of the genius of a people, its language, is neither the product of labour in isolation or unshared by other people. The language of our nation is also the language of a part of the great nation in India—Surendra Nath Banerjee's nation in the making. With us it is the language of a nation, a national language. With our neighbours across the border in West Bengal it is a regional language, a very important one but not a national language. The resultant literatures, since 1947, are noticeably distinct. Impact of ecumenical forces is strong across the border, as well as with us. Hopes and aspirations enshrined in our literature could and did impart a driving force behind our language movement, a movement that inexorably led us on to the founding of the Nation State of Bangladesh. The literature in West Bengal, a more sophisticated, a maturer literature, bears no sign which would prepare us for a language movement there. Bricks and mortars are there, but there seems to be no design which could result in an architecture. In so assessing the situation I take note of what is there, but I also take note of what is not there, in the great literature of west Bengal. It seems improbable that we shall again hear the voice of a Bankim or Dwijendra Lal or a Rabindranath [Bankim Chandra Chattopadhyay, Dwijendra Lal Ray, and Rabindranath Tagore were famous Bengali writers and poets] speaking of the *sat koti santaner, he mugdha janani* [O, affectionate mother of seventy million]. . . . The erudition of a Jadunath [the historian Jadunath Sarkar] speaking of the lonely furrow of Bengal away from the main stream of Indian life and civilization does not seem to have a hearer, not in West Bengal. West Bengal is a victim, perhaps a willing victim, of the siren call of Indian civilization.

The nation in Bangladesh is a nation because it intends to be a nation and nothing else. Enumeration of all that is peculiar to itself or all that it shares with a lot of other people, dead cargo or live heritage, would not explain or explain away the nation. The unbending pride, the shared identity with 80 million people in weal and in woe, the insistence on being a Bengali and nothing else, this is what makes the nation. Patriotism, a wise Greek had observed, is the act of falling in love with one's own country, its mountains and rivers, with whatever else God or nature has endowed it, including, of course, its people. A man falls in love with a woman or a woman does fall in love with a man not because she or he is the most perfect specimen of her or his kind[,] and he or she does fall in love and thereby begins the greatest adventure of life. It does not take a great deal of learning to know the greatness of heritage coming from Assyria, Chaldea, Egypt or Greece or Rome or Arabia or Iran or the more recent contributions of Red Russia, the nature and significance of which is being so hotly debated in Moscow and Peking, echoed all over the world, [in] Dacca too. This nation of ours has nothing to offer comparable to all this or any of these. Yet, what holds us together, makes of us a nation, is the exclusive passion of each to identify himself with this nation and nothing else. This, I believe, is what makes *Bangabandhu* [Sheikh Mujibur Rahman] the central figure of our time. In assessing the state of nation, the prospect the nation has before it, it is relevant to go a little into what may be called the driving force behind the phenomenon that is *Bangabandhu*. What made him tick? What are his claims to be the central figure in Bangladesh? Why did *Bangabandhu* do whatever he did? Why was the man so careless of his own safety? The least care could easily provide against this slapstick comedy drama which ended so tragically. But has it ended? That is the point one has to explore in any exploration of the state of the nation. Of course no one is, of however heroic a proportion, a hero all the 24 hours a day. With this reservation, there is no doubt that *Bangabandhu* was a man by love possessed, love of his own country in the widest sense of the term. This love that possessed the man, I am afraid, is considerably different from the rather tepid sentiment . . . all of us entertain for our country and try to pass off for the love of our country. *Bangabandhu* was a good enough Muslim, in certain respects almost puritanic. Earlier in life he was a loyal member of the Muslim League and an ardent supporter of the idea of Pakistan[,] doing his bit to actualize the idea. Long before the end he had absolutely surrendered himself to his last and lasting passion. He was by love possessed for that bit of the world that we call Bangladesh. Such love can be dangerous as it proved to be for *Bangabandhu*. This obsessive[,] possessive passion tends to render one blind to everything else, particularly when the love is requited. From 25th March 1971 to 10th January 1972 *Bangabandhu* is totally absent from the scene where unequal forces are locked in a deadly struggle. *Bangabandhu* and *Bangabandhu* alone is the symbol round which the adherents of the forlorn cause group themselves. And that is no accident. In those dark days, in that testing time, among the millions who would constitute the nation, there was no misunderstanding and there was no ambiguity. *Bangabandhu* alone was the symbol. But there have been other symbols in the long freedom struggle in the subcontinent. Between this one, the symbol in 1971, and others before him, there is a qualitative difference. To take only two examples: Gandhi and Jinnah. Either of them could sway millions, make them do their biddings. Jinnah, a man of the highest integrity, of very great forensic skill, a dedicated public man, had, after due deliberation, espoused a cause which he believed to be righteous and brought it to a more or less successful conclusion. It is rather difficult to associate Jinnah with that rather untidy passion, love, to motivate him.

Gandhi was different. He did preach and practise love. But that was because love was Dharma—Dharma for all men. He belonged to the world. It was accidental that he was an Indian. We denude it of all meaning when we try to assess his politics without taking note of the deep religious nature of the man. He did many things which pertained to this world. He was never out of politics. But whatever he did, he did it because it was religious duty to do it. He was a medieval man in the best sense of the term. Important as this life was, it was with him but a mere appendix to the far more important life to come, the everlasting life in God. Both of them counted adherents by the millions. It would not have entered the head of any of these millions to regard Jinnah or Gandhi as one of themselves. This is the difference, large as life, between *Bangabandhu* on the one hand and Jinnah and Gandhi on the other. *Bangabandhu* had forged an indivisible fusion between himself and the nation.

The millions who had identified themselves with *Bangabandhu* in 1971, what did they have in common with this man and were [they] not absent from the scene of action? There is no doubt that in 1947 these same millions had been swept by the idea of a Pakistani nation, millions who had not agreed to lose themselves in the identity of an Indian nation. That is the meaning of the Movement for Pakistan. It so happened that those who did not choose to lose themselves in the identity of a single Indian nation were Muslims, a fact which is not central to the idea of Pakistan. We can see that in Jinnah's first constituent Assembly address, his insistence that with the birth of Pakistan we are all citizens of Pakistan, whether Hindus, nor Muslims, nor Christians. By 1971 a section of these millions were equally determined not to lose themselves in the identity of a Pakistani nation.

This is, I believe, what is common between *Bangabandhu* and the struggling millions of 1971, the desire to stay distinct from the identity of a Pakistani nation or Indian nation. The English, the French and the rest of the Europeans who fought so hard against a single Europe that Hitler had designed may one day constitute a single European nation, but as of now, it will not take us far if we try to understand the realities of the European scene in terms of a European nation. The problems are still the problems predominantly of Englishmen and French and Italians and so on. And . . . in spite of the common class character of these distinct identities. That appears to be the situation in the subcontinent as a whole and in Bangladesh in particular too. There is a great deal we have in common of religion or of the class character of the society with the subcontinent as a whole or part of it, but cutting right across them all, there is the unmistakable will to retain the distinct identity. This is what *Bangabandhu* is a symbol of; this is what made the fusion of the man and the millions possible. In assessing the place of *Bangabandhu* it is irrelevant to make a catalogue of his virtues or gloat over his shortcomings: the millions took him to their hearts, word and all, because they found in him the expression of their innermost desire, the desire to retain their distinct identity of its own distinct nation. The epoch is still the epoch of the nation state, the problem is still the problem of the nation.

We have tried so far to explain what makes of us a nation. Obviously the nation has to have a habitat. It started as East Bengal, a province of Pakistan, rechristened East Pakistan, [and] is today Bangladesh, a nation state. I think it is futile to look for a rationale of its territorial limits. But Bangladesh is not unique in this cavalierly and rather difficult determination of its borders. The area could have been a little more or conceivably a little less. There are no strongly marked features which distinguish it from the neighbouring area. For better or worse these 55 thousand square miles contain a population not distinguishable from its neighbours, certainly [not] by foreigners.

This land that provides the people its homeland has features which appear to me important in determining the state of the nation today, tomorrow and perhaps for a long time to come. We have recently been told how the Mediterranean has been central to the shaping of the destinies of the peoples and countries surrounding it. The idea is not new. The geographical factors influence life, but they do not do it automatically. These factors and their forces can be studied, understood and aided to the attainment of results men consider desirable. Or they can be left alone, dead and inert matter with potentialities only. Iron, coal and oil have been available to man from the beginning of history. But it is only recently that they have grown into necessary and useful adjuncts of life. The capacity to make use of what nature has given man is a measure of the prospects of man, the state of his nation today and tomorrow.

Let me concede that [the] growing population in Bangladesh is the problem. Let me further concede that we are attaining a very considerable success in family planning. This, I do not think, particularly illuminates the question of the state of the nation today as an index of what is likely to be [to]morrow, when the entire exercise is on borrowed wisdom. All the policy decisions on the subject and their implementation may be good[,] but I am afraid . . . not good enough, for my limited purpose.

I propose to take the geographical, natural facts of life in Bangladesh, facts that may be said to have direct bearing on the state of the nation. Almost uniquely, the total land available for use in Bangladesh varies enormously from year to year. The annual alluvial accretion and the loss sustained each year by erosion is a fact of life which governs the lifestyle of a considerable fraction of the population. The legal framework which governs the use or loss of land was slowly built-up during the 19th century. The thrust of laws was designed to confer proprietorship of the land; practically dissociating ownership from actual use of the land. Secondly it was designed to bring about a formal equality before the law as between a man and a man. Thirdly, and not unimportantly, the Government was to be assured of a revenue. With a new insistence on written records and the ignorance of the rulers of the language or of the customs and the customary laws of the people, abuses which began to accrue to the system began to overshadow the possible benefits of the system long before 1947. Of the abuses which resulted, most probably litigiousness has proved the most costly, sustained principally by the entirely new profession of legal practitioners. It characterizes the practices and the habits of thought of the people more powerfully in the new or char lands than in the rest of the country. Today, now that we are in the grips of the idea of planning, most probably these are the parts of the country where experimental practices could be undertaken more easily than anywhere else. That would require a long look at the whole corpus of laws involving use, possession and determination of rights to these lands. So far, I do not see that any one has taken any notice of the situation resulting from this simple and noticeable natural fact of life in Bangladesh.

This relative abundance of new land each year is the result of the activities of the unique river system of the land. The character of Bangladesh and its people is dominated today, as it has always been dominated, by the river system and the water it carries or helps carry. The changes in the Teesta

during the late 18th and early 19th centuries, the changes in courses of the
Brahmaputra, Ganges or the Meghna during the last 200 years—these have
been more momentous facts in the life and labour of the people than all the
noisy labours of the governments during the same period. But this river system, this water system, the whole body of water that descends each year[,]
is capricious and has to be continuously wooed and taken notice of. During
the 18th century, the period of the breakdown of the Mughal system, this is
what was not done. As the Pax Mogola began to give place to anarchy, [dur-
ing] the century, [a] long time of trouble, the most precious casualty was in
the management of the water system. For, let it not be imagined that the
system managed itself; not even in Bengal where water is so abundant. Water no doubt is abundant, but so is silt. And you have to be continuously vigi-
lant before you can make proper use of the gifts of nature. Even during the
early years of the 19th century when the economy was in shambles those[,]
who had eyes to see could see that the prosperity of Bengal never depended
on its agriculture but on its trade and commerce and on the products of its
handicraft industries. All of which was possible on the proper maintenance
of its system of communications. Unlike any other part of the world this
was to us a gift from God which we received with acknowledgement. The
acknowledgement was in the labour, collective and individual, put in keeping the system in working order, in taming and training the rivers, in aiding
them wherever necessary. This was comprehensive labour providing the
foundation for the corporate life in the teeming villages.

During the 19th century the foreigners began first to notice the problems
connected with the management of water resources of the subcontinent.
Bengal was not the area which appeared to the foreigners to merit attention. There was so much of water here that it required detailed careful attention before it could be useful, . . . an idea which just did not occur, not
till the end of the British rule. During the Pakistan period the picture is not
very noticeably different. Is it very different now that we are all on our own?
The point I want to make is that water and its management is the heart of
the problem which is ours. The state of the Nation as an index to what is
in store for us in the future can be read in the priority we give to what we
call our central problem. And it is not so much a question of allocating this
or that percentage of our scarce resources to the development of our water
resources. The question is, do we make management of water resources
the focal point of our planning effort? As of now it does not appear that
there is that realization of the central role of the management of the water
resources.

Perceptions of Cultural Identity

Salma Sobhan

In Bangladesh, culture is at the forefront of politics. It has been a prime mover of political developments, the core of social movements, the focus of contestations, and the front line of political confrontations. The study here traces the main cultural strands that anyone wishing to make sense of Bangladeshi politics should be familiar with. It explains the all-important political question of identity. Even today, the main clashes on the battlefield of national politics concern the issue of Bengali versus Bangladeshi identity—or language-based identity versus religion-based identity. In the aftermath of a mass democratic movement against the autocratic dictatorship of General Ershad, the 1990s saw the rise of fundamentalist forces that contested secular notions of democracy and nationhood. Many scholars drew the conclusion that Bangladesh was surely on its way to becoming an Islamic state. This text, written in 1994, places this interpretation in a historical perspective and emphasizes the strongly contested nature of cultural identity in Bangladesh.

When independence movements in Asia and Africa against the colonial powers gathered momentum, the political parties involved in the struggle for independence frequently split along cultural lines. (The word *culture* here is used to include issues of religion and of language as well as others.) It is to be expected that the colonial powers were not loath to take advantage of the divisive potential of such issues. Unfortunately, the majority cultural group often could not free itself from cultural myopia. The politics of the sub-continent of India provide a particularly poignant illustration of this.

During India's struggle for independence from the British colonial rule the Indian Congress party and the All India Muslim League locked horns. Though the Congress had started life as an all India party, it was early on perceived as being unconcerned about the particular needs of the Muslims of India. The All India Muslim League came into being in response to that perception. The failure of these two parties to come to terms lead[s] to the partition of India in 1947 and the creation of the two states of India and Pakistan. At this time two major states in India were also partitioned; the state of Punjab in the West and of Bengal in the East. The state of Pakistan flanked India on the right and left and was separated by that state. The west wing of Pakistan was made up of the states of Sind, Baluchistan, the North West Frontier Province and a divided Punjab, and the east wing of Pakistan comprised the divided state of Bengal. East Bengal had always been the rural hinterland to West Bengal and Calcutta, but Dhaka—the capital of East Bengal—had been a Mughal outpost and had a culture of its own. It was not the cosmopolitan culture of Calcutta, but a composite of the cultures of Bengal and North India. In fact Dhaka is probably a good example of cultural synthesis.

Neither India nor Pakistan learned from the confrontation that led to the partition of India. In India the Congress went on to face confrontation after confrontation with others of its minorities—the Sikhs, the Nagas, the Tamils[,] not to mention the continuing problem with the Indian Muslims. In Pakistan, there was a similar myopia in the early 50s about the aspirations of Bengalis. This failure of understanding resulted in Pakistan breaking up in 1971, following a nine month long liberation war. Pakistan continues to be plagued by linguistic and tribal factionalism. Bangladesh, in its turn, has problems not only with its tribal population but also with its perceptions about itself.

In this paper I shall be examining aspects of the fluctuations in the Bangladeshi perception of identity. I have written elsewhere about the conflicts between Pakistan's East and West wings leading to the creation of Bangladesh in 1971. Here I also touched on the women's movement and the rise of religious obscurantism in Bangladesh. Since that article was written—in 1990—one has seen many changes in the political climate of Bangladesh.

In the earlier article the changes in perception were compared to the movement of a pendulum. I was then discussing the issue of the women's movement in relation to the phenomenon of the inaptly named fundamentalist movement and making the point that the perceptions of Muslim Bengalis about their cultural identity veered between the ethnic and the religious, though neither of these two categories is self-contained (thus in relation to the tribal groups in Bangladesh, the Muslim Bengalis assert themselves both as Bengalis—linguistically—and Muslims—culturally).

In this paper I will be examining in the present context the social and political results following these fluctuations in perception. I have deliberately used the word *culture* to include religion, because in this paper we are looking at the manifestation of religion rather than religious doctrines per se. In Bengal there has always been a tilt towards a syncretic version of Islam. Reformers tried to purge these syncretic elements from the religious practices of Muslim Bengalis but not with any great success. It should, however, be understood that not only do religious observances vary from country to country, but the laws derived from Islamic sources also vary. Such legal variations are, however, acceptable to jurists. The theme that Muslim Bengalis oscillate between seeing themselves as either Muslims or Bengalis is best . . . illustrated by a narration of historical events.

Bengali versus *Bangladeshi*

One of the many issues of contention in politics in Bangladesh is whether the citizens of Bangladesh should be known as Bengalis or Bangladeshis. . . . [O]n the face of it the latter terminology might seem to be more logical— the citizens of Bangladesh should be Bangladeshi, because that takes into account those who are not ethnically Bengali. The dispute has its origins in the identity crisis faced by the Muslim Bengalis for over a century before 1947. This crisis came to a head in 1971, when East Pakistan took a stand against the attempt of the western wing to subordinate the eastern wing to West Pakistani economic interests. One particular area of contention was the undermining of Bengali culture under the guise of promoting a unified Muslim cultural scenario. Such an onslaught was made on the culture of Bengal that those who remember this stick to the former—if illogical—nomenclature.

The period prior to the partition of India had seen the Muslim Bengalis asserting their religious identity very strongly. This was only partly a result of the Pakistan movement (the demand of a number of Indian Muslims for autonomy either within or without India). For it should be noted that in Bengal the political tensions between Muslims and Hindus were as much grounded in economics as they were cultural or religious. Even the reformist movement in Bengal—a movement to cleanse syncretic practices from Islam—was not alienated from the culture and language of the region. In fact, one of the initiatives of the movement was to translate the Quran into Bengali so as to make it accessible to the ordinary people. It is one of the ironies of the Pakistan movement that though the Muslim League was started in Bengal, and though it was the Bengali Muslim vote that was instrumental in getting the Muslim League enough support for the materialization of Pakistan, the cultural domination of the movement was North Indian. The reasons for this were historical. After the British established themselves as rulers of India, the Muslims of India had lagged behind the Hindus in acquiring English and finding employment with the new rulers of India; and when they woke up to the fact that they had been left behind, there was much leeway to be made up. So, in order to avail themselves of some space, the Muslims found it necessary to project themselves as fundamentally different from their Hindu compatriots.

At the same time the Hindu revival movement, which was particularly strong in Bengal, also worked in . . . turn to marginalize the non-Hindu. This lead the Muslims of Bengal, for political reasons, to espouse the language and culture of North India. This espousal was reinforced by the fact that much of the political leadership of Bengal at that time was dominated by men from families which though settled, sometimes for several generations, in Bengal were not indigenous. Many even asserted that for Muslim Bengalis their language of choice should be Urdu (Bengali and Urdu employ different scripts but most literate Muslim Bengali would have learned to read the Quran by rote in Arabic. Its similarity to the Arabic script meant that the Urdu could be easily mastered by them). But this consideration was not what prompted this assertion. Rather, it was the view that Urdu was a more Muslim language because of its script. Later there was a campaign that Muslim Bengalis should write it in the Urdu script rather as Urdu speakers in India use the Devangiri script interchangeably with the Persian script.

The Leaders

Though the Muslim League was founded in Bengal—at a meeting called by Nawab Salimullah of the Dhaka Nawab Family—the Muslim League did not immediately take off in Bengal at the grass roots. The movement that then united the largely Muslim peasantry was the Chirosthaee Bandobast movement against the imposition of land tax. The leader of the party—the Krishak Proja party—was a charismatic lawyer, Fazlul Haq, who was "a son of the soil"[—]that is to say an indigenous Bengali. The Nawab of Dacca's family were entrepreneurs from Kashmir who had been settled for a century in Bengal. He had the backing of a number of upper class Muslim Bengali both indigenous and emigrant, but Fazlul Haq's domination over rural Bengal remained absolute. It was another charismatic lawyer, Shaheed Suhrawardy, who was eventually to wrest this following from Fazlul Haq. But Suhrawardy himself, like Salimullah, was not a son of the soil either. His forebears had come as missionaries from Iraq to Bengal some three hundred years before. His mother tongue was Urdu, and though he used Bangla in his political life and was fluent enough, his accent betrayed his Urdu speaking origins to the end of his days. But unlike Salimullah, Suhrawardy's focus was Bengal. He had spent his early political life working with the renowned C. R. Das, and his focus was secular. So indeed was the focus of the man who became the leader of the All India Muslim League, Muhammad Ali Jinnah. Right up to the partition of India in 1947[,] the Muslim fundamentalist party, the Jamaat-e-Islam[,] remained opposed to the creation of Pakistan on the grounds that nationalism was un-Islamic, as true Muslims believe in the brotherhood of Muslims which transcends national barriers. (Once, however Pakistan became a political fact, the religious right did a volt[e] face and have been active in seeking political power within the state—this scenario can be paralleled in the case of Bangladesh.) In fact, the Muslim League in the 30s and 40s denied that they were anything but a secular movement. For Muslims, yes, but to safeguard their economic rights. For all the Muslim leaders of Bengal but the Nawab family and its followers[,] the partition of Bengal, at the insistence of the Congress, was a sad blow.

The Language Movement

The support and vote for the Muslim League in 1946, therefore, was never seen by the Muslim Bengali as a vote against the culture and language of Bengal. This became very clear early on following the partition of India. The issue of what was to be the national language of Pakistan brought about a major confrontation between the two wings. Though some Muslim Bengalis in British India might have chosen to put down Urdu as their chosen vernacular, the situation was quite different after 1947, when the proposition that only Urdu should be the national language of Pakistan was met by fury. The point was conceded in 1952 following an incident when the police fired on processionists protesting the proposed imposition of Urdu, killing three people. It marked the beginning of the divergence of paths being trod by East and West Pakistanis.

The War of Liberation—the Aftermath

The nine months of war between the two wings of Pakistan did not merely at the end establish Bangladesh as an independent sovereign state. It established the principles upon which the new state proposed to act. The Constitution of Bangladesh defined four binding principles, of which secularism was one. But the liberation of Bangladesh received no acclaim in the Muslim world, especially in the Middle East and Saudi Arabia. The culture of the west wing of Pakistan, tribal and hierarchical, was more easily comprehensible to them than that of the erstwhile East Pakistan, where music was part of daily life, and girls and women went around with their hair unbound. That as Muslims they should have actively broken up the largest Muslim state in the world was a reproach levelled at the citizens of the new country. This reproach neither took into account the atrocities perpetrated by the Pakistani army on its fellow citizens, nor that Pakistan was not a theocracy was laughable[,] but this rejection of Bangladesh by most of the Muslim world was a blow to the Muslim Bengali psyche from which it has yet to recover. Nonetheless most Muslims of Bangladesh cannot contemplate sacrificing their cultural identity to appease international Muslim sentiment anymore than the Indian Muslims would renounce their religion to placate Hindu fundamentalism.

The fact that much of the Muslim world saw the creation of Bangladesh as a victory of the anti-Muslim world has led successive governments into placatory acts. Those Bengalis who had collaborated against the liberation movement and who had as an act of clemency been let off lightly, or not punished at all by the new state of Bangladesh, took advantage of these sentiments to try to reclaim their position in society. Religion was a useful banner behind which to muster. Large sums of money poured into the coffers of the collaborators in an attempt to undermine the victory of 1971.

Bangladesh, of course, won liberation at a time of economic recession. Soon after the economically devastating conflict itself, the country was hit by disasters. There was a drought in 1972. The OPEC price hike in 1973 was followed by the floods of 1974, the aftermath of which was a famine, when food shipments from the U.S.A. which had been paid for were held back on grounds that Bangladesh's trade with Cuba brought within the ambit of the U.S.A. embargo against Cuba. This embargo was maintained until Bangladesh's last shipment to Cuba despite an undertaking by the then GOB [Government of Bangladesh] that thereafter trade with Cuba would cease. By the beginning of 1975 it was clear that the aftermath of the floods would result in a bumper crop on the river deposited silted fields, but by then the government had lost its grip, and the spiral of negative events started from which Bangladesh did not begin to emerge till 1990, 15 years on.

The Interregnum

During this period democracy in Bangladesh not only paid the price of the failure of the democratically elected government to deliver the economic goods and saw that government abandoning democratic principles, albeit under the impression that it was enlarging them, but it saw also subsequent governments rehabilitate the collaborators who had (in my opinion mistakenly) been pardoned in 1972/73. This was a fertile period for the religious obscurantists to start work on their agenda. Recently a member of parliament from the Jamaat-e-Islam (one of the religious right parties) was asked in an interview what his parties' agenda was. His answer was succinct "Power!" It is clear, however, even without this candid declaration that religion is their springboard for the very temporal goals of political power.

The Democratic Movement of 1990

This movement saw all the political parties come together under a common banner for elections under a caretaker government, because experience had shown that elections under the so-called civilian government headed by General Ershad would not be free. The Jamaat did not make the mistake of sitting on the sidelines. They had used the interregnum to their benefit—secularism had been removed from its place in the Constitution as one of Constitution's four binding principles, and Islam had been made the State religion. But the Jamaat needed legitimization. By participating in democratic elections it sought not only a voice in the parliament but also to gloss over its inglorious role in 1971. The Jamaat won about 12% of the vote in their usual strongholds[,] which netted them 17 seats. A coalition with the victorious BNP [Bangladesh Nationalist Party] . . . got them 2 more seats from the quota for women. But the real work of the religious parties is not in parliament.

The Anti-liberation Agenda

I have earlier written on the particular anti-woman focus of the religious right. This focus is being slowly widened to target for instance other vulnerable groups such as minorities; it has always [been] their intention to exercise control over society. Over the last two years (this is from 1992) there has been a rise of the pronouncement of *fatwas*—a *fatwa*, strictly speaking, is a jurist's opinion on a point of law. In Bangladesh it is an unauthorized pronouncement of punishment—mostly against village women who are accused of sexual irregularities. Most of the accusations are motivated by political or personal rivalry. In recent times the punishments have resulted in the death either by alleged suicide of or actual assault on the accused women. An open attack has been made on NGOs [nongovernmental organizations] [,] including the Bangladesh Rural Advancement Committee (BRAC—Bangladesh's largest NGO)[,] which has a vigorous programme for Non-Formal Primary Education particularly directed at girls, and the world famous Grameen Bank with its scheme for lending money to poor village women without collateral. The NGOs are seen as emancipating women[,] which is apostrophized under the head of irreligious behaviour. Men are instigated to act violently towards "wayward" wives, and to divorce them if they do not obey. The media concentration on the controversial poet Taslima Nasreen[,] accused of blasphemy[,] was to their advantage, as they seek to distract public attention from their real goals.

The Attack on Culture

During the Pakistan era, many aspects of Bengali culture were seen as alien by the West Pakistani. The Bengali language and women's way of dressing and the role of music in society were all contentious issues. The Bengalis reacted to these assaults very vigorously. Following liberation, however, and with the need for Bangladesh to take its place in the world as a sovereign state, other issues have come to the fore. Thus, despite a change in the medium of education to Bengali, there is a great demand for English teaching and a loophole in the law has enabled a large number of "Tutorials," where the medium of instruction is English, to flourish. Large numbers of young girls and women have abandoned the sari in favour of the tunic and pyjama as being more practical for daily wear than the sari[,] which retains its popularity as the garment for "dressing up." Much capital is made of the fact that in the matters of language and dress for example, Bangladesh seems to have moved away from its earlier defensive position. This attitude fails to see that a sovereign state has less to fear from such concessions than a partner in an unequal alliance as Bangladesh was after 1947. The Bengalis now face a much more serious assault. The assault on their freedom of speech and conscience. But the assault on the culture has not let up, for the attackers are well aware that these areas remain a bastion of self perception. The external fortifies the internal. Bangladesh still remains in harmony with its culture[,] priding itself on its tolerance and secularism and freedom of expression[;] with the iconoclast poet Nazrul Islam as the national poet, Modernism will take its toll as it does of all national cultures. It is unlikely that obscurantism will be able to do so.

Creating a Symbol of the Nation

Sayeed Ahmad

The Central Shohid Minar (Martyrs' Memorial, also spelled Shaheed Minar) is per-
haps the most loved and revered of all the national monuments in Bangladesh. Its
simple structure is replicated all over the country in schools, colleges, and govern-
ment institutions. Each replica is a site to pay homage to past glories of the nation
as well as to commit oneself to ongoing and future movements whose goals are de-
mocracy and secularism. The piece here, written in 1994, is an intimate account of
the creation of the monument in the late 1950s through the trials and tribulations of
its two extraordinary and talented creators: Hamidur Rahman and Novera Ahmed.

Hamidur Rahman, a pioneer painter of this country, had gone to Europe in
1951 to study painting at Beaux Arts in Paris. During his five-year stay in Europe, while coming under the influence of various western thoughts, media
and personalities[,] including painter Victor Pasmore, [and] art authorities
Basil Gray and J. Archer, he was able to realise deeply the wealth of his own
culture.

Sitting in a small flat in Cranleigh House a few hundred yards from
Euston tube station [in London] in 1956, Hamidur Rahman; Novera Ahmed,
the sculptress; and I were debating whether they should go back home or
utilise the opportunities already available in London. Hamidur Rahman
was my elder brother. Both artists had finished their academic life and
were now ready to embark in a competitive world. The picture of the then
East Pakistan was not a very happy one. Not many exhibitions were being
held, nor many commissions available. Painter Zainul Abedin was struggling hard to lead the art movement in Dhaka. Not many Asian painters
were working in London at the time. The racial colour bias was not so
pronounced then, therefore Hamidur Rahman[,] who had qualified from
the Central School of Arts, London, and Novera Ahmed from Camberwell
School of Arts, London, could have stayed back comfortably.

As the discussion went from aesthetic problems to economic problems,
the voice of Hamidur Rahman became sharper. I could see in his eyes a

grim determination to face an unknown future in his home-town. He was so convinced that he simply must go back. Europe was not suffocating nor dull, but the challenge felt by this youthful spirit led him to decide to return and immerse himself in the struggles of his country.

In the background of the 1952 Language Movement, no Bengalee could have remained unconcerned, least of all a fiery artist like Hamidur Rahman. He packed his small suitcase and boarded the plane for Dhaka. He did not choose to stay in Karachi where a lot of money was available for Europe-trained artists. His deep feelings, his roots, his convictions threw him into the difficult art world of East Pakistan.

Novera Ahmed followed suit to remain in his company for a long time. In the spring of 1957, Chief Minister of East Pakistan Ataur Rahman Khan requested Chief Engineer Jabbar and Zainul Abedin to ask Hamidur Rahman to prepare a plan for a Shaheed Minar [memorial to the martyrs of the language movement]. The idea charged Hamidur Rahman with tremendous enthusiasm. He found an outlet to express his commitment to Bengali nationalism. This was a complex demand. Never before had there been an agitation of such intensity as the Language Movement, nor was there any important example of a martyrs' monument in this tract of land. Therefore the artist Hamidur Rahman had to search for a new expression to convey the aspirations of the people. He presented a model of the Shaheed Minar along with 52 drawings and sketches, out of a hundred more he had worked out. There were other competitors who submitted their designs, but the Selection Committee composed of the internationally acclaimed Greek Artist Doxiades, Zainul Abedin and Jabbar chose the design evolved by Hamidur Rahman.

Hamidur Rahman started work in November 1957. He realised in a month's time that in order to complete the monument before February 1958, he must devote all his time to his work and be near the construction site. He therefore asked that two small tin huts be built next to the site, one to live in and the other to work in. He left his cosy Islampur house to live in this workshop so that he could breathe the atmosphere of the Shaheed Minar.

A pyramid, or a vertical column like Cleopatra's Needle, or an obelisk, or a Qutb Minar are the well-known forms of various styles of monuments. Hamidur Rahman designed a greatly different minar from the other, well-known structures. He went ahead untiringly and completed the first phase of the foundation, the raised platform and three columns[,] on time. He was grappling with two basic forms of horizontal and vertical to bring out the beautiful theme of revolt and peace, of love and grief, tears and solace. It can be seen that the vertical lines provide manifestation of the inner strength of

Central Shohid Minar in Dhaka. Photograph by Willem van Schendel, 2006.

a nation's conviction. The four columns reflect the tension of horizontal and vertical lines at different heights. The central column shifts away from the stated geometric shape, where the bowed head of the symbolic mother, bestowing protection and blessings on her children, leans forward at an angle.

Hamidur Rahman's design provided for stained glass to be used in the columns on which a pattern of hundreds of eyes were to be incorporated through which sunshine would glow. The floor was to be of marble, so as to show up, or reflect, the moving shadows of the columns as the sun crossed the sky, thus creating a mobile drama of geometric lines and colour from the stained glass. He had thought of inclusion of blood-stained footsteps of the Shaheeds [martyrs] and outside footprints in black of the aggressor, on the marble. He had kept provision for a clock tower and a well-stocked research library. In the basement gallery of the Minar, he had designed 1,500 sq. ft. of fresco depicting the scenes of the Language Movement, which was in fact one of his masterpieces. Hamidur Rahman had learned the technique of frescoes at London and Florence.

In this mural Hamidur Rahman portrays human figures brutally flattened and stretched into geometric forms, and unarmed marchers pushed back to the wall. Their last-ditch attempt to stand up for their rights transforms faces, arms, elbows and shoulders into sharp weapons. The single eye of a triangular face stares out and dismembered legs and feet continue their stance of unyielding challenge. Hamidur Rahman used earth colours from the folk palette—blue, yellow and earth red in pastel shades, deploying lime and egg yolk in the tradition of fresco work.

Unfortunately this beautiful work was erased by vandals. And the fact becomes downright tragic if we remember that this happened in 1972, in the month of February, when there was a general euphoria in the air as the first Ekushey [21 February] celebrations in the free Bangladesh were being planned. One of the disciples of Shilpacharja Zainul Abedin, Iqbal Ahmed, who is a noted leather craftsman himself, was going to the Shil-pacharja's house in the morning of 10 February along the Shaheed Minar road when he decided to drop in and see the progress of work at the Minar complex. The whole structure was being rebuilt and the area refurbished. He found some workmen of the Public Works Department at work in the room where the mural was. They were hacking at the mural and level-ing up the wall. Iqbal rushed to Zainul Abedin, who in turn sent him to fetch Hamidur Rahman from his house. When Hamidur Rahman came, the Shilpacharja sent him to the Government Secretariat to find out what was going on. There, in the labyrinth of the Secretariat, Hamidur Rahman found not one person who could tell him who had decided to deface the mural, who gave order and most importantly, why it was being done. Frus-trated, Hamidur Rahman came back to report to Zainul Abedin. Evidently, someone was responsible for this vandalism, but to this day, no one knows who. A single canvas [is] extant in my private collection of the same mural design, though this is in oil.

Novera Ahmed collaborated with Hamidur Rahman in the field of de-signing the fountain and embellishing the landscape with sculptures and design of plants and foliage. Both Hamidur Rahman and Novera Ahmed had spent time in Florence and Novera had studied sculpture under Dr. Vogel in London and the famous Italian Venturi in Florence. She was es-pecially fascinated by the great tradition of fountain sculptures abounding in Italian cities, such as the Fontana Trevi in Rome and Piazza Vecchio in Florence, and garden design as in Boboli Gardens and Villa Borghese. Mu-ghals had practised fountain art in India, but only in well-laid gardens, as part of the design of these gardens. In Europe, however, fountains had been a part of the aesthetic layout of cities. When Novera came back to Dhaka, she became the first practitioner of fountain art in the then East Pakistan. Obviously, she wanted to include a fountain as part of the structural design of the Shaheed Minar.

As an avant-garde artist she wanted to add a new dimension to the landscape of Shaheed Minar using the flow of water as a complement to the graceful moving shadows on the marble platform. Her sculptures were also to enhance the passion and pain of the martyrs through figurative works. She was the first sculptor who pointed out the importance of placing sculpture in the open air. Unfortunately, these aspects remain unfulfilled to a great extent even now.

In late 1958, following the imposition of Martial Law by General Ayub Khan, the Shaheed Minar plan was shelved and those connected with it had to undergo various tortures and harassments. I received a telegram in Karachi, where I was working at the time. Hamidur Rahman intimated that he was arriving on his way to the United States. I had anticipated this and therefore was mentally ready to accord whatever protection possible for his safety. Internationally acclaimed artist Sadequain and I went to receive Hamidur Rahman at the airport. He came out of the plane, completely shaken.

We talked of many things, except the painful subject of the Shaheed Minar. He said he was to fly out at the earliest, which meant the next day. He had got an assignment in [an art center at a university in Philadelphia], through the good offices of his friends in Dhaka. Things were unbearable for him. No one was allowed to work on the Shaheed Minar anymore. I could realise the frightful situation in Dhaka. The next day we saw him off at the airport. With tearful eyes he said, though his assignment was a long one, he would be back at the first opportunity to continue his work with the Shaheed Minar. His words came true. He cut short his stay without hesitation as soon as he heard that the situation was somewhat congenial and hurried back to Dhaka.

While in Philadelphia he executed a mural in Library Hall, depicting the Language Movement. It may be of interest for researchers that a substantial documentation of the Shaheed Minar basement mural is available in the Art Department of Philadelphia University, [but the mural] does not exist in Bangladesh.

In 1972, designs were called for to rebuild the Shaheed Minar (which was destroyed on the night of March 27, 1971[,] by the Pakistan Army). A competition was held and many people submitted their designs from amongst which Hamidur Rahman's layout was selected once again. I remember in 1973, sitting in my Circuit House flat, Shilpacharja Zainul Abedin narrated an interesting episode about the selection. He said that during several hours of deliberations the Committee kept on considering various changes. He was so exasperated that he raised his voice and in a firm manner said that the nation had owned and cherished Hamidur Rahman's design of the Shaheed Minar for many long years. Abedin told the Committee: "This is the face of my mother, I adore it. To some it may be a plain or a simple face, but it is my mother's face. I would not barter it for a hundred other beautiful faces." The result was that Hamidur Rahman's original design won the day. The much-loved symbol is replicated all over the country and has even crossed the border.

In due course of time the five columns of the monument were reconstructed, though he [Hamidur Rahman] had to go through much red tape and bureaucratic obstructions in fulfilling just a part of his total plan. The worst was that on December 7, 1973[,] when M. S. Jabbar, an associate of Hamidur Rahman, submitted the contract form for final approval of the Works Secretary, alas, no contract was signed, no contract could be signed! A horrible thing happened, the file got misplaced! Hamidur Rahman never got a farthing anymore.

I was further shocked when as recently as 1984, [when] a Finance Minister in the regime of H. M. Ershad, coming out of cabinet, told me that the government had decided to improve the Shaheed Minar. I posed the question as to whether it would be Hamidur Rahman's design. The minister smiled and said: "Not exactly. It will be somewhat similar, but not after the original." I don't know of any other country where designs are changed at will, without the artist's permission, particularly when the artist was alive and available.

Again in 1986 the Works Minister in Ershad's cabinet invited Hamidur Rahman to talk about the implementation of the plan of the Shaheed Minar. They visited the Shaheed Minar and Hamidur Rahman told the minister that he [could] spend as much as six months of his time if need be to execute his plan. The artist had envisaged a reading area in his original design, now he wanted to build a library for children behind the Minar, along the boundary wall, where a basement and an upper floor would contain the library and reading rooms. A lot of discussion took place but nothing concrete materialized. Once again, the government had attempted an eyewash.

Hamidur Rahman or Novera cannot implement their designs now. Hamidur Rahman passed away in 1989. And Novera Ahmed has simply left, with no forwarding address. No one knows where she lives now, or what she is doing. A pity such a gifted artist has vanished from amongst us.

Had Hamidur Rahman been alive today, he would have been happy to see that his humble offering has provided the central meeting point where people's songs and dramas are acted and where intellectuals and politicians go to place wreaths of homage to the departed souls of the martyrs.

Suppressing Student Protests in Dhaka

Meghna Guhathakurta

Ever since the 1940s, students' political actions have played an extremely important role in national politics. National power holders have good reason to fear student protests, especially when these link themselves to symbols of the nation. The text here describes students' anger on two adjacent campuses in Dhaka in 2002, showing how sculptures commemorating the Bangladesh Liberation War became centers of struggle between armed troops and students who had not even been born at the time of the war.

If one were to take a stroll down the campus of Dhaka University or the adjoining campus of the Bangladesh Engineering and Technology [BUET] during the past couple of weeks, one would be in for a shock. In place of bubbling students going about their business of studying or simply chatting away with friends or waiting for the bus, one would be met with the sight of student-less campuses filled with blue-clad policemen and -women dressed to the hilt in riot gears. Curiously, they would be clustered around monuments, which dot the campus of Dhaka University, commemorating historical struggles such as the Language Movement of 1952 (the Central Shohid Minar) and the Liberation War of 1971 (sculptures such as *Aparajeyo Bangla* [*Undefeatable Bengal*] and *Shoparjito Shadhinota* [*Self-Earned Independence*]).

The background to this story is the following. The triggering incident, which led to a mass upheaval of general students of Dhaka University, (i.e., students who are not cadres of the two mainstream parties, BNP [Bangladesh Nationalist Party] and Awami League) was a police raid of a female students' dormitory (Shamsunnahar Hall) during the night of 24th July 2002. The incident led to the injury and arrest of several innocent girls along with trumped up charges against them and the provost of their hall. It was allegedly reported that the provost who had been appointed during the Awami League regime and whose term was due to end in September had been unduly ousted by the new administration, and that she and some of her cronies had started a movement against the University administration and the government party cadres (*Jatiyotabadi Chhatro Dal*), which led to a law-and-order situation, which in turn compelled the police to raid the hall.

These allegations were proved false in the course of time, but what did happen was that the police worked in compliance with University administration and *Chhatro Dal* cadres to attack and abuse innocent girls in the middle of the night. No doubt from the next day onwards, streams of protest rent the air as students from all quarters demanded justice for the police atrocities and accountability of the University administration. As demands for the resignation of the Vice Chancellor [vc] and the Proctor [were loudly voiced], the administration decided to close the University for an indefinite period, with the order for immediate vacation of residential halls. Usually such steps are taken to defuse situations such as these, but this time the general students were not to be daunted. Instead of simmering down, the movement gained ground as students defied police barricades and took position in the Central Shohid Minar and declared a programme of fasting to death unless their demands were met. In the face of many threats from the police and *Chattro Dal* cadres, they stuck to their post and finally success came with resignation of the vc and the proctor on 31st July.

In the meantime students' movements were going on at the adjoining campus of the Bangladesh University of Engineering and Technology[,] demanding the trial of the murderers of Soni, a female student who fell victim in cross-firing between rival factions of the *Chhatro Dal* on campus several months earlier. But instead of taking any positive steps towards resolving the issue, the University administration committed the mistake of giving show cause notice [a court order] to the students who demanded justice for Soni's murder. This angered the students even more and although a new vc was instated, he proved just as intransigent to their demands. The situation on the BUET campus became even more volatile as the administration made use of the 1961 Act of the University, which prohibited any teacher or student to participate directly in politics. In the case of Dhaka University this law had been revised by the Act of 1973, which constituted Dhaka University as an autonomous institution. However, in the case of both BUET and Dhaka University, the government was trying to use the situation in an attempt to ban student politics on campus and hence the police had direct orders to quell any demonstration by using force. This power was exercised by the police when, with the growing involvement of civil society, their movement fuelled into the *gherao* [encirclement] of the administrative building. The police responded by *lathi* [club] charging and tear-gassing until the halls were vacated and BUET, too, closed down for an indefinite period.

But unlike the Dhaka University movement, which gained strength even after the closure of the University, the students of BUET were marched off campus under strong police vigilance and were not allowed to re-enter the campus area and take up positions anywhere. Nor were any other demonstrators or processions (be they students, cultural activists or civil society) allowed to use the central Shohid Minar as their platform, which is something unheard of in the whole history of Bangladesh . . . or perhaps not the whole history! This is where I reread the events mentioned above in the light of the history of democratic practice in Bangladesh.

The students' movement in Bangladesh has always been in the vanguard of progressive democratic protests against militarization, cultural repression and economic exploitation. This is witnessed by the role students played during the Language Movement of the 1950s, the Mass Uprising against the Ayub Khan regime of 1969, the Liberation War of 1971 and the anti-autocratic movement against the Ershad regime in 1990. Monuments commemorating these events, such as the ones mentioned above, have therefore time and again served as platforms to remind and inspire people to fight against regimes of oppression. Therefore a progressive tradition has been linked to these monuments. They provided cultural activists a platform to speak of a secular culture and practice in an environment overshadowed by fundamentalist fervour. They provided writers a space to speak about their rights to freedom of speech and beliefs. They provided students with a focal point through which to gain inspiration from history and to think critically and constructively about their future, about the kind of society they would like to see themselves living in. Any establishment bent on domination by force would naturally find these spaces of resistance a challenge to its authority and a threat to its existence. Hence their aim would be to restrict or even eradicate them as symbols of resistance from the minds of the people. This was exactly what the Yahya Khan regime of 1971 had in mind when they brought in the Pakistan army and started blowing up the Shahid Minar and cutting down the banyan tree (*botgachh*) beneath which students used to congregate. By the same logic they even massacred the family of Modhu who used to own the famous canteen on campus called Modhu's Canteen, where student leaders use to meet and plan their demonstrations! Is it not therefore in the same vein that the current BNP-Jamaat-led coalition government is instructing the police to make these spaces out of bounds for the students and the organized public at large! The evidence definitely points that way. Let us look at some of the antecedents and implications of the Dhaka University students' movement to explore this matter in depth.

Shoparjito Shadhinota, a war monument sculpted by Shamim Shikdar, stands in front of the Teachers-Students Centre of Dhaka University. This detail shows Pakistani soldiers raping a woman. Photograph by Willem van Schendel, 2006.

Although the police raid on Shamsunnahar Hall was the immediate triggering factor to the students' protest movement, certain incidents on campus had been responsible for generating sparks of dissent against the new administration, even prior to this incident. These incidents were essentially campus-related but had links with the overall ideological bias of the newly elected Government formed by the BNP-Jamaat alliance. First, the new administration had systematically tried to "clean" the Teachers-Students Centre (which was a focal point for cultural activists—poetry recitation groups, theatre groups[,] etc.) of all outsiders. It was mentioned that only those who were currently students and possessed ID cards would be able to hire rooms for rehearsals or even sit in the adjoining premises.

As benign as this step sounded in the language of administrative practice, it could not be denied that such measures also contained an ideological element. Cultural activism or the cultivation of secular and progressive ideals through various art forms have made a significant contribution towards the practice of democracy and free thinking in Bangladesh. As such they have often clashed with religious and orthodox thinking in politics and society. Therefore the struggle to uphold these values constituted a site of contestation in itself. For example, early this year, when the pro-Jamaati media started writing against the celebration of the first day of Spring (*Boshonto Utshob*) or the Bengali New Year (*Pohela Boishakh*) as being un-Islamic, students and young people celebrated in the streets with a vengeance, defying these strictures. Students have also been demonstrating on campus against the University administration cutting down trees to build a centre for Persian art and culture. It seems that the University was given a donation by the Iranian Cultural Centre for this purpose. The students' protest was based not only on environmental considerations but also against the unplanned way that the decision was taken. The final build-up was provided by another administrative measure, which angered the general student populace. This was the planned way in which the Proctor's Office tried to get rid of boy-and-girl couples sitting together around campus (the infamous *juti-uchhed obhijan*). The Dhaka University area has always been a place where there was less segregation between the sexes than in other public places. The administration tried to invoke a proctorial law from the colonial period, which stated that if a boy was seen to be talking to a girl without prior permission, he was to be fined. The evolution of Bangladeshi society has outgrown the uses of such a law, and its unjust invocation and crude implementation in the name of morality by the University administration fuelled the anger of the students. Many girls protested and were given a show cause notice by the proctor. At this point a police raid in a girls' dormitory, for whatever reasons, proved to be the last straw on the camel's back.

The fact that the students themselves invoked the basic premises of democratic practices, which were upheld by the symbol of our Liberation War, (the right to freedom of speech, the right to form groups and practice one's own cultural beliefs) was therefore an inevitable outcome. Many girls who were residing in Shamsunnahar Hall at the night of the raid expressed their fears in the following manner: "We were not born in 1971 and did not witness the Liberation War ourselves. But we have heard stories from our parents about the terror they felt when they heard the boots of the military marching outside or the dreaded thumping on the door." One girl said that she felt that same dread when they heard the boots of policemen on the corridor. Many girls had locked their rooms from the inside and when the police started shouting abuse and banged on the doors, their minds made a connection with a period of history which they personally had not witnessed but which was engraved deep in the collective mind of an oppressed people. It was little wonder therefore that in the protest marches that followed students did not shout partisan slogans but raised their voices against the collaborators of the 1971 war—Jamaat-e-Islam and Shibir, its student branch. They broke the police barricades to form what they called the *muktanchal* (liberated area) near the sculpture of *Shoparjito Shadhinota*. A daughter of a friend, a medical student, when passing by this area, witnessed a spontaneous performance of street theatre by the students of the Fine Arts Department. They were drawing satirical portraits of the power relations between the University administration and the ruling party cadres. The girl (in her early twenties) later admitted that she had felt she had been transported to a *muktanchal* of the Liberation War, i.e., the areas which the Mukti Bahinis (Freedom Fighters) had liberated from Pakistani Army occupation.

Thus one can understand that when, after the closure of BUET, the police and at times BDR [Bangladesh Rifles—a paramilitary force] were stationed in and around these historical monuments, it demonstrated a siege not only of those sites around which students might rally in protest, but also a siege of the very symbols of democratic practice and resistance that the people have cherished for so long; memories that have a capacity to release the flood gates of consciousness. This is something to be dreaded by power-driven establishments. Milan Kundera put it very succinctly in his *Book of Laughter and Forgetting*: "The struggle of man against power is the struggle of memory against forgetting!" The Pakistanis, with all their military might, had not been able to curb this memory. How can it be possible for a host of policemen and their masters to accomplish such a task?

The Chittagong Hill Tracts Peace Accord (1997)

Parbattya Chattagram Jana Sanghati Samiti
and the Government of Bangladesh

The Chittagong Hill Tracts War (1975–97) was a major challenge to the idea that the nation of Bangladesh equals the Bengali nation. Dozens of non-Bengali groups inhabit the country and their demands for full citizenship rights have been insistent. In the Chittagong Hill Tracts, traditionally an area with a large non-Bengali majority, anger at a lack of autonomy, at state discrimination, and at cultural marginalization led to a violent confrontation. The war pitted the Bangladeshi armed forces against the guerrillas of the Parbattya Chattagram Jana Sanghati Samiti (PCJSS; United People's Party of the Chittagong Hill Tracts). Dozens of massacres, thousands of casualties, tens of thousands of refugees in camps in India, and hundreds of thousands of illegal but state-assisted Bengali settlers from the plains turned the Chittagong Hill Tracts into Bangladesh's largest militarized region and human rights disaster. In 1997 a peace treaty sought to end the violence, restore order, and provide safeguards for the indigenous (non-Bengali) population. It turned out to be less than successful. Widespread violence and human rights abuses have continued, albeit at lower intensity, and many provisions in the treaty were never implemented. The area remains heavily militarized. Here is the abridged text of the Chittagong Hill Tracts Peace Accord (1997).

Under the framework of the Constitution of Bangladesh and keeping full and firm confidence in the sovereignty and integrity of Bangladesh, to uphold the political, social, cultural, educational and economic rights of all the people of Chittagong Hill Tracts region and to expedite socio-economic development process and to preserve and respect the rights of all the citizens of Bangladesh and their development, the National Committee on Chittagong Hill Tracts, on behalf of the government of the People's Republic of Bangladesh, and Parbattya Chattagram Jana Sanghati Samiti, on behalf of the inhabitants of Chittagong Hill Tracts, have reached the following agreement in four parts (A, B, C, D):

A) *(Ka) General*

1. Both the sides have recognised the need for protecting the characteristics and attaining overall development of the region considering Chittagong Hill Tracts as a tribal inhabited region.

2. Both the parties have decided to formulate, change, amend and incorporate concerned acts, rules and regulations as soon as possible according to the consensus and responsibility expressed in different sections of the agreement. . . .

B) *(Kha) Chittagong Hill Tracts Local Government Council/ Hill District Council*

Both sides have reached agreement with regard to changing, amending, incorporating and omitting the Hill District Local Government Council Acts 1989 (Rangamati Hill District Local Government Council Act 1989, Bandarban Hill District Local Government Council Act 1989, Khagrachhari Hill District Local Government Council Act 1989) and its different sections which were in existence before this agreement came into being. . . .

C) *(Ga) The Chittagong Hill Tracts Regional Council*

1. A Regional Council shall be formed in coordination with the 3 Hill District Local Government Councils provided that various sections of the Hill District Local Government Council Act 1989 (Act No. 19, 20 and 21 of 1989) shall be amended with an aim to make the three Hill District Local Government Councils more powerful and effective.

2. Chairman of this Council shall be elected indirectly by the elected members of the Hill District Councils, his status shall be equivalent to that of a State Minister and he must be a tribal.

3. The Council shall be formed with 22 (twenty-two) members including the Chairman. Two-thirds of the members shall be elected from among the tribals. The Council shall determine its procedure of functioning.

Composition of the Council shall be as follows:

Chairman	1
Members Tribal	12
Members Tribal (women)	2
Members non-tribal	6
Members non-tribal (women)	1

Men in the Chittagong Hill Tracts. Photograph by Willem van Schendel, 2003.

Among the tribal members 5 persons shall be elected from the Chakma tribe, 3 persons from the Marma tribe, 2 persons from the Tripura tribe, 1 person from the Murung and Tanchangya tribes and 1 person from the Lusai, Bawm, Pankho, Khumi, Chak and Khiyang tribes[.]

Among the non-tribal members 2 persons shall be elected from each district. Among the tribal women members 1 woman shall be elected from the Chakma tribe and 1 woman from other tribes.

4. Three seats shall be reserved for women in the Council, one-third of which will be non-tribal.

5. The members of the Council shall be elected indirectly by the elected members of the Hill District Councils. Chairman of three Hill District Councils shall be ex-officio members of the Council and they shall have voting rights.

Eligibility and non-eligibility of the members of the Council shall be similar to that of the Hill District Councils.

6. The tenure of the council shall be five years. Budget preparation and its approval, dissolution of council, formulation of council's regulation, appointment of and control over officers and employees and matters related to concerned subjects and procedures shall be similar to the subjects and procedures given in favour of and applicable for the Hill District Council. . . .

9. a) The Council, including coordination of all development activities conducted under the three Hill District Councils, shall supervise and coordinate the subjects vested upon the Hill District Councils.

. . .

c) Regional Council can coordinate and supervise in the matters of general administration, law and order and development of the three Hill Districts.

d) The Council can conduct programmes related to disaster management and relief, and also coordinate the activities of the NGOs.

e) Tribal laws and social justice shall be under the jurisdiction of the Council.

f) The Council can issue license for heavy industry.

10. The Chittagong Hill Tracts Development Board shall discharge its responsibilities under general and overall supervision of the Council. In case of appointment of Chairman of the Development Board, the government shall give priority to competent tribal candidates.

11. If the Regional Council finds any rule of the 1900 CHT [Chittagong Hill Tracts] Regulations and other related laws, rules and ordinances as contradictory to the 1989 Hill District Council Acts, then the government shall remove that inconsistency in law according to recommendation of and in consultation with the Regional Council. . . .

13. If the government wants to formulate any law regarding CHT, it shall do so in consultation with and according to the recommendation of the Regional Council. If there arises the necessity to amend any law that may be harmful for development of the three Hill Districts or for the welfare of the tribals, or to make any new law, the Councils may file a petition or put recommendation before the government. . . .

D) (Gha) Rehabilitation, General Amnesty and Other Matters

Both sides have reached the following position and agreement to take programmes for restoring normal situation in Chittagong Hill Tracts area and to this end on the matters of rehabilitation, general amnesty and other related issues and activities:

1. An agreement has been signed between the government and the refugee leaders on March 9, 1997 with an aim to take back the tribal refugees from India's Tripura State based on the 20-point Facilities Package. In accordance with the said agreement repatriation of the refugees started since March 28, 1997. This process shall continue and with this in view, the Jana Sanghati Samiti shall provide all kinds of possible cooperation. The Task

Force shall, after determination, rehabilitate the internally displaced tribal people of three districts.

2. After signing and implementation of the agreement between the government and the Jana Sanghati Samiti, and after rehabilitation of the tribal refugees and internally displaced tribal people, the government, in consultation with the Regional Council to be formed as per this agreement, shall start cadastral survey in CHT as soon as possible and after finalization of land ownership of tribal people by settlement of land dispute through proper verification, shall record their land and ensure their land rights.

3. The government, to ensure the land rights of the tribal families which are landless or possess less than 2 acres of land, shall provide two acres of land to each such family, provided that lands are available in the locality. If requisite lands are not available then grove land shall be provided.

4. A commission (Land Commission) headed by a retired justice shall be formed for settling land disputes. This commission, in addition to settling disputes of lands of the rehabilitated tribal refugees, shall have full power for cancellation of ownership of those lands and hills which have been so far illegally settled and occupied. No appeal can be made against the judgement of this commission and decision of this commission shall be final. This shall also be applicable in case of fringe land.

5. This commission shall be set up with the following members:
    Retired justice;
    Circle chief (concerned);
    Chairman of Regional Council/representative;
    Divisional Commissioner/Additional Commissioner
    Hill District Council Chairman (concerned)

6. a) The term of the commission shall be three years. But its term can be extended in consultation with the Regional Council.
    b) The Commission shall settle disputes according to the existing rules, customs and practices of Chittagong Hill Tracts. . . .

8. Allotment of lands for rubber plantation and other purposes: Settlement of land, of those non-tribals and non-locals who were given settlement of lands for rubber plantation and other purposes but had not undertake[n the] project within the past 10 years or had not utilized their lands properly, shall be cancelled.

9. The government shall allot additional funds on priority basis for implementation of increased number of projects in CHT. New projects formulated with an aim to make necessary infrastructures for facilitating development in the area shall be implemented on priority basis and the government shall provide funds for these purposes. The government shall, considering the

state of environment in the region, encourage developing tourism for tourists from within the country and abroad.

10. Quota reservation and scholarships: Until development equals that of other regions of the country the government shall continue reservation of quota system in government services and educational institutions for the tribals. For this purpose, the government shall grant more scholarships for the tribal students in the educational institutions. The government shall provide necessary scholarships for research works and higher education abroad.

11. The government and the elected representatives shall be active to preserve the distinctiveness of the tribal culture and heritage. The government in order to develop the tribal cultural activities at the national level shall provide necessary patronization and assistance.

12. The Jana Sanghati Samiti shall submit to the government the lists of all its members including the armed ones and the arms and ammunition under its possession and control within 45 days of signing this agreement.

13. The government and the Jana Sanghati Samiti shall jointly determine the date and place for depositing arms within the 45 days of signing this agreement. After determination of date and place for depositing arms by the members included in the list of the Jana Sanghati Samiti the government shall ensure security for return of jss [Jana Sanghati Samiti] members and their family members to normal life.

14. The government shall declare amnesty for the members who shall deposit their arms and ammunition on the scheduled date. The government shall withdraw the cases against whom cases have been lodged.

15. If anyone fails to deposit arms on the scheduled date the government shall take lawful measures against him.

16. After the return of all jss members to normal life general amnesty shall be given to them and to the permanent residents who were involved in the activities of the Jana Sanghati Samiti.

    a) In order to provide rehabilitation to all returnee jss members a lump sum of Taka 50,000/- shall be given to each family.

    b) All cases, warrants of arrest, held against any armed member or general member of the Jana Sanghati Samiti shall be withdrawn and punishment given after trial in absentia shall be exempted after surrender of arms and coming back to normal life as soon as possible. Any member of the Jana Sanghati Samiti in jail shall be released.

    c) Similarly, after surrendering arms and coming back to normal life, no case can be filed or no punishment can be given to any person for merely being a member of the Jana Sanghati Samiti. . . .

17. a) After signing of the agreement between the government and the Jana Sanghati Samiti and immediately after the return of the JSS members to normal life, all the temporary camps of military, Ansar and Village Defence Party shall be taken back to permanent installations except the border security force (BDR) and permanent cantonments (three at the three District Headquarters and Alikadam, Ruma and Dighinala) by phases and with this in view, the time limit shall be determined. In case of deterioration of the law and order situation, natural calamity and such other works the army can be deployed under the civil administration like all other parts of the country as per relevant laws and rules. In this case, the Regional Council may, according to the necessity or time, request the proper authority for the purpose of getting assistance.

    b) The lands of camps and cantonments to be abandoned by military or para-military forces shall be either returned to the original owners or to the Hill District Councils.

18. The permanent residents of Chittagong Hill Tracts with priority to the tribals shall be given appointment to all categories of officers and employees of all government, semi-government, councils and autonomous bodies of Chittagong Hill Tracts. In case of non-availability of eligible persons from among the permanent residents of Chittagong Hill Tracts for a particular post, the government may give appointment on lien or for a definite period to such posts.

19. A ministry on Chittagong Hill Tracts Affairs shall be established by appointing a Minister from among the tribals. An Advisory Council shall be formed to assist this ministry. . . .

This agreement is framed as above in Bengali language and is done and signed in Dhaka on the date of 02 December, 1997 A.D., 18 Agrahayan 1404 Bengali year.

On behalf of the inhabitants of Chittagong Hill Tracts
SD/- (Jyotirindra Bodhipriya Larma)
President, Parbattya Chattagram Jana Sanghati Samiti.

On behalf of the government of the People's Republic of Bangladesh
SD/- (Abul Hasanat Abdullah)
Convenor, National Committee on Chittagong Hill Tracts Affairs,
Government of Bangladesh.

Gender, Ethnicity, and the Nation

Kalpana Chakma

It is not easy in the heat of a nationalist or ethno-nationalist struggle to stand by your commitment to diversity and reflection. Yet Kalpana Chakma did just that. She was the organizing secretary of the Hill Women's Federation, representing the women of the Chittagong Hill Tracts in southeastern Bangladesh. Going against the grain of her own political movement, she used the issue of gender to interrogate basic premises and practices of freedom and democracy both within her own movement and beyond it. Her disappearance in 1996, allegedly at the hands of the Bangladeshi armed forces, is commemorated every year on 12 June. Kalpana's diary, which was discovered after her disappearance, bears testimony to great issues: the question of representation, as a member of the Chakma community and as a woman.

Pioneer Club, Khagrachhari, 21 May 1995. We know that all over the world in backward countries and societies, repression within the family and society is almost the same. But I think that women are more repressed in our country, because here they are repressed through the word of law. In addition to that are the heartbreaking events that occur in the corners of the Hill Districts.

Women are victimized and trivialized in each and every corner of the Hill Tracts. On the one hand is the steamroller of rape, humiliation, and torture being committed by the army and the Bengalis; on the other hand is the discrimination between the sexes in a tradition-bound society. In yet another dimension lie the brutal massacres of ethnic oppression.

In such a situation women no doubt have a difficult position to maintain as political activists. It is through trials and tribulations that we have to continue to pursue our political mandate. Until now our women have participated in a broader political movement from an independent position. Our claim for self-determination has been translated into the movement for gender equality. We know that women's liberation cannot take place outside the context of liberation of the downtrodden classes and sections of society. An oppressed people cannot ensure the rights of another, nor can

On a foggy winter morning, women in Bandarban (Chittagong Hill Tracts) are washing pots and taking water from the Sangu River. Photograph by Willem van Schendel,
2003.

they guarantee their personal security. That is why, sisters, we have to fight
for equal rights by emphasizing our fight for national self-determination.
We have to bring about social transformation. We cannot deny our own
tradition-bound, decadent patriarchal society. In this sense the struggle of
our Hill Women's Federation is not only a political one; it is at the same
time a struggle against male dominance within our family and society.

That is why we need social transformation. For this we need to have
progressive-minded brothers and sisters on our side. And that is why our
women activists must become more aware and acquire the necessary capacity and skills for effective leadership so that they play a significant role in the
struggle for equal rights.

Translated from Bengali by Meghna Guhathakurta.

The Two Meanings of "Bangladeshi"

Amena Mohsin

You would think that there would be no problem in referring to inhabitants of Bangladesh as Bangladeshis. But things are not so simple. In the first years after the birth of Bangladesh, the term Bangladeshi *was not current. It was only during the first postindependence military government of Ziaur Rahman that* Bangladeshi *became the official term to refer to inhabitants of Bangladesh. But the term did not refer to citizenship or residence as much as to a specific religio-linguistic category— Bengali Muslims. The main point was to distinguish Bengali speakers in Bangladesh (overwhelmingly Muslims) from Bengali speakers in India (mostly Hindus) and to claim nationhood for the former. Since then, the use or rejection of the term* Bangladeshi *has signaled different party-political positions regarding identity, as issues of citizenship, nationhood, and ethnicity became the stuff of power struggles between two dominant sections of the country's national elite. In this text, Amena Mohsin explores the contested terrain and reminds us of the early sidetracking of an attempt to introduce* Bangladeshi *merely as a marker of citizenship.*

The Bangladesh Nationalist Party's manifesto (BNP, the political party floated by Zia[Ziaur Rahman]) defines Bangladeshi nationalism as follows:

> Religious belief and love for religion are a great and imperishable char-
> acteristic of the Bangladeshi nation . . . the vast majority of our people
> are followers of Islam. The fact is well-reflected and manifest in our
> stable and liberal national life. . . .[1]

Proponents of Bangladeshi nationalism further point out that Bangladeshi nationalism is territorial; it draws a line between the Bengalis of Bangladesh and the Bengalis of West Bengal. This gives it a totality, which is precisely lacking in Bengali nationalism. This however is a mere exercise in semantics for Bengali nationalism . . . [, which] explicitly had a territorial dimension [because it focused on East Pakistan/East Bengal]. Moudud Ahmed, the Deputy Prime Minister during the Zia regime, pointed out its [Bengali nationalism's] integrative character in arguing that the concept of Bangladeshi nationalism is identified with the state and not with the origin of the people. He pointed out that the people of CHT [the Chittagong Hill Tracts] will not accept the Bengali national identity, but will accept the Bangladeshi national identity. . . . Moudud obviously was referring to [Manabendra Narayan] Larma's contentions in the Bangladesh Parliament in 1972. Incidentally, Larma, the nationalist leader from the CHT, had coined the word[s] Bangladeshi nationalism during the constitutional debate in 1972, but Larma's conception of Bangladeshi nationalism was at variance with the BNP's. In 1972 Larma was talking in the context of a secular Bangladeshi nation wherein the contours of nationalism would have been political and territorial. This was supposed to dampen the dominance of the cultural and linguistic elements then so pronounced in Bengali nationalism, in order to enable the Hill people of CHT to integrate themselves with the Bengalis in a political not cultural sense. Bangladeshi nationalism as it evolved in 1975 was in essence a reassertion of the Muslim identity of the Bengalis of Bangladesh. Thus instead of being an integrative force it deepened the division between the Hill people and the Bengalis; now religion as well as culture were being used as tools of domination. Accordingly changes were brought about in the mass media, education and the Constitution to expedite and legalise the process of this new construction.

Note

1. Bangladesh Nationalist Party, "Ghosanapatra" [Manifesto], Dacca, 1978.

Secularism as Religious Tolerance

Amena Mohsin

Secularism, one of the four pillars of the Bangladesh state as laid out in its first constitution, carries a special meaning. The constitution does not indicate the separation of state and religion, as in the West. Instead, it refers to state acceptance of diversity of religious belief, tolerance of the coexistence of several religious communities, and a ban on the use of religion for political purposes. It was a clear reaction to the Pakistan elite's misuse of Islam as a political tool in the pre-1971 period. Amena Mohsin explains the meaning and significance of secularism in Bangladesh's first constitution.

Apart from language and culture, secularism too was a plank of Bengali nationalism. In the context of Bangladesh, [Sheikh] Mujib defined it in the following words:

> Secularism does not mean absence of religion. Hindus will observe their religion; Muslims will observe their religion; Christians and Buddhists will observe their religions. No one will be allowed to interfere in others' religions, the people of Bengal do not want any interference in religious matters. Religion cannot be used for political ends.[1] . . .

In order to implement the above, Article 12 [of the constitution of Bangladesh] stated:

> The principle of secularism shall be realised by the elimination of:
> a. communalism in all its forms;
> b. the granting by the state of political status in favour of any religion;
> c. the abuse of religion for political purposes;
> d. any discrimination against, or persecution of, persons practising a
>   particular religion . . .

Article 18, para 2, further stated:

No person shall have the right to form or be a member or otherwise take part in the activities of any communal or other association or union which in the name or on the basis of any religion has for its object, or pursues, a political purpose. . . .

In the construction of nationhood in Pakistan religion had been used as the main tool of domination of the Bengalis by the Pakistani regime. Again in 1971 the Pakistani regime had employed the rhetoric of religion in carrying out one of the worst genocides of the century. Secularism was therefore a logical outcome of the spirit of the liberation war in Bangladesh. It also accommodated the religious minorities in Bangladesh. But while religious communalism was prohibited, the Bengali elite failed to take note of the communalism that its own assimilationist nationalism could breed.

Note

1. *Parliamentary Debates* (Dhaka: Government of the People's Republic of Bangladesh, 1972), 452.

The Tablighi Jama'at

Yoginder S. Sikand

The growing tendency to speak of Islam as a single global category obscures the fact that there are many different Islamic groups, movements, and identities. One of the most popular movements in Bangladesh is the Tablighi Jama'at (TJ; Islamic Outreach Group). This is not a local movement but a vast and dynamic transnational one. Its sprawling annual world assembly is held in Tongi, a town just north of Dhaka. In this contribution, published in 2001, Yoginder Sikand takes a look at the recent history of the Tablighi Jama'at in Bangladesh as well as its current geographical distribution and social-support base. He shows how the Tablighi Jama'at differs from Islamism or political Islam (represented by the Jama'at-i-Islami) because it has neither interest in political power nor concern with textual religion. He also shows that it is distinct from Sufism because it rejects its mysticism and worship of saints. As Sikand points out, Islamic movements among Bengalis are hardly insignificant in global terms: "With a Muslim majority of 85 per cent and a population of over 120 million, Bangladesh is home to one of the largest numbers of Muslims in the world. Taken along with the Muslims of the neighbouring Indian state of West Bengal, Bengali speakers are, after the Arabs, probably the world's single-most populous ethnic group."

By the late nineteen sixties, the TJ [Tablighi Jama'at] seems to have established a firm foothold for itself in East Bengal. According to informed sources, however, it was only in the 1970s—with the emergence of East Pakistan as the independent Republic of Bangladesh in 1972—that the TJ witnessed its most rapid expansion in the region. One major reason for this seems to have been the changing role of Islam in public affairs wrought first by the bloody events of the 1971–72 Liberation War and then, particularly in the post-1975 era, by consistent attempts by ruling elites to use Islam as a political weapon to help legitimise unstable and unpopular regimes. We turn first to a discussion of the events leading to and during the Liberation War of 1971, to see how, ironically, the militant secular nationalism of the

Bangladeshi independence struggle appears to have opened new spaces for the further expansion of the TJ in what is today Bangladesh.

Islam and the Bangladeshi Liberation War (1971–75)

... The events leading up to the creation of Bangladesh had critical implications for the future of Islamic groups in East Bengali Muslim society. Not the least of these was the active involvement of staunchly pro-Pakistani Islamic groups within East Bengal in the killing of large numbers of Bengali Freedom Fighters, particularly the intellectuals who were the guiding force behind the liberation struggle. Most actively involved in these killings was the Jama'at-i-Islami. Led by Professor Ghulam Azam (who ... was earlier associated with the TJ), the Jama'at-i-Islami openly collaborated with the Pakistani forces in their attempt to crush the Bengali freedom movement. During the war itself, Ghulam Azam shifted his base to West Pakistan, from where he directed his deputy, Abbas Ali Khan, to form the Razakars, the dreaded paramilitary outfit whose task was to identify and kill Freedom Fighters. A similar group, al-Badr, was launched by the Islami Chhatra Sangha, the students' wing of the Jama'at-i-Islami. Not to be left out, the Muslim League formed its own armed group, al-Shams, which, along with the Razakars and al-Badr, worked in tandem with the Pakistanis.

The active involvement of Islamic political outfits such as the Jama'at-i-Islami in the large-scale massacre of Freedom Fighters had a tremendous impact on the minds of many Bengalis. Not surprisingly, then, when Bangladesh finally won independence, public opposition to Islamic political groups, especially the Jama'at-i-Islami, was intense. In declaring Bangladesh to be a secular state, the country's first prime minister, Shaikh Mujib-ur-Rahman, was only responding to widespread public demands. Secularism, however, did not mean rejection of or hostility towards religion or any particular religion. It meant, instead, that religion and politics would be kept apart, that no political parties based on religion would be allowed to exist and that in the eyes of the State all citizens, irrespective of religion, would be considered equal. Following this proclamation, the Jama'at-i-Islami and all other Islamic political groups were banned.

Implications for the TJ

These developments—the involvement of Islamic political groups in the massacre of Freedom Fighters, the declaring of Bangladesh to be a secular state in which religion and politics—*din* and *siyasat*—would be strictly kept apart, and the banning of the Jama'at-i-Islami and related groups, seem to have actually worked greatly in favour of the TJ, which is why, according to *tablighi* [sources from the Tablighi Jama'at] sources, it was only after the liberation of Bangladesh that the movement really rapidly took off, spreading to almost all parts of the region. While the Jama'at-i-Islami and similar Islamic political groups had evoked tremendous hostility among ordinary Bangladeshis for their role in the events of 1971, the TJ, by remaining completely aloof from political involvement in the course of the war, had endeared itself to many. For the tablighis the war over *duniyavi* (worldly) spoils was, at best, irrelevant—neither did the movement as such support the liberation struggle and nor did it oppose it. Even at the peak of the fighting, [tablighi] *jama'ats* carried on with their preaching tours and in their speeches made no reference to the dramatic happenings around them except to exhort Muslims to "follow in the path of Allah" in this time of crisis. If Pakistani soldiers would sometimes come in mufti [civilian clothes] to listen to the *bayans* (sermons) at the *markaz* [center] at Kakrail, Bengali Freedom Fighters would approach *tablighi muballighin* [preachers] to offer supplications to God for them. Steering clearly away from this duniyavi conflict, they appeared in the eyes of many Bengalis as true men of God, in contrast to the Jama'at-i-Islami or the Muslim League, for instance, who were now seen as power-hungry politicians donning an Islamic garb. This seems to have made a lasting impression on the minds of many Bangladeshis, an impression that lasts till this very day.

Secularism, as it came to be understood in the immediate aftermath of Independence—the separation of religion and politics—fit in comfortably with the distinction that many tablighi activists tended to make between *din* and *duniya*, religious and temporal affairs, a distinction that Islamic political groups looked upon as itself un-Islamic. This disassociation from politics as conventionally understood enabled the TJ to freely carry on with its activities even as groups like the Jama'at-i-Islami were banned. Interestingly, several Jama'at-i-Islami activists, fearing arrest or persecution, are reported to have actually begun participating in TJ activities after the ban on the Jama'at-i-Islami came into effect. This does not mean that all or even many of them actually gave up their allegiance to the Jama'at-i-Islami or necessarily changed into active tablighi supporters. According to Ghulam Azam, for many of these individuals, participating in tablighi activities such as jama'ats was simply a way to evade the authorities and to avoid being recognised by the State and the public as a member of a banned, pro-Pakistan organisation.

Islam, the Bangladeshi State and the TJ (1975 to the Present Day)

If the official policy of "secularism" of the Bangladeshi state under Shaikh Mujib-ur-Rahman (1971–75) provided new opportunities for the TJ to expand and flourish, the active espousal of Islam by Bangladeshi rulers in the years following Mujib's assassination in 1975 has only helped to further strengthen the movement, among other Islamic groups, in the country. In the aftermath of the 1975 coup which brought to power the army led by General Zia-ur-Rahman, Islam began being projected as the official ideology of the Bangladeshi state, even though there seems to have been no strong public pressure from below to do so. Zia introduced a number of measures that gave a powerful fillip to the Islamic forces in the country. Zia's policies were carried even further by his successor, Lieutenant-General Hussain Muhammad Ershad, one of whose first steps on assuming power was to declare Islam as the state religion of the country in 1988. The government now began to spare no effort at patronising Islamic groups and organisations. Rejecting completely the composite secular Bengali nationalist spirit of the liberation struggle, Ershad publicly declared:

> Islam is our ideal and it is the only way to our emancipation. The existence of the Country will be at stake if we fail to establish Islam in Bangladesh. We, the nine crore [90 million] Muslims (of Bangladesh) will certainly speak about Islam, think about Islam and dream about Islam. This is our only way for emancipation.[1]

The growing salience of Islam in public life, especially after the military takeover in 1975, has been attributed to several factors. According to some, Islam was seen as a convenient tool by the military dictators, enjoying little public support, to legitimise their own regimes and to combat the powerful secular opposition, particularly the Awami League. [Badruddin] Umar opines that the patronising of Islam by the Bangladeshi state coincided with and, indeed, actually reflected, the growing crisis of the ruling classes in the country, with socio-economic inequalities growing at an alarming rate, pushing down the real incomes of the poorest of the poor. Islam, then, was seen as an effective counter to radical groups among the dispossessed, who, at the same time found in the promises of "Islamic justice" their only source of hope and solace. One top bureaucrat, who was later to go on to become the Director-General of the government's Islamic Foundation, the main body concerned with the regulation of Islamic affairs in the country, even went on to suggest that Islam, in particular the TJ, could in this context "be the only effective means to combat the looming threat of communism in the country."

Besides these internal developments and domestic political compulsions, there seem to have been international factors at work that provided an additional stimulus to the Islamic forces in Bangladesh and to government efforts at promoting Islam in the period following the 1975 military coup. Bangladesh had gradually emerged as a major exporter of cheap, unskilled and semi-skilled labour to the oil-rich Arab states. The official display of its Islamic credentials has been seen as an effort to please its Arab patrons as well as to ensure a continued flow of Arab financial assistance. Moreover, being home to among the world's largest Muslim populations, Bangladesh could not expect to remain untouched by the growing salience of global Islamic reassertion that began manifesting itself in the seventies. Added to this was the growth of strong anti-Indian feelings among many Bangladeshis for a variety of reasons which, given the communal underpinnings of national identities and nationalist ideologies in South Asia, were reflected in the increasing importance that began being placed on Islam.

The TJ, as we had noticed earlier, received a great impetus in Bangladesh in the aftermath of the liberation struggle. Numerous respondents trace their association with the movement to the early years of the country's independence, when they turned to it for solace and comfort amidst the terrible destruction wrought by the war. The years that followed, especially after 1975, were an era of great frustration for many, when chaos ruled supreme, with military coups and dictatorships, natural disasters and economic decline, bringing in their trail immense suffering, torments and uncertainties in people's lives. Bangladeshis now began to flock in larger numbers than ever before to the TJ, finding in it an anchor in the otherwise anarchic and shattered world around them. A leading Bangladeshi scholar notes that the increased salience of Islam in public life in Bangladesh particularly after 1975 itself owes much to the rapid expansion of the TJ in the country in this period. . . .

Regional Concentration

Although the TJ is active almost all over Bangladesh, and now has a markaz in every district and most sub-district or *thana* headquarters, the movement is particularly strong in some parts of the country and relatively weak in others. All available evidence suggests, and this is attested to by many senior tablighi leaders, that the TJ has its strongest presence in the area around Mymensingh, particularly in the district of Netrakona. According to leaders at

Participants at the world assembly of the Tablighi Jama'at in Tongi. Photograph by Willem van Schendel, 2003.

the tablighi markaz in Dhaka, the Mymensingh district in northern Bangladesh ranks first in terms of the number of tablighi activists. This is an area with a rich history of peasant revolts inspired by charismatic Islamic heroes. Tablighi work in Mymensingh started in the early 1950s, considerably before it began to spread to many other parts of East Bengal. Mymensingh's easy accessibility from Dhaka, with which it was linked directly by road and rail, requiring no major rivers to be crossed, made it one of the earliest foci of tablighi work in the region. One reason for the strong presence of the TJ here, then, is simply because it has been active here for a relatively longer time.

Interestingly, the TJ focus on Mymensingh might also be related to the fact that, starting from as early as the 1870s, the area had grown into a major centre for Christian missionary activity. Even though the evangelical zeal of the Christians was directed primarily at the animistic Garo tribe that lived in the hilly tracts of the district, it is possible that Muslims, including the tablighi authorities, were apprehensive of poor Muslims living in the area going over to Christianity. The TJ is said to have won the support of many influential Deobandi *ulema* [scholars of the Deoband Islamic movement] in Mymensingh, thus ensuring that it would encounter no serious resistance from the local religious authorities.

According to TJ sources, next to Mymensingh, centres of tablighi influence and strength in Bangladesh are, in roughly descending order, Dhaka, Noakhali, Comilla, Sylhet, Chittagong and the northern-most as well as the southeastern districts. Noakhali and, to a somewhat lesser extent, Comilla are known for a marked Deobandi presence and so the fairly strong presence of the TJ here is not surprising. Sylhet's case is somewhat atypical, for unlike in the rest of Bangladesh, Islamic "reform" in recent years here has been linked, to a considerable extent, with the migration of large numbers of people to Britain. Chittagong is still heavily suffused in Sufism, centred around the cults associated with the saints of various mystical orders and has, therefore, not proved to be fertile ground for the TJ, which is known for its hostility to popular Sufism. Instances are known of tablighi activists being forcibly prevented from preaching in the area and of being physically assaulted by local Muslims. North Bengal, as well as the southeastern Khulna-Jessore region, is cut off from the rest of the country by a series of massive rivers. This communications barrier is said to pose a hurdle in the TJ's efforts to expand in the area. Moreover, North Bengal has had a strong tradition of radical and secular peasant movements, which, according to Mujahidul Islam, General Secretary of the Communist party of Bangladesh, may make its people relatively less responsive to Islamic appeals.

Social Support Base of the TJ in Bangladesh

Bangladesh still remains an overwhelmingly rural society. Not surprisingly, many tablighi activists come from rural backgrounds. They may reside in villages or may be recent migrants to the towns while still maintaining close links with their relatives in their village homes. In the villages and among rural migrants to towns, tablighi support is hardly uniform among all classes. It seems to be particularly strong among middle peasants and small rural entrepreneurs and people from such backgrounds who have taken up temporary or permanent residence in towns. Reflecting a phenomenon that has been observed over much of the rest of South Asia, and not just among the Muslims, newly emerging lower-middle classes in Bangladesh, in both villages and towns, seek to translate their recently achieved economic prosperity into claims for a higher social status within the traditional social hierarchy. Thus, indigenous names are discarded in favour of Arabic or more Islamic-sounding ones. The external symbols associated with sharia-centred Islam are now given particular stress, such as the beard, and Islamic dress for men as well as women. If one has accumulated enough money, one goes on the *haj* [pilgrimage to Mecca], in which case when one returns, one begins to be held in great respect as a *Haji* [person who has completed the pilgrimage to Mecca]. And, often, now that one has the money and can afford to take time off from one's work, one also gets involved in the TJ, going off, from time to time, on tablighi tours, with the result that one comes to be held by one's neighbours as a pious, holy man.

Adding to the obvious attraction that the ethos that the TJ deliberately seeks to cultivate would hold for lower-middle-class Bangladeshi Muslims is the central role of the oral tradition in the tablighi enterprise. Unlike, for instance, the Jama'at-i-Islami, the TJ places no importance on the written word. There seem to be few tablighi-type books in the Bengali language, and most of those that do exist are simply translations of works penned by Indian tablighi leaders. In a country where most people are illiterate, and where even among those who have had some access to education literacy skills are poorly developed, the oral tradition, with its stories of the dazzling miracles of saints and holy men, the awesome powers of supernatural beings, the sensuous pleasures of Heaven and the bone-chilling horrors of Hell, plays a central role in the transmission of ideas and knowledge. Not surprisingly, then, lower-middle-class Bangladeshis, with little or no formal education, can readily identify with the TJ's unconcern for the written word as well as with the spectacular stories that are narrated in tablighi sessions.

The marked presence of lower-middle-class Muslims in the TJ in Bangladesh, as in many other countries, then, owes much to its ethos and style and the content of its message, all of which, taken together, are seen to provide an attractive channel for the articulating of claims to higher status within the traditional social hierarchy. In some sense, then, one could perhaps speak of the lower-middle class as being the "natural constituency" of the TJ, not just in Bangladesh. Recent years, however, particularly from the early 1980s onwards, have witnessed a noticeable dilution in the earlier overwhelmingly lower-middle-class composition of the TJ in Bangladesh. Today the TJ counts, for instance, several active workers among the teachers and students at the Bangladesh University of Engineering and Technology [BUET], Dhaka, and some institutes of higher education in Mymensingh. This can be largely attributed to the pioneering efforts of Mohsin Ahmad, who brought several of his students into contact with the movement during his several years in the Dacca Engineering College. Some of his students are now on the faculty of the BUET and other engineering institutes, where they actively canvass the tablighi cause among their colleagues and students. Besides, today a small, though growing, number of business people and professionals also seem to be taking an active interest in tablighi activities.

This development appears to have resulted, at least in part, from a conscious decision on the part of tablighi authorities to reach out to these groups. One tablighi source mentions officers in the government bureaucracy, doctors, students, especially of engineering, medical and technical institutions and cadet colleges, besides the police and the armed forces as groups among whom tablighi efforts should be specially made. The reasoning behind this was simple. "It is quite natural," wrote this tablighi activist, "that leading persons in the community be made special target of the *Muballigin*. If the leaders of the community swing towards *Tabligh*, it is easier for others."

Despite their relatively small numbers, business people and professionals who are actively involved in tablighi work tend to occupy positions of responsibility and authority as *zimmedaran* [responsible persons] at the national, district and thana-level markazes of the TJ. At the Kakrail Mosque markaz, the *shura* [council] of seven persons who are responsible for the overall functioning of the TJ throughout Bangladesh includes three professionals who retired from top-level posts in the government service: Haji Abdul Muqid, brother of Mohsin Ahmad, a retired engineer; Sirajul Islam, retired chief engineer of the Department of Roads and Highways in the Ministry of Communications; and Azizul Maqsud, who retired as a high-ranking official of the Bangladesh Agricultural Development Corporation. Many of the other zimmedaran at the Kakrail markaz, as indeed in other markazes, are also retired professionals.

Note

1. Sayyed Tayyeb-ur Rahman, *Global Geo-Strategy of Bangladesh, OIC and Islamic Ummah*, (Dhaka: Islamic Foundation, 1985), 2.

Islamist Women Activists Discuss Jihad

Maimuna Huq

In Bangladesh, as elsewhere, Islamic activists have emerged as vocal critics of the current social order. Their remedy, to reform everyday life and the state according to their interpretation of Islamic scriptures, has been at the center of heated altercations. These debates have a special edge in Bangladesh because the Islamic or Islamist solution is in stark conflict with the ideals that inspired the Bangladesh Liberation War—nationalism, democracy, socialism, and secularism—ideals that provided the charter for the new state. The result is mutual scaremongering, rhetorical hyperbole, and social panic. The absence of solid knowledge about the different groups of Islamic activists, and their evolving ideas and practices, seriously hampers a more composed understanding of the processes underlying the groups' rise. In a rare study of middle-class women Islamic activists, however, Maimuna Huq provides a window to their world and aspirations. She studied members of a women's Islamist student group (Bangladesh Islami Chhatri Shangstha, or BICSA). In the excerpt here, we can hear the voices of these women as they grapple with the notions of gendered pious labor and nonviolent jihad, framed by Huq's perceptive analysis.

Women's Islamic activism in Bangladesh can be understood partly as a response to the perception that local and global life-worlds are increasingly wracked by violence, injustice, and oppression. Bangladeshi Islamists believe that the liberal state's failure to deliver on its promises of socio-economic security for all is evidenced by increasing violence, corruption, and class disparities. The Islamist movement therefore deploys a scripturally referenced emphasis on "social justice" in calling for the establishment of a "pristine" Islamic polity through *jihad* (primarily non-violent). BICSA, for example, offers a systematic path to "peace and success both in this world and in the hereafter" (a phrase often repeated in its official discourse), a path offered as a refreshing contrast to the overwhelming threats that inundate Bangladeshi women today through print media, street violence, and satellite TV images. A small but growing number of educated women are persuaded by this Islamist vision of a salvific, pristine polity to be achieved through the cultivation of pious, pristine selves. BICSA harnesses their anxieties by interweaving religious texts with narratives pertaining to local and global current events and issues in its study programmes. It uses global and local forms of violence to constitute a landscape of suffering, insecurity, and disorder in the nation and the world at large, with orthodox Islam explicitly construed as the only hope for cure.

This combined appeal to visceral insecurity and pious desire to ground oneself in orthodox Islam is manifest in key BICSA discourses and practices. Veiling and other forms of pious modesty, for example, are construed as not only religiously correct but also personally protective in a context where Bangladeshi women from the middle and especially the lower-middle classes (including most BICSA activists) are more vulnerable to violence than are elite women. Secular women's groups and the daily newspapers increasingly provide a platform for addressing the more overt forms of physical violence against women, but various "covert" forms of sexual harassment and "the violences of everyday life" to which average Bangladeshi women are subjected are virtually ignored in such venues. BICSA steps into this gap, hitching practical concerns about everyday violence and its attendant anxieties to religious concerns about bodily modesty and mental peace. It proposes a prevention-orientated approach to safety that is based on self-protection (secluding oneself through veiling from the predictably objectifying, potentially harmful male gaze), moral reform of society (including men), and reaffirmation of women's contributions as sisters, wives, mothers, and homemakers to nation-building and the construction of the global Muslim *umma* (community of Muslims). BICSA's project of social-ethical change is best summarized in its trope "security of life, property, and dignity." It is this particular project of reforming the quality of daily life in present-day Bangladesh within an Islamic framework and living with the sacrifices that undertaking such a reformist project might entail that undergirds BICSA's notion and practice of *jihad* as essentially opposed to all forms of violence, including violence in the very structures of one's articulations, thoughts, emotions, desires, and imaginings.

[At a BICSA study circle in Dhaka in March 2003], attended by eight members including the chairwoman (a higher-level BICSA member), a participant named Tanya was asked by the chairwoman and moderator, Nabila, to launch the discussion by commenting on the pre-assigned Qu'ranic verses (*sura as-Saff*), which deal with the issue of *jihad*. Following traditional Islamic scholars, Tanya suggested that there are two kinds of *jihad*, namely *jihad akbar* (the greater struggle) and *jihad asghar* (the lesser struggle). The greater *jihad* is that against one's *nafs* (baser self, animalistic instinct), which, being subject to the *waswasa* (whisperings) or influence of Satan, constantly tries to divert one from righteousness. Tanya tied this distinction to another, which she made, between mere "believers" and "*true* believers." *Nafs*, she suggests, thwarts a believer's efforts to become a *true* believer. A believer's constant struggle to overcome her *nafs* is therefore her most important battle, and socio-political struggle is *internal* to this larger struggle against desires of the self: that is, a pure self is more easily achieved in a pure society. Socio-political struggle is therefore lesser struggle, *jihad asghar*. In particular, Tanya defined lesser *jihad* as struggle waged in the cause of Allah through the commitment of one's life and property, and argued that time, career, intellect, and creative talent are at least as important for the success of the contemporary Islamic movement as the sacrifice of wealth, even life itself. . . .

In reflecting on Tanya's comments, one of her fellow participants, Bilkis, questioned the comparability of the sacrifice of life with that of time, energy, or wealth. A fellow participant, Nur Jahan, responded as follows:

> One can die in combat at a whim, or for glory, or personal vengeance. Anti-Islamic forces such as the boys of Chatra Dal kill and die for their cause as well. In Islam, however, to be rewarded by Allah as a martyr, one's intention must be pure and exclusively to defend Islam for the pleasure of Allah alone. We know the *hadith* that in the course of a battle, Ali [the Prophet's son-in-law and the fourth caliph] was about to kill an enemy soldier. At that moment, the soldier spat on Ali, who then released his adversary. At the soldier's puzzlement, Ali explained that if he were to kill his foe at that moment, he could not be certain that part of [his] motivation was not personal anger, since the soldier had spat on him. Thus Ali could not bring himself to kill an enemy because he could not be certain that his only intention at the moment of killing was to defend Faith. It is virtually impossible to muster this kind of purity of intention today. Also, it is a sin to realize an Islamic practice such as martyrdom but for the most just of causes. Therefore, it seems tome that conducting *jihad* in other ways that entail living rather than dying is much more fruitful today.

Another participant, Najma, commented:

> I think there is another reason why living rather than dying entails greater commitment to Allah's cause today. When one dies, everything ends. One must no longer deal with the troubles of life. One may *think*

that sacrificing one's life for the sake of Allah is the most difficult thing to do, since life seems to be the most precious thing we have. But I feel that spending one's wealth for Islam, for example, requires greater love for Allah since one must *live* with the consequences of that, one may have to face a lifetime of economic hardship. . . . Thus these kinds of sacrifice involve greater hardship for the cause of Islam. Dying takes but a moment. There are no consequences to suffer.

Rikta added that given the dearth of Islamic workers (in Bangladesh) today, the Islamic movement needs live workers much more than dead ones. In her view (and in that of many other activists I spoke with), it is not on the conventional battlefield that Muslims face today the most serious of attacks, but in the spheres of culture, the arts, and media indoctrination and in the temptations of upward socio-economic mobility. "The Prophet Muhammad said that the pen is mightier than the sword, and this is more true than ever before today," she reminded her audience. Nowadays, she said, activists can serve Islam best through study of a wide range of books, writing articles and books, and through preaching among family, friends, fellow students, and neighbours. . . .

BICSA's policy of non-violent *jihad* does not go unquestioned among junior activists, however. One participant asked: "If Islam can be served best through writing and speaking, then why did the Prophet Muhammad engage in so many battles? Why did even some among female companions (*mahila sahabi*) accompany him to the battlefield? Why did they not simply continue to preach?"

Nabila, the chairwoman, responded that to her knowledge the Prophet fought only where the Muslim community was under physical attack and, later, whenever ruling elites would not allow the Prophet to preach the message of Islam peacefully. This, she explained, was not the situation facing BICSA—yet. "Violence is a last resort, when one's very survival is in question, and that moment has not arrived," said Nabila. Despite being banned from certain key campuses such as Dhaka University, she argued, there was still much scope for BICSA activists to propagate the Islamic message peacefully. The media offer the most effective means today for propagating the call for an Islamic revolution. These means for getting past oppressive rulers and gaining access to publics were not available in the time of the Prophet. "But do we not emulate the Prophet?" asked a participant. Nabila responded that to propagate the divine message of liberation, practical strategies for propagation must change with context.

Rikta responded that it is humiliating to have to flee from the dormitory when faced with the possibility of violence from rival activists (e.g. in the aftermath of violent conflicts between BICSA's male counterpart group Chatra Shibir and the student wings of the ethno-secularist Awami League and the conservative-liberalist Bangladesh Nationalist Party). Sometimes it is important to stand and fight so that one's opponents do not consider one weak and try to terrorize one into silence. "They consider us timid, in our veils," she fumed. Not only does this dishearten activists, she argued, but unopposed secularist shows of strength discourage women who might otherwise join BICSA.

Despite Rikta's dissent, many BICSA activists are content with BICSA's normative avoidance of violence. Furthermore, neither BICSA authorities nor the parent organization Jamaat have thus far relaxed the policy of strictly non-violent *jihad* for women, which bans even verbal violence. Why?

Importantly, BICSA's non-violence helps it attract members. In Bangladesh, politics is often violent, and many families oppose participation in politics by young sons and daughters (especially the latter). BICSA's meticulous avoidance of violent encounters with secular and liberal-nationalist groups helps activists garner and retain familial support.

But how does BICSA distance itself ideologically from violence, given its own emphasis on *jihaad fii sabiilillah* (struggle in the way of God) and, for that matter, the Prophet Muhammad's own willingness to wage literal war in the latter part of his life, following his migration to the town of Madina from his hometown Makka?

As partly seen in Nabila's responses to questions, BICSA does this in a number of ways. First, it effectively recasts South Asian Islamist Abul Ala Maududi's vision of socio-political *jihad*, which emphasizes Islamization of Muslim polities equally for hegemonic and self-defence purposes, as a vision justified primarily by self-defence against and socio-political resistance to "un-Islamic socio-cultural influences and anti-Islamic political and economic domination." In this context, self-defence means cultural, political, and economic self-defence.

Second, it shifts the popular understanding of *jihad* as violent resistance to liberal-secularist, Indian (Hindu), and Western domination to an understanding of *jihad* as the investment of one's time, effort, money, influence, credentials, skills, and creative and performative abilities, a form of *jihad* that I call civic persuasion. The object of civic persuasion is the Islamization of the polity simultaneously from above (through moral-ethical reform among the social and political leadership and Islamization of the state) and from below (through the Islamic socialization and politicization of ordinary citizens).

Third, having constituted themselves in opposition to the multiple forms of violence that afflict Bangladeshi women, BICSa activists are reluctant to reproduce other forms of violence. They therefore tend to privilege notions of peace, patience, and reasoning in both ideology and praxis.

Finally, the painstaking cultivation of feminine Islamic virtues by BICSa, including "shyness" (*lajja*) and "modesty" (*shalinata*), "humility" (*binay*), and the related, urban attributes of "politeness" (*bhadrata*), "decency" (*shalinata*), and "civility" (*shabyata*) in deportment and interpersonal relations disinclines BICSa women to any kind of violence. This holds for public situations where "talking back" to verbally aggressive rivals and sometimes even physically repulsing aggressors instead of seeking refuge in BICSa offices might boost group morale. Withdrawal and non-confrontation accord better with *lajja* and *bhadrata* than does brawling in the street or on campus.

On the other hand, BICSa staunchly defends and glorifies the violent engagement of its male organizational counterpart, Chatra Shibir, on the ground that its members have no choice: they operate openly as a political party, and political culture in Bangladesh is such that one is disempowered, even annihilated, if one refuses to fight back. Violence, BICSa argues, cannot be altogether renounced in an essentially violent world, but must be used judiciously and authorized by "authentic Muslim leaders." Indeed, the violent encounters of Shibir men empower BICSa members with a rousing repertoire of tales of sacrifice and martyrdom, which provides them with a moral vocabulary of justification for mobilizing against and dislodging from power those perceived as oppressors. In these circulating tales of Islamist men's sacrifice of life or limb, anti-Islamists are always understood to instigate the violence.

Some scholars have characterized the violence practised by Islamist men in South Asia as essential to political Islam. In showing that Islamist women affiliated with these same male Islamist groups and studying virtually the same texts on *jihad* as their male counterparts studiously avoid violent behaviour, my fieldwork points to the need for cultural contextualization of violence in the name of religious ideology. BICSa women are just as Islamist as Chatra Shibir men. Nor is it clear that Qur'anic verses mobilizing violence are addressed specifically to men. Nevertheless, BICSa women are strictly non-violent in practice. There is, in effect, a culturally specific, gendered division of pious labour, with women specializing in virtues such as "shyness" and men taking on what is seen as the heroic, necessary work of defensive violence.

The Nation and the Military

Ayesha Siddiqa

This piece, published in a Pakistani newspaper in 2007, seeks to warn Bangladeshis. Since its birth, Bangladesh has experienced several coups d'état, and military regimes ruled the country from 1975 to 1990. Ayesha Siddiqa argues that the restoration of parliamentary democracy in 1991 did not end military interference. Rather, the armed forces acted as the power behind the throne of successive civilian governments. In 2007 a military-controlled "caretaker government" took power and ruled without legislative authority until it allowed elections and a return to parliamentary rule in 2009. Siddiqa suggests that recent developments have made it more dangerous for civilian politicians to flirt with the military.

Talk to an average Bangladeshi about civil-military relations and they will tell you that their country is not like Pakistan and that they will never allow the military to take control of politics. Unfortunately, in their eagerness not to be compared to Pakistan, the Bangladeshis have failed to notice that they are slowly creeping towards a situation subtly comparable to Pakistan and that if they are not careful the military would soon begin to play a decisive role in the country's politics. They must also realise that the elite of any country might be as myopic as that of any other country and may push the country to political disaster.

Bangladesh started its transition to democracy in 1991 when public protests put an end to the rule of General Ershad who had taken over after the assassination of his predecessor General Ziaur Rahman. Since then, the army has not returned to politics. Bangladeshi political historians always forget the botched coup attempt of 1996 when Generals Naseem and Hilal Murshad conspired to take over. Had the military been fully professional then, which means tightly organised as a hierarchy, it would have managed to take control of the government. The fact that the conspiring generals did not have good communication channels with the battalion guarding Dhaka and could not convince some generals to move from strategic positions saved the country. So, in 1996, there were elements in the army who had the ambition to gain power.

However, the civilian rulers entered into an informal partnership with the military[,] according to which the government would ensure the military's interest in return for the latter staying out of politics. This arrangement could be managed because the armed forces were not completely professional. The legacy of the Bangladeshi military is a mix of freedom fighters and officers repatriated from the United Pakistan armed forces. The friction between the two schools of thought did not allow for the kind of consolidation of perception and interests, which would result in the building up of a praetorian military. The officer cadre was further enticed into submission through the opportunities gained from participating in the UN peacekeeping missions. Apart from the defence budget, the military depends on the UN to obtain resources for the gratification of its personnel.

Some of the UN money was later re-invested in exploring other possibilities for economic expansion by the armed forces. The Bangladeshi military has used some of this money as venture capital and established stakes in business and industry. . . .

Since the past ten years, there have been three developments in Bangladesh that have had an impact on its politics.

First, the military has consolidated its corporate ethos and culture, which means that the organisation is building cohesion within itself, which it lacked earlier. Along with this, the military has also become more conscious of its interests, which includes personal stakes of the officer cadre. For a military which was basically meant to provide security against external threat to Bangladesh, the bulk has now become engaged in the UN peacekeeping missions. Whether peacekeeping missions are the core task of a professional military is a moot point.

Second, a gap has emerged between the people and the political leadership. The politicians have become more intensely authoritarian and myopic in their thinking. Such a transformation is not new but dates back to the times soon after the country was born. However, the predatory instinct of the politicians has intensified[,] resulting in policies that would destabilise the country.

Third, there is the development of an equally predatory middle class that is willing to use the military as a secondary partner to change the current political arrangement. Since the Bangladeshi political system is patronage-based, the common man is not able to look beyond Sheikh Hasina and Khaleda Zia. The problem of the educated middle class, on the other hand, is that while [they are] not willing to "soil their hands" in the "dirty game of politics," they would like to take power away from these two female leaders. Resultantly, the educated middle class is quite happy to use the military and unfair political means to change the domestic scene.

For instance, while making a speech in Canberra the Bangladeshi advisor on foreign affairs claimed that the caretaker setup in the country [the military-controlled interim government that ruled Bangladesh in 2007–8] denoted the rule of the "Baudhulouk" [bhadralok]. This term means educated and more capable; it was traditionally used by the Calcutta elite to refer to themselves. The underlying message of the gentleman, which more or less represents the perception of the educated middle class, is that there are new groups that are ready to replace the old leadership. Since mass politics is too dirty a game, these new power aspirants will use unfair means and the military to negotiate power. These people would rather have the military help them with some rigging than let Sheikh Hasina and Begum Khaleda Zia return to power.

Surely, the two ladies must share their part of the blame for letting things come to this point. The misuse of power and ill-conceived policies rarely bring fruit. For example, the BNP [Bangladesh Nationalist Party] strategically encouraged the Jama'at and other religious extremist factions to their own advantage. Interestingly, Khaleda Zia was not the only beneficiary of cultivating religious extremism. The military benefited both directly and indirectly. A more rightist society is bound to be more nationalistic in a narrow sense.

However, the problem is that using the military is never a good option. This is not an organisation which can be trusted to remain a junior partner once the civilian policymakers and stakeholders begin to use it to gain power.

Pakistan's example is a case in point. The 1958 coup by the civil bureaucracy was not meant to bring in the military. But once General Ayub [Khan] decided to take over power, there was nothing that could stop him. Sadly, we are still unable to check the military from gaining power.

Amending the Constitution

Saqeb Mahbub

During forty years of independence, Bangladesh has witnessed many changes in its political system: from parliamentary to presidential and back to parliamentary, and from military takeover to rubber-stamp Parliament to sovereign Parliament. Understandably, its constitution has undergone changes too, and not all of them were made in a democratic context. In 2010 the Constitution of Bangladesh has been put under the microscope—for the fifteenth time since 1972. With the annulment of the Fifth Amendment of the constitution through a judgment by the Supreme Court in 2010, the constitution is to revert to some of the core values behind the formation of the original 1972 version, whose four main pillars were democracy, socialism, nationalism, and secularism. The judgment also declared illegal the proclamation of martial law, as had happened on 8 November 1975 after the assassination of Sheikh Mujibur Rahman and his family. The lawyer Saqeb Mahbub (a partner at Mahbub and Company, Dhaka) put the following summary of the judgment on the blog Unheard Voices.

The most significant part from the long-awaited judgment of the Appellate Division:

1. Secularism reenters after thirty-three years. It will reappear in the Preamble, Article 8, and Article 12, just as it did in 1972.
2. "Bismillah" [Islamic term that means "in the name of God"] in the Preamble is out (despite [Prime = Minister] Hasina's promise; in her defence, this was not her decision).
3. People of Bangladesh can continue to be called "Bangladeshi" (High Court's decision to rule the amendment replacing Bangalee with Bangladeshi is overruled).
4. The old Article 10—fundamental principle of achieving a "socialist economic system"—is back in place.
5. Socialism will not mean "economic and social justice" any more. It will mean socialism.

Wearing the nation on the skin. A young man in Dhaka wears a T-shirt proudly proclaiming his country's name, in Bengali and English. Photograph by Willem van Schendel, 2011.

6. The proviso to Article 38 prohibiting religious politics is back. Does not mean Jamaat[-e-Islami] is automatically banned, but if this sticks, they will surely be taken to court.

The Bengali Sense of Victimhood

Rahnuma Ahmed

In Bangladesh, political humor has been used effectively as a form of resistance. Political cartoons have been very much part of that trend. But the cartoon discussed here stems from a different genre. The message is that external powers are plotting with "tribal" insurgents to break up the nation-state of Bangladesh by sawing off the Chittagong Hill Tracts from the rest of Bangladesh. In her column in the newspaper New Age, *Rahnuma Ahmed foregrounds the Bengali nationalism inherent in the cartoon by revealing the politics of silence that surrounds Bengali oppression in the region.*

A cartoon had caught my eye. Published in a Bengali national daily, soon after the recurring incidents of ethnic violence in Rangamati and Khagrachhari in February this year [2010], it shows a map of the southeastern part of the country. The land mass is coloured a sea-green. The letters forming the word "Bangladesh" are printed in black. An iridescent grey shades off into black in parts it presumably represents, but indistinguishably so, both Indian territory and the Bay of Bengal's waters.

It shows the Chittagong Hill Tracts—with the districts of Khagrachhari, Rangamati and Bandarban clearly marked out—being sawn off by arms clutching wooden handles, fixed to both ends of the saw. To the right side of the cartoon, extending into Bangladesh as it were, are two arms, while on the left, three. The arms on the left side of the map are clothed. The first two hands reach out of their coat-covered shirt-sleeves. Clothed. Civil. The last one juts out of what seems to be a clerical coat-sleeve. The topmost coat-sleeve has "European Union" written on it. The second, "Chittagong Hill Tracts Commission." And the third, "Christian missionary." Both arms to the right are bare. Uncovered. One has "UPDF" (United People's Democratic Front) scrawled on it, while the other, "JSS" (presumably referring to the PCJSS, *Parbatya Chattagram Jana Sanghati Samiti*). No clothes. Barbaric.

A nation besieged by enemies within and without. The cartoon thereby evokes a sense of crisis. Fear. Anxiety.

Bangladesh victimized. Cartoonist unknown. Published in *New Age*, 5 April 2010.

It is, I thought to myself, a perfect example of all that which bedevils the nation nearly forty years after independence. There are many signifiers. There are both presences, and absences. Those present—and named—are the enemies. These foes are both internal, and external, to the nation. They are out to destroy the nation. To sever its limb. Only those present (in the cartoon) wield power, and malevolently so.

The Bengalis are absent. It is this absence which captures very well, I think, how Bengalis increasingly prefer to portray themselves when confronted with their power as ethnically dominant, and overwhelmingly so, within this nation. The act of absencing makes Bengalis appear powerless. As a victim, one who is defined in the dictionary as:

—a helpless person, somebody who experiences misfortune and feels helpless to remedy it.
—[victimhood:] fall victim to somebody or something, to be affected, harmed, or deceived by somebody or something.

Bengalis are the victims of regional and international machinations. Of forces who are infinitely more powerful. Forces external to the nation, with whom bad elements within the nation, the "tribals," have ganged up.

I cannot help but think, how would the cartoonist have portrayed 1971? East Pakistan, being cut asunder by, who? Aided by, who? But of course, let me add, when I compare the situation in the CHT [Chittagong Hill Tracts] at present to the situation confronting Pakistan in 1971, I do not do so from any ulterior motive of advocating a break-up, or secession, or any such thing. I do it because *ekattur* [1971] has taught me that to survive as a nation, one must not only be able to accommodate cultural differences, but to welcome them. That what the centres of power label a "conspiracy" is most likely, a political problem, one that must be resolved politically, never, ever, through the deployment of brute force. That genuine attempts must be made to undo historical wrongs. Before it is too late.

That lives matter. That homes matter. That justice matters.

I muse to myself, why are there no Bengalis in the cartoon? Probably because however hard one tries to depict them innocently, the very labels, "government," "army," "police," "settlers," are heavily-laden with power. With Bengali power, and historically so. The nation's history is built on ethnic domination; it is one that continues in the historical present. I muse to myself, the cartoonist must have realised that putting in Bengalis just wouldn't do. The victim myth would have become unsustainable. That it would be better to leave them out. Altogether.

But the absence has been made present through other means. Very distinctively so. The letters printed on the land mass. Bangladesh. Bangla + desh, the land of the Bengalis. A literal rendering. It homogenises differences among Bengalis, differences to do with class, gender, religion, regional, linguistic (many Sylhetis think of themselves as Sylhetis and not Bengalis), historical. And among indigenous peoples too, Chakma, Marma, Tripura, Santal, Bawm, Tanchangya, Rakhain, Garo, Lushai, and many others. The construction of a Bengali sameness becomes an ethnic norm, one to which others must aspire. Must wish to belong.

Soon after independence, we had been too heady to grasp the wisdom that lay behind Manabendra Narayan Larma's words, "Under no definition or logic can a Chakma be a Bengali or a Bengali be a Chakma . . . As citizens of Bangladesh we are all Bangladeshis, but we also have a separate ethnic identity, which unfortunately the Awami League leaders [the then ruling party] do not want to understand." The change that Ziaur Rahman had effected after coming to power had to do with nationality, with national belonging—"Bangladeshis" instead of "Bengalis," the latter had been held to be universally applicable for all citizens regardless of their ethnic belonging. It was a technical correction, having been accompanied by the military occupation of the Chittagong Hill Tracts. By death and destruction. By rape. By the settlement of landless Bengalis on *pahari* [hill] land. It led to the flight of indigenous peoples in large numbers, to neighbouring India where they sought refuge.

In order to portray "the" Bengali as victim, the cartoonist must suppress the Bengali presence. That, surely, is interesting?

Bengali writers, however, are more forthcoming. Some claim Bengalis are indigenous, have been so for centuries, or better still, since time immemorial. It is the *paharis*, who are settlers. The "tribal" rulers are exploiters. Hilly people are extremists. They did not take up arms to resist Bengali oppression, to regain cultural autonomy, but because they are . . . [and] have always been . . . for many centuries . . . bandits and criminals. They abduct and kidnap Bengalis. Others write, some foreign NGOs have ulterior motives. They want the army to withdraw before amicable relations have been restored between *paharis* and Bengalis. Foreign forces, such as the European Union, some foreign members of the CHT Commission, have become active under cover of the Peace Treaty (1997). There are plans afoot to sever the CHT from Bangladesh, to re-make it on the lines of a Christian East Timor. Bengali settlers are being slaughtered. Their houses are being razed to the ground. Even military personnel are being attacked. Muslims are being prevented from entering their mosques. From praying. A large conspiracy is in the offing.

Can such paranoid ramblings, whether depicted visually through cartoons or written out in articles, counter imperial politics? Concerns over national sovereignty are real, are justified in these times when US-led imperial terror, one in which western European nations are fully complicit, has been unleashed worldwide. To save the nation, a genuine leap of imagination is needed. One which does not confuse the roles of "perpetrator" and "victim."

Images of Post-1971 Politics

Liberation War memorial in Khulna (southern Bangladesh). Photograph by Willem van Schendel, 2006.

Today, the Liberation War of 1971 lives on as the foundational moment for both nation and state in Bangladesh. All over the country monuments celebrate the war's glory and valor. This one, titled Heroic Bengalis (Bir Bangali), is a good example. It shows three Freedom Fighters (Muktijoddha)—a peasant in a sun hat, a military man in uniform and helmet, and a shirt-wearing civilian—joining a battle with the enemy. They surround the first flag of independent Bangladesh (after the war the yellow map of the country was dropped from the national flag).

Politics in Bangladesh continue to be enthralled by the war. In their quest for power, political parties are constantly evoking their contributions to the war. They nurture elaborate narratives of their senior (or deceased) leaders' valiant roles in it. Wartime one-upmanship is essential in claiming legitimacy and, as a result, competing readings of key war events are the stuff of everyday politics. Forty years on, the Liberation War is still the major theme in Bangladesh politics.

"Stop communalism! The call of the Committee for the Uprooting of Traitors and Collaborators of the War of 1971." Poster, 1999. Used by permission of the Heritage Archives of Bangladesh History, Rajshahi.

After the Bangladesh Liberation War of 1971 there were plans to try war criminals, but these soon came to naught. In the 1990s, however, a citizens' committee was formed to insist that justice be done after all. This is one of its posters. It demands the formation of a special tribunal to put war criminals on trial and a prohibition of the "communalist politics of the Jama'at-Shibir [Islamist] groups." The image is especially emotive. It shows the dragon of communalism (religious sectarianism)—dressed as a conservative Muslim man wearing the colors of Pakistan—trampling on skulls and pulling down two key symbols of Bangladesh: the flag and the National Monument for the Martyrs of the Liberation War (Jatiyo Smriti Soudho). Punishment for war crimes continues to be a live issue in national politics.

"Vote for Jewel and Babu! The Bangladesh Islamic Students Camp [Shibir]—Bangladesh Institute of Technology, Rajshahi." Poster. Photograph by Willem van Schendel, 2006.

After the war, the ruling Awami League prohibited the Jama'at-e-Islami (an Islamist party that had sided with Pakistan) on the ground of treason. In the late 1970s, however, the military government of Ziaur Rahman allowed the Jama'at-e-Islami to return. Since then it has played a distinctive role in politics, although in national elections it has never received more than 9 percent of the vote.

Its student organization, the Islamic Students Camp, became very active on university campuses, and at times controlled them. It often clashed violently with student organizations of other political parties, especially during elections to student bodies. This poster seeks the vote for fourteen positions, from deputy chairman to sports secretary, in a central student council.

"We want Al-Hajj Sheikh Mohammad Abdullah to be elected as Member of Parliament for Munshiganj!" Poster. Used by permission of the Heritage Archives of Bangladesh History, Rajshahi.

In Bangladesh, elections are contested with great enthusiasm, and invariably dozens of parties take part in them. Since 1990 two parties have dominated the scene: the Awami League and the Bangladesh Nationalist Party. To most voters, it is not the relatively vague ideological differences between these parties that are important but the fact that they represent contending factions of the ruling elite.

Both parties use transmitted charisma rather than policy pledges to appeal to their voters. This election poster for a local Bangladesh Nationalist Party candidate in Munshiganj (a town in central Bangladesh) is a case in point. There is no mention of the candidate's ideas or policy aspirations but the vignette in the upper-right-hand corner contains essential information. It shows the late Ziaur Rahman (the army man who took power after a coup d'état in 1975 and was assassinated in 1981); his widow, Begum Khaleda Zia (prime minister from 1991 to 1996 and from 2001 to 2006); and their son Tareque Rahman (who was being groomed for leadership in the Bangladesh Nationalist Party)—all showering their power and blessing on the candidate.

"The indigenous peoples of Bangladesh must be given constitutional recognition!" Poster. Used by permission of the Heritage Archives of Bangladesh History, Rajshahi.

In the wake of the Chittagong Hill Tracts War (1975–97), a national movement took shape to demand basic rights for minority groups in Bangladesh. It was able to put the issue of minority rights on the national political agenda, especially after it forged links with majority-group activists and with international indigenous peoples' organizations.

"Stop the U.S. imperialists' reign of terror and looting! Self-interested imperialism and its supporters are ruining the industrial and agricultural economy. And stop the export of gas!—Communist Party of Bangladesh." Poster. Used by permission of the Heritage Archives of Bangladesh History, Rajshahi.

There are many left-wing political parties in Bangladesh. The Communist Party of Bangladesh is one of them. This poster shows hellish hounds, representing the United States and the United Kingdom, pawing Afghanistan, Palestine, Iraq, and Bangladesh. It also takes up a hot issue in national politics: the possible export of Bangladesh's considerable reserves of natural gas to neighboring India. Popular support for left-wing politics was high in the late 1960s and 1970s but is currently at a low ebb.

VII

Contemporary Culture

Bangladesh's complex culture is deeply embedded in its distinctive oral and literary traditions. The outside world has been largely unaware of these traditions. It tends to see Bangladesh through dichotomous lenses: the illiterate rural masses versus the educated urban elite, the religious versus the secular—especially religious nationalism versus linguistic nationalism—and tradition versus modernity. But the cultural universe of Bangladesh goes way beyond such juxtapositions. A heritage of multilayered cultural fusion lies at the basis of an aversion to orthodoxies of many kinds and a willingness to embrace disparate ideas and beliefs. To understand Bangladesh we must be aware of this openness to complexity, conciliation, and creativity and of its impact on political and social processes in the country.

In this part we look at some examples of today's compound culture. They form a medley of cultural expressions, presenting festivals and celebrations (both religious and secular), popular culture (both traditional and emergent), and high art (both literary and visual). We also explore the sensual earthiness of the local cuisine, the growth and styles of cultural establishments, and the critical space occupied by minority cultures.

Cultural space in Bangladesh is always political. The politics of culture are apparent when we view the contested terrain between religious orthodoxy and syncretistic cultural trends. In the context of global Islam, Bangladesh is a "moderate" Muslim nation. In the context of nationalism, a hegemonic and state-supported Bengali identity subordinates indigenous cultures.

The political is also expressed in cultural practices that signify resistance. For example, the popular protest songs, which the Bangladesh independence movement produced, continue to echo as they inspire analogous songs created by the indigenous people of the Chittagong Hill Tracts in their battle against state oppression.

In this part we concentrate on texts that bring out some of the facets of Bangladesh's diverse culture; there is also a collection of images depicting the country's cultural diversity.

An artist at work at the Dhaka University Faculty of Fine Arts. Photograph by Willem van Schendel, 2010.

The Raw, Frank, Funny Eid Parade

Henry Glassie

*The end of the Muslim fasting month of Ramadan is marked by the festival of Eid
(also spelled Id), which is celebrated with great fervor throughout Bangladesh. Apart
from its religious significance, for most revelers Eid means visiting relatives and
friends and eating lavishly. Historically, processions were taken out on the streets
of Dhaka to celebrate Eid. This custom faded away, but it was revived in the mid-
1990s. Henry Glassie gives a lively eyewitness account of the carnival atmosphere
that characterizes the parade in Dhaka. He tells us about the imaginative and
sometimes hilarious floats that inhabitants from Old Dhaka put on view—and
what they communicate: wit and humor, criticism of political wrongs, surprising
interpretations of history, and pride in Bangladesh's achievements.*

During the month of Ramadan, trade increased gradually in the streets of
Dhaka. Sweet shops packed at dusk with people buying delicacies to break
the fast each night. Booths opened to sell Eid cards that commingled the
sentiments of Easter and Valentine's Day. Shoppers sought new clothes, and
editorials in the papers expressed the hope that Eid might boost the economy as Christmas does in the West. Though half the city's people had returned to rural homes for the holiday, crowds on the day before Eid rivaled
any Christmas Eve throng. At New Market, in the press of shoppers, there
was no way to stop or go quickly. In touch at all times with the bodies of
two other people, women and men drifted in the thick human tide, bearing
bundles of new clothing.

The night was shattered with fireworks. Ramadan ended, and it was Eid.
Early in the morning, I joined eighty-five thousand men for prayer in the
open field by the High Court in downtown Dhaka. We wore snowy prayer
caps and loose, new *panjabis* [loose-fitting upper garments] in white, cream,
ivory, fawn, buff, beige, and the most delicate shades of lemon, peach, and
apricot. An amplified voice led us through *namaz* [prayer] at a stately pace. It
felt good to repeat the familiar postures, standing, bowing, kneeling, lower-
ing the head in massive oneness. We sat for a long prayer of peace for the na-

tion, the wide community of Muslims, the whole tortured world, and then, not suddenly or hastily, but without delay, the crowd dispersed, walking. The rest of the day was spent indulging in the great Bengali delights. We sped from home to home in order to sit, to feast, to be in company.

On the afternoon of the next day, I went to see the Eid parade with Shamsuzzaman Khan. As old paintings attest, Eid was marked by processions in the last century. The parade faded away during the tense Pakistan period. In 1994, the mayor invited the parade's revival.

In this, the second performance in the new series, the people of Old Dhaka march into New Dhaka. They come with banners, the first wishing peace, love, and happiness to the citizens of Bangladesh. Brass bands, uniformed in fantastic parody, provide the sound, a thumping, wailing blend, as in New Orleans, of carnival and martial regularity. The pace is set by floats, mounted on trucks or pulled by bullocks, but most often powered by a man pedaling some variant on the rickshaw. It is not the architecture of the float that demands attention, but its human tableau. Men and women perform a brief skit, over and over, or they hold theatrical postures in representational exactitude. Realism is the aim. Pleasure for the audience lies first in the precision of portrayal, the costume, the makeup, the perfect gesture. Mimetic accuracy prompts the laugh of recognition, stimulating the mind into understanding, troubling the matrix of emotion where pleasure meets pain.

Filtering from two sides, joining the long line in the expedient order of chance arrival, the floats gather, clot, then move forward, presenting to the people—and to the dignitaries on the reviewing stand—glimpses of the world as it is seen from old Dhaka. Like those on rickshaws in traffic, the pictures come in no order. Each is a colorful, engaging work on its own. But for the rickshaw artist, multitudinous images gather into a small number of significant categories—mosques, say, movie stars or village life—and, as I watched, the images flowing in the Eid parade clustered into a few categories in which they became meaningful, through which, like rickshaws in the aggregate, they connected into a view of Bangladesh. The Eid parade offers one more introduction to Dhaka.

History segments in Bangladesh by shifts of political power. Periods are not embraced arbitrarily by turns of the century, but, as in Japan, by events that separate stretches of time, unequal in length, but consistent in tone. These pieces of time do not fit easily into transnational schemes, but they hold immediate meaning for the people of the country.

The historical floats in the Eid parade concentrate at two points of transition from one period to the next. One clutch of floats evokes Mughal grandeur. Before the Mughals began the conquest of Bengal in 1575, there had been distinct periods in Muslim command, and before the Muslim conquest in the thirteenth century, the Hindu Senas, the Buddhist Palas, and the Hindu Guptas had ruled. But that is all prehistory to the creators of the Eid parade. Their tale begins in Mughal opulence.

Opulence sets the tone. In oriental splendor with a Persian accent, powdered to pale aristocratic complexions, people sit, swaddled in folds and tucks of glittery fabric. Men wear the turbans and curly silver slippers of the classy modern Muslim wedding.

Three floats carry *nawabs*. The parade's most lavish presentation, borne on a truck and accompanied by horsemen, is a painting come to life: the *nawab*, the ruler of Bengal, sits easily on his magnificent throne, attended by elegantly attired, deferentially disposed ambassadors from the Middle East and Europe. The assembly incarnates the period when the wealth of Bengal stunned the visitor and excited the greed of England. This is the last great *nawab*, Ali Vardi Khan, who died in 1756, and whose grandson and heir was defeated in the next year at the battle of Plassey by Robert Clive of the East India Company. The Mughal period ended. The British period began.

The aftermath is not depicted, as it might be, by British atrocities, but by the *nawab*, transmuted into an instrument of alien power. There he sits, richly dressed and complacently smoking his *hukka*. Before him, a woman pleads with passion. Behind him, her husband is flogged with a whip. The couple represents the people of Bengal, requesting justice, beaten without mercy, while their leader puffs in luxury. The lash goes on.

No float recalls the end of the British period, in 1947, when India was partitioned and Pakistan erected; the colonial period was not over for the people of East Bengal. After 1757, when Mughal rule ended and the British period began, the next date that matters is 1971, when Bangladesh was created.

Young men in military uniforms, with powdered faces and fake moustaches, are enough to bring to mind the terror of the time when the Pakistani army cracked down and millions were massacred in 1971. But the story is made explicit in the wooden boat, borne on a float, filled with women and children while Pakistani soldiers beat them with the butts of their rifles; and by the boys, their bodies caked with clay, frozen into the postures of a statue commemorating the freedom fighters, the guerilla warriors who resisted to the death; and by the sad little girls, dressed as the grieving mothers of the heroes who fell in the liberation of their nation.

The shift from the Pakistan period to the Bangladesh period is marked by a banner reading, "Our freedom was the greatest accomplishment of the

Bengali people." Behind it march men, holding above the earth a gigantic flag, the banner of the new nation, in design like Japan's, but in the colors of Bangladesh: the green field centered by a red hot sun.

The story is brought to date in a float labeled, "Our political leaders." On it women impersonate the women currently vying for power: the prime minister, Khaleda Zia, and the chief of the opposition, Sheikh Hasina. Surrounded by supporters, waving to the crowd, both speak interminably into microphones. They exemplify the dominant style of the parade, for they are neither lampooned nor lionized. It is the very accuracy of representation— the saris, the makeup, the gestures—that spreads smiles among the spectators, who stand in the street, playing the part of masses.

At the end of history's stream lies modern life. Two floats depict the population. This is the view from Old Dhaka, so the prime distinction is not between rich and poor, but between Muslim and Hindu. On one float sits the Muslim family, the father in prayer cap and beard, the wife and children in placid decorum. Their serenity contrasts with the float portraying Hindus. A drum pounds. A boy dances in sensual abandon. He wears a wrapped and rolled *dhoti*, the emblematic dress of the Hindu male, though most Hindu men, like most Muslim men, wear the simpler sarong called a *lungi*. Even men who wear trousers at work are apt to relax at home in the loose, comfortable *lungi*.

This is a parade on a Muslim holiday in a nation that is eighty-eight percent Muslim, but the Muslim view of the world would be incomplete without the Hindu presence. Only eleven percent of the population is Hindu, but Muslims till the soil and, leaving the land, fill the apartment buildings and *bustis* [slums] of New Dhaka, while Hindus mix in large numbers among the merchants and manufacturers who are the parade's authors. (It follows that Hindus will be overrepresented in any book featuring artisans, like this one of mine.)

It is a parade on a Muslim holiday, but it does not celebrate Islamic law nor assert an Islamic politic. Only a few of the parade's pieces hold peculiar interest for Muslims. A long line of rickshaws, wrapped in cloth, wholly enclosed, recalls the bad old days of the Pakistan period when women traveled the streets in hiding. A boy and a girl snuggle openly in the last rickshaw to illustrate the enlightened present, to suggest the progress made by women within Islam. (And remember: both of this Muslim nation's principal political leaders are women, a thing apparently impossible in the liberated, Christian West.)

On one float sits a *pir* with a long beard, tangled up in chains. The *pir*, the living Muslim saint, might be a holy man, guiding his disciples on a profound mystical quest, or he might be a fraud who extracts their cash to live in luxury. The parade's *pir* is a hilarious, patent fake. Implicitly, he provides a warning to the gullible, compatible with that issued from the float on palmistry. The mad palmist searches with an enormous magnifying glass through a big book of secrets, while two men, good sports amid rough humor, hold up the handless stumps of their arms, and the sign beneath them comments that if palmistry determines what kind of luck you have, then we have no luck at all. We, the ones without luck, are the dupes who surrender our cash to false *pirs* and palmists, and we are the men without hands, and we are the people watching, standing on the ground within our own tragedies.

The parade's main topic is the troubles we share, Muslim and Hindu alike. In comedy crossed with anger, the parade raises issues for consideration by the city's people, who crowd the streets, and by its mayor, watching from the reviewing stand. One banner reads, "The Dhaka electricity supply: rubbish." Those people are annoyed by periodic disruptions in the flow of electricity, and these by the city's unhealthy water: "Boil your water or die." One man lies stupefied, crushed by a mountain of bags labeled "traffic jams." Two floats show men disappearing into open manholes. Manhole covers are stolen and sold for scrap, and, were it not for conscientious citizens who flag the holes with leafy branches, and for the adroit operators of agile rickshaws, open manholes would cause endless accidents. There is one man with a blue papier-mâché mosquito on his head and plasters all over his body, and another with a sign saying, "The mosquitoes will drive us crazy." Thirty years ago, I am told, a city health inspector eliminated mosquitoes from Dhaka, but today with every sunset they return in blood-thirsty swarms. Only mosquito netting and smoking coils make sleep possible, and experience in this place teaches you why the mosquito is the lowest incarnation in the Hindu chain of rebirth.

Medicine is the subject of four floats. On one, surely clear enough, a gloomy doctor sits with his black bag shut, surrounded by sick and dying children. The sign reads, "If you have no money, you will get no cure." The label on another, in reference to a notorious local case, reads, "Not a medical center, but a love center." Above the sign, a doctor with a stethoscope over his shoulder chats up two pretty nurses, all of them uniformed in studied detail, while a man on the bed behind the doctor writhes in histrionic agony.

Five of the parade's little dramas show muggers, locally called hijackers, the highwaymen who infest the city's streets at night. One represents dacoits, the bandit bands of the countryside.

Solutions to the problems of mosquitoes and foul water, greedy doctors, and street thugs . . . lie beyond the control of the people. These are complaints addressed to the oblivious *nawabs* of the present. But other problems lie within control, and the parade confronts them directly. One float excoriates wife beating, another prostitution, another narcotics addiction. Four raise the evils of alcohol. Boys, enjoying the role, stagger like drunks. A battered daughter turns on her drunken father and beats him, upsetting all order in the chaos wrought by drink. In truth, alcohol is not a grave problem in Dhaka. There is one bar for every two million people. But alcohol is a focus here, as tobacco is in America, because it is something that remains within the command of the individual will, absorbing the frustrations engendered by more serious problems that lie beyond, and becoming the urgent, symbolic embodiment of wrongness itself.

In the raw, frank, funny Eid parade, the celebration of what is right—the heroic achievement of the nation—is set into tension with criticism of what is wrong: the failures of the government and the people, the trustees and heirs of the achievement. To appreciate the wit and courage of the people of Old Dhaka, imagine their parade winding through the streets of Washington, D.C., on the Fourth of July. Some of the floats would serve quite well—the profiteering, philandering men of medicine, the muggers, drunks, and dope fiends—but others would need translation. There might be a historical float of a slave auction, perhaps one of the president jogging in his shorts, another with a lobbyist for the gluttonous insurance industry showering a congressman with dollars. The point is that the people of Dhaka have their own picture of history, with its stirring, disturbing relevance for the present, and they understand their problems. They understand, complain, and endure.

A Visionary of Rural Beauty

Burhanuddin Khan Jahangir

If there is one name in the world of art that epitomizes the quintessential Bengali and has universal appeal, it is Zainul Abedin (1914–76). Born in rural Mymensingh, Abedin grew up in a peasant community and found inspiration in the landscape of his childhood. But his art is not merely idyllic. He mastered the modernity of the Calcutta Art School, and his work is intensely political. In a study of Zainul Abedin's oeuvre, Zainul Abediner Jijnasa *(published in English as* The Quest of Zainal Abedin*)—from which we include a chapter here—Burhanuddin Khan Jahangir hones in on this. Abedin's quest is for alternatives, not only in the world of aesthetics but also in the real world of poverty, hunger, religious chauvinism, and exploitation. His sense of beauty is therefore rural, real, and trendsetting. It challenges both elite disdain of rural Bengali culture and the artistic and aesthetic conventions of the day. As the director of the first school of fine arts set up in East Pakistan, and as a pioneering and widely admired artist, he left his mark on the design of things to come.*

Abedin learnt to dream within the confines of the village: amid the rural landscape and amid the joys and struggle of the peasant family. From there he learnt to see, from that seeing flowed his drawings of the men and women and the bullocks of that village.

To enter the world of Zainul Abedin and see how he lived, one has to discard many set notions of beauty (beauty implied a beautiful face) or labour (labour was ugly) or about the rusticity of peasants and bullocks: or that the existence of bony men and women were indicative of the nature of social justice prevailing in the world. The world of Zainul Abedin teaches us that among the ten doors of present society, nine are closed and all the villagers, the crises-ridden villagers, the uprooted urban settlers, all mill together at this open door. They are a protest against the recognized notions of beauty, an opposition to what has been standardized as beautiful. Abedin saw them with ease. Abanindranath's [Abanindranath Tagore (1871–1951), a painter] dreaminess was not apparent in this "seeing," nor was the historical episodes of Jamini Ray [(1887-1972), another painter]. The mythologies of Nandalal [Nandalal Bose (1882–1966), another painter] too [were] absent: instead, there was reality: from the beginning to the end, the reality of peasants, boatmen, women and men.

Zainul Abedin came from a particular tradition. This tradition was that of the lower suburban middle-class, or more realistically, of the lower middle-class Muslim society, where most of the professionals came mainly from suburban towns with a rural peasant background. It was impossible to draw a line between peasant society and suburban townships. Mymensingh town blended into the rural scene, and the unmetalled roads of the village led to the metalled roads of Mymensingh town. The villagers produced rice and jute, sold them in the market. In dire times they borrowed money, and sometimes tried to become rich by cheating others. And sometimes they came to town for public trials and cases and saw before them the *babus* and the *miah sahibs* [Hindu and Muslim gentlemen] of British Bengal of the thirties, acting as their spokesperson and fighting their legal battles. In such a way had simplicity and complexity, empathy and exploitation, the clarity of the simple and the immediacy of the complex, the simplicity of empathy and the complexity of exploitation been captured in the mind of Zainul Abedin. In his consciousness therefore, one did not notice any confusion. His earlier works especially could be likened to the lucidity of his well-known Brahmaputra river: clear, lucid and strong.

What he saw, he drew: rivers and boatmen, boats and ferry-ghats[,] the obstinacy of the bullock and the river overflowing, the beauty of the village belle and the struggle of scrawny starving people. Through his eyes he participated in his surroundings, through his eyes he wandered in his mind. He was not representing scenes, events, objects or subjects; he was seeing. It has become urgent to analyse this "seeing."

The way in which [the art critic] John Berger tried to analyse the way of seeing in the case of Caravaggio, I will try to proceed in the same way in the case of Zainul Abedin. Caravaggio was first an artiste of life. He experienced life in the same way as common people, dwellers of the wayside, the lumpens, the hooligans. In the tradition of European art, the urban elites were either criticised or appreciated from the point of view of power. Many have worked in the line of Caravaggio: Hogarth, Goya, Gericault. Each have shown how these luckless vagabonds survive. Only Caravaggio was the exception. He did not try to represent the life of the luckless and homeless, he did not act on behalf of anyone; instead, he saw, and through his seeing, he tried to relate his own life with theirs.

Caravaggio's candle in the dark, over-ripe melon, the smell of damp

Landscape in central Bangladesh. Photograph by Willem van Schendel, 2003.

cloth in the dark stair well, the gamblers' den, the cheap mess remind us of a sudden confrontation. His [chiaroscuro] unfolds terrorism, pain, expectation and death and this unfolding is intimate. Only daylight and loneliness remain exiled. The people below fear both these things. That is why there is no sense of space in his work.

On the other hand, in Abedin's work, the sense of space dominates. His work is filled with light as if the whole village, the whole river, the whole field, people, boatmen, fishermen, peasants and bullocks are spread out in the open. There is no [camouflage], no class-based interests, no centre of attraction. Everything is open. This is the expression of the contradiction and deepfelt need of rural society. The centrepoint, basis and source of colonial and post-colonial rural life is poverty and starvation; poverty and starvation are etching lines in the faces of people, in the appearances of women and men, in the body of bullocks and boats and in the process is creating tension; and the tension is creating the inevitability of a special type of expressionism, where the space is being filled at the hint of a posture, a gesture: where any wish is expressed through a look. This is a way in which the space is filled with tension. We look at Abedin's eye and we see a revelation, an unfurling, without [camouflage], without pieties, without betrayal—the whole village society, the whole landscape, the whole as content: men and women, the bullocks driving the plough and boats. The expression of this reality is both centred and boundless.

How did he do this? Abedin grew up in a rural culture in which was manifest the signs and symbols of living. Everything was a legend; the girl, the boy, or the bullock driving the plough. [P]*unthi* [narrative verse], folk songs and daily living: everything had to be read with the eye. From the symbols emerged similarities, metaphors, sympathy and empathy; and each one carried its own message. The totality of all messages was rural life, and that was sufficient for the interpretation of the word rural. With this cultural consciousness he articulated the education of the Art School of the British Raj. There he learnt measurement and differentiation. For this reason the symbolic similarities manifest in each of his work[s] became dependent on folk material. On the other hand each of his work[s] became independent due to reason of measurement and differentiation. In this way his figures transcended the . . . Mughal-like figures of Chugtai and Abanindranath Tagore, or the epilogical figures of Jamini Ray's historical legends or the mythological figures of Nandalal Basu.

It has become very urgent to analyse Zainul Abedin's final resolution. The Calcutta Art School legitimized a mid-Victorian essentialism in painting. Due to this legitimization, theory became estranged from application. Zainul Abedin learnt the theory of measurement and differentiation from this school. But because of the populist source of his work, the application of this theory to his work reaped contradictory results. In the villages he had seen the work of craftsmen. They work on the basis of a prototype and in their work principles remained implicit. These principles differed from place to place. This was the way in which the particular was created, which

at times could change general rules. Abedin in his work applied a traditional
theory of art to a particular example or model. As a result, his work did not
become conformist due to social and artistic reasons. The principles arising
from and imposed by the Calcutta Art School changed from time to time.
The neoclassicism of the early years made space for safe romanticism, and
romanticism in turn eroded in favour of a type of a narrative naturalism.
For that reason, the students of this school learnt more about how to draw
rather than what to draw, which was why in all their work it was the selection of the content which was important not the content itself. In Abedin's
work, it was the content which became the work, the content destroyed all
artistic principles. He applied to his subject the different theories which he
learnt at the School, neoclassicism, romanticism and narrative naturalism.
They are all there in his work, but everything has changed because of the
content. He did not select his content, he veered towards it. This itself was
revolutionary, for him, for his time and for his society.

In his time the conflict between colonial British capitalism and the
landed aristocratic class created on the one hand indebtedness among the
peasantry and on the other hand led to the commoditization of agricultural
produce. Rural poverty increased through indebtedness and capital penetrated agricultural commodities. Also the rural economic sector resisted the
growth of the indigenous market. Factories sprung up in selected urban
sites. In this way colonial capitalism became articulated to the capitalism of
West Europe.

In his time too, the movement for Pakistan was under way under the
leadership of the Muslim League. Under colonial capitalism, Muslim capital had lost the competition with strong competitors such as British and
European capital and secondly with Marwari and Hindu money lending
capitalists. The interest of this Muslim capital joined hands with the interests of the landed and career interests of Muslim society. These two interests joined together in the Muslim League and Pakistan movement. They
strengthened religion as an ideology. These developing yet weak interests
though not strong as competitors were able to express their ideals and power
through political and business organisation. The political organisation was
the Muslim League, and the business organization, Ispahani and Adamjee.
The business organisations had spread their influence through the political
organisation and the political organisation in turn had influenced the peasantry through middle-class Muslims. The two-pronged use of the religious
ideology: business and political, had a hypnotic effect on Bengali Muslims.

As opposed to the ruling philosophy of contemporary politics, Zainul
Abedin through his work made a different statement about the political

and spiritual future of his independent homeland. He did not draw pictures of Muslim glory, he did not support the Mughal School like Chugtai. Nor did he select a subject from feudal society. He returned to his content, and his content was the life of peasants, boatmen, fishermen, the faces of their wives, mothers, daughters, the plight of the peasants and their courage.

In this way he captured the dynamism of the Bangladesh society. From the backwardness of a peasant society he looked towards the future: a future which was not about communal and religious blindness, nor about the inhumanness of the European bourgeois. The present, he wanted to say[,] was crises-ridden. That is why Bengali society had only a past and a future. In this way he rejected the Pakistan movement, destroyed the past of Muslim feudalism. He brought as his subject peasants, boatmen, fishermen and peasants tilling the land, and boatmen, fishermen plying the rivers were what constituted the society of Bangladesh. This was the political and spiritual future of his motherland. In this way he and his friends in art and literature (Qamrul Hasan, Shafiuddin Ahmed, Shaukat Osman, Gholam Quddus and others) differentiated themselves from the political leaders of their own class and upheld a different interpretation about their own society and country. Later during the Pakistani period, this differentiation and interpretation prepared the way for a cultural alternative.

Translated from Bengali by Meghna Guhathakurta.

A Dancer's Mission

Bulbul Chowdhury

Bulbul Chowdhury (1919–54) was born in undivided Bengal. His ancestral village was Chunti, in the district of Chittagong. Bulbul's childhood was spent traveling with his father, who, as a service holder, was posted to various places in Bengal: Bandel, Bankura, Bogra, Asansol, Manikganj, and so on. Coming as he did from a Muslim family, Bulbul Chowdhury's friendships were mixed and he was close with children from other religious backgrounds. Just as a child in any other Muslim family, Bulbul received education in Arabic and Koranic teachings, but lodged inside his mind were the words of the poem he memorized from his father:

> *You gave no instructions*
> *To destroy the temples of others*
> *O Constant One,*
> *You had said that in this world*
> *All were equal*
> *Equally your children.*
> *We did not follow your message*
> *Forgive us O Hazrat*

In this sense, Bulbul Chowdhury was not unique; he reflected prevalent social trends. When he became a recognized artist in Pakistan, he retained this perspective. As a choreographer and dancer, he combined themes from Bengali folktales and history with new dance forms. After his early death, the Bulbul Lalitakala Academy (Bulbul Academy for Fine Arts) was established in Dhaka to carry on his mission. At a press conference in a Karachi hotel in 1953, Bulbul Chowdhury expressed his cultural concerns.

No doubt Islam's eternally rich heritage is one of the most important components of our national heritage. But a few of my friends seem to think that it is the *only* component of our national tradition. If that were so, then there would be no existence of separate traditions of Arabic, Iranian, Egyptian, and Turkish cultures. If Islam were the only tradition that they would have

Bulbul Chowdhury dances with Lakshmi Roy. Used by permission of *The Daily Star*, Dhaka.

followed, then they would have merged into one. But they did not. That only proves that Islam may be one important feature of our national tradition, but it is definitely not the only one or even the most important one. Rather it is a fact of life that that there exist in Pakistan different nationalities—the Bengali, Punjabi, Sindhi, Pathan, Baluchi—each with their own intrinsic regional features shaped by their respective ecological and geographic characteristics. . . . In the light of this fact, we can say that in order to develop an All Pakistan national culture it is not necessary to dissolve the specific characteristics of our provinces. Rather the characteristics should be developed for the very same purpose. . . . In this context there naturally arises the issue of Bengali versus Urdu. If we agree that the various regional features are fundamental for our national culture, then we must also agree that anything that creates obstacles to the development of regional languages must also create obstacles for our national culture because it is through these regional languages that we express our literature, art, and culture. If the voice of the Bengali language is constricted, it will only lead to bitterness, protest, and rebellion, creating crisis in our national expression.

Translated from Bengali by Meghna Guhathakurta.

Preferences

Shamsur Rahman

A key figure of Bangladeshi literature, Shamsur Rahman (1929–2006), was a self-conscious modernist with a secular outlook. He was much loved in a country with a deep appreciation of poetry, and he became the target of Islamist anger and barely survived an assassination attempt by members of Harkat-ul-Jihad al-Islami (Islamic Struggle Organization) in 1999.

পক্ষপাত

ঘাসের নিচের সেই বিষাক্ত সাপকে ভালবাসি,
কেননা সে কপট বন্ধুর চেয়ে ক্রুর নয় বেশি।
ভালবাসি রক্তচোষা অন্ধ বাদুড়কে,
কেননা সে সমালোচকের চেয়ে ঢের বেশি অনুকম্পাময়।
রাগী বৃশ্চিকের দংশন আমার প্রিয়,
কেননা সে দংশনের জ্বালা অবিশ্বাসিনী প্রিয়ার
লাল চুম্বনের চেয়ে অধিক মধুর।
আমি কালো অরণ্যের সুকান্ত বাঘকে ভালবাসি,
কেননা সে একনায়কের
মতো কোনো সুপরিকল্পিত
সর্বগ্রাসী শত্রুতা জানে না।

PREFERENCES

I love the venomous snake hidden in the green
because it is not more malignant than a deceiving friend.
I love the blind vampire bat
because it is a great deal more compassionate than the critic.
The angry scorpion's bite is dear to me
because its agony is sweeter
than the red-lipped kiss of a faithless sweetheart.
I love the graceful tiger in the dark forest
because the dictator's
calculating all-consuming viciousness is alien to it.

Translation from Bengali by Kaiser Haq.

The Adventure of Editing a Magazine

Noorjehan Murshid

Women writers have a long and celebrated history in Bangladesh, with names such as Rokeya Sakhawat Hossain, Shamsunnahar Mahmud, and Sufia Kamal included in the canon. Literature was a space where Bengali Muslim women felt free to express themselves, and yet, whenever women took to launching their own journals and magazines, they did not find it an easy task. Even as recently as the mid-1980s it was hard—the political situation became more and more ominous and the absence of democratic practices fueled conservative and orthodox tendencies in society. In this piece, Noorjehan Murshid (1924–2003), a rights activist, describes the trials and tribulations as well as the thrills that accompanied her literary venture.

I edited a journal called *Edesh-Ekal* [This country and this time] for some years and have indeed a story to tell. Before I start my story I would like to tell you who I am and what was the setting in which I conceived the idea of publishing a journal. I am Noorjehan Murshid, as you have already gathered, and I come from Murshidabad. My surname Murshid, of course, has nothing to do with Murshidabad. My name is not from Murshidabad but from an accident with which I have been living for slightly over four decades now.

I was educated at the Victoria Institution in Calcutta and the Universities of Calcutta and Boston. My first job after my graduation from Calcutta was that of Headmistress of a Girls' High School in Barisal at the ripe age of twenty-two. While I was waiting for the result of my M.A. examination, I was appointed Superintendent of a Post Graduate Women Students' Hostel in Calcutta known as Mannujan Hall. At the same time, I joined All India Radio as a broadcaster.

With partition I opted for Pakistan which meant for me Dhaka and my destiny. I joined politics in 1954 and got elected to the East Pakistan Legislative Assembly on a United Front ticket by defeating a distinguished Muslim Leaguer and educationist, Begum Shamsunnahar Mahmud. Since 1954 I have been actively involved in politics both in and out of power. But with the assassination of Bangabandhu Sheikh Mujibur Rahman and the murder in jail of my colleagues Tajuddin Ahmed, Nazrul Islam, Monsur Ali and Qamruzzaman, I lost heart and sort of withdrew from politics. All over the subcontinent there was turmoil. Zulfiqar Ali Bhutto was hanged, Indira Gandhi was assassinated and we were deeply depressed.

The military in power in Bangladesh formed political parties to get support from the people and gave rise to a kind of politics for which I had only repulsion. During the long night of military rule in one guise or another, which only ended recently, the country was politically debased and economically ruined. Greed, violence and unemployment created a situation of lawlessness and general insecurity which hit women specially hard.

My journal was born in these circumstances and in response to my own need for a worthwhile occupation as well as to the situation in the country, When I brought out my journal I felt that there was a need for it. You bring out a journal at a particular time when you believe strongly you have something special to say and that there are people in society who want it said. Most of our people are poor and without rights and exploited. Even so, women are poorer and more exploited and deprived than men. The idea of social justice was accepted and current but it did not seem to include the notion of equal rights for men and women. The journal wanted to draw attention to this default of long standing and to work for the equality of woman and man. This we thought would be possible only in a sane, civilized and just society, and our aim was to contribute to the creation of such a society. The concept of the journal and its range of interests were expressed through its different sections which were: "The World," "Country," "Society," "Interviews," "Literature," "Miscellaneous Reflections," "Debate," "T.V.," the "Theatre" and "Letter from Abroad."

I recall with pleasure that the first issue contained articles on the origin of the dowry system in Bangladesh, women workers in industry, women's representation in Parliament, a long extract from Simone de Beauvoir's *The Second Sex* in Bengali translation, and a discussion on the subject of women and development. The allocation of space among the various interests reflected the balance we kept in view. We wanted *Edesh-Ekal* to say something to all citizens and at the same time to maintain a strong focus on women and their problems. We hoped thus to avoid giving the impression of representing a female "ghetto." When the journal came out it was indeed well received. The editor got dozens of congratulatory letters. It was reviewed favourably by the newspapers and periodicals. I used to send my journals to the cities, district towns and even to rural areas. But the actual readership of the journal was limited to a small section of the middle class. I was surprised to notice that I was receiving letters not only from different parts of West Bengal but also from Bengali readers from Bombay and had a few readers in the U.K. and America as well.

I started the venture without any institutional support. Most of the support came from my family. I created a fund with contributions from my husband and children and my own savings. When I decided to bring out the journal I was optimistic, indeed, too optimistic. I wanted to print 10,000 copies. After a great deal of persuasion by Obaidul Islam, head of the Bangla Academy Press and by my husband, I agreed to reduce the number to 5,000 and soon realized that even that would be too large a print and scaled it down to 3,000 copies with great reluctance and annoyance. The first issue came out in August 1986.

We approached our friends and other sympathetic people for contributions and I must say we were pleased with the response. From the start I wanted to lay a strong emphasis on women and women's issues and contacted almost all women writers in the country. I received some articles, stories and poems from them, but most of my contributors were men and I feel sorry to say that some of our women writers, who of course rightly call themselves writers and not women writers, were rather cool towards the magazine. They promised and never delivered.

My target groups were educated middle class men and women, who form the back-bone of our society. Unless they are aware of the causes—personal, social, national and international—behind their backwardness and exploitation they will not be able to overcome them.

Our women are doubly exploited, for being members of an unjust society and for being women. I know cases where husbands and wives are educated and well placed in society and the wives have not only their own income but they have fortunes inherited from their parents, and still the wives are treated like slaves and some times get beaten up by husbands and sons, that is by the male members of the family. What could be the reason? One view is that men are interested in the money of their wives or mothers and not in them. So, you see, education alone cannot help us to protect ourselves and our interests. Intellectually, if we cannot bring ourselves to believe that if necessary we should leave husband and family to save our life and dignity, we can never be equal to men. In a male dominated society this is the worst thing that can happen to a woman. Through my journal, I wanted to reach these types of women and men.

I brought out my journal from the Bangla Academy Press. One morning Nirmalendu Goon, the poet, came to the place, sat down at my table and appointed himself my assistant. He helped with proof reading and also contributed an interesting personal column. So, I started with one assistant and a chauffeur. For the distribution of the journal, I contacted the "Hawkers' Association" and gave them 1,000 copies to sell, only to find out later that most of these were destroyed by white ants and rats. When I protested, they said no one wants to buy this type of intellectual magazine. They showed me some cheap and glamorous magazines of cinema and sex and asked me to bring out something like these; otherwise, it would not sell. So the "Hawkers' Association" proved useless for me in the matter of distribution of the journal. Nirmalendu Goon could only assist me for two hours a day in proof reading; he could not help me in any other way. So I appointed a very bright girl called Sabera and a boy named Tareq to help with the distribution of the journal, collection of articles and ads, answering and mailing letters, etc.

Soon I felt the need for an office assistant who would maintain files, answer telephone calls and record messages, keep an account of the expenses under different heads. To bring out the magazine regularly every month was my headache. Besides, of course, I had to keep an eye on everything concerning the journal. Soon I found that my overhead expenses were becoming too much for me to bear. Within two years, the resources, with which I had started, were nearly exhausted. I was bad at collecting ads. I noticed from a distance how confidently Dr. Mustafa Nurul Islam, the editor of the quarterly journal *Sundaram*, went through the gates of different business houses and organizations and got hold of their chiefs and came back with very lucrative and regular ads. Obviously, I did not have his flair for business, but I know, I was being discriminated against. I was a woman and an ex-minister of a former government whose members were not in great favour in the commercial district of Motijheel in Dhaka.

The first step I took was to reduce my expenses. Printing charges at the Bangla Academy Press were high. So I thought of changing the Press. I hired some wayside printers, but the atmosphere in these places was rather uncongenial unlike at the Bangla Academy Press, where one could have a place to work for hours, have tea, converse with almost everybody present and meet well-known literary people. The idea of sitting on a stool for long hours with my back towards a busy road didn't appeal to me. So I bought a small composing unit and hired two compositors. As is evident, the more I tried to reduce my expenditure, the more I put myself in a situation where it increased. But in spite of all these troubles, I never thought of giving the journal up. The journal used to come out regularly but understandably with very few ads. My daughter Sharmeen came forward to help me in collecting ads and she really tried. She and Sabera both worked for the journal with dedication. They never thought any work for it beneath their dignity. One day the poet Nirmalendu Goon left as suddenly as he had come and took his column with him. Tareq also disappeared, probably for reasons of health. I recruited the young poet Maruf Raihan and later Raqib in their places.

After four years I started to feel I was failing. At this moment a young man walked in from nowhere and claimed that he knew the secret of running a magazine and making a commercial success of it—in which respect my record so far was dismal. He said that if I gave him a chance he would bring out the journal on a particular date every month and until he could do that he would not take a penny as wages—that is he offered to give me free service until my paper had a regular income and came out regularly on a particular date. An attractive offer, but I was rather skeptical, and know now that I should have obeyed my instinct. Instead, I saw him draw up an impressive chart, showing the details of his plan of operation: strategies were devised for increasing circulation, deadlines were fixed for the collection of contributions from writers and ads, an uncompromisingly firm date was set for the publication of the journal every month, and as for costing it was impeccably done. He embarked upon an expensive campaign of addressing letters to people all over the country urging them to subscribe to the magazine. In his zeal he distributed all the copies of its back issues, including my office copies, free. He employed hawkers to do the job. I was out of Dhaka at the time for some months. He explained to my office staff that the journal should reach every educated home where there were people to read it—a laudable idea that was defeated by its originator. When I came back from abroad I found him still struggling with the issue whose printing process had begun five months ago and which was alleged to have got mysteriously lost in the computer. The young man in question eventually brought out an issue but he took six months to do so. On top of everything, it was so badly printed and so full of printing mistakes that, in despair and anger, I literally drove him out of my office. I had the whole issue reprinted but at that point the journal went totally broke.

And what is the moral of the story? I must play down the hilarious denouement to the affair. The switch-over to computer technology need not have been the undoing of the journal—I obviously should not have entrusted the publication to a stranger of completely untested ability. He merely represented an avoidable mischance. The truth is I was weary of the effort to keep the journal afloat as a deficit proposition and of the dependence on ads. I acknowledged earlier that the intellectual support I received was not unsatisfactory. The readers too responded well to the journal, enabling us to maintain the circulation at a reasonable level for some time. The real reason for the failure of the journal to stay alive longer than it did is to be ascribed to certain social and economic factors. I do not know of any serious journal in this country with the exception of *Sundaram* which has sustained itself for long without either institutional support of some sort or commercially or politically motivated financial backing from some source or other. When times are hard the lower and middle classes are not very keen on spending their scarce cash on things like *Edesh-Ekal*. The slump in the sale of the journal, which began with the great flood of 1988, coincided with the growing strength of religious fundamentalists, a group seeking power and control over society, especially educational institutions, with ferocity. I however think, in retrospect, that despite all this, some of the problems I spoke of would not have existed for a person with greater business acumen than I possessed. I also think that the values for which the journal stood are not only valid but basic to our conception of the society we want to build. These values and forces inimical to them are at present engaged in a deadly conflict. What is needed is not surrender but a reincarnation of the spirit of *Edesh-Ekal* as a form of intelligent and assertive group action rather than lonely individual effort.

The Short-Film Movement

Tanvir Mokammel

Postindependence Bangladesh has witnessed the growth of many creative move-
ments, such as the group theatre movement, the art movement, and the short-film
movement. Enthusiastic young artists formed these to test the frontiers of their art
and to represent the values, dreams, and expectations that their generation derived
from the Bangladesh Liberation War. These movements allowed personalities and
institutions to emerge and left an indelible mark on contemporary culture. Tanvir
Mokammel is a filmmaker, one of the pioneers of his generation and a front-line ac-
tivist in the short-film movement. Here, in excerpts from a piece titled "Problemat-
ics of Alternative Cinema in Bangladesh: An Introspection," he sketches the context
in which the movement developed and the problems it has faced since its inception.

Alternative cinema, parallel cinema or second cinema, whatever one calls
it, takes off differently in different countries. The differences lie in the scale
of support from the government and non-government financial institutions,
level of taste among the audience, state of democratisation in the polity of a
given society, availability of technical infrastructure, nature of censorship
and so on. [N]one of these prerequisites are [conducive] to develop an alternative cinema in contemporary Bangladesh.

[Al]though there were some sincere endeavours towards realism in the
feature filmdom [during the 1960s], alternative cinema truly began in Bangladesh during our liberation war when, during the 1971 war, the duo Zahir
Raihan and Alamgir Kabir made *Stop Genocide* and *Liberation Fighters*. It is
impressive to see that in such an arduous war situation and with such a
paucity of funds, the exiled government came forward to support serious
films. It is a pity that successive governments after independence, though
commanding many more resources, totally discontinued that spirit.

The pity is more, as due to massive illiteracy (only 24 per cent of our
people being literate), the power of written words in Bangladesh is bound
to be limited, whereas film, television, video or any format of life-image has
immense potency. But unfortunately, since independence, although the sky-

line of Dhaka has changed so conspicuously, and so much water has flowed through the Padma and the Meghna, . . . mainstream cinema of this country has managed to remain as philistine as ever, if not worse.

The days of social realism in celluloid during the 1960s are now gone. Gone are the days of *Titas Ekti Nadir Nam* (1973) and *Palanka* (1977). *Surjo Dighal Bari* (1979) was perhaps the last of the Mohicans. In a poor third-world country like ours, government being the most potent social organisation, the responsibility of this failure is squarely on the government. Government itself is actually a problem. With non-perceptive and non-sensitive bureaucrats at the helm, during the tenure of the last successive governments, cinema has often got tossed between the Ministry of Culture and the Ministry of Information. A naive newcomer is often at a loss to find under which Ministry cinema is now, by the way, honest, where is it now? Really?!

It is a pity that even two decades after independence, a democratically elected government still lacks any clear policy guideline regarding promoting good cinema in Bangladesh. Ministers come and go! Talking about, no, *not about Michelangelo*, but about—better films! But alas, nothing happens. Lack of an enlightened cultural policy, and almost as a convention, always the most cantankerous person of the cabinet being the Information Minister, and with the pot-bellied yes-minister bureaucrats ruling over there, the situation in the Ministry is simply—Kafkaesque.

Lack of vision, a sense of complacency and corruption and due to the inherent inadequacy of any government body, the *Film Development Corporation (FDC)*, which churns out all those run-of-the mill commercial films, has now pathetically turned itself into a mere lumpen dream factory. Abhorrent violent films, branded as "social action" (!), "action" (!!) and "superaction" (!!!) with no reference to Bangladesh reality at all, regularly crop up from there.

Recently teenage love has become the most lucrative theme, understandably, as in each decade a new generation of teenagers appears and by catering to them, new teenage love films turn out to be good money-spinners. Actually film-making business in mainstream feature filmdom of Bangladesh has long been deteriorating into mere shady deals in [laundering] black money. So no wonder that, although around seventy full-length feature films annually are produced in such a resource-poor country as Bangladesh, none of these films are at all palatable. These films are made by the lumpen to satiate lumpen taste. Due to the fatuous nature of these films and the awful viewing atmosphere in the cine-halls, the alienation of sensitive people from the local film industry has become complete. . . .

Since 1984–85 . . . a new vista opened up in the alternative horizon of Bangladesh filmdom. Though still in an embryonic stage, these young film-

makers have even succeeded in building up an alternative distribution channel of their own. From raising funds to run the projector by himself, an
alternative film-maker in Bangladesh has to undergo the whole cycle from
visualizing a film up to managing its proper distribution.

Generally these films are shot in 16 mm. The question of the choice between 35 mm. and 16 mm. has turned out to be not just a choice between
two formats, but a choice between two approaches of film-making, two
attitudes—two ideologies. . . .

During the late 1960s and the 1970s a kind of alternative cinema emerged
in Calcutta centring around a symbol: an angry young man amidst the deca-
dence of middle class idealism. . . . In Dhaka, the symbol is often a youth
amidst the decay of the values of the 1971 liberation war. It is curious to see
that most of these short-film-makers began their careers by venturing at
least one film on the backdrop of 1971. The reason seems self-evident as during the 1971 war most of these young film-makers were in their boyhood,
in their most sensitive and formative years. So the trauma they had experienced resulted in the 1971 war appearing again and again in their films,
almost like a leitmotif. . . .

In Bangladesh it is . . . the sensation of challenging the existing political taboos which makes these films popular. But these political nuances
are so typical and topical of Bangladesh that outsiders can hardly find out
what are the exceptional points in these otherwise flawed and poorly made
films. Audiences in Bangladesh have also by now [l]earned to transform
any subversive element in a film which has escaped censorship into a plea-
surable entertainment. No wonder that these short films are screened more
during the months of December–March, the months of hectic political activism in Bangladesh. . . . Actually we know pretty well that whether it is
the *Jatiyos* or the *Jatiyotabadis* who are in power, the ethos of Bangladesh
statehood remains the same—communal, bureaucratic and philistine. So
by becoming a film activist each of us essentially ends up being a political
activist too. At the same time, we refuse to be marginalised and patron-
isingly patted as mere "short-film-makers" by the establishment. We are
independent film-makers, realistic film-makers, true film-makers, the rest
are—businessmen. . . .

Our movement is often compared with the Group Theatre Movement
in Bangladesh, which by now has come of age and has carved a niche at
home and abroad. But I think the conditions between the two are organi-
cally different. Film is a much more expensive and cumbersome medium
than theatre. Besides, film is a technological medium, and in Bangladesh,
the technology is monopoly-owned by a philistine government. But the

most significant difference between the two lies in the fact that the theatre groups in this country, like alternative cinema, do not have to compete with any established commercial theatre, which is simply non-existing in Bangladesh. But alternative film-makers, in their every step, have to confront the enmity of a powerful and entrenched commercial film establishment. . . .

Half a decade ago we rightfully felt that the bond of good camaraderie among us has to be institutionalized and hence we are now an organised body. One success that this body can boast of is the alternative distribution network that we envisaged and, though still in an embryonic form, has become quite operative now. Cultural organisations, student and youth organisations, trade unions and mass organisations in the districts and sub-districts have provided us an off-cine-hall [non-commercial] parallel network. We were pushed to a corner, but have ended up learning a few tricks to outmanoeuvre a philistine censor board and a lethargic bureaucracy, perhaps in a little guerrilla way (!). Then remember, during 1971, this was a land of gritty guerrillas!

Ilish in Mustard Sauce

Shornomoyee

Ilish *(or hilsa) is a fish. But this statement does not begin to describe the meaning of ilish in Bangladesh. It is the official national fish, the queen of fishes in a fish-eating society, the delight of taste buds, and the star of local cuisine. Bengali palates— famously discerning—yearn for the superlative taste of ilish.*

So do not be surprised to come across grand ilish festivals in the country's five- star hotels and posh supermarkets, or to hear marriage brokers extol the ilish- cooking skills of a prospective bride. Ilish plays a central role in cultural politics as well. In the eternal contest between West Bengal and East Bengal, which revolves around dialects, food, and football (soccer), ilish has come to represent the east.

Naturally, there are countless ilish recipes. You can steam, bake, fry, or smoke it, and you can combine it with numerous spices, vegetables, and other ingredients. Some recipes are closely guarded family secrets; others are regionally specific. Here Shornomoyee—who is from Bikrampur in central Bangladesh, a region historically known for many things, including prospective brides with incredible cooking skills that mesmerize the most finicky of palates—reveals her very own recipe of shor- she bata ilish *(ilish in mustard sauce). It is a family tradition, passed down the generations.*

Ingredients

> 1 medium-size ilish fish, cut into five pieces (excluding the head and tail)
> 1/2 cup of black mustard seeds, ground into paste with water and a pinch
>   of salt
> 2 teaspoons of turmeric
> 1 teaspoon of chili powder (optional)
> 3 or 4 whole green chilies (according to your taste)
> 1/4 cup of ginger paste or crushed ginger
> 1/2 cup of mustard oil
> salt as needed

Preparation (cooking time 20–25 minutes)

Marinate the pieces of fish in turmeric, chili powder, salt, and a little bit of mustard oil. Heat the rest of the oil in a pan, and then lightly fry the fish pieces (they should not be deep-fried). Set the pieces aside.

Using the same mustard oil in the pan, stir-fry the ginger paste and then put in the mustard paste. Add salt to taste and stir, adding small amounts of water so that the mixture is not too dry. Gently place the pieces of fish in the liquid paste and let it simmer for a while in low heat. Then, with the heat turned up, add water (according to how much gravy you want) and put in the whole green chilies (slit in the middle if you wish the curry to be hot). Cover and simmer in medium heat until the fish is done. (An alternative process is to steam the fish in the prepared gravy instead of cooking it. In that case the fish should be marinated but need not be light fried beforehand.)

As a final touch you may want to take off the lid and add a few extra drops of fresh mustard oil and then cover and simmer for a second or two. This adds the pungency of mustard to the dish.

Rickshaw Art

Joanna Kirkpatrick

The anthropologist Joanna Kirkpatrick was among the first to study the colorful decorations that adorn the ubiquitous cycle rickshaws of Bangladesh. Observing this popular art over a number of years, Kirkpatrick—who prefers the spelling rick-sha as it is closer to Bengali pronunciation—noticed how political change was mirrored in its themes.

In this article from 1997, she argues that rickshaw art can be read as a social comment, as reflecting "ordinary people's interest in what's going on politically in the country . . . and also in the world."

The three-wheeled pedicab or cycle ricksha of Bangladesh has been around at least since the late forties and the partition of India. In those days they were left more or less undecorated. Sometime in the sixties heads of movie stars began to appear as decorative motifs on the golboards, or small round shields attached to the back of the rick, along with floral designs, in Rajshahi and Dhaka. . . . One finds the most glamorous ricksha arts in Dhaka, with Rajshahi being a runner up for elaboration, color and range of thematic content. In Dhaka in the eighties (I was last there in 1987), about eighty percent of the rickshas were decorated. Chittagong and Comilla areas, where I checked the ricksha art scene in 1986, revealed less enthusiasm about decorating them at all, and, if decorated, fewer human images, more floral or scenery images. Chittagong is considered to be a more pious town than Dhaka, while in Sylhet, considered to be religiously even more pious, the rickshas were completely undecorated. A sub-type of pious ricksha art in and around Comilla is the plain ricksha with [a] beautiful dark blue or green hood on which is sewn an applique of a minaret or floral design enshrining the word "Allah," or a ricksha with hood deco showing a mosque with minaret, sickle moon (Muslim moon) above and "Alla hu" appliqued in Bengali.

Ricksha art began to flourish during the freedom struggle with Pakistan in the early seventies. During this war there were patriotic images showing people saluting the Bangladesh flag, or an astronaut planting a Bangladesh flag on the moon! This period also inspired war atrocity scenes, where the crime was painted on one side of the picture: Paki soldiers raping women and killing; and on the other side the punishment: valorous Bengali Mukti Bahini [Freedom Fighters] bayonetting the Paki enemy. Other panels showed only the crime. One ricksha artist told me that the government became aware around 1972 that in-country foreigners were taking a huge interest in atrocity images by purchasing panels in the market, so the government sent round the word to the artists and makers to stop painting these scenes. By 1975, when I first went to Bangladesh, one could find a few faded atrocity pictures. In Rajshahi at that time, only worn, old war-scene panels of fighting tanks, planes and ships remained.

I first saw the ricksha art in fall of 1975 as I got settled in Rajshahi, where I was attached as a researcher and visiting professor of anthropology at the Institute of Bangladesh Studies, Rajshahi University. At that time Rajshahi ricksha art was not flourishing, but there were some wondrous animal scenes, including animals unknown to Bangladesh such as giraffes and kangaroos! My favorite was a panel of parrots playing *sangeet* [songs] with harmonium. Alas for me, in 1975–76 I was not in Dhaka often enough to see much ricksha art, but I did notice a lot of scenes with animals, and one featuring the American film actress Jayne Mansfield. It was a variation on the "waterhole" scene of animals in threat postures on both sides of a stream, only in this case the animals were saluting the actress, the elephant with raised trunk, the hippo with mouth agape showing its knobby teeth.

I began a focused study of ricksha art on a return trip to Dhaka in 1977–78, when I met artist Alauddin (art name "Naj"), one of Dhaka's finest ricksha artists. He was busy making various animal fable pictures. At this time Dhaka was going through an "official" reaction against film stars and human images on the rickshas, so the artists were painting myriads of fantastic birds, either just congregating, or billing and cooing like lovers. Animal fable scenes were also very common. One which I saw in passing and could not photograph showed a cat dressed in business suit talking on the phone while a rat servant brought in the tea. Was this a "fat cat" lampoon? When human images submerge, the animal fable rises. Another fable showed a VIP parading in an open car, with animals holding garlands [and] presenting them in raised salute. The VIP was a lion wearing a turban. Satirical?

Back in Dhaka in 1982, I found a resurgence of popular movie imagery, with marvelous renditions of movie stars, but also continued interest in perennial themes such as the waterhole, the city scene, peaceful animal scenes, animal fables, country village scenes with cow and calf, mosques,

Rickshaws waiting for customers in Dhaka. Photograph by Willem van Schendel, 2006.

the Taj Mahal on a lotus, [and] an elaborate design of the flower vase used as a seatback decoration. A charming feature at this time were the "disco" ricks, which sported an inserted tape player into the base of the seat, which could be activated to play disco music.

In 1986–87, one could find every type of painted imagery in Dhaka—from "filmi" (of the movies) to pious—and the rickshas in Rajshahi were at their most elaborate, featuring movie stars galore but also beautifully decorated hoods and hood *"rumals"* (rear curtain of the hood). In Dhaka I found many examples of the "femme fatale" theme, including hood paintings or ricksha panels showing Dosshu Fulon (famous Phulan Devi of India) the female bandit, holding an AK47, or brandishing a pistol. In Rajshahi, the "Nag-Nagini" movie theme—of a brother and sister who could transform themselves into cobras—was also very popular. The artist Robu produced especially attractive pointillist paintings of Nag-Nagini. In Chittagong I found ricksha panels with human faces—movie material—in the makers' shops, but did not see them on actual ricks. Instead I saw mostly scenery images or peaceful animals. Assisted by fine artist Mr. Chandresekhar, from Chittagong Arts College, I was able to find and visit the *mistri dokans* (maker shops) which made and sold ricksha decorations, hoods and decorated parts of ricksha bodies. I found the mostly floral vase designs of the hood rumals to be colorful and technically expert sewn appliques of various plastic materials in colors and scintillating gold and silver plasticine fabrics.

In 1992, my collaborator Kevin Bubriski . . . found some ricksha panels featuring a hero (to some) of the Gulf War, Saddam Hussein, in prayerful pose, surrounded by fighting airplanes. Other types of imagery noted before were still popular. The artist Ahmad, of Ahmad Art in Old Dhaka, was Bubriski's guide for this trip. . . . The Saddam images indicate to me one of the most interesting aspects of ricksha art, which is that it often reflects the ordinary people's interest in what's going on politically in the country (*muktijoddha* or liberation war images, animal fable lampoons) and also in the world (landing on the moon, the Gulf War images). As social comment, it resembles Trinidadian calypso songs or rap music.

Generally speaking, in the eighties the elites of Bangladesh scorned ricksha art as vulgar while at the same time many fine artists of the country took it seriously as an expression of the taste and interests of the masses. I know this because I visited Dhaka Arts College and Chittagong Arts College and spoke with fine artists in those institutions. When I asked rickshawallas [rickshaw drivers], ricksha artists and sellers of ricksha decor who was the audience for this art, they all replied one way or another, "the ordinary people." One man even used the English word "ordinary," as in "*ordinari lok*."

What sort of art *is* ricksha art? From my outsider point of view, I consider it "people's art." It is not necessary to force it into a unitary category as it combines folkloric, movie, political and commercial imagery and techniques. It serves the expression of heart's desires of the man in the street for women, power and wealth, as well as for religious devotion. Ricksha art also serves prestige and economic functions for the people who make, use and enjoy it.

In 1975–76 in Rajshahi, most of the painted panels on the rickshas were signed with the maker's name. In Dhaka, artists signed their own names. Nowadays, rickshas sport both the maker names as well as artist names. The artists are not formally trained, but had learned their art either from a parent, another ricksha artist or on their own. Their imagery sources included calendars, book illustrations, children's books, movie posters, other rickshas, advertisements and their own imaginations. Some ricksha artists also paint movie posters and calendars. Movie banner artists specialize in just banners, but they too follow poster material. Some imagery appears to have rather old sources: the fantastic city scenes, which show modern and traditional styles of architecture and planes, trains and ships, appear to have originated in commercial trade imagery popular in the thirties in the west. Locating primary source material depends on guessing or luck, because the artists who painted rickshas in the early days are now gone from the scene.

But let the ricksha artists have the last word: When I asked Alauddin in 1986 if he thought of ricksha art as fine art or as commercial, he said it was commercial art, which to him is art to be seen at a glance, not art to be studied and thought over, such as "fine art." That year I also visited an artist in Rajshahi (having first met him ten years earlier). The man is a prominent sign painter, ricksha artist and decorative interior wall painter to whom I put the same question. He told me a witty story about his puzzlement with modern art. He said he had been visiting the Rajshahi University campus to keep a business appointment with one of the professors. While there he noticed a painting hung up on a wall whose subject he could not decipher. It seemed merely a hodgepodge of painted swirls. He asked the professor to tell him what the painting represented and the professor replied, "A girl dancing." Trying to understand, the sign painter asked, "But, how do you know this?" and the professor replied, "The artist told me!"

Three National Festivals

Abul Momen

Bangladesh is often described as a land of fairs and festivals. In the rural areas there is a long tradition of seasonal fairs (mela) that have strong regional appeal and draw thousands of people. Then there are manifold religious festivals, not surprising in a country that is home to the most diverse religions: Sunni and Shia Islam, Hinduism, Buddhism, Christianity, and several local religions. In this text, the journalist Abul Momen searches for festivals that are truly inclusive and bring together all Bangladeshis, thus expressing their unity as a nation. He identifies three. In Bengali, Ekushe means "the twenty-first." This term is used as shorthand for 21 February, Mother Language Day, a day of mayhem in 1952 but now a joyful countrywide celebration of freedom and identity. On this day many people dress in black, white, and red. The second festival is Bengali New Year (Noboborsho or Nababarsha, Pohela Boishakh) on 14 April, when festive crowds turn out dressed in red and white. And the third is Victory Day (Bijoy Dibosh) on 16 December, when the streets color green and red.

[What] options do we have to express our holiday and festive moods? Bengali Muslims do not have community songs and dances. A festival is a community participatory outdoor event. The *Jamaat* [Eid prayer] is an outdoor and participatory exercise, but truncates the society by prohibiting women from participating, . . . and secondly, it is a purely religious prayer. . . .

And in a poverty-stricken society, religious events take a festive look only among the haves, who form only a small section of the population. The bulk remain unfed, unclad, not to speak of good food and new clothes. And again, as we have a sizeable number of religious and ethnic minorities in our country, any religious programme becomes sectarian in this country. So Eid, for various reasons, falls short of a national festival. It is at best a religious festival of the Muslim community.

Puja is full of festivity. With songs, dances, art-works and daylong outdoor celebrations, it is a festival. But as a religious one it is limited to the Hindus, who are the largest minority community in the country.

Celebrating Victory Day on the streets of Dhaka. The young man in front sports the national flag and the words "Bangladesh, 16 December" on his cheek. Photograph by Willem van Schendel, 2010.

As a traditional agrarian community, Bangalis are deeply attached to nature[;] . . . rural folks not only depend on the bounty of nature but perhaps this long active association with nature has kept alive in their mind the pagan passions for nature and natural elements. People believe in nature's supernatural powers, see behind nature's every act of fatal consequences the hand of God. . . . [They organize] at least one event a year, drawing people from far and near. These occasions often grow into big events, taking almost the shape of a festival, with a fairly good part of a fair in it. These are, however, all local festivities. . . . In this sense Bangladesh could be termed a land of fairs and festivals.

But where are the festivals that people all over the country celebrate together? Like any other country, we have some national days, such as *Shohid Dibosh* [Martyrs' Day], *Swodhinota Dibosh* [Independence Day] and *Bijoy Dibosh* [Victory Day]. In some countries Independence Day is observed with great pomp, like a festival. But in our case the formal state functions are the day's main events. After all, festivals are not state functions but totally social events. In fact, festivals are successful only through people's spontaneous participation.

In a very unique development, one of the most tragic incidents of our history finally took the shape of a festive occasion for the nation. Just as some of our local fairs gradually crossed the barriers of their religious roots through people's spontaneous participation, so it is the case here. What was originally an occasion of mourning became, in course of time, an occasion of remembrance, and then from remembrance to paying respect, and eventually, covering all aspects of Bengali art and culture, took the shape of a real national festival.

Ekushe, the Mother Language Day, has its symbol in the monument [the Central Shohid Minar, or the Martyrs' Memorial, in Dhaka] and, as this has been replicated throughout the country, specially in all educational institutions, gradually educated Bangalis have developed a deep involvement with the spirit and culture of *Ekushe*. . . . All through the sixties we have seen *Ekushe* embodying all the creative and intellectual fervour of a rising nation. Innumerable songs were tuned, poems composed, essays written, so many programmes held, so many people participated in all those activities that the occasion became one of national rejuvenation. Originally the issue in this case was language[,] . . . but finally it became an occasion for searching our roots and waking up as a nation. . . . People spontaneously organised fairs and chalked out day- to month-long programmes. *Ekushe* February today is our national festival—a secular cultural festival.

Some leading Bangali intellectuals have always felt the necessity of a secular festival for nation-wide celebration, and they selected Bangla *Nababarsha* [New Year] for the event. . . . Chhayanaut, the popular cultural group of Dhaka, introduced a morning musical programme at Ramna Park to invite and receive the New Year. The significance of the New Year, the scope to come closer to nature, the special environment of the morning musical programme, the novelty of dress and food, and the holiday mood gave it a festive colour and quality. . . .

The third national festival, I believe, could be Victory Day. Victory in a liberation war is by far the biggest occasion for any nation, and when it comes at the cost of three million lives, the exodus of crores [tens of millions] of people, two hundred thousand women being raped, and above all, if it comes through transformation of a seemingly idle, home-sick nation into a brave warrior, then the occasion is a great one. . . . Moreover, the time is beautiful for holding a festival. December is dry and cool, traditionally our season of festivity. With the annual examinations over, young and old alike are ready to have festivities at that time of the year. With the popularity of *Bijoy Mela* [Victory Fair] we can see that already the nation is participating in a festival of national scale. . . . Because of anti-liberation forces becoming powerful in society there are still some misunderstandings and unwanted debates in society that make it hesitant and confused about celebrating Victory Day in the same joyous spirit and mood. However, we know history will march forward, the nation will go ahead, and all confusions and hesitations will wither away. The nation will one day find back its rhythm and will celebrate at least three festivals a year as a nation. In fact it is already celebrating them. Yes, unfortunately not always as a [unified] nation at the moment.

Wangala, Christmas, Pre-Christmas

Ellen Bal

The cultural variety in Bangladesh is enormous. Dozens of languages, different kinship systems, competing worldviews, and all kinds of combinations between these make for an overlapping mosaic of cultural nuances and identities. And none is static. We get a glimpse of this complex, shifting universe if we look at the Garos, a population in northcentral Bangladesh who never identified with the dominant language, Bengali, or religion, Islam, and who have followed a cultural trajectory all their own. In this text we can trace this through three parallel annual festivals, each celebrated in December.

Garos have maintained a distinct identity throughout the twentieth century. The introduction of Christianity has played an important role in this. . . . The traditional Garo religion and its followers are called Sangsarek. Some of the old Garo are still Sangsarek. But unlike a couple of decades ago, outward signs of this religion are difficult to find. . . . Sangsareks believe that the world is populated by *mite*. [The term] [m]*ite* is generally referred to as "spirit," but some *mite* were so powerful that they would better be translated as gods. . . . [The best] known festival, *Wangala*, was held at the beginning of the cold season, after the harvest had been completed. In Bangladesh, real Sangsarek festivals are rare. These days Garos are reviving Wangala in a whole new fashion, with a Christian prayer meeting taking a central role. . . .

Christmas has become the most important annual festival and is widely celebrated. For days, or even weeks, before the actual occasion, excitement runs through the area. It is not for nothing that people call it *Boro Din* (big day). During the days before Christmas, hundreds of Garos can be seen at Mohakhali bus station in Dhaka, where buses leave for Tangail and Mymensingh. The feast is general celebrated in one's own village.

In recent years, another celebration has become popular: "Pre-Christmas," which was introduced by city Garos. As such people would be in their vil-

Decorating the Christmas tree in a Garo village home. Photograph by Pierre Claquin. Used by permission of the photographer.

lages for Christmas, they would organize celebrations some weeks before Christmas with their Garo friends in the city. At present, pre-Christmas parties are gaining popularity in the villages too. Church associations and other organisations like to arrange special pre-Christmas feasts. It is especially popular to present a cultural show and to invite the people for a meal.

Songs for an Endangered Homeland

Kabita Chakma and others

The people of the Chittagong Hill Tracts have many folk songs that highlight how individuals are intimately connected with their natural surroundings. The homeland implies both physical space (the hills, the forests, the sky, the stars above, animals, birds) and hill dwellers' personal connections to it. The first two songs here are examples of this personal relationship with the homeland.

During the Chittagong Hill Tracts War (1975–97), songs about the homeland took on a different meaning. "Someday" by Kabita Chakma (the third song) expresses a deep yearning for the return of peace to the homeland. The final song is a protest song. Parents of many young girls and boys were at first hesitant when their children started joining the resistance movement, but later the parents themselves encouraged it, because they realized that it was the only way they could walk the streets safely and with dignity. In this final song children address their mothers to let them join the struggle.

1.

O, stars from faraway land
The beautiful moon of the skies
Come down to our land
And listen to our songs of yore.
I will show you around
And will sing to you
Gleefully I will dance
And sing to you our tales of yore.

2.

I will not ever leave this land
Here I will stay lifelong

This drawing shows Bangladeshi army personnel and lungi-clad Bengali settlers attacking hill people in the village of Naniarchar in the Chittagong Hill Tracts in 1993.
It appeared on the cover of a locally published booklet titled "Chitkar" (The scream),
which commemorated the massacre. Anonymous artist. Used by permission of the
Hill Women's Federation, Chittagong Hill Tracts.

It is eternal in my heart.
Here the blackbird sings its songs
The *biju* bird chants, "Biju! Biju!"
The *katol pakhok* bird calls, "Katol pakhok" [the jackfruit ripens]
And the *puia* bird announces that guests have arrived.

3.

Someday my heartland
Will light up in the sun—this hill field, this forest
Will be full of light, wonderful light.
The Kassalong River will overflow its banks
Sweeping away the hurt and humiliation.
Then may this land, the forests of my heart
Drench ecstatically in showers of love.

4.

We cannot survive without opening our mouths,
How long are we to lock up our voices?
The time has come to take to the streets.
So, Mother, don't prevent us anymore.

Mother, we have to go
Join the demo in the street
We have to face the bullets.
Oh, Mother, don't forbid us
Don't pull us from behind.
The streets quake
With the slogans
And the sound of protest.
We all have to fight!
Mother, don't worry about us
Stay calm and happy.
If we are killed
Then consider yourself to be the mother of a martyr [*shahid*].

Translated from Chakma by Meghna Guhathakurta.

Oh, Sad One, Do Not Lament!

James (Nagar Baul)

Since the 1970s Bangladesh has developed a vibrant youth culture of which Bangla Band music is the keystone. This music has become an important symbol of the sensibility of young adults and a highly popular means of emotional expression. It connects easily with the heavy metal, rock, and grunge of the global music scene and yet manages to stay rooted to its locale: it draws much of its inspiration from the richness of Bengali folk songs and the philosophy of mystic and Sufi traditions such as Baul and Maijbhandari. These bands draw huge audiences and now tour the world. Here are the lyrics to a hit from circa 2005 titled "Dukhini Duhkho Koro Na!" (Oh, Sad One, Do Not Lament!).

Look, a new sun has arisen
On the pathways and highways.
The play of colors unfolds,
Why stay indoors?
With abandoned [loose] hair let's take to the street, let's dance with joy!
Oh, sad one, do not lament; Oh, sad one, Oh . . .

Wind your way through darkness, into the light,
Unveiling your eyes on the moonlit carpet.
Come out! Come out of doors!
Catch sight of the rainbow; the sight of the seven colors.
Oh, sad one, do not lament; Oh, sad one, Oh . . .

Forge your way through the milling crowd,
Turn the leaves of sorrow; and find the garden of dreams.
Pray, why stay indoors,
Hand in hand let's sing together.
Oh, sad one, do not lament; Oh, sad one, Oh. . . .

Translated from Bengali by Meghna Guhathakurta.

VIII

The Development Gaze

In the forty years since Bangladesh gained its independence, the outside world has observed it primarily through development-tinted glasses. Most outsiders who visited the country, or lived there for some time, were linked to donor agencies, the media, development organizations, or international corporations. These outsiders played a pivotal role in projecting an image of Bangladesh internationally as essentially a bundle of development challenges.

The development gaze on Bangladesh has been an intense one. Development practitioners—both foreign and domestic—have highlighted problems such as mass poverty and the gap between rich and poor, and they have prescribed and administered various remedies for these ills. Bangladesh has been a test ground for various imported development models, fashions, and styles: from rural cooperatives to integrated development, from village government (*gram shorkar*) and self-reliant villages (*shonirbhor gram*) to sustainable development, and from women in development to social forestry. Meanwhile Bangladesh turned into a breeding ground for many innovative development ideas, some of them highly influential. The most talked about is microfinance.

The role of development interventions in the considerable improvements that have taken place in Bangladesh is contested, despite the interventions' self-glorification. For many years, there has been rampant criticism of the dominant top-down approaches to development and their negative impact on natural and human resources. Critics consider other factors to be more important in explaining the change, for example the resilience and creativity of people against all odds, as expressed in ventures that are taken up spontaneously and not at the behest of bilateral or multilateral donors. Mass migration has led to mass remittances; entrepreneurship has blossomed, leading to new industries and export earnings; and agricultural productivity has increased.

Street scene in Dhaka. Photograph by Willem van Schendel, 2010.

The texts in this part have been selected to reflect these themes. The first texts present and interrogate the development context and the role of development experts and nongovernmental organizations. These are followed by texts on rural microfinance and the gap between rich and poor in Dhaka that critically look at the challenges that innovative interventions may face from the local elite, both rural and urban. The remaining texts follow two strands. The first considers the broad critique, from several perspectives (gender, ethnicity, environment, and urbanization), of the negative impact that development interventions have had. The second depicts positive experiences that hint at the potential inherent in Bangladeshi society—for example, schools for girl laborers who work for a living, or the care that a village demonstrates in nurturing the young and vulnerable.

Despite challenges, Bangladesh has had a long learning curve in the field of development. In the early years of independence, it had the reputation of being, if not a basket case, at least a test case of development. Four decades on, development experts consider it to be transitioning to a middle-income country. For many, the development gaze continues to be a major perspective on Bangladesh, but it is less dominant than it used to be.

From Poverty to Progress?

Just Faaland and J. R. Parkinson

When Bangladesh became independent, scholars and policymakers around the world felt that this newly independent country needed large doses of aid to survive, and not only because of the colossal damage to the infrastructure that was a legacy of the Bangladesh Liberation War. Bangladesh was seen as suffering from geophysical, economic, and demographic conditions that were extremely hostile to development. It was this suffering that made Bangladesh a prime challenge to the skills of development experts. Just Faaland and J. R. Parkinson captured the mood of the period in the title of their book, Bangladesh: The Test Case of Development, *published in 1976. The text here is from the introduction to their book. It outlines the harsh conditions that Bangladesh inherited and assesses the prospects of development in the newborn country.*

It must be the fond hope of most educated people that man can control events and his own future. There is little to give credence to that view in the situation of Bangladesh. There can be little prospect of a spontaneous movement to reduce the increase in population and it is impossible to see how a much larger population can be given any prospect of attaining the type of living standards to which the Western world has become accustomed. Nature, not man, is in charge of the situation in Bangladesh.

The starting-point from which economic development must be attempted is unpromising. Income per head in 1972 was estimated at us$70. In terms of consumption this means a diet mainly of rice with very little to supplement it. In the famine of 1943, when 1 1/2 million died in Bengal, it was necessary to consider what tonnage of ships could be diverted from the transport of munitions to the carriage of food to India. The calculations of need were based on consumption of cereals of 1 lb. per head per day. The same basic calculations are made today, but the calculations are more often based on 15 oz. than 16 oz. a day; fractions of an ounce make a great deal of difference to the amount of imported food required by 80 million people—such fractions also make a great deal of difference to the daily lives of the population.

A diet largely based on minimal amounts of rice, besides providing insufficient calories, is deficient in other ways. Rice contains less protein than wheat and there is inadequate consumption of pulses and animal products to supplement it. The most important source of protein is fish, but even so consumption amounts to only about 4 lb. per head per year and consumption of milk, another source of protein, to about 20 lb. per head per year. Over half the households in Bangladesh get too little protein. Fats are also scarce, average consumption of cooking oil amounts to about 5 lb. per year. A diet of rice is deficient in various vitamins which are not supplemented by consumption of other foods; shortage of vitamin A in the diet is particularly serious. Inadequate nutrition leaves the way open for disease and combines to reduce the expectation of life. Child mortality is particularly high: about one-quarter of all children die before their fifth birthday; those that survive are smaller and lighter than they would be with better food.

With too little money available for food it is not surprising that few other consumption goods are available to remove the monotony of life. In 1969–70 the consumption of textiles was estimated at 7 1/2 yards per head; in the circumstances of 1972–3 this had dropped to 5 yards per head and apparently has remained at that level since, well below the 9 yards that might be regarded as reasonably satisfactory in the circumstances of life in Bangladesh. For the men solace is traditionally given by tobacco. Consumption of cigarettes in 1969–70 was estimated to be about 265 *per capita* per year. This at least must have given the adult male some respite.

Other indications of the standard of living of the population tell the same story: about 300 petrol pumps, less than 20,000 private motor-cars, about 5,000 buses, about 70,000 motor vehicles in all, including motorcycles, less than 2,000 miles of railway, 50,000 telephones, 300,000 radio sets and 10,000 television sets. All the indices reveal a standard of living bearing little resemblance to that of Western countries and yet at the same time they show the anachronisms of the development process: the modem businesses with telephones, the favoured few with electric light and radio and television sets, the highly privileged with cars, contrasting as much with the impoverished landless labourer as the maharajahs of not so long ago.

Deprivation of the world's goods is not perhaps the most important aspect of the impoverishment of the people; in the long run the deprivation of access to the world's knowledge may be far more serious. Development will not proceed without a massive education effort. If anything, educational statistics overstate the educational effort that is being made. Some 80 per cent of the population is illiterate; it is said that 60 per cent of the primary age group of the population is enrolled in the schools but it is evident that

Agricultural workers in the 1980s. Photograph by Willem van Schendel.

the dropout rate is such as to leave little permanent impact on the adult population.

Life in Bangladesh is, of course, very different from that of industrialised countries. There are a few large towns, and most people live in 65,000 small scattered villages of a few hundred to 1,000 people, in houses constructed mainly out of mud and bamboo. There may be a tube-well for the provision of drinking water but this is much more likely to be drawn from a tank or pond. Most of the villagers rely on cultivation for their subsistence but some have no land or too little to do this and earn what living they can by casual labour, while others follow subsidiary occupations such as weaving, handicraft, and fishing if they live near to rivers or the sea. Possessions are few; it is exceptional to have tables, chairs or cupboards, though half the households might have a bed, and earthenware cooking utensils abound. The village family is a very strong influence and arranged marriages are the custom. Few people travel much outside their village except to market; the women observe purdah and seldom leave their homes. New ideas have little influence and percolate only slowly; it is hard for all to see how life can be improved.

In the *World Bank Atlas* [1974] only Rwanda was tentatively estimated to have a smaller per capita income than Bangladesh; another two countries were bracketed with it, but none of these has anything like the population of Bangladesh. Only Indonesia has a population larger than that of Bangladesh, and a *per capita* income not much greater; but Indonesia increased its *per capita* income by over 4 per cent per annum in the period 1965 to 1972 while per capita income in Bangladesh declined. Since then Indonesia has gained significantly from its new oil wealth and from improved terms of trade, while Bangladesh's relative position deteriorated markedly; war and its aftermath held back any increase in real income; population has continued to increase and real income to fall.

All this would not matter if Bangladesh were rich in natural resources and underpopulated, if it were effectively governed and if its social order and economic system were geared to growth, but none of these things obtain. The terrain, in relation to the number of people that inhabit it, is inhospitable and often hostile. It is dominated by mighty rivers which in depositing silt both form and flood the territory over which they flow; in the monsoon the rainfall is intense and unpredictable; the one certainty is that much of the land will be covered with water, and loss of life and interruption to production from flooding may be considerable. Even more dangerous are the cyclones which unpredictably can inundate vast areas of land and cause great damage and loss of life. The cyclone of 1970 killed 200,000 people and their animals, and devastated much agricultural land.

The years since 1971 have been a period of experiment with different styles of government. To begin with there was no constitution, and Sheikh Mujibur Rahman, who had led resistance to West Pakistani influence, assumed government with the backing of his Awami League supporters. When a new constitution was established, elections were held and the Sheikh was returned to power in a parliament that included only very few members of opposing parties. The imposition of a presidential system of government and dissolution of parliament (with its own consent) followed in January 1975. Overwhelming support and little in the way of effective opposition did not give rise to strong government, rather the reverse; little was done to come to grips with the administrative, economic and development problems facing the country.

The brutal assassination of Sheikh Mujibur Rahman in August 1975 and the subsequent *coups* and turmoil are evidence of political instability which may have unpredictable effects on the economy. The basic problems remain the same, as does the need for effective government to deal with them. Until a clear lead can be given by government, there is not much hope of improving the lot of the inhabitants of Bangladesh. In the last resort it is the efforts of Bangalees that will determine their economic and political future but a large amount of external assistance will be needed if Bangladesh is to succeed. In the future, as in the past, the outside world cannot fail to be affected by the misery of Bangladesh.

In the face of the devastation of the cyclone of 1970 the world showed its readiness to come to the aid of those suffering cataclysmic disaster. In the civil war of 1971, when refugees poured over the Indian border, the need to intervene in her affairs was manifest. During and after the War of Independence the United Nations through its Relief Operations, Dacca, and later through its Relief Office in Bangladesh, mobilised assistance on a large scale for Bangladesh. Once again the international community supplied substantial support to alleviate suffering caused by the 1974 floods. The long-drawn-out inability to improve the lot of the people and the need to remove the constant threat of starvation is not, however, a problem that the world feels compelled to solve. For Bangladesh, growing dependence on the rest of the world for food is a dangerous position and one which is bound to make it increasingly difficult to find the resources needed for development. A positive approach to the development of Bangladesh on the part of the international community is necessary. Trade *and* aid is still a valid slogan and the world has a responsibility for providing export opportunities for Bangladesh's jute; but this alone will not go very far in dealing with Bangladesh's problem, which is basically one of insufficient capacity to generate resources for development while maintaining minimum consumption levels.

Nothing short of a continuing massive injection of aid is likely in present circumstances to get the economy off the ground sufficiently quickly to give real impetus to the development effort. It is not easy to see how donor countries can be persuaded to maintain an effort on the scale needed. Bangladesh is not a country of strategic importance to any but her immediate neighbours. Perhaps its only importance politically, lies in its availability as a possible test-bench of two opposing systems of development, collective and compulsive methods on the one hand, and a less fettered working of the private enterprise system on the other. It might be considered worthwhile by some countries to give aid to demonstrate the power of one or the other system, but it can scarcely be felt that large gains are likely to result from such an exercise, to Bangladesh or to potential contestants. If aid is to come for the development of Bangladesh it is more likely to be for economic reasons or on general humanitarian grounds. In the long run it is the latter that is important. Assistance from other countries must be seen as an endeavour to solve the world's most difficult problem of economic development. If the problem of Bangladesh can be solved, there can be reasonable confidence that less difficult problems of development can also be solved. It is in this sense that Bangladesh is to be regarded as the test case.

Being a Development "Expert"

Brigitte Erler

It was during a so-called mission to Bangladesh in 1983 that Brigitte Erler, an experienced development professional at the German Ministry for Economic Cooperation and Development and erstwhile member of parliament, suddenly realized that she was part of an "unholy alliance." The development aid that she had so fervently sought to bring to the poorest people in the world was causing them more harm than good and benefited those who needed it least. She quit her job and wrote an insider's story about her experiences. The book, stridently titled Lethal Aid, *caused a furor in Germany. Here she describes her isolation from those whose interests had formed the mainstay of her commitment.*

As a representative of the Ministry for Economic Cooperation and Development arriving in "your" developing country, you are met at the airport by a member of the embassy staff. . . . You wait in the VIP room for the luggage to be sorted and then an air-conditioned car whisks you off to your deluxe hotel. You will get reimbursed for this, even though the cost may far outstrip the regular accommodation allowance, because more modest hotels are considered unacceptable. You find yourself in the sterile atmosphere of an Intercontinental or Holiday Inn. The only local color provided here in Bangladesh is the view of the slums. Cleverly, the top-line Sonargaon Hotel with its vast marble entrance hall has been built right near the slums and not, as is usual, in the upscale neighborhood. Funded with Japanese development aid, it is probably intended to encourage the slum dwellers' enterprise and initiative.

The representative of the United Nations Development Programme in Dhaka once tried to make arriving experts swiftly rent a house rather than spend the usual months in the Sonargaon Hotel, but to no avail: the government feared that the hotel would stand empty.

Right from the start, you move among the upper crust. From the hotel an embassy limousine conveys you to ministries for talks with high officials whose social position is somewhere between landlord and middle class. . . .

Then you begin to rush through the projects. Usually you have about half a day, or a day, per project but long trips frequently use up most of that time. It goes without saying that each project leader, and almost every expert, is at pains to present the project in the best possible light. After all, their jobs depend on my impression. And even if they are honest in presenting the entire set of problems, it still is the point of view of the white expert that you get to hear. Usually they are deeply immersed in their problems and successes and hold forth without pause. They rarely have the opportunity to describe their work to an interested listener who also holds the key to the planning and future of the project.

This thoroughly understandable behavior seldom gives the "counterparts," or local project workers, any chance to speak. And if they do, you speak with them only in the expert's presence; and they will present everything as previously agreed with the project leader—unless they are completely at loggerheads with each other, which I have never experienced.

If you want to speak with a counterpart—not even with the peasants concerned—alone, you have to perform a psychological feat of strength. The project leader will unfailingly interpret any separate talk with a Bangladeshi as a sign of distrust. It was in Bangladesh that I first understood this clearly. The more congenial and committed I found an expert to be, the more difficult I found it to cope with this uncalled for demonstration of distrust. During earlier trips I had certainly always tried to speak with the locals, but only in Bangladesh did I become aware of the mechanisms with which we constantly deceive ourselves.

Often, after exhausting journeys across the country, or the third project visit of the day, you simply find it less strenuous to speak German than English. It also sounded pedantic when I asked to continue a German discussion in English for the benefit of the counterparts in attendance. It was easier to explain complicated things in German, and often I did not understand technical terms in English, so we ended up with German once again. Sometimes counterparts would speak poor English and—intimidated by the power of the German ministry and the presence of a woman with authority—spoke it so softly that I had trouble understanding them. As a result, I frequently misunderstood a counterpart and the expert would have to step in to clarify things. And so I would prefer to stay with the expert. On top of this there was the obvious psychological closeness to another German in a strange environment. You trust him automatically and think you understand his reactions and interpretations better than those of somebody from another culture.

Moreover, it takes a lot of time to win a local's trust because he has no reason to trust a stranger. Any critical remarks may jeopardize his own job, either because he will be called to account, or because his information will lead to the demise of the entire project or a part of it.

I also had to learn how Bangladeshis communicate. It was by quietly hearing them out rather than by firing questions at them that I learned the most. I found it especially hard to bear long silences. Perhaps the scales fell from my eyes during this particular mission precisely because Bangladeshis are so amazingly communicative.

Translated from German by Willem van Schendel.

NGOs—Modern Landlords with a Global Vision

Lamia Karim

In contemporary Bangladesh the prominence of NGOs is a fact of life. The country hosts thousands of active NGOs and has long been the world's exemplar of nongovernmental development initiatives. It is a prime breeding ground for all kinds of development experiments, models, and practices. Therefore, what NGOs do in Bangladesh matters globally.

In this critical piece, the anthropologist Lamia Karim poses the question of how NGOs got to be so powerful in Bangladesh. She points to their access to lavish external resources during a neoliberal phase of capitalism—as well as to the weakness of the Bangladesh state, especially in the rural economy. NGOs were able to provide crucial financial and employment services, thereby forging links of global patronage and dependency not only with poor peasants but also with young professionals and public intellectuals. Karim sees NGOs as new landlords.

NGOs that were aided by western donors largely facilitated the process of globalization. Through micro-credit operations, rural people and NGOs in Bangladesh have become mutually dependent, and rural people and multinational corporations have become connected for the first time. Through NGOs, micro-credit recipients have become consumers of products of multinational corporations such as finance capital, breeder chickens, [and] cell phones, and as producers, they remain dependent on multinational corporations for physical inputs such as seeds, fertilizers, and pesticides. But NGOs are not passive agents of capital. NGOs are also active producers of new subjectivities and social meanings for people through their various economic and social programs. Thus, the relationship between rural subjects and NGOs is contradictory and varied; they instrumentally exploit each other. However, the balance of power is with the NGOs. Yet very little ethnographic work has been done to examine how this micro-credit model might intersect with local patriarchal norms and cultural practices. . . . NGO staff and local and international consultants hired by NGOs and aid organizations do the bulk of the research on micro-credit NGOs in Bangladesh. . . .

There are several critical factors that allow the NGOs to play such a decisive role in rural life in Bangladesh. Firstly, there is the virtual absence of the state in the rural economy. NGOs dominate the rural economy from rural credit to telecommunications to primary education. Secondly, the NGOs provide two-thirds of the institutional credit in rural areas. In Bangladesh, neither the government banks nor the traditional moneylenders loan to the very poor because they lack physical collateral. This financial dependency on the NGO[s] has given them the power to act as patrons of the poor. They constitute a modern landlord with a global vision. Thirdly, the NGOs are a major source of employment in a country with limited job opportunities for its burgeoning young population. . . . NGOs are seen as the future—a promise of a better life and, for the better educated, an opportunity to go abroad for training. Fourthly, the NGOs have silenced dissent in the public sphere by inducting a large number of university professors and researchers as consultants in their various programs; public intellectuals who might otherwise have spoken out against the excess of NGOs. . . . Finally, the work of NGOs fragmented the left political parties from the 1970s onward when both groups struggled over the adherence of the poor. The resource-rich NGOs won.

Rich-Peasant Resistance to Development Organizations

Ainoon Naher

It is estimated that microfinance currently covers about 60 percent of all poor house-holds and 37 percent of total households in Bangladesh. When it first started its journey in rural Bangladesh, microfinance (or microcredit) was not universally wel-comed. On the contrary, both fundamentalist Muslims and rural rich people con-demned it. The rural rich have always acted as moneylenders, using poor people's dependence to their own advantage. They perceived microfinance as a direct threat and organized to oppose institutions such as the Grameen Bank, the Association for Social Advancement (ASA), and BRAC, sometimes violently. In this text, the anthro-pologist Ainoon Naher highlights the political aspects of development by focusing on the power struggles that result from development organizations getting active in local arenas.

In rural Bangladesh, rich peasants who function as informal community leaders are called *matbors* [Muslim religious leaders]. Most such individuals are likely to view NGOs entering their domain as rivals who are there to or-ganize poor people in a way that goes against their interest. Thus it comes as no surprise to find such people's views on NGO activities converging with that of the Mullahs. In Jiri, Bodrul Haider Chowdhury of Subedar Bari, a village matbor holding important positions like member of the govern-ing bodies of two local schools, secretary of the mosque of his *bari* [village home] and a leader of Awami League, told me: "Though Grameen Bank are helping the poor women, it is true that women have become *bepurdah* [not keeping purdah]."

About the burning of BRAC schools, he had this to say: "The *alems* (ma-drasa teachers and other religious leaders) agitated against BRAC. They burnt the schools. I did not myself see any mark of the turtle on anyone or the pushing of injections [mentioned in stories about forcible conversion]. But I heard it from different people of the village. As it has spread so much, I think something must have happened somewhere."

One Jamat [Jama'at-e-Islami, a political party] supporter told me that NGOS are trying to destroy the existing social structure of the village. He said: "They want to destroy our traditional system of arbitration and the position of the matbor." Then he recited a verse meant to stress the importance of the matbors:

Bap chara put,
Shorgo chara bhut,
majhi chara nao,
matbor chara gao
Son without father,
/ Ghost without heaven,
/ Boat without boatman,
/ Village without matbor [all are the same][1]

The rich peasants, who lost sources of cheap labor, due to different developments, seemed as critical of women's participation in weekly Grameen or ASA meetings as the mullahs did. The village elite constantly bemoan the increasing difficulty of "finding good help" as young women from families who have supplied domestic servants for the local landowner for generations are now taking advantage of self-employment opportunities provided by garment industries and various NGOS; those who do not join NGOS or [a] factory are at least aware that they can charge higher wages. Members of the Grameen Bank credit groups told me that, as [these young women] did not work in the houses of the rich peasants, [the village elite] attacked the Grameen "Center."

Nasir, member of an affluent family and a long-time migrant worker in the Middle East, expressed this resentment in this way: "Nowadays because of the two 'G's,' Grameen Bank and the Garments Industry, we do not get servants. Five years back we used to have four to five maidservants in our home. But this time I have seen that even if you call the women for any family occasion, they do not come. All of them are 'busy' with their Bank."

Traditionally the powerful rich peasants hold the important posts (e.g., secretary, member) of different institutions, such as school, mosque, *madrasa* [Islamic school], etc. of the villages. This is a symbol of their power as well. But NGOS, specifically BRAC, on the contrary recruited poor people in the management committee of the schools. This exclusion surely caused resentment of the *shomaj* leaders (matbors), most of whom remained indifferent as the "fundamentalists" began to attack BRAC. That this class of people had the power to contain the fundamentalist elements if they so chose was illustrated by the role of Mohammad Ali, the richest person and a *"murubbi"* (patron) of South Jiri, who played an active role against the "fundamental-ists" in his *para* [village neighborhood]. BRAC set up their schools in South Jiri with his help. Mohammad Ali [told] the owners of the land (selected for the BRAC school) to build schools, arranged a meeting between guardians and BRAC officials, etc. Though he lived in town, every Friday during his visit to his bari, he kept in touch with BRAC. He was also the secretary of both schools . . . [and] of his para. When the agitators began to burn the BRAC schools in his area, he called a meeting in his para and told the people that he had brought the BRAC schools to his area and they belonged to him, so if anybody would damage the schools they would have to pay for that. Once he threatened the imam of the bari mosque that he would be dis-missed from his job if he started speaking against BRAC and other NGOs during the *jumma* (Friday) prayer. The imam did not say anything further as Mohammad Ali was paying him. Mr. Ali also visited the madrasa and quar-relled with the principal about the attack on BRAC. Despite further attacks on schools, both of the schools in this para remained open in the end.

In Bangladesh villages, there has also been a long tradition of affluent families doing "charity" work, as for example providing relief during natu-ral disasters. Some rich peasants help the poor through *zakat* [alms] and other traditional modes of redistribution, practices that help rich peasants gain and retain social prestige. But since the NGOs have entered villages like Jiri, they have also encroached on such traditional domains of the rural elite. For example, after the cyclone of 1991, [the international NGO] CARE promptly distributed relief among the affected people. They provided wheat and saline solution to poor people. And later they set up tube-wells and sani-tary latrines in many baris in Jiri. During my fieldwork, Grameen Bank [GB] and ASA approved a special long-term interest-free loan for repairing houses very quickly. In the case of ASA, a member receiving such aid paid back Tk. 3 [Tk. is short for Taka, the Bangladesh currency] per week and the GB mem-bers paid Tk. 8 per week. A GB member, Rokeya, told me that, although one member of the Union *Parishad* [UP; Union Council] had listed the names of the affected families, they only got 4 kg of rice per household, after 21 days. "Neither the UP Chairman nor any wealthy person visited us. Nobody helped with one taka! That's why Grameen Bank has become our *ma-bap* (i.e., providers, literally, 'parents')!"

Note

1. Brackets in the original.

The Birth of a Megacity

Until the 1960s Bangladesh was one of the most rural societies on Earth. It had a population of fifty-five million and no less than 95 percent of them lived in villages. Dhaka, the largest town, only had some seven hundred thousand inhabitants. Although this image of the nation as an essentially rural society lingers on, urbanization has changed the face of the country and the life of its citizens.

The graph here shows that towns and cities have expanded enormously since the 1960s. Today forty-five million Bangladeshis live urban lives, and Dhaka has twenty times as many inhabitants as it had fifty years ago. It is growing rapidly, and demographers expect Dhaka to reach the twenty-five million mark by the mid-2020s. It will be one of the world's true megacities. Other Bangladeshi cities are also growing as more and more Bangladeshis find it impossible to make a living in the countryside. Most of them end up in slums (which are growing at twice the overall rate). Following worldwide trends, well-to-do city dwellers increasingly ensconce themselves in gated communities, shun the run-down public transport, and try to distance themselves from the poor in many other ways.

A Century of Urban Growth in Bangladesh, 1911–2011

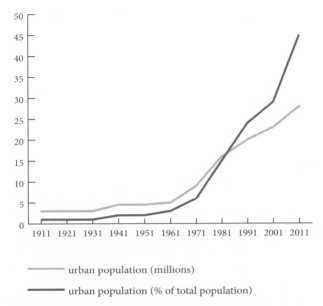

——— urban population (millions)

▬▬▬ urban population (% of total population)

A century of urban growth in Bangladesh, 1911–2011.
Source: population censuses.

The sky over a Dhaka city neighborhood. Photograph by Shahidul Alam/Drik.
Used by permission of Drik Picture Agency.

The Wealthiest People of Dhaka City

Kamal Siddiqui, Sayeda Rowshan Qadir,

Sitara Alamgir, and Sayeedul Huq

In the 1980s a group of social scientists carried out a social survey of Dhaka city. At a time when the focus of social research in Bangladesh was almost exclusively on the rural and the poor, these researchers provided an unprecedented insight into the lives of the urban rich. What is particularly striking in their account is the very recent emergence of a vernacular group of extremely wealthy people and the means by which they amassed their fortunes.

In 1947, that is[,] at the time of Pakistan's establishment, there was no one from the Bengali Muslims in the richest stratum of Dhaka city society. It was either Hindus or Marwaris who constituted this layer. After 1947, this group of people soon migrated to India, but the vacuum left was filled not so much by the Bengali Muslims as by the non-Bengali Muslims like the Adamjees, Bawanis, Ispahanis, etc. The first stage for the Bengali Muslims in their upward mobility was to graduate from the ranks of lower middle class and rural background to urban middle class through filling the vacuum in the sphere of professional jobs and urban real estate property left by the departing Marwaris and Hindus. Some upward mobility was also ensured through education. This phase was completed in the 1950s. The 1960s witnessed an attempt by the Pakistani ruling class to create a rich class in Bangladesh (then East Pakistan) through what Hamza Alavi [1972] called "contacts and contracts." The state was heavily involved in this process and the new rich came up as junior partners of the Pakistani ruling class. Obviously, since Dhaka was the capital, it had the highest concentration [but] of the 22 richest families of Pakistan, only one was from Bangladesh, who was, however, a resident not of Dhaka but of Chittagong. . . .

The independence of Bangladesh drastically reduced the preponderance of non-Bengali Muslims in the richest stratum of Dhaka society. Many of them, in fact, left for Pakistan after transferring their liquid capital. On the

Jewelry store in Dhaka. Photograph by Willem van Schendel, 2010.

other hand, the new state machinery together with [an] increased flow of aid provided new and expanded opportunities for both the old rich [and] many new families to graduate to the ranks of the richest in Dhaka city. . . .

Interviews with selected respondents showed that the first big amount of money (i.e., primitive accumulation) was acquired by the Dhaka city richest in one or more of the methods described below:

a. Theft, embezzlement, forcible occupation, etc., involving government funds and stores and abandoned property; and heavy kickbacks taken by bureaucratic power holders against favours dished out.
b. Involvement in smuggling, narcotic trade, hoarding, black marketing, currency racketeering, under- and over-invoicing, etc.
c. Defrauding and permanently defaulting big loans taken from NCBS [nationalized commercial banks] and DFIS [development financial institutions].
d. Commission agency out of million-dollar "projects" or purchases financed generally by foreign aid and in collusion with the state power.
e. Unearned income through reselling of permits, imposition of sanctions, issuance of arbitrary notifications and creation of artificial scarcities.

In all these methods, some sort of support or cover from power holders was essential, either openly or covertly. The pivotal role of power holders in class formation through primitive accumulation, in other words, plunder, was thus well established. . . .

What is . . . unique to Dhaka city and Bangladesh is not that the rich are getting richer, but the fact that theft and plunder as means of accumulating capital are showing no signs of yielding place to economic means of accumulation, namely profit maximisation through productive investments in various sectors of the economy.

A Girl's Life:

Work and School

Staff writer, Women Magazine of Bangladesh

Most data on women in Bangladesh paint a dismal picture of their situation, but data on female school enrollment, especially in primary schools, provide an exception. One study from 2010 mentions that girls have overtaken boys in enrollment, attendance, and completion in primary schools. Even so, many young girls are excluded from formal schooling because of domestic duties and limited family resources that are often expended for the advancement of male children. The Child Learning Centres initiated by the Dhaka Ahsania Mission—a local NGO that has been active since the 1950s—are innovative in making it possible for young girls who have to work for a living to still exercise their right to education.

In Bangladesh, family poverty and poor-quality state education force millions of children out of primary school. Girls in particular lose out, as they are often the first to be called on to get a job or help their parents at home. But a new project of flexible learning centres is hoping to change this as Aasha Mehreen Amin found when she visited two centres run by the Dhaka Ahsania Mission.

A maths class is in full swing inside a Child Learning Centre (CLC) in a slum area of Sheorapara, Dhaka City. There are four tables where students, aged eight to twelve, sit immersed in their work. Jannatul (which means "heavenly" in Arabic) is a round-faced, wide-eyed twelve-year-old girl wearing a threadbare shalwar kameez [tunic and pants].

Jannatul Akter works twice as hard as many children and had to fight to come to school. Every morning, after setting up a fruit stall on the main road of Sheorapara, she comes on here to read and write in Bangla and English, study maths and take part in reciting poetry and singing and dancing.

"I like everything about school," she says, "the dancing, poetry, singing. Madam [the tutor] also teaches us how to stay clean and comb our hair." Jannatul is one of the lucky ones. Every few steps along the alleyways near

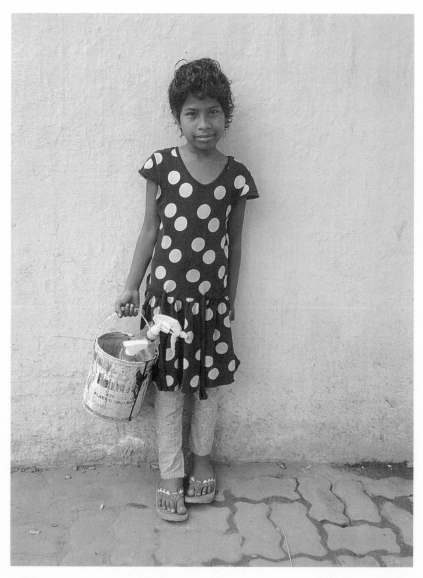

A young girl earns her living in Dhaka by cleaning cars' windscreens. Photograph by Willem van Schendel, 2011.

the learning centre, there are clusters of little children playing in the dust. Many of the older ones say they don't go to school.

Jannatul's tutor first saw her working on the fruit stall when she was ten and asked her mother to send her back to primary school. Initially her mother, Tajmohal Begum, was reluctant, fearing her daughter would lose her job. "Then Madam (the school's teacher) came and convinced me," she says. With her husband dead, and six children, Tajmohal's daily concerns are getting a decent meal for the family and how to provide for the future. "I have to save, and I have to give dowry for their marriages," she says. "We have no choice."

Jannatul gets up in the early hours and works before going to school at nine, returning to the stall after school and finishing around 9 PM. Dark circles under her eyes betray the long days she puts in carrying the heavy crates of fruit, which she must sort, unpack and sell. For all her hours, she takes home only 20 Taka a day (less than 20 pence). One day, Jannatul hopes to land a highly prized office job but she must stay at the fruit stall for as long as her family expects it. She smiles as she remembers the moment she was allowed to go to school, "Before the stall owner did not let me go to school—but then Madam came and talked to him and even Ma told him, you cannot stop her from going."

Part-time attendance at the centres gives children a fighting chance of staying in school. Professor Rezina Sultana, former principal of a teacher training college in Dhaka, says the scheme is likely to provide new opportunities for girls—"Families still have high hopes for their boys, but don't expect so much for their daughters, so if they see something is more flexible they are willing to give their girls a chance."

The centre in Sheorapara runs from 9 to 12, while another in nearby Ibrahimpur runs from 11 to 2 PM[,] where Helena, a teacher with the project works. "Sometimes the students have to leave in the middle of the class, but we always finish the lesson the same day, so they don't have to study at home. I can give personal attention to each student as the class size is small. In government primary schools it is impossible to do that as there are 40 to 70 students in each class. There are also some costs such as admission test fees and school uniforms that these parents cannot afford."

Helena, in fact, is quite a celebrity among her students who are obviously deeply attached to her. "They are so good and if I fall ill, they will go to a phone shop to call up and ask how I am and if I will be coming to school or not. It is amazing." Meanwhile, if a child doesn't turn up, the class teacher will visit the child's house to ask her guardian why she didn't attend class and then writes the reason in a "home inspection" book.

Ibrahimpur's learning centre is in a small rented room within a cluster of one-roomed houses; Helena's classroom is clean and cheerfully adorned with colourful posters, alphabets, numbers and motivational words, as well as an array of drawings by the students. Each class generally has 25 students and is divided into four subject groups which roughly translate into the first, second and third grade of school.

"It is a multi-grade system," explains G. F. Hamim, the coordinator of this project (called UNIQUE) run by Dhaka Ahsania Mission. "It allows each child to be assessed and taught according to his or her proficiency," he says. "If, say, a child has reached Class 3 competence in mathematics, but has Class 1 proficiency in Bangla[,] then the teacher will teach her accordingly, until her Bangla reaches Class 3 level." The set books are all National Textbook Board texts taught in the formal system and the project, [which] aims to help these children to continue their education by enrolling them into regular primary schools after they complete the CLC course.

At Ibrahimpur Centre, it is Thursday and "cultural day." Two sisters take the lead in a number of song and dance numbers. They go on to perform a song, "We are the future citizens, we will lighten the darkness, we will carry the torch of knowledge," they sing. For the children at these centres there is a good chance they will.

Messages of Development

Bangladesh Red Crescent Society and NGO *Forum*

All over Bangladesh the eye meets billboards, posters, banners, and other signs that development agencies, eager to communicate with local people, have put up. These signs' messages are varied, as are the ways in which they are packaged. Quite often they adopt a distinctive naive painting style. Here are two examples.

Cyclones are a frequent hazard in exposed Saint Martin's Island (Jinjira) in the far south. This sturdy concrete billboard from Bangladesh Red Crescent Society instructs locals to seek cover in specially built cyclone shelters as soon as they hear the alarm. Photograph by Willem van Schendel, 2003.

In a tourist spot—the Mujibnagar mango orchard where the first Bangladesh government was proclaimed—this signboard from the NGO Forum for Drinking Water Supply and Sanitation advises visitors to use sanitary latrines at home. Photograph by Willem van Schendel, 2006.

Migrants in Barisal

Jeremy Seabrook

Barisal is a district town in southern Bangladesh that has been described as "the Venice of Bengal." Cradled in a network of rivers and canals, it hardly rises above water level. Like most towns in Bangladesh, it is surrounded by rich and densely cultivated alluvial plains. Despite this natural opulence, the plains are home to intense deprivation. If you do not own land, life can be unbearably hard. Many despair of making a living in the countryside and move to the towns and cities. The enormity of this movement is reflected in the fact that Bangladesh's urban population has increased from seven million in the 1970s to about fifty million today. Jeremy Seabrook sketches the life of two groups of temporary denizens in Barisal, "a melting, melancholy place": migrants on their way to bigger cities and nomads clinging to a lifestyle that has become increasingly precarious.

Barisal awakens to a dawn chorus of crows. They perch, gleaming and malevolent, on stinking metal containers of waste or sagging loops of electricity and telephone lines, a stave of discordant morning music.

The city is a halting-place on the road to Chittagong or Dhaka for people who have lost land, their most precious possession. Land in Bangladesh is a source of constant violence—land seized by the powerful, deeds of ownership falsified by corrupt officials, subdivided into uneconomic parcels by inheritance. But the most ferocious dispute of all is the constant struggle between land and sea. Barisal is a melting, melancholy place, battered by storms from the Bay, its waterways and canals overflowing, so gorged with water that the sea spits out land it cannot swallow and, in another mood, eats up what had been until recently fields of grain.

Water floods the plain, sweeps the city in tidal surges, drips in an irregular heartbeat from the tree canopy. Water turns Barisal into a fluid, mythic place: it is the edge of the world, its seventeen rivers streams of forgetfulness, which the dead must cross in order to wash away the memories that attached them to life. And, indeed, people here must forget all they knew about rural life, as they are born again into the urban penumbra of Barisal, a life after the death of a countryside which made and then expelled them. A frieze of the dispossessed makes its way through the waterlogged landscape towards this improvised city.

In a marshy field on the outskirts of town, a group of nomadic families have set up their brief camp—hoops of bamboo enclosing black polythene. These, unlike the unwillingly uprooted, are perpetual migrants. They live an archaic culture of catching snakes, selling their meat, skins and venom for traditional medicines. Their relationship with snakes is mysterious, since the creatures respond to their voice without the use of flute or any other instrument. They gather herbs which they weave into the fabric of amulets, proof against the evil eye and the spells of ill-wishers. Those who wander have a knowledge withheld from settled people, out of whose credulity they make a living. Kasha Ali had ten children, of whom four died. Allah gave them this life, so why should they settle? If the children go hungry, and have not enough to sustain them, they live or die by the grace of God. Shameto Begum's husband has gone into the city to sell charms and to practise *singha*, a traditional medicine using buffalo horn: they grind the horn, and cure the sick by cutting their veins and blowing the powder into the bloodstream; the blood that flows is black, and as it emerges, the evil that has poisoned it is made manifest.

These traditional nomads are different from the reluctant migrants of Barisal, the crowds besieging the terminal for steamers on the turbulent river and the bus-stand, where battered Bedfords with dented chassis and modern Hinos with panoramic glass windows bear the people away to sell their labour, their youth and vitality, the produce of their land, the skill of their fingers; transactions in which they are always the losers. It is not only the fragile land that is eroded by restless rivers and tides; ways of life, culture and tradition are also washed away. Even the people appear thin and two-dimensional, emblems of poverty, subject of reports, abstracts and inquiries that have been stored away in monsoon-stained files half-eaten by white ants. Micro-credit initiatives, aid programmes and development projects have come and gone, but the poor remain, bony rickshaw-drivers, emaciated elderly maidservants up before dawn and still cleaning vessels when the family retires after midnight, children breaking bricks in desolate yards, faces powdered with red dust, while in the drenched villages they lure birds and fish into bamboo traps, a work increasingly necessary in the city of hunger, which cannot provide sustenance for its people.

A Day at the Hospital

Shahaduz Zaman

*In a closely observed portrayal, Shahaduz Zaman (a medical doctor turned an-
thropologist) brings to life the daily routine of an understaffed and underresourced
government hospital in Bangladesh. In this excerpt he focuses on patients in an
orthopedic ward, how they cope with their misfortune, and how they struggle to
deal with a universe populated by doctors, nurses, ward boys, and cleaners. In many
ways, the power relations in the ward reflect those in the wider society.*

As the study hospital is the cheapest option for tertiary-level treatment, the
hospital is occupied chiefly with patients from lower economic background.
During my fieldwork I encountered several violent cases. . . . One man
crushed his legs and hands when a bomb he was making at home to cause
panic during a political demonstration blew up accidentally. Another man
almost had his hand cut off by two workers whom he had dismissed a day
earlier. A lady arrived with a gunshot wound in her leg caused by a mugger
who snatched her gold necklace. A young boy of about 14 lost his legs when
another boy with whom he had a quarrel, pushed him out of a train. An
elderly lady broke her hip when her neighbour kicked her because her bean
tree's vines had climbed into his mango tree's branches.

Every day I would hear such harsh stories. At the end of my fieldwork the
ward's medical officer suggested, "Why don't you wait a few more weeks.
As you know the national election is coming. The fighting between the two,
rival, political parties will intensify and you will see many more handless
and legless people in the ward."

The head of the orthopaedic department told me, "Decades ago when
we were young doctors, we did not see so many crime-related cases in the
ward. But now, every week there are such cases. I believe the rapid urbanization occurring in the last decades, the competitive market economy and
the population increase have made people more intolerant and aggressive
which has resulted in these increased cruelties."

However, most ward patients are victims of traffic accidents. . . . A number of cases were related to accidents at work. There is a big ship-demolition industry nearby, as the hospital is located in a coastal city. Many workers from that industry are admitted with broken or severed limbs caused by falling, heavy objects. Factory workers whose limbs have been cut off by a machine are also brought in. Construction labourers also appear with broken hips or legs after falling from work sites on high-rise buildings.

Of note, there were a small number of female patients in the ward and the majority of the patients were young males. The restricted mobility of Bangladeshi women in the outside world probably explains this disparity. Bangladesh is a predominantly Muslim country where the concept of purdah (seclusion) for women prevails. Although Islamic rules are not strictly followed in everyday life, it is generally discouraged for women to work outside the home, and there are few employment opportunities for women outside of their own domestic sphere. As the mobility of women outside the home is limited, they are not often exposed to the dangers that can cause orthopaedic casualities.

The physically crushed patients of the orthopaedic ward were found to be mentally crushed as well. They suffered from a host of uncertainties. Most of the patients were uncertain about their condition. Diagnosis was not of much concern for the orthopaedic patients, because they all came to the hospital with a very obvious injury. Instead, patients were mostly concerned about the treatment plan the doctors had assigned to them, and their prognosis. The staff of the ward hardly explain either of these to the patients. Patients are not sure what the doctors and staff members of the ward are doing with their broken hands or legs, for nothing is clearly communicated with them regarding their condition. During the professor's round the patients remain a passive audience. Medical discussion goes on over the patient's bed, [and] he or she is not allowed to speak but only to answer the questions directed at him or her. Patients are not supposed to ask anything to the doctors during the round. If someone dares to ask a question, he or she is immediately scolded by the doctor for hampering the round, and asked to keep his or her mouth shut.

Ramjan Ali is a bus helper (an assistant to a bus driver) who hurt his legs in an accident. Since his admission he has been sceptical about the treatment procedure in the ward. Doctors told him that both his legs are broken and that he will need an operation in one of the legs. But Ramjan thinks that doctors have diagnosed him incorrectly, and that he did not break two of his legs but only one. He is anxious that the doctors will also operate on his right leg, the one he thinks is healthy, because he was having traction in his left leg. The hospital made X-rays of both of his legs, which show the fractured sites. However, Ramjan thinks that one of the X-rays is not of his legs but put into his file by mistake. He tried in vain to convey his suspicion to the staff members. First he told them to a ward boy who chided him for such thoughts: "Don't you dare say it to the doctor; he will just beat you up." Ramjan still tried to persuade the nurse. The nurse also became very angry and said: "Don't try to be too smart. Doctor will see whether the X-rays are correct or not. If you don't like the treatment here, just leave." One day when he was trying to see the X-ray plate against the light, a duty doctor was passing by and told him: "You! What are you doing with the X-ray? Want to be a doctor? Keep those in the file and don't mix up with other papers." Ramjan did not dare to tell him about his suspicion.

Boka (scolding) is one of things that patients receive from all the staff members, from cleaners to professors, regardless of their rank. Scolding the patients and their relatives is an integral part of the ward scene; they are scolded for a multitude of reasons, especially when they do not act according to the expectations of the staff. The scolding starts right from their admission, when patients are scolded for delaying their visit to the hospital and for visiting local bonesetters instead. Doctors scold the accident patients for their carelessness and ignorance that caused the accident. Doctors also scold patients if they cry or make sounds during their examination. As mentioned before, patients are also scolded if they show interest in their medical records or ask questions, because the doctors think it is unnecessary. The nurses scold them for not following the medication and other instructions properly or for attempting to elicit any information regarding the treatment. Scolding by the ward boys is directed mostly to the relatives of the patients, as the ward boys are responsible for clearing the relatives from the ward, but the patients are also scolded by ward boys for the misdeeds of their relatives and for not cooperating properly with the ward boys' jobs, such as changing the patients' beds, taking the patient to the X-ray department or changing a dressing. Cleaners also continually scold the patients and their relatives for making the ward dirty. On a few occasions I saw doctors slap the patients.

In addition to physical injury and medical uncertainty, patients also suffer from anxiety about how to cope with the economic loss caused by their hospitalization. Their economic loss is manifold. First, there are the expenditures involved in being in the hospital. Though the government hospital is virtually free of charge (officially, the admission fee is 5 taka), there are many costs involved in the hospitalization process. The patient must buy almost all of the medicines and other materials for daily use in the hospital.

The hospital generally has a regular supply of some analgesic and antimicrobial drugs, and, irregularly, antibiotics. None of the drugs are sufficient enough, either in quantity or in strength, to cover the treatment course of the patients. A small portion of the required drugs are given by the hospital and the rest must be bought from the shops. Cotton, gauze and X-ray films are irregularly available and most of the time are bought by the patients. Injectable drugs and medicines required for operation are almost never available in the ward. I also encountered incidences when the lower level staff stole medical and non-medical items from the patient and sold those to the drug shops outside the hospital for low price. The patients had to buy the drugs again.

There are other sorts of informal payments in the ward. Informal payment begins upon entry to the hospital. The liftman demands money for taking the patients to their respective wards, the ward boy demands money for bringing the patients from the outdoor patient's consultation room to the ward, the gate keeper asks for money for allowing the relatives to enter the ward a little earlier then the official visiting time or to stay past the official visiting time, the X-ray technician wants money for taking the X-ray to the patient and cleaners demand money in exchange for helping the patient to go to the toilet in the absence of his or her relatives. All these informal payments are known as *bakshees* (tips).

The second level of economic loss is the loss of personal income. The patients' profiles indicate that most of them are day labourers, low salaried employees or small businessmen. In most cases their inactivity means a complete loss of income, which is a huge economic burden for most of the patients. In most cases, it completely devastates the economic well-being of the patients.

Rahmat Ali is a rickshaw puller. He was severely injured when his rickshaw was run over by a public bus. He had an operation on his leg and was in the hospital for about 6 weeks. He says, "Only when I am on the road with my rickshaw do I have money in my pocket. But now, for more than a month I am stuck here. I have no earnings at all. My only younger brother could help me financially but he also had to close his small cigarette shop in the bazaar in order to attend me in the hospital." I asked why his wife did not come to attend him instead. He replied, "She works as a maid, that's how she is feeding our two children as I have no income. If she comes, who will take care of the children? Moreover, you can see that it is very difficult for a woman to stay in this hospital." I then asked how he met the operation's cost. He told me that he had taken a loan from the proprietor of the rickshaw that he used to pull:

I borrowed 10,000 Tk (approximately US$150) from him, which is a huge amount for me. I can't sleep at night when I think about how I will repay his money. Shall I ever be able to pull the rickshaw again? Even if I succeed, it will take years for me to repay him from my rickshaw income, moreover, I will have to starve to pay him back. Now I think the only solution for me is to sell my small piece of cultivatable land that I have back in my village. Then I am a pauper. These thoughts worry me all day while I am lying in this bed.

Despite all these miseries, patients rush to this hospital because it is the only public (and therefore the cheapest) tertiary-level hospital in the locality for thousands of poor Bangladeshi patients.

The Children of Katni

Betsy Hartmann and James K. Boyce

Humanity is not usually the lens through which allegedly overpopulated Bangladesh is viewed. Demographers and development scholars tell us that Bangladesh's expanding population forms a major stumbling block on the road to national progress and prosperity. Most Bangladeshis are young and most of them live in villages. Usually they remain faceless to the transitory "development experts" of international organizations whose duty it is to make a quick assessment. In the piece here, Betsy Hartmann and James Boyce portray the lives of the youngest Bangladeshis. They got to know them in the 1970s, when they lived in a village (Katni) and studied the day-to-day life of the villagers. Their observation of the children of Katni focuses not on problems of population growth or poverty but on the children's humanity and how adults care for the children and take responsibility for their welfare.

Many Westerners think of Bangladesh's children as the joyless inheritors of their parents' fate: grinding poverty and the prospect of early death from starvation or disease. Those who stress the evils of over-population see in the country's children the basic cause of poverty as well as its most pathetic victims. But the smiles on the faces of Katni's children quickly shatter the image of Bangladesh as a desolate, hopeless place, and invite the outsider to look beyond those stereotypes.

As naturally as rice seedlings take root in the soil, Katni's children grow in the village, embodying its hardships but also its beauty. The village is their entire world—its soft, dirt paths carry them from house to house, its patches of jungle contain the spirits which frighten them in the dark, its fruit trees and lush fields form the backdrop of their lives. Each season brings new crops, new work and new play. Katni's children seldom lack physical attention, for if their parents are busy, they have grandparents, aunts and uncles, sisters and brothers to look after them. Loneliness is an alien concept—a cry is sure to draw attention. "There is a special kind of love for children," the villagers told us. "Without it you can't be whole. You will understand when you have children of your own."

Children dressed in warm clothes on a cold winter morning in northern Bangladesh. Photograph by Willem van Schendel, 2010.

This love extends even to those children who in other societies might be outcasts, confined to special institutions. Azi, known to the villagers as "the crazy one," is a retarded boy who at the age of 12 cannot speak a full sentence. He spends his days wandering naked through the village, singing mumbled songs to the white cranes perched in the reeds. The younger children sometimes tease him but the adults treat him well, giving him food when he is hungry. One day when his stepmother beat him, other women rallied to his defence, saying, "The boy should not be beaten—he doesn't understand anything. Allah gives a child like that for a reason, and he should be loved."

Love, however, does not fill empty stomachs, and early in life poor children learn that while their parents provide affection, they cannot always provide food. For these children survival means gleaning in the fields during the harvest, or running to a mango tree when a strong summer wind blows in the hope of catching a few falling fruits. As foreigners, we were naturally objects of great curiosity to Katni's children. At first most of them were afraid of us, but Shahida's irrepressible younger sister Amina soon led gangs of children to our house to watch us. One day Amina summoned up her courage and threw a potato at us while we were eating lunch. Jim chased her around Ali's house, to the amusement of many onlookers, until he finally got hold of her. Amina was sufficiently intimidated to stop her mischief, and before long we began to estaplish friendships with the children. Standing shyly at the front door, Lebumia asked for empty matchboxes from which he fashioned toys; neighbourhood children used our house as a hiding place in their games of cops and robbers. On many late afternoons, we sat on the bamboo bench outside our house and watched the children play. They devised their own toys and games, making miniature *dhekis* and trucks out of banana-tree stalk, linking puddles with ingenious miniature irrigation systems, sketching board games on the path, and designing hats from jungle leaves. Children of all ages played together, and quarrels were remarkably rare.

Born into a world where everyone knows them, where they do not have to prove themselves or compete for love and social acceptance, Katni's children fill the village with a buoyant happiness. Not yet old enough to be oppressed by adult worries, their spontaneous joy shines forth as a natural human birthright.

Education

Although there is no rigid separation between work and play, Katni's children are expected to do their share of household chores. In fact, their labour is an important part of the family economy. In landed households, their help in harvesting and processing crops often saves their parents the expense of hiring outside labourers. Poorer children frequently work for other households, sharing their modest wage with the rest of the family. As they work alongside adults, imitating their actions, Katni's children learn the basic skills of village life—the most important part of their education.

Besides learning practical skills, Katni's Muslim children receive religious training early in the mornings at the village *madrassah*, a one-room bamboo building with a thatched roof. The village *jamat* [religious council] maintains the building and provides a small salary for Mofis, the *madrassah* teacher. We often woke to the sound of children passing our house on the way to the *madrassah*. Young girls who spent most of the day half-naked covered their faces demurely with their mothers' saris, while boys wore their fathers' oversized caps, which kept sliding down their foreheads. In their arms they clutched the family copy of the Koran and Arabic alphabet books. The poorest children of the village were conspicuously absent, for, lacking decent clothes, they were ashamed to attend.

Sitting on burlap bags, the children recited Arabic lessons for an hour and then listened to Mofis lecture on subjects ranging from the story of Abraham and Isaac to the reasons why they should not attend Hindu festivals. As soon as Mofis recessed the *madrassah*, all trace of seriousness vanished from the children's faces and they burst out to join younger brothers and sisters who waited impatiently outside. They raced down the village paths, stopping by our house to make sure we were awake.

For most of Katni's children, the *madrassah* is the only school they will attend and Arabic the only written language they will study. Their native language will remain mysterious print on newspaper pages and painted signs, out of reach to all but a few. Literacy in Bengali is the key which unlocks the door between the village and the outside world, but formal education is expensive and few of Katni's parents can afford to send their children to the government school. Although tuition is free for the first few years, books, paper, slates and pencils cost precious *taka*. As Abu, a poor peasant, told us, "How could I ever send my children to school? I cannot afford rice, so how could I buy books?" After third grade, tuition and exam costs begin and rise steadily grade by grade. The matriculation exam at the end of tenth grade, the last year of high school, costs 300 to 400 *taka*, a huge expense for any family in Katni.

About 10% of Katni's school age girls and 30% of the boys attend government school. Most go to the nearby elementary school, a white cement building with a corrugated metal roof, located on the outskirts of the Hindu village beyond Amtari. Huge mango and banyan trees used to shade the school, but they were cut down during the 1974 famine in a government "food for work" project. The walls of the school's three classrooms are whitewashed, bare of any blackboards, colourful posters or maps. Sitting in rows behind wooden tables, the children learn their lessons by endless recitation. "In the sky are black, black clouds. In the river swims a silver fish," they chant, abandoning the familiar accents of their village dialect for the polished sounds of standardized Bengali.

Although 211 students are enrolled in the elementary school, on any given day about 100 attend classes. Sometimes for several months at a time, no children from Katni go to school. When we asked the children why, Anlina explained:

We don't go because the teachers beat us too much. If you miss a day or two of school, the teachers will beat you for not coming. But even if you go every day, they'll think of another reason to beat you. The headmaster is the worst—he loves to beat children!

Anis added,

Most of our schoolmasters don't really want to teach school, they just do it for the money. They'll come to school for an hour or two in the morning and then announce that school is closed. They want a holiday so they can plough their fields. Or they beat the children so they're afraid to come to school and then say, "Oh, today there aren't enough pupils. We can't hold school." When the school inspector is coming from town, the teachers will tell the students that free biscuits or milk powder will be distributed on that day, so all the students come. While the inspector is there, the teachers act very nice—they tell long stories and don't beat anyone. But once the inspector has left, everything goes back to normal. Who can learn anything at such a school? Myself, I didn't learn anything until I went to high school in Lalganj.

Most village children leave school before reaching the fourth grade either because their parents can no longer afford it or because their help is needed at home. Those who continue in school are usually boys from relatively prosperous families. Both Anis and Jolil went as far as high school. As is customary, their fathers hired private tutors for them—students at the Lalganj college, who helped Anis and Jolil with their studies in return for free room and board. However, even with tutoring, both boys failed the expensive matriculation exam; they were unable to compete with boys raised in town.

Sultan also failed his matriculation exam, but his rich peasant father could afford for him to take it twice more, until he finally passed. Though known for his inane remarks and slow wit, Sultan is now Katni's only college student. His brighter cousin Talep also passed the matriculation exam, but he could not afford college tuition fees. Coming from a family with only one acre of land, Talep financed his high school education himself by serving as a private tutor in a neighbouring village. He saved enough money to attend college for one year, but then had to leave. Talep is bitter:

You've seen how stupid my cousin is. But because his father has money, he can go to college. He failed his matric exam twice, while I passed the first time with honours. But I'm poor—my father is dead and I have to support my mother and sister. I'll never be able to finish college.

Girls seldom study past sixth grade, even if their parents have sufficient funds. Since village women are not expected to take outside jobs, little incentive exists for their higher education. Parents also worry about their daughter's reputation: walking to school every day, sitting in class with boys and learning from a male teacher may turn her head the wrong way. Villagers often tell stories about female students eloping with their teachers and about scandalous love marriages between Muslim girls and their Hindu classmates. Nevertheless, for many mothers sending a daughter to school is the fulfilment of a dream. Many women wish they could read and write; as Betsy practiced Bengali script or wrote letters in English, women looked over her shoulder, marvelling at the motions of the pen. "I always wanted to learn to read," said Amina's mother, "but I couldn't. My mother had a deformed hand and I had to do all the housework. Now I send Amina to school so at least she will know how."

The main reason to educate a daughter, however, is to improve her chances of attracting an educated husband with a government job. A young man with a steady salary commands a high dowry on the marriage market. Such a son is a valuable asset to his parents, for his job can serve as a vehicle for upward mobility, as well as insurance against hard times. But many parents worry that their son may later refuse to share his prosperity, forgetting the sacrifices they made to finance his education.

You Have 30 Minutes to Evacuate

Shahana Siddiqui

Dhaka is one of the largest and fastest-growing cities in the world. In 1980 it had three million inhabitants and in 2010 about fifteen million. By 2025 it is expected to have twenty-five million inhabitants—it will then be one of the five largest cities in the world. To many the symbols of the growth of Dhaka are a changing skyline, high-rises, choking traffic, and rows of imported air conditioners in fancy new shopping malls. But to the majority of Dhaka's inhabitants—rural migrants who seek a safe haven in the anonymity of the urban jungle—growing urbanization means risky livelihoods, insecure homes, and being at the mercy of real estate owners and their henchmen, often in the form of law and order agencies. The newspaper report here describes a moment in which state agencies swooped down on the inhabitants of a Dhaka slum in 2010 without prior warning, leaving the people defenseless and vulnerable.

The police assure concerned *basti bashis* [slum dwellers] of Sattala, Mohakhali, that no eviction would happen. The people believe the police officers and go on with their daily activities. The noon prayers end. Riot police suddenly appear, armed and ready to go. Demolition workers from nearby slums accompany the enforcements.

A high-up government officer takes a microphone and obscurely tells the people that their homes will be demolished. You have 30 minutes to evacuate. The race against time starts . . . NOW!

Chaos takes over. Two bulldozers appear. Riot police take position to put anyone out of line. Because to protest against the destruction of one's home would be wrong, would be illegal.

Oh wait, that's what they are—illegal. Thousands of people, homes, households are all illegal. They should not have been here to begin with.

Go back to where you came from. If you are not going to go on your own, our bulldozers will help pave the way for you. Few hours [was] all that was needed to destroy 2.5 acres of households, communities, homes.

A poor inhabitant of Dhaka selling rat poison in the city's financial district. Photograph by Willem van Schendel, 2002.

Approximately 8,000 men, women, and children, about 2,400 households evicted, destroyed one fine Thursday afternoon.

The evictees take whatever they can. Personal belongings, construction materials, electrical wiring—anything they can live on or sell to get them through the next few days.

The question is then, where are the activists, where are the well-off neighbours? Where are all [those] cultural, political and religious ideals of pro-poor, pro-people, socialism, inclusion, Constitutional rights?

Bangladesh is a leading example in post-natural-disaster relief [and] yet, we don't know what to do in manmade disasters. Suddenly mandates, policies, project limitations chain our basic sense of citizenry and humanity. Yet, manmade destruction is in many ways worse—a human consciousness is at failure here, a choice is made, humanity and respect for fellow humans are purposefully left aside.

Bengali *bhadraloks* [educated people] romanticise the rural poor and despise the urban ones. We see the latter as freeloaders and their living spaces as dens of all evils. Our decent Bengali way of living is always under threat by these bastis.

Our sons would never get into drugs if it wasn't for the dealers living in the slums. Neither would they ever be tempted by carnal sins if it wasn't for those street prostitutes. And of course women from good families are never to be seen on streets that are roamed by these *meyera* [women] of dubious character. Our cities would be safe if the *mastaans* [thugs] did not emerge from these shanties.

Our footpaths would be cleaner, our lakes prettier, if it wasn't for these makeshift homes and latrines. Because of them, there is such pressure on our electricity, water and other amenities. Not to mention how inconvenient it is to have these beggars, *ferriwallahs* [hawkers], street vendors, hustling us to buy or give something while we sit in traffic, go for a walk, or enjoy a plate of *phuchka* [a crisp snack].

It's all their fault that they are poor and trying to just survive one day at a time. It's their fault that they do not have the education, options and orientations to lead the bhadralok life. It's their fault that government and non-government provide band-aid solutions and no long-term economic and social opportunities to the urban poor. They will leave soon, so what's the point of investing?

Millions of urban poor both in Dhaka and in secondary cities have been living in those areas for generations. Yet, they are not our equals as city dwellers. To be a basti bashi, no matter how many years of residency, immediately means you are an illegal occupant and therefore do not have any rights. The threat and reality of eviction are constant without any protection from government or non-government.

Yet it is these basti bashis that run our homes and industries, our society and the economy. They break their backs every day to clean our streets, drive our vehicles, build our fancy apartments and commercial buildings, carry goods from one end of the city to another, maintain our households and raise our children, [and] watch over our homes while we sleep so peacefully at night. And it is these thousands of basti bashi men and women (whose minimum wage we refuse to pay), who are generating the highest export earning for Bangladesh.

The informal economy constitutes . . . over 65% of all employment in the city. Those employees live in over 3,000 slums and squatter settlements throughout the capital. Of over 2.5 million . . . slum residents and other poor segments of the city, less than a third own land or have access to decent housing.

In all our talk of saving people and establishing a democratic, accountable governance system, the *bhadralok shomaj* [society of cultured and decent people] of the city fail to take a strong stand against evictions and atrocities against the urban poor. Just because we depend on them, does not mean we have to like them, right?

While the largest NGO in the country has been raising money in the past week for the Pakistan flood victims, at the heart of Dhaka city 8,000 people (and rising) are now homeless—yet no single Facebook update on that.

Within days of the Nimtoli fire, friends and families rushed to the site to stand by the victims. One week into [the] Sattala eviction and not a single human cry for help, justice. Difference—Pakistan is a misfortune, Nimtoli a tragedy, Sattala is illegal.

Will we sit back and allow such human rights violations to happen in our backyard? Are we to accept the government's blatant disregard and disrespect of High Court stay orders? Will we not hold our civil servants, politicians and policymakers accountable [for] why these people who support our entire economy are not given adequate housing?

Is it not our Bengali value to stand up against atrocities? Is it not our religious duty to fight for social justice and help the less fortunates especially during the month of Ramadan? Are these duties and values not the foundation of our bhadralok shomaj?

How They Are Developing Us

Aung Shwe Prue Chowdhury

The inhabitants of the Chittagong Hill Tracts are acutely aware of the dominant development paradigm. Whether the development agency is international or national, it is most likely to be oriented toward the construction of infrastructural works rather than toward tuning in to local needs and livelihoods. There is a long history here of development being carried out "for the people" but without their participation or consent. In this interview, Aung Shwe Prue Chowdhury, the Bohmong raja (chief of the Bohmong Circle in the southern Chittagong Hill Tracts), voices his frustrations about the counterproductive policies of international development agencies, which are based on an arrogant disregard of local realities. The example he uses is interference in the administration of the Chittagong Hill Tracts, traditionally based on headmen reporting to the circle chief. He also points to another major grievance in the Chittagong Hill Tracts: the government's disrespect and willful marginalization of the region's customary laws.

Development activities in the Chittagong Hill Tracts (CHT) are taking place in two ways: through the government and through NGOs. There is no coordination between these organizations. Hence there is a lot of overlap. We do not get a comprehensive report of what kind of development is taking place. Each organization gives its individual report. There is a need for a coordination committee that will undertake regular monitoring activities. Actually what is responsible for all this is the lack of an overall vision of development and a tendency to undertake and implement short-term projects.

Once the United Nations Development Programme (UNDP) proposed to all [three] circle chiefs that they construct about ten offices for headmen [local administrative heads under the circle chief] in the three districts of the CHT. There would be three in Khagrachhari, three in Bandarban, and four in Rangamati. But there are about 350 headmen in the CHT.

I asked an official in UNDP, "Why are you trying to do this? Is it a test case?"

He replied, "No, it is not a test case."

Then I asked, "If so, then how can this be realistic? We have *X* number of headmen. There may be differences in orientation and educational background among them, but they *are* all headmen. They have the same status. Who am I going to leave out?"

Then they countered me by saying that the Chakma Circle chief had said yes, so why won't you agree to it? I thought for a while, then I responded: "There are twenty-five *upazilas* [subdistricts] in the Hill Tracts. At least give twenty-five offices, one for each upazila. Then all the headmen will be covered." But even then the UNDP stuck to their old decision and built ten offices. These offices are not functioning at all. They provided only the infrastructure support but not the manpower support needed to maintain them because that would raise the issue of salaries. This is the cold reality of our development.

There are about forty to forty-two NGOs working in Bandarban [the southernmost district of the Chittagong Hill Tracts]. I know that CARITAS gives free agricultural inputs to *jum* [swidden] cultivators. BRAC, ASA [Association for Social Advancement], IDF [Integrated Development Foundation] [all national NGOs] are giving loans to widows and destitute people. But no real development results from this because they are not able to make weekly repayments fifty-two times a year. The loans are offered at steep interest rates and no sooner has the first installment been taken, pressure is applied for repayment. Apart from these NGOs, some religion-based NGOs, like the Christian Community Development of Bangladesh (CCDB) and World Vision, are also working in this area.

The land in the Hill Tracts is divided into four circles. They are the Chakma Circle, the Bohmong Circle, the Mong Circle, and the Maini Valley. The Maini Valley is under the Forest Department. The remaining land in the circles is self-administered by the *adibashi* [indigenous people]. But even so, the government invokes state laws to intervene in almost all aspects of land administration. This is not right. I think customs are more important than law. It is immoral for the government to think that it can possess everything, just because the hill adibashi have no written laws. In most societies we observe customs against incest; they are social customs. They are not written down and yet they are foundational to our society, and it is from these social customs that many laws have emerged. That is why I think that it is by giving priority to and integrating customary laws that one should resolve the land problems of the CHT. Customary processes should not be neglected in the constitution of development institutions.

How can peace be expected to come to the CHT? It all depends on the political will of the government. The government can make it all happen if it wants. We are not getting the benefits we were supposed to get. Our dreams are not materializing.

It is important to remember that jum cultivation is the mainstay of the indigenous people. At one time about 100 percent of indigenous people of the area were dependent on jum cultivation. Now the population of the CHT is increasing, and the land allocated for jum is gradually decreasing. Currently 35 percent of the population of Bandarban is no longer dependent on jum cultivation. Forests are being degraded and deforested. The government should pay attention to it. Fruit orchards should be cultivated for the benefit of the poor. Local varieties of mangoes and other fruits can be cultivated. Appropriate livelihood options must also be there that are appropriate according to the geographical and anthropological realities of the region.

Translated from Bengali by Meghna Guhathakurta.

Poverty, Gender, and Shrimps

Meghna Guhathakurta

In 1997 UNESCO declared the Sundarbans—extensive mangrove forests along the coastal belt of southwestern Bengal and adjacent India—a World Heritage Site. According to the UNESCO website, the area is "an excellent example of on-going ecological processes, displaying the effects of monsoon rains, delta formation, tidal influence and plant colonization. The area is known for its wide range of fauna including 260 bird species, the Royal Bengal tiger and other threatened species, such as the estuarine crocodile and the Indian Python."

International recognition has not, however, stopped the decline of the Sundarbans. Environmentalists deplore their degradation, caused by many factors. One of these is state encouragement of shrimp monoculture, the second-largest foreign-exchange earner for Bangladesh. But it is not only the serious degradation of the natural environment that is worrying. The rapid spread of a cash economy has had far-reaching negative effects, not least on local human relations, and especially on gender relations. This text explores some of the vulnerabilities to which women of the region are exposed.

It was a spur-of-the-moment decision for me to accept an invitation to go and visit a local NGO in the southwestern part of the country, bordering the Sundarbans in the south and West Bengal in the west. To be more exact it was a trip to the Kaliganj and Shyamnagar thana of Satkhira, an area traditionally well known for its bio-diversity but gradually succumbing under the influence of the mono-culture of shrimp cultivation. The fact that the area skirted the rich mangrove forests of the Sundarbans was an extra incentive for me to go and visit the area.

The journey from Dhaka to Kaliganj by bus is smooth but long and arduous. As one approached Kaliganj one could notice the change in the air and environment. Along one side of the road the bright green vegetation and the golden mustard flowers were giving way to stretches of dark stagnant, brackish water and mudflats. These were the sites of the famous *"chingri ghers"* or ponds for shrimp cultivation, a major foreign exchange earner.

The markets skirting the roadside sported freshly painted signboards announcing the sale of shrimp fries from the local rivers. People boarding the bus cracked jokes about the salinity of the water in Kaliganj, which rang like a friendly warning for visitors to the area.

Sushilan (the organization I went to visit) is a non-governmental development organization working for the sustainable socioeconomic development of the under-privileged resource-poor communities of Kaliganj, Debhata and Shyamnagar thanas of Satkhira district. These areas are in the vicinity of the Sundarbans, Bay of Bengal and the Indian border and ecologically unique compared to other regions of Bangladesh. This tidal plain with mangrove forest is the most complex ecosystem with the highest biological productivity in the world. Sushilan thinks that understanding these specific ecological features and incorporating them in local development initiatives is of primary importance. More often than not macro-level development policies do not reflect this importance. There is therefore a strong advocacy component rooted in Sushilan's work. Since my visit was short, lasting only about a day or so, there was no time to look at all their activities. But of what little I saw I noticed the intricate intertwining of environment and peoples' lives and livelihood, almost like the region itself where lush vegetation interlaced with rivers such as the Kakshiali, Chunar, Kholpatia, and Kalindi.

The dominant income earner in the region is now shrimp cultivation. Yet this used to be a rich rice-growing region. It still is in places where the shrimp cultivators have not taken over agricultural land. Besides rice, other crops like mustard and *rabi* [dry season] crops grow in abundance. In the Kaliganj area itself not many green leafy vegetables are grown, although just a few miles away this is quite common. Sushilan through a demonstration farm is helping to train local farmers to explore new techniques to grow crops in existing soil conditions. In this they try to find methods of cultivation that work around the conditions like salinity and waterlogging[,] which practices of shrimp cultivation in the area are causing.

But the impact of the shrimp cultivation on people and lives are not so easily circumvented. The poor as usual are the most vulnerable of all. Shrimp cultivation is expanding so fast that it is taking up not only agricultural lands in the area, but also much of the *khas* or government land by the roadsides, which by law is to be distributed by the local government to the landless. Many of Sushilan's group members feel deprived of their rights to this land, and therefore feel the need to put pressure on the government. But this is not easy, given the fact that many of those who own the shrimp farms are not only members of the local power structure but also involved in national politics at the highest level.

Laborers working a shrimp pond in southwestern Bangladesh. Photograph by Willem van Schendel, 2006.

Another important deprivation is the loss of grazing land. Kaliganj is situated on a slightly higher plane than Munshiganj (Shyamnagar thana) in the south, which skirts the fringes of the Sundarbans. Traditionally, farmers of Kaliganj area seasonally used to send their cattle down to graze in the lowlands where poor families often earned an income by looking after the livestock. But from Kaliganj to Munshiganj, an hour-long drive, all along on one side one looks at a bleak landscape of shrimp farms, without trees, without vegetation[,] in fact without a single scrap of grass in sight. On the other side of the road, by contrast, green fields interweave gracefully with full flowing rivers, the edges of their banks adorned with the leafy branches of the Sundari trees. But it is not only cattle-rearing that is affected. Lack of fodder also prevents poor people from raising goats and poultry as income-generation activities. This has often left only one opening for income generation in the area and that is fishing for small fish fries in the numerous rivers of the locality. This is not without its danger, as we shall see later.

Women of the area particularly are victims of the socio-economic transformation described above. When I visited a local group of 18 women who were members of Sushilan, they all turned out to have been married but without husbands. Only three were widowed, their husbands killed by tigers in the forests while foraging for their living. The rest of the women were either divorced or deserted by their husbands who, due to lack of agricultural land, could not find any work as labourers and hence, not being able to cope with managing a family, either crossed the border or migrated elsewhere looking for jobs! Yet we are told that the more we integrate with the world-economy the higher our chances are of full employment! Shrimp cultivators do not use local labour for their farms. Moreover, their work is seasonal for which they bring in labourers from another region. As a double curse for the destitute and deserted women, many of these men enter into relationships and marry them only to desert them again when the season is over.

The women are left to fend for themselves and their children, for of course the men do not take the children with them. As mentioned before the only way open to them is perhaps fishing for fries in the rivers. This they have to do in knee-deep water pulling their nets behind them. The rivers[,] being very near to the coast[,] also respond to tides. When the water is warm, sharks and crocodiles also find their way upstream and accidents are not infrequent. The group told me of their fellow member whose legs had been torn apart by a shark. Another told of the time she had been abducted by robbers in the Sundarbans who demanded ten thousand *takas* in ransom. Her brother's family who was too poor to pay the sum in full had to sell her fishing net, the only source of her income to gain her release. What a vicious circle if ever there was one!

If one raises the question as to what the local authorities are doing in such cases, then one is likely to be laughed at very sarcastically. Local authorities[,] especially those in charge of law and order[,] are more than likely to be recipients of the booty. Women of the group told me of various instances when they were allegedly apprehended by the police and charged of smuggling sarees [saris] across the border. Women[,] once caught by the police[,] were often trafficked across the border to be sold as housemaids and prostitutes in India, Pakistan and the Middle East. Therefore women are always on the alert not to fall into such a trap. They also narrated stories of resistance when they occupied a piece of *khas* land and built a structure for their very needy group member in the face of opposition from very powerful people. The law-and-order authorities had to comply in the face of their solidarity. The poor women driven to a corner have therefore found their own answer to their problem: resistance! But how strong are they in the face of a predatory state with high stakes in pocketing the lion's share of foreign exchange earning industries?

As I made the journey home, my heart felt heavy. I kept hearing the echoes of the plaintive voice of a village woman singing her heart away to her husband going into the forest, wondering whether he will ever return. A few years ago, she had only the tigers to fear. Today men looking for work are driving these tigers out of their natural habitat because of gradual depletion of forest resources. In addition a new breed of tigers is being introduced into the social landscape for whom women are becoming even more of a prey. Have we all turned a deaf ear to her cries?

The Happiest City in the World

Harry

A blogger from Tasmania, Australia, contemplates the reasons that may explain why Rajshahi in western Bangladesh emerged as the "happiest city" in the world in a 2006 survey.

Well I'm back in Dhaka, having just spent 24 hours in what was voted the happiest city in the world in the 2006 World Happiness Survey—Rajshahi, Bangladesh. In the same survey Bangladesh was voted the happiest country. So what's Bangladesh got that other places like the United States (ranked 46) and Great Britain (at 32) don't have?

Money? According to 2010 International Monetary Fund figures, Bangladeshis enjoy a gross domestic product (GDP) at purchasing power parity (PPP) of US$1,487 per person per year, ranking its national wealth at 155. (The Democratic Republic of Congo rates lowest at 182 with $330; the world GDP PPP is currently $10,500). In contrast, and making it relevant to the readers of this blog, Australia ranks 10th ($38,663), the United States 6th ($45,934), the United Kingdom 19th ($34,388) and South Africa 77th ($10,229). Luxembourg rates the wealthiest at $78,409. So money obviously isn't the reason for Rajshahi's happiness.

How about wide open spaces and lack of overcrowding? Bangladesh has an estimated 165 million people on a land area of 147,570 km^2; that's double the size of Tasmania, which has a population that has just reached 500,000, and 1.5% the size of the USA (9,826,675 km^2), which has a population less than double that at just over 300 million people. To put that into figures that can be comprehended, the USA has a population density of 32/km^2 while Bangladesh has one of 1,099/km.^{2} Australia, admittedly not a fertile country, has a population density of 2.8/km^2! Visit Bangladesh and that population density cannot be ignored.

Enough of the figures. Why am I writing about Bangladesh on [my blog] *a gentle place*? Bangladesh, with its poverty, extreme weather patterns and its number 1 rating as the country most likely to be devastated by climate change (were the earth's temperature to rise by just one degree Celsius, 11% of Bangladesh would be submerged[,] displacing 55 million people)[,] seems anything but a gentle place. But that's not what you feel when you visit here. You experience gentleness in everyone you meet. Everywhere you go. And you see colour. Bright colour.

Dinner last night, had at Aristocrat roadhouse halfway between Rajshahi and Dhaka, was a perfect illustration of this. After my favourite Bangladeshi meal, dhal makhani [lentil sauce], was served, I watched as each of my Bangladeshi colleagues served each other before serving themselves and, having noticed the plate of the person next to them emptying, stopped eating mid-mouthful to add yet more naan [flat bread] to their culinary neighbour's plate. Such displays of caring and gentleness cycled around the table throughout the meal, naturally amongst the customary pleas of "No, no, that's too much." But it would be rude to deny the friendship and, after approaching proficiency in eating with my hands (right hand puckered into the shape of a badminton shuttlecock as it gathers up the food and elephant trunks it into your mouth; left hand avoiding direct food contact but used to spoon yet more dhal [lentil soup] onto your plate and the plates of those around you)[,] we rolled down the ornate Aristocrat stairs and into the waiting minibus. It was time to see more of Bangladeshi's colour, and the road was as good a place as any to observe it.

Bangladeshi trucks must be of the most colorful in the world. With a framing coat of canary yellow, each panel is painted with utopian scenes of snow-capped mountains, meandering rivers, enchanted forests and fairytale palaces; verdant greens, royal blues, crimson reds and burnt oranges. No pastel shades for vibrant Bangladesh. Even the central hub of the rear differential is painted, usually mimicking that of half a large soccer ball.

Whereas the trucks are simply glaringly colourful, the passenger rickshaws are both colorful and ornate. Gold, silver and bronze are added, as is the standard shocking pink. The flat-tray rickshaws don't escape colour either: the slatted sides are painted in alternating blocks of yellow, red, blue, green and orange. Even the twin-light Victorian-style Rajshahi lampposts get the colour treatment with one bulb shining pink, the adjacent one green.

All this colour is augmented by the "colour" of travelling on Bangladeshi roads: 90% of the 6 hour trip was spent in the middle of the road (whether on the straight, heading up a rise or rounding a corner) trying to pass the overladen truck in front (that was itself passing another overladen truck) as a battered old passenger bus, sinking roof loaded with luggage as well as passengers that could not squeeze inside, tried to pass us. Once it passed I'd watch as a rooftop passenger crawled to the back of the bus, hung down over the rear window, and lit a cigarette! Flashing headlights, honking horns, and pedestrians and cyclists on the side of the road, seemingly oblivious to the danger we posed, completed the scene.

And the conversation? "Harry, You've been here so often now [4 times][1] you must make Bangladesh your home." I chuckled. "OK, your second home. You already love the food, we now find you a good Bangladeshi wife to make you happy here!" Raucous laughter all round this time . . . including from Sue when I relayed this to her.

At 1 A.M. when they dropped me back at my hotel each one, despite being exhausted, got up, shook my hand and wished me the "best night's sleep." "See you tomorrow my friend." As they drove down the road I watched their smiles filling the side mirrors—gentle smiles further brightening the faces of gentle people.

So how accurate was the 2006 World Happiness Survey? Pretty spot on I reckon. Perhaps had [rock band] REM visited here they would have penned *Gentle Happy People*.

Note

1. Brackets in the original.

Village Scene. Painting by S. M. Sultan, 1989. Photograph by Niko Richter. Image © NETZ Bangladesch, Berlin. Used by permission.

S. M. Sultan (1924–94) is one of Bangladesh's best-loved painters. The son of a village mason in Narail (southwestern Bangladesh), he ran away from home and led an itinerant artist's life abroad until he returned to his home district in the early 1950s. He was described as "wayward, . . . a fugitive from material pursuits, . . . a maniac"; and later in life he pronounced: "I went around the world led by my whims" (Sadeq Khan, *S.M. Sultan* [Dhaka: Bangladesh Shilpakala Academy, 2003], 9, 27). Often living as a recluse and far from the country's cultural elite, he developed an instantly recognizable style. His rural surroundings provided him with the main topics for his powerful oil paintings and watercolors.

"Fortieth Annual Death Anniversary Commemoration [Urs Sharif] of Khan Bahadur Ahsanullah." Poster, 2004. Used by permission of the Heritage Archives of Bangladesh History, Rajshahi.

Death anniversaries of Islamic spiritual guides are important cultural events that are celebrated throughout Bangladesh. Some commemorate men who lived many centuries ago. This poster announces the death anniversary of Khan Bahadur Ahsanullah (1873–1965), to be celebrated in his native village of Nolta in Satkhira (southwestern Bangladesh). He was a well-known education reformer, Islamic thinker, and social worker who, as a high official in the colonial administration, improved the higher *madrasa* (Islamic school) curriculum in Bengal and was active in the movement to establish a university in Eastern Bengal (the University of Dhaka, 1921). He also started numerous institutions, among them the Ahsania Mission and a publishing house.

Cover of the debut album *Ajob* (Strange) of the fusion band Ajob, 2006. Used by permission of Ektaar Music.

Bangladesh's thriving band music scene successfully mixes local themes and styles with international trends. Popular bands draw enormous crowds of young fans and the bands tour the world. Some of these bands have been around for a long time, but many others come and go, trying to attract attention with creative novelty. Imaginatively designed album covers are an important element to this, as this play on Bangladesh's transport art demonstrates.

A decorated truck in Jhenaidah, a town in southwestern Bangladesh. The signature shows it to be the work of Mithu Art. Photograph by Willem van Schendel, 2006.

On streets all over Bangladesh, transport art is a very popular art form. Everywhere trucks, buses, rickshaws, and scooter taxis are decorated with pictures, tassels, flags, appliqued pieces, panels, and calligraphy. The local artisans who make these decorations have an enormous repertoire. Floral motifs, folkloric themes, movie scenes, portraits, political commentary, and religious imagery are common. This truck shows two other popular forms. On top is an example of what may be described as modern aspirational. Here it is a row of villas and an immaculate road; other images of this kind show surging airplanes or fast cars. Below is an example of animals in nature. Elephants, birds, and fish are often depicted, but perhaps the most popular animal is the Royal Bengal tiger, Bangladesh's national animal. Here it is shown in its natural habitat.

"We pray for the nation's prosperity, peace, and welfare and send our heartfelt wishes and congratulations to all citizens on the occasion of the festival of Lord Krishna's birthday 2006—The Bangladesh Hindu-Buddhist-Christian Welfare Front." Poster. Photograph by Willem van Schendel, 2006.

The cultural complexity of Bangladesh gets expressed in many ways. The country's official calendar is peppered with holidays pointing to the four major religions: Islam, Hinduism, Buddhism, and Christianity. One of these is Jonmastomi, the birthday of the Hindu deity Lord Krishna, celebrated in August.

High Risk. Film poster in Jessore, 2006. Photograph by Willem van Schendel.

This film poster on a wall in Jessore, a district town, promises cinemagoers the thrill of violence and sex. It is full of titillating images: shooting guns, scantily clad women, trickling blood, a villain with an eye patch, and tough men on fast motorcycles—all set against a blaze of fire. This is a must-see movie!

The Dhaka film industry produces about a hundred movies a year. It is facing competition from foreign films, television, and new media but retains a large niche market in the melodramatic segment. Bangladesh also produces art films, distinct from these cheaply produced commercial movies for the local market, that are distributed internationally and have won major awards.

Sämäi chaw chi bala che haw ni
khuyung moh thika a phaw hnäh.

ᚻᒪᐟᐁᐜ ᑭᐁ ᛏᕀᕀᕑᚿ ᑕ‡ᕀᚻ ᚽᚼ‡ ᚿᚻ ᛃ ᑭᕀ ᚻᐁᚻ
ᕀᑮᚻ ᚿᐁᚾ ᐁᛏᕀᑲ ᐁᚻᐁᐜ ᐺᛃᑭ ᛏᕀᚾ.,,

Two examples of children's books in languages spoken in the Chittagong Hill Tracts.
Above: a page from *Flying in the Sky* in Khiyang. Below: a page from *Shinglok's Field* in Mro,
2009. Used by permission of Save the Children UK, London.

In recent years the importance of teaching young children in their mother languages
has become an issue in Bangladesh, and private initiatives have been undertaken to
support basic education in the country's various minority languages. These examples
are from a series of publications intended for young children in the Chittagong
Hill Tracts. The two languages shown here belong to the Tibeto-Burman family
of languages and are not related to Bengali, the language of instruction in primary
schools. The Mro (or Mru) language shown has its own newly developed script.

Tokai befriends a pigeon. Cartoon by Ronobi, n.d. Used by permission of Rafiqun Nabi.

One of Bangladesh's best-loved cartoon characters is a poor street kid. His name is
Tokai. Tokai, created by the cartoonist Ronobi (Rafiqun Nabi), is dressed only in
a checkered *lungi* (sarong). He roams the streets of Dhaka, scavenges for a living,
and sleeps wherever he can. Witty and cheerful, even though usually ignored by
his better-off countrymen, he is an uncanny observer of the follies of the powerful.
And he is not shy to tell the truth, playfully exposing the hypocrisy around him.
He has become a Bangladeshi institution because he speaks for the country's social
conscience. In this tranquil scene, Tokai bonds with a nonhuman friend.

SMS. Acrylic painting by Kantideb Adhikary, 2008. Used by permission of the artist.

Bangladesh has a thriving art scene, with artists exploring a wide variety of media and approaches. This painting in acrylic, shown at Kantideb Adhikary's (b. 1980) first solo exhibition in Dhaka, is done in a style known as oriental art. By playfully combining well-established conventions of South Asian miniature painting with cartoon techniques, this work focuses on a ubiquitous gadget of modern life.

Wherever the Forest Department Is, There Is No Forest

Tasneem Khalil

North of Dhaka lies Modhupur, an area that used to be an island before it was en-veloped by the Bengal Delta, thousands of years ago. Slightly raised above the level of the surrounding floodplains, it was covered in dense forests inhabited by ethnically distinct groups such as the Mandis (or Garos) and Koch. As state institutions and development organizations moved in, both the forest environment and the people of Modhupur came under threat. The journalist Tasneem Khalil made a short visit in 2007 and reported his shock in the Dhaka newspaper the Daily Star.

Here goes an open invitation: come and see the game, visit one of the most attractive zoos in Bangladesh, spread over 478 square kilometers of land that is home to the largest *sal* [tree yielding hardwood timber] forest in the world. On display: more than 25,000 Mandi and Koch *adivasis* [indigenous people]. Welcome to Modhupur, best described by an independent observer as: "An open laboratory where the adivasis are the guinea pigs suffering endless experimentations at the hands of the Forest Department, multi-national corporations and their guardian institutions, the church, Bengali settlers, and the Department of Defence."

For us, I and photographer Amirul Rajiv, it was pretty much of a shock and awe experience to take endless motorbike rides deep through the sal forest. For two days and nights we raced from one village to another, docu-menting the lives of the people whose woe we were investigating, the extent of their suffering, the ruthless oppression they have to endure, the mindless rape of their motherland which they so dearly refer to as *ha•bima*.

This is the story of how the Bangladesh state, through its Forest Depart-ment, is treating one of the most colourful ethnic minorities in the country as easily dispensable burdens. This is the story of how the Asian Develop-ment Bank and its evil twin the World Bank is financing projects of mass destruction in the name of development, destroying acre after acre of sal forest. This is the story of how multi-national chemical merchants like Syngenta, Bayer, and ACI [Advanced Chemical Industries] are marketing deadly poisons to the unaware farmers. This is the story of how pastors and *maulanas* [Islamic scholars] are leading a campaign of cultural invasion taking away the very identity of the Mandi population. This is the story of how the Bangladesh Air Force goes on a daily bombing spree in Modhupur, endangering the ecological life of the area.

And then, this is the story of resistance, how the Mandi adivasis, persecuted for hundreds of years at the hands of civilization are now resisting and trying to turn things back, to desperately make their voices heard by an uncaring country.

It all started with the Forest Department taking over "conservatory" duties in Modhupur in 1951. In 1955 the area was declared a "restricted forest." In 1962, declaration of a "national park" came in. What exactly happens when the ownership of a sal forest is forcefully taken away (without any consultation) from the very people—Mandi and Koch adivasis who worship it as their motherland, and is handed over to a union of corrupt guardians at the Forest Department? Reverend Eugene E. Homrich, pastor at Saint Paul's Church, Pirgacha, Modhupur[,] has a quick answer: "Wherever the forest department is, there is no forest."

To date, officials of the Forest Department—a wing under the Ministry of Environment—religiously engaged themselves in illegal timber logging with absolute impunity. Acre after acre of sal forest—our priceless ecological treasure—was handed over through handsome under-the-table deals to timber merchants. Within 50 years, since the Forest Department took charge of Modhupur, it made sure that the forest was cut to half of its original size. And 60 species of trees, 300 species of birds? Peacock, fowl, leopard, wild pigs? Extinct. Bio-diversity, ecology? Destroyed.

And the people? Well, they became easy target practice for the forest guards and victims of a thousand false poaching cases every year. Indiscriminate shooting at Mandi people in Modhupur is a regular affair. Ask Sicilia Snal who was collecting firewood on August 21, 2006. Without warning forest guards, five or six of them, opened fire on three Mandi women around 7.30 in the morning. Sicilia was injured with hundreds of shards of cartridge piercing her back. Her kidneys were badly damaged. One of the worst victims of oppression in Modhupur, Sicilia[,] cannot walk or move her hands properly. "Looks like the Forest Department is competing to win a gold medal in shooting," Pavel Partha, environmentalist and human rights activist best known for his authoritative work on Modhupur, commented to us.

And then, after destroying the forest, killing its bio-diversity and enforcing a regime of terror and oppression on the people, the Forest Department came up with an ingenious plan to erect a wall around 3,000 acres of Mandi land, in the name of "Modhupur National Park Development Project." That, anti-wall activists cried out, would destroy the lives of thousands of Mandi families in the area. "They are talking about a zoo and we all will be caged inside the wall," one adivasi activist told us.

"They came here, the Forest Department, and served us with an eviction notice," Jerome Hagidakh, an octogenarian Mandi leader, described how it started in 1962. "The government has handed over this forest to us, we were told. The Mandi people will be uprooted and we will plant trees instead."

This is "development" ADB (Asian Development Bank) style: finance projects that destroy thousand-year-old natural sal forest and plant exotic species, all in the name of preserving the ecology of Modhupur. So, 8,000 acres of sal forest got wiped off the face of the earth and a rubber plantation project (that later turned out to be unprofitable, what a surprise) took shape in 1986 through 1989 with ADB finance. An ecological disaster followed as nearby paddy fields became infertile, ground-water level fell, hundreds of species of birds and animals were overnight extinct. "It's poisonous, the rubber garden. You will smell poison there in the air. It's a life-threatening place where workers die every year because of poisoning," Eugene Nokrek, a Mandi activist, told us.

However, good guys in ADB and their angel friends in the Forest Department and Ministry of Environment did not stop there. And "social forestry," another model for destroying bio-diversity, was imported to Modhupur. Now, again, thousands of acres of sal forest had to be wiped out to make way for eucalyptus, acacia, and manjium plantation: all exotic species threatening to local ecology. Plus, hybrid, genetically engineered banana and pineapple. "So-called social forestry has destroyed bio-diversity in Modhupur and has crippled the Mandi people's livelihood," according to Pavel Partha.

These days, the banana that you have for your breakfast in Dhaka comes from Modhupur. And its nutrients: Theovit, Tilt, Karate, Ridomil, Sobricon, Gramoxcon, Rifit, Score, Ocojim, highly toxic insecticides and chemical hormones used for banana plantation.

Multi-national corporations like Syngenta, Bayer, ACI, Auto Equipment, and Agrovet have made sure that poisons—labeled "Toxic: Do not inhale, eat or touch with bare hand"—make their way to our tables through hybrid banana production in Modhupur. Every year, four to five Mandi workers, mostly women, die of poisoning at these plantations, Eugene E. Homrich estimated. "We don't eat these bananas ourselves. How can one risk eating something cultivated with so much insecticide and injected with so much chemical hormones," Anthony Mansang, a Mandi activist, told us.

Bangladesh beyond Borders

In this part we look at Bangladesh beyond the national territory. People in the Bengal Delta have always been very mobile, migrating within the region and settling far beyond it. Historical patterns have been complex and multidirectional. For example, during the colonial period, sailors from Bangladesh created communities in port cities in Britain and the United States, and large numbers of agricultural settlers and laborers began to move into neighboring regions, such as Assam and Tripura (now in India) and Arakan (now in Burma/Myanmar). The political upheaval of partition in 1947 led hundreds of thousands to leave the delta for newly independent India—and hundreds of thousands to migrate into the delta from India. These migrations continued from the 1940s to the 1960s. The Bangladesh Liberation War spawned an even larger group of refugees; most of them returned home after the war was concluded.

Beginning in the 1980s a worldwide diaspora began to gather force, and Bangladesh's society became a truly global network with particularly strong nodes in North America, Western Europe, the Gulf, and Southeast Asia. Important migrant groups are contract laborers, professionals, and students, among others. However, by far the most expatriate Bangladeshis live as unauthorized (and often vulnerable) labor migrants in India and Pakistan.

Today, with vastly improved communications, Bangladeshi communities abroad find it easier than ever to stay in touch. This has a major impact on Bangladesh's society. Migrant workers, especially in the Middle East, are now sending home so much money that remittances have become a major driver of economic growth. Expatriate Bangladeshis also became a significant force in cultural change in Bangladesh—from fashion to religion to artistic expression to family relations.

We have selected entries that introduce a range of emigrant experiences. The part begins with five contributions dealing with people from Bangladesh crossing the border into India at different times. They came as parti-

Gulf-bound contract laborer at the Dhaka airport. Photograph by Willem
van Schendel, 2002.

tion migrants, as settlers, and as visitors and found themselves the object of
state policies and popular actions.

The following four contributions touch on the lives of overseas migrants and their descendants. These explore how the migrants combine
life in a new social environment with enduring but transforming links to
Bangladesh.

The final section of this part is concerned with how Bangladesh as an
entity has been represented abroad—as a victim of war, a young state, a site
of transnational class struggle, and a source of new ideas. We see how the
Concert for Bangladesh first made the country a household name around
the world in 1971; how the state's international activities ranged from an

initial struggle for recognition to a successful campaign for International Mother Language Day; how a worldwide labor-rights campaign focused on working conditions in factories in Bangladesh; and how the made-in-Bangladesh development concept of microcredit or microfinance became a global bestseller.

Dispersing Partition Refugees in India

Joya Chatterji

The Bengal Delta has always had a mobile population, with considerable flows of migrants moving in and out of the region in search of employment, land, or education. Added to this from the 1940s, however, was migration resulting from the spectacular and violent process of state formation that tore British India apart. Large groups of people left newly independent India to settle in newly independent Pakistan, and vice versa. These people, often referred to as partition refugees, settled wherever they had friends or relatives and wherever they found houses and jobs. Many ended up in refugee camps. Among the hundreds of thousands who migrated to India from what is now Bangladesh, many settled in the state of West Bengal. In India the central government (in Delhi) and the state government (in Calcutta) had different views on how to handle the influx. While the central government largely looked the other way, the dispersal policies devised by the state government turned out to be both misguided and draconian. As the historian Joya Chatterji shows here, these policies ignored refugees' interests and led to excesses such as starving the inmates of refugee camps who refused to be sent to former penal colonies and barren tracts of land.

The context in which the Bengal migrations took place, and government policies towards refugees evolved, was the outbreak of communal violence between Hindus and Muslims in the late summer of 1946. The Great Killing in Calcutta in August 1946 left at least three thousand people dead. That autumn and winter, it was followed by tit-for-tat pogroms by Hindus against Muslims in Bihar, and by Muslims against Hindus in Noakhali and Tippera in eastern Bengal. Early in 1947, savage killings in the north Indian town of Gurgaon left many thousands dead. In March 1947, the city of Rawalpindi in the Punjab witnessed horrific carnage. On 15 August 1947, British India was partitioned. Two days later, the Radcliffe line, which defined the new borders between India and Pakistan and divided the provinces of Punjab and Bengal, was published. Violence now assumed genocidal proportions in the Punjab and in parts of north India.

By contrast, Bengal's partition did not spark off violence comparable with the Punjab holocaust. There was much tension between Hindus and Muslims in the two halves of truncated Bengal, but the killings tended to be sporadic and localised, and never assumed the scale of the massacres in the Punjab. Early in 1950, however, there was another bout of widespread violence in East Bengal. This was followed by reprisals against Muslims in West Bengal, particularly in Howrah on the outskirts of Calcutta.

These patterns of communal violence critically influenced the flight of refugees and the directions in which they moved between India and Pakistan, as well as government's responses to these events. Immediately after partition, huge numbers of Hindus and Sikhs fled from West Pakistan, as did Muslims from north India more generally to the western wing of Pakistan. Between August and December 1947, some fifteen million people crossed the western borders between India and Pakistan, half of them Hindus and Sikhs seeking refuge in India, and roughly the same number of Muslims escaping to Pakistan in the opposite direction. By contrast, the refugees from eastern Pakistan did not flood into India in one tidal wave. Rather, they came into India over a period of many years, sometimes in surges but more often in barely perceptible trickles. In the end, however, they added up to an enormous total. By 1973, in the quarter of a century after partition, six million Hindus from the east had come as refugees into West Bengal. Significantly, the number of Muslims who decided to join their co-religionists in the east was much smaller: perhaps no more than a million and a half, in roughly the same period between 1947 and 1970.

The sharp contrast between these migrations helps to explain why the Government of India viewed the refugee problem in the east and west in such different ways. From the start, New Delhi had accepted that partition would result in large and irreversible transfers of population across the western border with Pakistan. The Government of India realised that refugees from the west would have to be escorted safely out of Pakistan and be fully and permanently rehabilitated in India. It also swiftly decided that the 4.5 million acres of "evacuee" property, abandoned by Muslims who had fled to Pakistan, would be given to the refugees. The transfer of Muslim property of those who left India to incoming Hindus and Sikhs became the cornerstone of official policies and programmes to rehabilitate the refugees from the Punjab and western India.

The influx of refugees into West Bengal was seen as a different problem altogether, both in its scale and its nature. [The prime minister Jawaharlal] Nehru was convinced that India could not cope with another refugee crisis of Punjabi proportions, and with the flawed reasoning that so often marked his response to complex problems, continued to maintain, all the evidence notwithstanding, that Bengal had no refugee problem. To justify his case, Nehru insisted that conditions in East Bengal did not constitute a grave danger to its Hindu minorities. Well after the Hindu exodus had begun, he remained adamant it could be halted and even reversed. All that was needed, according to Nehru, was for the government in Dacca [Dhaka] to deploy well-conceived "psychological measures" to restore confidence among the Hindu minorities. This indeed was the aim of the Inter-Dominion Agreement of April 1948 between India and Pakistan. It followed that the Government of India was against relief, let alone rehabilitation, of the Bengali refugees, since it was felt that handouts would attract economic migrants, as opposed to genuine refugees, to India. Delhi also set its face firmly against the redistribution of the property of Muslim evacuees from Bengal to incoming Hindu refugees. In contrast to its policies in the west, the plan was to hold their property in trust until Bengal's Muslims too, returned home. Delhi's line was that refugees crossing the Bengal border in either direction should, and eventually would, be persuaded to return home. Long after it had become obvious that the refugees in Bengal were there to stay, Delhi clung to a stance where expedience triumphed over experience. The result was that the centre [the government in Delhi], to which the Constitution of 1950 had given powers to dictate rehabilitation policy throughout India, did little to assist the West Bengal government to deal with its "refugee problem," even after Delhi finally and grudgingly acknowledged that such a problem did indeed exist.

The Government of West Bengal, however, could not afford to take such a panglossian view of the crisis. The partition of the province, by splitting the administration of West Bengal into two, crucially affected Calcutta's capacity to govern effectively. Partition had also exposed huge underlying schisms within the ruling Congress party, as the various West Bengal factions tried to win control over an organisation which had previously been dominated by delegates from eastern Bengal. The first Congress government of West Bengal, headed by the East Bengal Gandhian Dr Prafulla Chandra Ghosh, fell in January 1948 after only six months in office, a victim of factional in-fighting. The ministry which replaced Ghosh was led by an erstwhile society doctor, Bidhan Chandra Roy, and it too was neither stable nor secure. Dr Roy, therefore, did not have the luxury of ignoring the refugee problem and simply pretending it did not exist. By the middle of 1948, over a million refugees had entered West Bengal. By the end of 1950, the number had risen threefold to almost three million. Since the entire population of West Bengal at the time of partition was 20 million, this influx of refugees in two years had driven it up by almost a sixth. In 1947, the province was already densely populated, indeed by any standards, overcrowded. By 1951 West Bengal had an average of almost 800 people per square mile, and the province did not grow enough food for its own people, let alone for the incoming refugees. In the critical years after independence, West Bengal could not rely on help from the centre to cope with the traumas of partition and with the grave problems which came in its wake. The state government had thus every reason to be desperately worried by the economic and social consequences of the continuing influx of refugees.

The initial response of the West Bengal government . . . was to try artificially to keep down the numbers of people who were officially recognised as refugees, and therefore eligible for whatever meagre assistance government gave them. To be classified as a refugee, Calcutta declared, a person had to have migrated to West Bengal before the end of June 1948; and in addition, he would have had to have been registered as a "bona fide refugee" before January 1949. *Bona fide* "registered" refugees, moreover, were entitled only to "relief," but not to "rehabilitation," given that policy was based on the premise that the refugees were not there to stay. The next phase in government's reactions was to cut back severely on such exiguous "relief" as was doled out, even to those relatively few refugees who had "registered" on time. It declared that able-bodied males who had been at a camp for more than seven days were not entitled to any relief, part of its drive to shut down the relief camps as soon as it could. These policies, unbending and brutal though they were, were driven by the West Bengal government's imperious need to limit the potentially huge financial liabilities of helping the immigrants from east Bengal. . . .

Dr Roy was particularly alarmed by the fact that the great majority of these refugees had flocked to Calcutta, the political heart of West Bengal, and its surrounding districts. Making their way to Calcutta made good sense to the refugees. Naturally they gravitated to places where they had kin and connections, and where they had a chance to find work. Educated middle-class people, who were prominent among the first refugees, were drawn to Calcutta and its suburbs because it was the hub of administration, education, trade and commerce, and offered the best prospects of finding employment. Calcutta also had another attraction: long before partition it had provided a home to a quarter of a million or so migrants from eastern Bengal. In consequence, many of the refugees from the east came to Calcutta because they had friends, caste-fellows and sometimes relatives in the big city who, so they hoped, would give them shelter while they looked for work and a more permanent home. Artisans, who also were numerous among the refugees in the first wave, came to Calcutta for similar reasons. . . .

A powerful logic thus dictated the decision of refugees to go to particular parts of West Bengal. They went to those places where they calculated they had the best chances of rebuilding their lives. But the West Bengal government found it convenient to close its eyes to this simple fact. In the thinking of the official mind, ensconced as it was in the warrens of the Writers' Building [secretariat of the West Bengal government], the "painful swarming" of the refugees on its doorstep represented a grave threat to social and economic stability and to the ministry's very survival. Unquestionably, the refugees placed an enormous strain on the already inadequate infrastructure of the city. But it was also clear that they were discontented with government. The bhadralok [educated middle-class people] of eastern Bengal brought with them a lively tradition of political activism; indeed these refugees saw themselves as the true heirs of Bengal's nationalist legacy, the people who had made the greatest sacrifices for the Hindu homeland. Not surprisingly, they felt betrayed and angry at being received so coldly and so grudgingly by the beneficiaries of their selfless politics. B. C. Roy could see that these sentiments could easily be turned against his government by his many enemies, both inside and outside the Congress party. As he explained to Nehru, the refugees were "in a state of mental excitement which enables the careerist politician to get hold of them and to utilise them for the various types of propaganda against the Government and the Congress."[1] His point was dramatically proven by the huge and heated demonstrations which met Nehru when he visited Calcutta in July 1949. Angry protestors, refugees prominent among them, hurled stones and shoes at Nehru's car and a bomb exploded at a public meeting he was addressing. Nor could Roy disregard the fact that the dense concentration of refugees in relatively small clusters made them an especially numerous and dangerous constituency in the places where they had chosen to settle. In June 1949, the shock defeat of a Congress candidate in a by-election [special election] in South Calcutta almost brought Roy's government down. From the end of 1949, another ominous trend was that refugee groups began forcibly to occupy privately owned property, as they had done at "Azadgarh," seriously alarming government and the propertied groups on whose support it relied. Whether "registered" or not, the refugees had become an awkward fact of life in Bengal with potentially serious political implications which government could no longer afford to ignore. . . .

This was the context within which Roy's government formulated its policy of rehabilitation. It helps to explain why the central plank of that policy was to *disperse* the refugees from the areas in which they were concentrated, and in particular to get them out of Calcutta. The chief priority was to break up refugee clusters, dilute these dangerous and combustible concentrations, and drive as many of the refugees as possible out of the metropolis. The goal was to resettle the refugees elsewhere, either in "empty" tracts as far away from the city as could be contrived, or preferably to send them outside Bengal. Already in 1948, Dr Roy had mooted the idea of transporting some refugees to the infamous former penal colonies in the Andaman Islands in the Bay of Bengal. Now he began to put pressure on government at the centre to persuade reluctant governments in other states to accept some of Bengal's refugees. Inside Bengal itself, the government embarked on a programme of setting up refugee colonies well outside Calcutta, situating one or two of them in each surrounding *thana* [police station or subdistrict]. At the same time, it made vigorous efforts to disperse the refugees to camps and colonies further away in the outlying western districts of West Bengal, particularly in Bankura, Birbhum, Midnapore and Hooghly, where there was wasteland [that] government could acquire for the purposes of resettling refugees. The core of the policy was to spread the "problem" as widely and thinly across the province as possible, diluting the political impact of these unwelcome "trouble-makers" by scattering them in far-away districts.

In practice, however, this policy was easier to enunciate than to implement. Refugees showed a stubborn unwillingness to leave the camps and pavements of Calcutta for the places picked for them by government, and demanded to have a say in where they would be rehabilitated. Well before another influx in 1950 added a new and even more urgent dimension to this intractable problem, Government's harsh response showed how seriously it took the dangers: it fell back on the ugly device of restricting the right to relief to only those refugee families who fell in line with its plans. Time and again in 1949, orders from Writers' Building directed camp superintendents to deny relief to "able-bodied" refugees who failed to cooperate with its plans to be sent from Calcutta for rehabilitation. Memorandum after memorandum insisted that refugees could not be permitted to "hold up rehabilitation"; and stressed that "as soon as lands have been allotted and tents offered and railway warrants issued, refugees [were] expected to go to their new places of settlement."[2] By the time the riots in Khulna began to push new waves of refugees across the border into West Bengal, it was already a standard practice in the camps to starve the inmates into complying with government orders. Inevitably, it was the weakest and poorest among the camp population—refugees totally dependent for their survival on government's meagre "doles"—who were most vulnerable to these pressures and became the focus of the government's drive to disperse them. . . .

In the case of the refugees of West Bengal, government thought it knew better than the refugees themselves what was in their best interests, and stubbornly refused to accept any evidence to the contrary. When refugees proved reluctant to be "dispersed," government dismissed their resistance as "irrational." When the camps failed, it was not because they were the wrong solutions in the wrong places, but because the refugees had "regressed" to a state of "child-like" dependence. Government found it convenient to believe that refugees had clustered in and around Calcutta not as considered decisions based on intelligent assessments of where they could best survive and prosper, but out of some unthinking "herd" mentality which made them gather together in urban ghettos. Likewise, the official mind brushed away the clearly expressed preference of refugees to stay on in West Bengal, or to return there from unpromising places like Dandakaranya on the barren borderlands of Madhya Pradesh, Orissa and Bihar, as sentimental and irrational desires, to be taken no more seriously than the "clinging of a child to its parents." When its camps failed to deliver even a semblance of the goods of rehabilitation, government clung against all the evidence to its view that the fault lay in the refugees' deep-seated apathy. As more and more of its camps failed, government grew more deeply convinced about the failings of the "refugee character" and more determined than ever to disperse the incoming refugees. The tragedy was that the more patently its policy failed, the more vigorously it was pursued by government.

Notes

1. Dr B. C. Roy to Nehru, 17 April 1951, cited in Saroj Chakrabarty, *With Dr B. C. Roy and other Chief Ministers. (A Record up to 1962)*, (Calcutta, 1974), 182.
2. Memo No. 8637 (13) Rehab., from J. K. Sanyal, Assistant Secretary to the Government of West Bengal to all District Officers, dated 9 December 1949. Intelligence Bureau File No. 1838/48, Government of Bengal; West Bengal State Archives, Kolkata, India.

The Nellie Massacre

Makiko Kimura

In the course of the nineteenth century, settler migrants from the Bengal Delta be-
gan to move north to sparsely populated Assam in search of agricultural land. This
stream—encouraged by a colonial government keen on tax revenues and landlords
looking for cheap labor—expanded in the twentieth century. It continued after the
partition of 1947, when Assam became a part of India and most of the Bengal Delta
became East Pakistan, and then Bangladesh. Now migrants from the delta had
become foreigners and their entry was unauthorized. In Assam there was grow-
ing resentment against these newcomers, who were mostly Muslim Bengalis. In the
1980s they became targets of a powerful Assamese nationalist movement that sought
(and continues to seek) to exclude them from citizenship and electoral politics. The
antiforeigner campaign used judicial, legal, and political instruments as well as
violent intimidation. One of the best-known examples of the latter was the killing
of hundreds of Muslim Bengalis in a rural area of Assam.

On 18 February 1983, immediately after the state legislative assembly election of Assam, a large-scale massacre took place in Nellie, a rural area in Assam. At the time, there was a movement in the state against the inclusion of
foreigners (mostly East Pakistani and Bangladeshi immigrants) in electoral
rolls. The movement was led by the All Assam Students Union (AASU), and
the All Assam Gana Sangram Parishad (AAGSP), who called for a boycott of
the election forced by the central government. It is widely acknowledged
that the movement was an outcome of the continued immigration to Assam
from the East Bengal region since the colonial period.

The Nellie massacre was not the only violent incident at the time. There
were numerous violent incidents before and after the election period, and
both local and immigrant people fell victims. In terms of the number of
the dead, however, the Nellie massacre was the largest one—it is said that
around 1,600 people died because of the attack. In this incident, the local
people, including the Assamese and tribes such as the Tiwas, the Karbis,

the Mishings, the Rabhas and the Kochs, attacked the Muslim immigrants from East Bengal.

In 1978, because of the death of Member of Parliament Hiralal Patwari, a by-election [special election] to the Lok Sabha [India's Lower House of Parliament] became necessary in the Mangaldoi parliamentary constituency. In the process of holding the by-election, it was discovered that the number of voters in this constituency had grown phenomenally. Soon after, the AASU demanded that the election be postponed and the names of the foreign nationals be deleted from the electoral rolls. This marked the beginning of the six-year-long movement, the anti-foreigners' movement in Assam.

The main aim of the movement was to detect illegal immigrants from East Pakistan and Bangladesh, to delete their names from the electoral rolls and to deport them from Assam. The movement gained mass support from the people, and was very active from the end of 1979. In early 1980, several talks were held between the AASU leaders and Prime Minister Indira Gandhi. But no agreement could be reached in the talks because of the movement leaders' demand that those who entered Assam after 1951 should be deported, while the government proposed 1971 as the cut-off date. In the latter part of 1980, the central government became oppressive towards the movement. Also, mass support did not last long, and from 1981 to 1982 the movement stagnated. From the end of 1982, the movement was revived again because the central government decided to hold the election in Assam without revising the electoral rolls. The organisers of the movement called for a boycott of the election, and during the election period, numerous violent incidents occurred, the Nellie massacre being one of the biggest.

The election and the massacres, especially the one in Nellie in 1983[,] was the turning point of the movement. After the Nellie massacre, some of the Muslim student leaders parted with the AASU because they opposed the anti-Muslim tone of the movement. The anti-foreigners' movement in Assam was one of the biggest ethnic movements that threatened the national integration of India. Before the movement, Assam's plain areas were relatively peaceful compared with other northeastern regions such as Nagaland or Mizoram, and it seemed that the Assamese people were well integrated into the Indian nation. However, after the movement, various movements emerged, including militant ones. Also, it was rare that pan-Indian media focused on an issue in Assam. However, the movement, and especially the Nellie incident, was widely highlighted and brought the matter to the attention of people not only in India but also worldwide. . . .

Contrary to my expectations, the explanations on the sequences of the events relating to the massacre that were given by the Muslim immigrants, the Tiwas and the local movement leaders were relatively consonant with one other. The basic "agreements" among all interviewees are as follows: [T]he incident started in the morning (timing given varied from 5 AM to 10 AM). At first, the attackers started burning houses, and then the immigrants noticed that their villages were gheraoed [surrounded] from every side. After burning all the houses, the perpetrators started killing the inhabitants by using guns, bombs and daos (axes traditionally used by tribes). The violence continued into the afternoon until the police and army arrived, at which point the attackers left. Attackers were local people, including tribes such as the Tiwas, Karbis, Mishings, Rabhas and Kacharis, etc., and also the Assamese. Some people, including the Tiwas, said that the Tiwas were the largest group in number.

The emphases and some of the details such as timings and the grouping of the attackers differed from each other but, generally, their explanations did not contradict, and it is possible to find common factors and descriptions of the sequence of events. However, the opinions on the cause of the massacre are widely different.

Operation Pushback

Sujata Ramachandran

Bangladeshis form the largest group of immigrants in India. The vast majority are unrecorded. The Indian government has claimed that there are twenty million unauthorized migrants from Bangladesh in the country, but the factual basis of this figure is unclear. Indian politicians and the mass media have depicted these immigrants, who work mostly in poorly paid low-skilled jobs, as infiltrators who threaten the social fabric. Attempts to stop migration from Bangladesh by means of fencing the border, shooting border crossers, issuing identity cards to bona fide Indian citizens, and exerting diplomatic pressure on the Bangladesh government have had no noticeable effect. This has prompted the authorities in several Indian cities to resort to forced deportation, a tactic that has been employed several times since the early 1990s. The Bangladesh government does not recognize individuals presented at its border as its citizens unless they can provide documents to that effect. Other markers, such as being a Muslim or speaking Bengali (even in an East Bengali dialect), do not distinguish Bangladeshis from Indians because there are millions of Indian citizens who are Bengali-speaking Muslims and not a few of them speak East Bengali dialects. Operation Pushback—derided in the Bangladeshi media as Operation Push-In—was the first highly publicized attempt to deport Bengali-speaking Muslims from an Indian city. Sujata Ramachandran, who did field research among Bangladeshi immigrants in India, describes what happened.

The aggressive campaign to deport undocumented Bangladeshis from the capital city . . . was carried out in New Delhi on September 9, 1992. In this . . . highly publicised endeavour, a group of 132 persons, 87 men, 23 women and 22 children were identified as Bangladeshi nationals and roughly removed from a large resettlement colony called New Seemapuri in east Delhi. Accosted by several police officers from the Seemapuri police station, these unauthorised immigrants were taken to the old Delhi railway station. Fifteen officers, including two females from the Delhi Armed Police (DAP), escorted the deportees on the ninety-seats coach in the Sealdah Express train during their 36-hours journey to Sealdah in West Bengal. Once there, after being handed over to an advanced party being led by the Foreigners' Regional Registration Office (FRRO), they were delivered by two Border Security Force (BSF) and army trucks as well as Kolkata [Calcutta] police bus to the Haridaspur check post before being sent across the border. An official with the FRRO further explained this elaborate procedure: "We have already informed the Border Security Force. These chaps would be deported by the push back system."

Rather astonishingly, in the beginning the local administration vehemently denied that "Operation Pushback" was being coerced upon the helpless immigrants. In fact, in a newspaper interview at this time, Seemapuri police station SHO (Station House Officer) Rathi, who accompanied the deportees to the railway station, openly avowed that the deportees were enthusiastically ready to return to their country. "They are here because they want to go, all of them are volunteers," he espoused. But another unidentified officer from the same station let it slip that the police had forcibly rounded up people for three days and held them under detention for deportation. "There is no section under the Indian Penal Code to arrest such individuals. They are detained under Section 3C of the Foreigners' Act and served Quit India Notices," the official admitted.

By the same token, all the unfortunate deportees ascertained the involuntary nature of "Operation Pushback." *"Ham apni marzi se nahi ja rahen hain* (We are not leaving of our own free will)," they affirmed. To highlight one case, Khalid, a *"kabadiwala"* (rag picker) being discharged, candidly divulged: "I am being forced to go. I am the only one from my family who is being sent away. My two kids and wife are still here." Another deportee, Shamsuddin, added: "Given a chance, I (will) return . . . I am going (to Bangladesh) because I was unlucky to be on the road when the police came looking (for us)." It appeared that Khalid and Shamsuddin were not the only deportees to leave behind their immediate families. Reportedly, more than three fourths of those dismissed from this country still had close relatives in the same *basti* [slum]. Many of these detainees also claimed that they possessed ration-cards and had exercised their votes in previous elections.

The fundamental objective of "Operation Pushback" was transparent, that is, to deter new "infiltrators" and intimidate existing ones. But what was arresting was its repulsive ritualised script. These evictions, it is concernedly noted, were instigated on the Islamic Prophet Mohammed's birthday and, not surprisingly, a great majority if not all of those who were deported belonged to the Muslim faith. And as if the symbolic nature of these expatriations were not already self-evident, the unfortunate deportees had their heads shaven and their meagre belongings burnt in front of them before being cast out of Indian territory through the North 24 Parganas district of West Bengal. As mentioned in the newspaper *Ananda Bazar Patrika* of Kolkata, when asked why the few clothes, bedding and even utensils of those being sent back were being destroyed, a BSF officer reportedly responded: "So that they can tell people there that nothing can be brought back. We are even burning their money." Over and above, this officer informed the *Patrika* reporter, the poor deportees would be soundly thrashed in advance of the final shove.

Geographical locations in close proximity to the actual border, it seems, would provide the appropriate sites for this unnecessary brutality. Again, the message permeating the violence of this final practice cannot be easily ignored. As the officer explained, this unkind treatment would be carried out in plain view of Bangladeshi citizens across the border, actively discouraging them from entering India at any future date. Ultimately though, the ceremonious tonsuring while humiliatingly degrading its victims, exemplified the purging of Indian soil from the insidious effects of infiltration through the purification of the unclean bodies of these Muslim immigrants. The raw rejoinder of the requiting Indian state was being forcefully and metaphorically written on the physical frames of its victims.

Snake Charmers in Limbo

Satadru Sen

In this indignant piece titled "Border of Insanity," the historian Satadru Sen rallies against the lack of empathy and respect for human rights that Indian intellectuals and the media display when it comes to the forcible deportation of suspected Bangladeshis from Indian soil. He takes the example of a group of snake charmers— men, women, and children—whom Indian border guards drove into the rice fields that make up the no man's land at Satgachi on the northern border with Bangladesh in January 2003. The Bangladeshi border guards refused to let them in because of lack of proof of their Bangladeshi citizenship, and stalemate ensued. For a week the snake charmers had to survive in the no man's land. Sen uses this brutal episode to show the urgency of rethinking what he calls "our fundamentally warped concep- tion of Indian citizenship" and "the meaning of citizenship in South Asia today."

If there was something horrifying about the recent drama at the Satgachi border between India and Bangladesh, it seems to have escaped the notice of the Indian media. The basic facts are so absurd that they could have come from the imagination of S. H. Manto [writer of short stories in the Urdu language]: over 200 frightened snake charmers, their children and snakes rounded up in India, herded into the no-man's-land between the Border Se- curity Force [BSF] and the Bangladesh Rifles, and eventually pushed into their "legal" homeland in the middle of the night. Throughout the dura- tion of the drama, I looked through the mainstream newspapers for a sign of outrage. These were conspicuous largely by their absence. This is nearly as ominous for the state of Indian society as what was done to the snake charmers. The small episode raises serious questions not only about the Indian intelligentsia's (and media's) sense of its responsibility when con- fronted with issues of human rights, but also about the nature of the state and the meaning of citizenship in South Asia today.

That the Satgachi incident was a grotesque violation of the most basic notions of human rights would appear to be self-evident. This in itself is not new or surprising; given the perennial tension between democracy and authoritarianism that marks Indian political society, we have become inured to the sight of men with guns and uniforms terrorising the unarmed and the disenfranchised. Even by that standard, this particular drama was so public, so well documented and so protracted that one might have expected a reaction, even if the reaction was only embarrassment. Nothing of the sort was forthcoming. What we got, instead, were expressions of anxiety about those "illegal immigrants" who have not yet been discovered and escorted to the border, and who seem to pose an imminent threat to the health of our healthy nation. Deputy Prime Minister Advani talked about rooting them out, as he often does. The press accepted the premise of his promise, although some reporters muttered sympathetically about dying snakes and sick children. My academic colleagues who spoke out eloquently against the pogrom in Gujarat did not appear to have recovered from their exertions in that matter.

This silent acceptance was unfortunate, because there is an urgent need to visit the question of just what an "illegal alien" is in India, and whether the concept can and should be applied in the peculiar context of a South Asian nation state. My grandparents came from across the border, as did Advani himself. I do not believe they needed visas to enter India, to live in India and to be safe from the BSF. My brother—born in West Bengal in 1972—grew up speaking Bengali in a Jessore dialect, thanks to the migrant woman who took care of him. Neither he nor the servant was accused of any illegality of identity or geography. They were of course Hindus, like Advani. As such, they could be viewed as "Indians" whose border had receded before them, forcing them to follow. Hindus who trickle across the Bangladesh border today are usually accepted as "refugees," provided they are not shot by the BSF in the process of crossing the line. But if Muslims who come from "that side" are automatically illegal, then perhaps the Indian state needs to come clean on where it stands on the Two-Nation theory. I do not mean an exercise in contemplative self-mortification; the complicity between Indian nationalism and the Hindu Self is too well established for that to be necessary, let alone productive. What I have in mind is an act of juridical honesty: a statement from the Supreme Court, perhaps, that will spell out the legal and ideological basis for these selective deportations.

Surely the possession (and non-possession) of passports and visas cannot be the basis of citizenship in countries like India, Bangladesh and Pakistan. How many "citizens" in these states have passports? For how many of them is the concept of an identity that ends at the border, and that must be constantly validated by the state, ideologically meaningful? That kind of identity still belongs to a limited segment of Indians and their neighbours: it is the monopoly of those who Partha Chatterjee calls "proper citizens," i.e., individuals who are able to participate in our underdeveloped civil societies. It is not the identity of migratory snake charmers in their various avatars and gradations, who are still a very large part of the population of South Asia. At the risk of patronising the subaltern, I would venture to say that they do not understand the illogic of citizenship. That, in fact, is what was most painful to see in the Satgachi incident: the sheer incomprehension on the faces of those who are "Bangladeshis" and not "Indians," and who were nevertheless caught between two monstrosities.

The question why they must comprehend has been neither asked nor answered. Has there been a decision or even a debate as to why those who are marginal to modern citizenship must be forced to kneel (quite literally) before the sanctity of borders and passported identities? What benefit do they gain from this subjugation to an extraordinarily undemocratic process of policy-making and implementation? What benefit do "proper citizens" obtain from this brutal assault upon the nature and history of South Asian society? It might be argued that by appropriating terminologies such as "illegal alien," and forcing the non-national and the semi-national into the mould of the modern citizen at gunpoint, the rest of us experience our modernity as a nation and a gratifying membership in the club of modern nation states. This, after all, is what the Americans do with dirty Mexicans, what the British do with the human refuse that clogs Sangatte, what the Australians do with Afghans who float unbidden towards the Great White Land. We unquestioningly accept the morality and the universality of their performances of nationhood, citizenship, borders and violence, as if the realities of our demographics and history are identical to theirs.

The hunt for "illegal" Bangladeshis in India is, obviously, an easy way for Advani and Balasaheb Thackeray to score points with the fascist brigade and its sympathisers. In a world in which they have already capitulated before the power of the American empire, it allows them to highlight the boundaries of their manly resolve, and of the nationhood that rests upon that masculinity. It allows them to appear protective of "bona fide" Indian workers and the Indian economy, although there is little evidence that Bangladeshi migrants have seriously harmed either. Where "undocumented" migrant labour is present to any significant extent, migrants tend to supplement the local labour force, rather than "steal" the jobs of deserving citizens. It is unlikely that the snake charmers of Satgachi had deprived Indian snake charmers of their legitimate livelihood, or endangered Indian snakes. They had not defrauded the Indian state of welfare benefits; such benefits are a pipe dream even for the "legal" poor in India. They were not terrorists; there is no evidence that their snakes had bitten anybody. The red herrings of terrorism, economic drain and unfair competition from illegal immigrants[,] have been the standard rhetorical tactics of xenophobes, bigots and, of course, ardent middle-class nationalists. The real reasons why people are being pushed back and forth between India and Bangladesh today, with barely an audible word of protest, have to do with our fundamentally warped conception of Indian citizenship, and our fatally colonised sense of ourselves, our states and our societies. The saving grace in all this are the villagers on the Indian side of the border at Satgachi, who—not being proper citizens—provided the "foreign" snake charmers in the no-man's-land with some measure of comfort and sustenance. Perhaps they should be shot for treason.

The Green Passport

Zakir Kibria

When traveling abroad, Bangladeshis carry green passports emblazoned with the outline of their country surrounded by the words "Government of the People's Republic of Bangladesh" ("Gonoprojatontri Bangladesh Shorkar"). Usually the passports are full of visa stamps because few foreign countries allow Bangladeshis in without a visa. Even so, being identified as a Bangladeshi may be a problem, as this story of a hapless visitor to Guwahati, the main city of the neighboring Indian state of Assam, reveals.

It was 4 o'clock in the morning in Guwahati, Northeast India. The Kanchanjangha Express arrived on time. I landed on the platform and tried to reboot my senses after a twenty-one hour journey. . . .

What I experienced for the next few hours was beyond my anticipation. . . . I was trying to adjust to the sudden change in temperature. I can't say that I liked the smell of the station but the crowd of passengers sleepwalking looked surreal. For a moment I felt disoriented and didn't know where I was. There was an announcement in a language very similar to Bangla, and yet it sounded different. But I didn't have time to think about the origins of the Assamese language or its relation to Bangla. I still had a three-hour taxi ride to Shillong.

Bargaining with taxiwallas at train stations and airports is never easy. I knew that I had to pay more than the usual fare. Early morning traffic was thin and it took only a few minutes to get to the Shillong taxi stand. Frustration about paying a steep fare to the taxiwalla vanished in a moment when I was told that political parties in Meghalaya had called a *bandh* [general strike] till the evening and there was no taxi to Shillong till evening. It was election time in India and Sonia Gandhi was scheduled to address an election rally in Meghalaya. Apparently, she wasn't welcome in the hills.

I bought all the English newspapers I found in the newsstand. News and information suddenly seemed urgent to me. It's always a little uncertain in the Northeast, I remembered my friends had warned me in Kolkata [Calcutta]. I opened my *Lonely Planet* travel guide. It's not that I ever follow

Detail of a Bangladesh passport. Photograph by Willem van Schendel.

travel guides, but I carry my *Lonely Planet* wherever I go because it does come handy. I leafed through the pages. The first hotel I found in the budget section was only a few paces away. I climbed the stairway with my carry-on luggage, which started to feel heavy. I had to wake up the old man at the reception desk. I couldn't understand what he said in Hindi. I was used to being taken as an Indian. I replied in English. He showed me a room. It was nothing fancy but the rate was lower than my estimate. I started to fill in the registration form. Sleepy but friendly, the old man asked for my ID and I gave him my passport and showed him the visa. My green passport usually doesn't bring a smile on the faces of airport immigration officials. It took a long time, but over the years I became used to the indifferent and often hostile reactions to my passport. The sleepy-friendly old man suddenly became alert, as if he woke up for the second time and astounded me.

"You are a Bangladeshi? We can't allow you to stay here."

For a moment I was blank. I asked, "Why?"

"There is instruction by local police." He replied, "We have problems in Assam all the time and Muslim militants from Bangladesh often come and plant bombs. There are also Pakistani agents carrying Bangladeshi passports."

I could argue with him and tell him that till date the Indian state hasn't convicted a single Bangladeshi for acts of "terrorism" in India. Nor have they even arrested one! I could implore him to let me stay but somehow I had the feeling that it was not going to work even if I played nice.

I turned my cell phone on and tried to call my friend from Manipur who was going to join me in Guwahati. I bought an Airtel sim card in Kolkata (had to submit a photo and xerox copy of my passport and visa page). There was no signal. I remembered the cell phone advertisement on TV. "Air? Yes. Water? Yes. Network? Always." Was it an Airtel ad or was it Vodafone? I turned off the automatic network selection and tried manually. It showed several networks available. None of them recognised my sim card. For the next couple of hours I roamed around the area near the train station and tried to check in to nine different hotels. *Lonely Planet* lost its relevance. They have no section on surviving when you are profiled as a potential Muslim terrorist. I tried every decent looking hotel (even a few not-so-decent ones). I was just going in and asking if they were taking in guests from Bangladesh. They all parroted the same instructions from police.

I thought that I should go back. The next train to Kolkata was in the evening. Tickets are rare. I could afford to fly back to Kolkata and I decided to take one last chance before I took a taxi to Guwahati airport. One early rising guest at a hotel lobby was kind enough to find a hotel for me. How did I know that it would be one of the expensive ones? By now the taxiwalla has become sympathetic to me and confessed that he is from Chittagong. His family has been living in Assam for three generations. They still have relatives in Chittagong. He started to speak in Bangla but the Chittagong dialect was not familiar to me.

The exterior look of the hotel confirmed that it must be in the league of star-rated hotels. The reception desk was manned by a person speaking "standard" English and was wearing a nice suit. He seemed familiar with the miseries of travellers carrying Bangladeshi passports and told me that probably they are the only hotel in Guwahati that allow Bangladeshis. But I have to report to local police station as soon as possible. I started to fill in the registration form and tried to imagine what awaited me at the police station. What if they are not satisfied with my explanation that I am going to meet friends in Shillong? Is it wise for me to tell them that a friend from Manipur will join me? The Indian media blames Bangladesh all the time as a safe haven for militant groups fighting for freedom in Manipur and other states in Northeast. I left my passport at the desk to be xeroxed and checked into my 2,000 Rupee-a-night non-AC room.

I couldn't figure out how to make a call outside the hotel. I called the PABX [switchboard] operator to connect me to the cell phone number of my friend in Manipur. I felt happy to hear his voice. My ordeal seemed not to have surprised him too much. He told me that we are lucky that I could call him because he would enter Guwahati in three hours and his cell wouldn't work here. If I had called him later I might not have reached him and he didn't know where I was staying.

I turned on the television and browsed the channels for a few minutes. It's all election news and Bollywood songs and dance routines. Some of them familiar to me, as the cable operators provide the same channels in Bangladesh. I browsed for a few moments, perhaps trying to find a Bangladeshi channel. I couldn't find one.

Fast-Footed Sylhetis

Katy Gardner and Zahir Ahmed

Today remittances from migrants are Bangladesh's largest foreign-currency earner, replacing foreign aid and export earnings as the national economy's powerhouse of change. People from the Bengal Delta have long tried their luck abroad, and many different migration flows can be identified. In terms of remittances, three types of migration are currently important. The oldest is overseas labor migration. Sailors from Bangladesh (especially from the districts of Sylhet, Noakhali, and Chittagong) were employed on European ships for centuries and from the eighteenth century onward communities of stranded sailors developed in port cities such as London and New York. By the mid-twentieth century, Britain, facing labor shortages, began to import cheap workers, mostly from the Caribbean and South Asia. Within Bangladesh, Sylhet became the prime sending area. Today Britain's large Bengali population is overwhelmingly Sylheti. As British migration policies tightened and new opportunities arose, overseas labor migration from Bangladesh found new destinations, notably the Gulf region and Southeast Asia. The second type of migration builds on the tradition of the delta's middle-class families educating their children in important centers of learning. In the colonial period, they would go to Dhaka, Kolkata (Calcutta), or London. Today they go to North America, Australia, Europe, or the Gulf—and often secure well-paid jobs in the world's most prosperous economies. The third type is cross-border migration, often on foot, to India and Pakistan where cheap Bangladeshi labor is welcomed by employers but not authorized by the state. This migration flow is by far the largest and involves many of the poorest migrants from Bangladesh. All three types of migrants yield remittances for relatives back home because many migrants continue to cherish their roots in Bangladesh. Here is a sketch of the transnational ties that bind Sylhet and Britain.

The territory [of Bangladesh] has always been characterised by high degrees of fluidity, both within and across its shifting political borders. From pre-colonial times migrants from the west settled the highly fertile but often waterlogged lands of the east, whilst other historical evidence points to movement in the other direction, a continual flow of people, regardless of national borders. These constant, crosscutting migrations are both a result of the region's turbulent history, and its turbulent environment, in which floods and cyclones mean that "belonging" can never be guaranteed. Ranabir Samaddar writes movingly that the country is "an insecure environment, inhabited by insecure families." Such families dream constantly of escaping insecurity. "This dream has made Bangladesh a land of fast-footed people, people who would not accept the loss of their dream, who would move on to newer and newer lands. . . ."[1]

Today, these fast-footed people are moving both internally and overseas, predominantly to the Gulf and to South East Asia. The scale of this movement is vast; . . . from 1976–2002 official figures show that over three million Bangladeshis migrated overseas, mostly on short-term contracts. Whilst some are middle-class professionals, the vast majority of migrants are wage labourers, often inhabiting the most vulnerable and lowly paid sectors of the international labour market. Many more move illegally, and are thus not captured by official statistics. These migrants take huge risks in their attempts to access foreign remittances, and many are either caught and deported before they have a chance to earn, or are cheated by unscrupulous brokers.

In Sylhet, international migration has a distinct character. Whilst many men from the district have migrated to the Middle East, far more influential has been the movement of people from particular areas to Britain. Indeed, approximately 95 percent of the British Bengali population is Sylheti in origin. From the nineteenth century onwards, Sylhetis worked on British ships leaving from Calcutta as *lascars* (sailors). Some of these men ended up in the docks of East London, where they jumped ship and searched for new livelihoods in London.

There is no single reason why Sylhetis rather than other Bengali groups dominated ship work, or why it was they, rather than others who, many years later, were able to monopolise the "labour voucher" system which brought people from ex-colonial territories to work in post-war Britain. One factor may have been the colonial system of land administration. Whilst over much of Bengal, *zamindars* (landlords, who paid taxes directly to the British) owned large tracts of land which were worked upon by their tenants (*raiyat*), until 1947[,] Sylhet was administered as part of Assam. Here, in contrast to the *zamindari* system, many smaller farmers were independent owner-occupiers of land (*talukdar*) rather than tenants on the large estates owned by *zamindars*. Possibly this contributed both to an entrepreneurial spirit as well as the capital reserves required to travel to Calcutta in search of ship work. Another factor may be the riverine geography of the region, which produced a population experienced in boats and shipping. Crucially too, particular individuals may have dominated the recruitment of labour, thus leading to a "chain" effect whereby men from particular villages and lineages gained employment through the patronage of their relatives and neighbours. Whatever the reasons, by the time work permits were being offered by the British government to men from the subcontinent in the 1950s, Sylhetis were well placed to gain maximum advantage. With a small but rapidly growing network of men already living in Britain, the chain effect continued. Such was the demand for the "vouchers" that . . . an office of the British High Commission was opened specially in Sylhet.

Most of the men who left for Britain in this period lived and worked in cities such as Birmingham and Oldham, finding employment in heavy industry. Some went directly to London, working in the garment trade as pressers or tailors. Usually living in lodging houses with other Sylhetis, this was a period of relentless hard work with as much money remitted home as possible. In today's terminology, the men were "transnationals" *par excellence*: they worked and lived in Britain, but returned as often as they could to their villages where they were still heavily involved in social networks of kinship and community, as well as regional and national political activities.

Over the 1970s and into the 1980s conditions started to change. Britain's heavy industry was in decline and many Sylheti men moved to London to seek employment in the garment or restaurant trades. Crucially, a growing number started to bring their wives and children to the United Kingdom. This shift was partly the result of changing immigration laws, which many rightly feared would soon make primary migration to Britain (without it involving marriage to a British citizen) impossible. It also reflected wider changes in the areas where many Bengalis were settled, in which mosques, shops selling *halal* meat and other community facilities were becoming established. Today, the Bangladeshi population is the youngest and fastest growing in Britain. The 2001 Census enumerated a total population of 283,063 of which 38 percent were under sixteen. Fifty-four percent of the Bangladeshis live in London and nearly half of these are situated in Tower Hamlets where they form over a quarter of the resident population. (In some areas within the borough, this figure is higher.)

Whilst there is still some movement and settlement back to Bangladesh from Britain, the character of transnationalism has therefore changed radically over the last few decades. The predominant form of migration to Britain is now through marriage, and visits "back" to the *desh* [home country] may include children born in Britain who have never been there before. Whilst some households are still being reunited, the majority are now together in Britain.

Jalalgaon Village. Situated only a few kilometres from Biswanath Town, with its resplendent shopping malls, fast food outlets and multi-storied community centres, Jalalgaon is a "Londoni" village *par excellence*. Alongside the humble single storied houses of those who never went to the UK, the village is filled with the mansions of successful migrants. These may be up to three storeys high and are invariably surrounded by high brick walls. The architectural styles are reminiscent of the housing developments one might find in Dubai or Saudi Arabia, or in Baridhara, a rich (some may say *nouveau riche*) district of Dhaka. Many have satellite dishes and some have smoked glass windows, an embellishment that until recent years was unseen outside of the US or Saudi Arabian consulates in Dhaka. Others refer directly to the migration experience of the owners: just as one might see stone lions guarding the gates of British homes, here stone aeroplanes adorn walls and roofs. In another house in Jalalgaon, Manchester United's strip [shirt] is painted on the outside wall. None of this would be so remarkable were it not for the stark contrast with the rest of rural Bangladesh, in which mud and thatch (*katcha*) houses are the norm. [M]any of these houses are empty. Others are lived in by caretakers, often poorer relatives of departed families.

Note

1. Ranabir Sammadar, *The Marginal Nation. Transborder Migration from Bangladesh to West Bengal* (New Delhi: Sage Publications, 1999), 83–87.

Sending Money Home

Alastair Lawson

In the late twentieth century large numbers of migrant workers left Bangladesh for the booming economies of the Gulf, Southeast Asia, and beyond. By the early-twenty-first century it was clear that they were sending so much money home that Bangladesh seemed to have moved decisively beyond the era of foreign-aid dependence. Rapidly expanding flows of remittances brought about the revival of an ancient system of money transfer, known in Bangladesh as hundi *or* hawala. *Based on trust and personal linkages, it was quicker, cheaper, and more convenient than official banks. It was also invisible to the state, which deemed the method illegal. With state support, banks have attempted to deflect remittances to their own channels, as the news report reproduced here demonstrates.*

For decades, the Hundi system of money transfer has been the fastest way for expatriate South Asians to transfer cash to their relatives back home. A payment is made in Europe or the Gulf to a middleman and usually within 24 hours the recipient gets the money in India, Bangladesh, Pakistan or Sri Lanka. It is fast, efficient and has stood the test of time. There is only one problem. It is illegal in all the countries concerned. Now the Hundi system is being challenged by a Bangladeshi bank that claims it can deliver money just as fast but legally.

Down a dirt track near the town of Comilla in central Bangladesh, Morzina Akhter is sweeping her front yard when BRAC Bank's motorbike courier roars up with a consignment of money from her relations in the Gulf. Ms Akhter's money has been sent under the Secured Easy Remittance Service, or SERS, which was set up by BRAC Bank earlier this year. If this system of money transfer catches on, it could bring an end to the centuries old Hundi network.

BRAC is one of the country's largest non-governmental organisations, with offices all over Bangladesh. That, says BRAC, puts it in a good position to out-perform the Hundi system by delivering remittances from abroad to remote locations just as fast, but legally. Ms Akhter is impressed by the new

Bangladeshi enterprises in Singapore, including one advertising itself as "devoted to the ultrafast and cheap remittance of Bangladeshi migrants' hard-earned money to Bangladesh." Photograph by Willem van Schendel, 2006.

system. "If cash is sent through a normal bank there's lots of officialdom and bureaucracy to overcome and we can wait up to ten days to receive our payments," she says. "But this new system is much more efficient and convenient. As soon as we are informed that some money has been sent, it's delivered to us in our villages with the minimum of paperwork."

The Hundi system has flourished because it is quick and simple, involving a network of middlemen who deliver the cash in return for a commission. But Hundi is illegal because it undermines official exchange rates. Bangladesh's banking system is thought to lose about $240m (£150m) a year because money is not being transferred through official channels. Critics say that Hundi is also used to shift laundered money from extremism and crime.

"To overcome the Hundi system, we have to create the motivation among the people who are getting money from abroad," says BRAC Bank spokesman Sirajuddin Mondol. He says the bank is "trying to mobilise the people against the Hundi business" because it is "bad for the people, as well as the country also." With about 40% of foreign remittances entering Bangladesh through Hundi, he admits it is "a big challenge."

Economist Debapriya Bhattacharya also believes the Hundi system's future is uncertain because of its association with crime. As South Asian economies grow, he says, financial regulations and law enforcement will become tighter. "The Hundi system is going to reduce over time because of the sheer logic of economics," he says, citing improved institutions and better management of the exchange rate. "The issue is that it should not play a major role in the mainstream transaction process and should not create a disincentive for the normal market players to invest and also make savings." This he sees as more important than rumoured links to crime, saying drug money can "pass through any country . . . under the current globalised system."

But many villagers are reluctant to trust a bank to step into Hundi's role, remaining doubtful that it could deliver as quickly or as efficiently. While such views persist, it seems that Hundi, even if it is illegal, will remain as important as ever in rural Bangladesh.

Bangladeshi Activists in London

John Eade and David Garbin

Today, tens of millions of people of Bangladeshi origin are living abroad. In many places they have formed distinct communities with well-established cultural and political organizations. These organizations are very dynamic in their response to local, national, and transnational transformations, as the example here demonstrates. Factionalism, generational change, the emergence of new ideological choices, and the political and economic evolution of Bangladesh all contribute to this dynamism.

In their struggle for acceptance and a decent life in their new homes, migrants and their descendants debate the merits of two strategies: how can we best combine integrating into local institutions with building up our own? The outcome of this debate will determine their future relationship with their society of origin, Bangladesh. Here is an example of intergenerational change among Bangladeshis in London.

The war of independence against Pakistan in 1971 resonated deeply in London where first generation leaders engaged in fund raising, campaigned against Pakistani institutions and worked for the (inter)national recognition of the "liberation war." Although the ties with Bangladesh remained strong, political orientations changed at the end of the 1970s with the involvement of the second generation in the struggle for local resources. Some alliances with local white activists were secured during this period of anti-racist resistance and mobilization against discrimination in the housing, educational and cultural spheres. These alliances were justified in terms of the language of struggle and sometimes the practice of public demonstrations.

Consequently, by the end of the 1980s a group of second-generation secular activists had entered the Labour Party and sought to break into local political and administrative institutions. They challenged their elders as community representatives through seeking to forge an alliance between the Bangladeshi nationalist heritage and Bengali cultural identity, on the one hand, [and] with class and other ethnic identities on the other. The political fragmentation of the community and the adoption of different community discourses thus reflected the diversity of Bangladeshi interests.

The division of the political arena through the factionalization of secular politics, produced by the competition for ethnic leadership and positions in various public organizations, is today reinforced by the existence of two interdependent levels of community representation. While the second-generation activists have integrated in local council institutions, the members of British branches of Bangladeshi political parties—Awami League and Bangladesh Nationalist Party—are active in building networks through kinship and village links with Bangladesh, particularly with Sylhet, their district of origin. . . .

The nature of the relationship between Bangladeshis in the UK and their country of origin has to be understood . . . according to different interconnected arenas (local, regional, national, transnational). The first generation living in London might have kept a strong attachment with their ancestral villages through regular visits, the improvement of their family properties and regular remittances. Since the mid-1980s this financial involvement has been institutionalized through the work of many "development groups" (*Jonokollan Shomittee*) controlled by lineage leaders closely linked with the activities of Bangladeshi political parties in London, in particular the Awami League. The objective of these organizations was to support the construction of educational or religious facilities in rural Sylhet. The creation of these groups coincided with a sub-regional decentralization of governance in Bangladesh which reinforced the role that *probashis* (expatriates) could play in local Sylheti politics. The networks established across the transnational space, in turn, provided a political platform for Bangladeshi leaders coming to the UK and seeking alliances with *probashi* organizations for electoral purposes in Bangladesh . . .

The intense competition for the leadership of the Awami League in London highlighted the factionalization of the political space where business interests, regional affiliations and kinship belongings were embroiled. The claim for a need to occupy a strong position in British mainstream politics through their participation in local authority institutions led the second-generation secularist leaders to re-examine the role of their older élites. The latter were criticized mainly for their inability to mobilize their political resources and the strength of their social networks for the social/economic advancement of the local "Bangladeshi community" in Tower Hamlets. . . .

The increasing importance of the Islamization of space in the East End of London shed light on the new involvement religious actors intend to show in the local arena, particularly the leaders of East London Mosque. The purpose-built mosque offers many activities, including providing Islamic literature, study groups, conferences and social support to the local Bangladeshi and also Somali Muslim community. The close links established between the East London Mosque activists and youth groups—mainly the Young Muslim Organization—and their participation in publicly funded bodies and various anti-drug projects legitimated their claim to occupy a central role in the local landscape of community representation which had been dominated by secular activists up to the late 1980s.

At a religious level this claim to centrality was contested by other well-supported mosques in Brick Lane and St Katharine's ward, as well as by the plethora of prayer rooms and mosques scattered across the borough. In the political context the debate over political representation has also been connected with the prioritization of Islam as a unique and encompassing identity linking Bangladeshis in the UK with the *umma*, the global Muslim community. While the Brick Lane Mosque remained associated with first generation nationalist politicians, the East London Mosque benefited from the financial support of Middle East countries and Pakistan. The Brick Lane Mosque's local politicians helped to gain financial support from the Bangladesh government for an internal refurbishment after President Ershad's visit in 1985, while the East London Mosque's leaders emphasized their multinational support, in terms of financial support and congregation, and their role as East London's "central mosque."

For the East London Mosque activists, the prominence of a Muslim identity rooted itself both in the complete code of conduct that Islam has to offer and in the "authenticity" of values often opposed to the "syncretic" cultural practices of the Indian subcontinent. With high rates of unemployment, poor housing conditions and drug problems young Bangladeshis in Tower Hamlets were described as increasingly attracted by Islamist alternatives to the "gang culture." Violence, crime-related behaviour and the development of an informal economy would be perceived as a reaction to their very limited local prospects. At the same time they could also be seen as the product of the deficiency and "lack of morality" of secular western education. College unions and youth groups thus became the sites of increasingly polarized identity politics as new forms of social control based on religious principles have emerged among the second- and third-generation Bangladeshis. To counteract these Islamist initiatives, secularists strengthened the idea that a Bengali cultural heritage remained central to an educational approach aimed at a greater integration of young British Bangladeshis. . . .

The division of the political arena over transmission of values and the prioritization of religious or cultural identities became embroiled in a process of competition for the appropriation of space. It is important to note here that during the last decade public funding in Tower Hamlets for the organizations managed by secularists declined, while support for mosques and Islamic community organizations increased. On its adjacent site, the East London Mosque is now engaged in a large-scale expansion programme. Worshippers can purchase a piece of land and donate it to the mosque following the injunctions of the Islamic property law known as *Waqf.* The planning permission on the site previously owned by a private developer was secured after an intense campaign against secular councillors on the grounds that religion provided the unique basis for community identity. For the East London Mosque activists, the successful conclusion of a 2-year conflict over the disputed land demonstrated their strengthening position both within the community representation sphere and in the struggle for local resources. However, in a context of rapid urban change and increasing public–private partnership through regeneration programmes, secularists are still forging powerful alliances with public agencies, local entrepreneurs and important City firms. The organization of various local "multicultural" festivals and, above all, the introduction of a reinvented tradition, the Baishaki Mela, celebrating the "Bengali New Year" on Brick Lane, reflected this trend. The Baishaki Mela affirmed even more powerfully than before that Tower Hamlets' western wards—and Spitalfields in particular—were the cultural heartland of a local, national and global Bangladeshi "community." The New Year events deliberately evoked those celebrated in Dhaka, Bangladesh's national capital, but they also set an example for Bangladeshis elsewhere—in North America, other parts of Europe and the Middle East, for example.

In Spitalfields the new urban image of a local space renamed officially "Banglatown" was also designed to provide a sense of multicultural identity which would attract tourists and visitors from outside the area, following the successful model of Chinatown in Soho. Along Brick Lane, Bangladeshi entrepreneurs and restaurant owners participate in the "exoticization" of local places despite the fierce competition between them. . . .

The growing polarity between secular nationalists and Islamists was not restricted to the political arena . . . because more and more young British Bangladeshis found it hard to identify with the ideology that characterized the liberation war despite the legitimating efforts of the secularists. The commitment of their elders to the Bangladeshi politics through kinship and business networks was also perceived as a distant concern compared with their perspective of the future in the UK. For those who defined themselves first and foremost as Muslim, the traditional form of Islam in the subcontinent based on syncretic practices and the cult of holy men (*pirs*) seemed irrelevant to their present economic and political environment. The issues of discrimination and social exclusion were far more important to them. Furthermore, the fight against Islamophobia replaced the older anti-racist campaigns, which had helped to stop the National Front and British National Party activities in the western part of the borough. The mobilization surrounding the publication of Salman Rushdie's *The Satanic Verses* was also a key moment for many who could unite under the banner of a universal and global Muslim identity in order to act publicly and express their religious attachment. . . .

The conflicts, as an expression of the relationship between self-determination and struggle, also raise the issue of local/transnational/global collective memory. As those who can remember the events leading to the birth of Bangladesh get older, they are faced with the challenge of what memories should be passed on to the second and third generation of British Bangladeshis and for what purposes. This involves, of course, the contemporary politics of Bangladesh and the role of the Awami League leader, Sheikh Hasina, who is the daughter of the murdered "Father of the Nation," Sheikh Mujibur Rahman. The self-seeking and "corruption" of her supporters can establish the moral high ground for Islamist opponents who have to resist the accusations of supporting Pakistan (now or in the past). As Bangladesh becomes more formally Islamicized in response to local and wider global developments, so Bangladeshis in London and elsewhere in the West come under pressure to conform to everyday practices which reflect this local/global Islamicizing development. These political and ideological changes clearly influence people's daily lives at the local level through, for example, how they dress, who they mix with, what kinds of books they read and the television programmes they watch.

A Lungi with a Zip!

Emdad Rahman

*How does one deal with being rooted in two cultures? In this exhortation to "deshi/
Brit boys" or "coconuts," Emdad Rahman champions the lungi. This is the sarong
that Bangladeshi men wear around the house (if they are middle class) and outdoors
(if they are not). Why be ashamed of it? Be a proud lungi-wearing cosmopolitan!*

"What is the height of fashion? A lungi with a zip!"

Once upon a time *deshis* [Bengalis] used to be proud of their ability to
wear the clothes of the venerable English gentleman. Outside *desh* those
who aspired to the same thing were known decisively as 'booted and suited'
and denied the status of the westernised *deshi* babu. These days you receive
an invite to a mate's wedding in Sylhet, which is full of *deshi* traditional
garb. No problem there. The 64,000-dollar question is: do you wear a lungi?
You are probably on holiday on a beachy resort in Sylhet being laid back,
relaxed and doing what the locals do, which is probably watching Indian
films on cable/satellite TV. Do you wander round in a Becks-style [the soccer player David Beckham] sarong on your way to the olive grove eatery?
You are a normal sort of bloke so think, would you wear a lungi on the tube
on your way to work? Of course not; you'd be scorned, ridiculed, derided,
laughed at, almost as much as if you admitted to owning a Morris Minor,
enjoying *Big Brother* or listening to Kumar Sanu. Even the Reformist Jyoti
Basu hates them. He told the Times News Network in September 2002 that
he did not like lungis any more. The quintessential Bengali babu, now feels
that India will go to the dogs unless people give up wearing the lungi. "This
country will surely be ruined if we do not stop wearing lungis. How can
you travel in a bus or a tram in a lungi? How can you work?"

Designer Lungis . . .

Lungis, I would like to say[,] are a great form of clothing. I don't usually wear them outside, but [they] are great for around the home. How-

ever, funny things happen in London, and you do, very occasionally, see a man in the street so attired. But do not forget we are talking about a *deshi* in Sylhet here. This is despite dozens of attempts by modern fashion designers—including Jean Paul [*sic*] Gaultier, famous for his, er, open-minded designs—to prove that a bloke in a skirt can look good. However it should be said that a "Mokles" brand lungi does not somehow have the same appeal as a pair of Gucci's.

Legend has it that once a Chacha caught the gravy train to England. On one of his infrequent jaunts into the city it was noticed that he was wearing a lungi. An English toff asked him, "What is this, old chap?," by catching his lungi from behind. The Chacha caught the gentleman's tie and asked him what it was. The Englishman replied, "It is a tie." Chacha replied: "This is a back tie."

A Distressing Childhood Experience . . .

I can recollect an incident from when I was a young whippersnapper involving one of the hardest blokes in the East End. For my own personal safety I'm going to refer to him as *"Bhaisaheb." Bhaisaheb* was a community role model who also happened to be trained in the "finer" aspects of martial arts instruction. One day a group of my friends and I met him near our local youth club and badgered him endlessly to show us some of his kicking skills. After repeated pleas, *Bhaisaheb* relented and proceeded to put us all out of our misery. To spice up the story I would like readers to note that those were the days when *Bhaisaheb* was a fashion icon with a mullet hairstyle, who dressed in white Farahs, red Japanese silk shirts, white tennis socks and Dunlop squash trainers. With a war cry ("Yaaaaleeee") *Bhaisaheb* produced a (un)majestic scissor kick as portrayed so well by Guile on the Street Fighter games. (Believe me when I say I've seen elephants kick higher). Unfortunately *Bhaisaheb*'s Farah trousers where a wee bit tight and he ended up splitting them from ear to ear, and guess what (no *chuddis* [briefs])! Almost twenty years on and me and my homies still haven't recovered. Despite the years the questions continue to roll: Why did he not wear a lungi . . . a lungi . . . a lungi! Hollywood's screenmake of the book *Sleepers* involving Brad Pitt and childhood ghosts bought all the memories flooding back.

Dear Bhabiji . . .

Ancient fashion garments generally used no stitching although, *deshis*, like their Indian counterparts, knew about sewing. Most clothes were ready to wear as soon as they left the loom. The lungi has never really disappeared and continues to be part of *deshi* fashion. For *deshis*/Brit boys in the UK to admit that they wear a lungi is a serious coming out and I would like to encourage other men to give it a go. (If you are going to come out don't be shy—talk to Bhabiji or email me for personal, professional and moral support). This now leads nicely up to the final straight. If the lady of a typical *deshi* house wears the trousers what do the blokes do? Wear a lungi of course! When women wear trousers are they trying to get in touch with their masculine side? Are they pushing the gender boundary? OF COURSE NOT! So why are these assumptions applied to men wearing lungis? Cynics and coconuts should try wearing one in the house at first. Having said that, although a lungi is male attire, you need to tie it or whatever just to keep it from falling off! And where are all these guys that DO want to wear lungis? Some of them haven't had the nerve to try it in public yet. Some are guys at the office, and some are here, reading this article. However, there are not enough of us demanding lungis designed for men to have a big pull on the real drivers of mass production, like Gap, Gucci and River Island. There is some interest on the part of fashion designers who have sent guys down catwalks in skirts, but I feel that the way the lungi is going to catch on is not from a runway phenomenon—it will evolve from streetwear. When I was in school and becoming image-conscious, I asked my PSHE [personal, social, and health education] teacher if it was true that clothes make the man. "You're a man on two feet," he said, disgusted, rolling his eyes a bit. "Man makes the man." Back then I had an eye for classic style and got laughed at because of my allegiance to different brands, but I wore "fine" suits that I considered well ahead of the curve: well ahead of my time. Twenty-odd years later, fashion sheep will be loyal to any tag with a name on it, but I am still the urban style iconoclast. This summer, I am bigging up [promoting] the lungi almost exclusively.

Fashion comes and goes, but style is timeless. And here I am: well ahead of the curve, well ahead of my time. I'm pretty sure this style won't catch on, but maybe it should. My teacher at school was right: clothes don't make the man ([t]hink about *Bhaisaheb*). A man can stand on two feet—lungi and all.

The Concert for Bangladesh

Ravi Shankar

In August 1971—while war was raging in East Pakistan/Bangladesh—a memorable concert was staged in New York. The Concert for Bangladesh was in aid of the suffering people of the war-torn region. It was the first benefit concert to bring together major world artists for a common humanitarian purpose. As such, it was the forerunner of recent global fundraising performances. The musicians Ravi Shankar and George Harrison initiated it, as described in Harrison's song "Bangla Desh":

> *My friend came to me with sadness in his eyes*
> *Told me that he wanted help*
> *Before his country dies*
> *Although I could not feel the pain,*
> *I knew I had to try*
> *Now I'm asking all of you*
> *To help us save some lives.*

In 2005 the concert album and accompanying documentary were rereleased, and Ravi Shankar wrote the following introduction.

It makes me so happy that the Concert for Bangladesh is being released again. Hailing from Bengal, my heart went out to the Bengali-speaking people of Bangladesh and it was natural for me to reach out and want to help the refugees and the hundreds of thousands of little children.

I expressed my concern to George Harrison. He knew about the turmoil of my mind and a concert to raise funds was initiated. An enormous amount of money was collected and this could never have been achieved without the help of dear George. What happened is now history: it was one of the most moving and intense musical experiences of the century.

Again and again I am asked which concerts stand out in my memory, and it is very difficult to remember all the prominent ones as my career spans over seventy-five years of performances; but the Concert for Bangladesh was very significant to me as the conception of the idea came from me and the people needing aid were very close to my heart; some of them, of course, being distantly related to me. Ali Akbar Khan and Alla Rakha joined me on stage for the first half and George Harrison played the second half, joined by other eminent musicians including Bob Dylan and Eric Clapton. George closed the concert with "Bangla Desh," the special song he wrote for the occasion.

As a result, overnight the name of the country Bangladesh came to be known all over the world. Millions of dollars were raised and given to UNI-CEF who distributed milk, blankets and clothes to refugees. It touches my heart very deeply to know that this event is not to be forgotten, and that with the re-release of the film and the album people in Bangladesh will continue to be helped. I am sure that the music of this electrifying concert of 1971 will move the listeners even today.

Displaying Statehood

Anonymous

Independence made Bangladesh a new player in the world state system. Its leaders suddenly had to perform on the international stage. They sought to gain official recognition of Bangladesh by countries and international organizations around the world. Despite widespread sympathy for the new state, this was not always easy because Pakistan continued to thwart Bangladesh for several years after the war. As a result, Bangladesh could not become a member of the United Nations or the Organization of the Islamic Conference until 1974. Memberships in other international associations were celebrated in Bangladesh as diplomatic successes. In 1973, Prime Minister Sheikh Mujibur Rahman traveled to Algiers for the fourth summit of the Non-aligned Movement. There he met with heads of state and government leaders from around the world and enrolled Bangladesh as a member state.

Sheikh Mujibur Rahman speaks with Fidel Castro, prime minister of Cuba, at the summit of the Non-aligned Movement in Algiers in 1973. Used by permission of the Heritage Archives of Bangladesh History, Rajshahi.

UN Peacekeepers from Bangladesh

Ilyas Iftekhar Rasul

Since 1988 Bangladesh has been a major contributor of troops to the peacekeeping operations of the United Nations. The troops have been deployed in conflict zones in Africa, the Middle East, Asia, the Caribbean, and Europe. Peacekeeping, a source of pride for the country's armed forces, also provides international prestige and legitimacy—besides earning them very good incomes.

The international (and domestic) legitimacy of the armed forces had been seriously compromised after they repeatedly intruded into national politics. Military coups brought undemocratic regimes to power from 1975 to 1990—and from 2007 to 2009 the military controlled a "caretaker government" without legislative authority.

Here a former military advisor to the Permanent Mission of Bangladesh to the United Nations gives his assessment of the involvement of the armed forces in international peacekeeping.

Since 2003, the United Nations (UN) has been observing "International Day for UN Peacekeepers" on May 29 every year. The purpose of this day is twofold; one, to honour the memory of UN peacekeepers who lost their lives in the cause of peace; two, to pay tribute to all men and women who have served and continue to serve in the UN Peacekeeping Operations (UNPKO) for their high level of professionalism, dedication and courage.

Bangladesh, as an active member of the UN and as a top Troops Contributing Country (TCC), also observes the day in a most befitting manner, expressing solidarity with UN activities and programmes. What does this day mean to the UN vis-à-vis Bangladesh? What lessons can we draw from it?

The responsibility of maintaining world peace and security is enshrined in the UN Charter. Peacekeeping, although not explicitly mentioned in the Charter, has evolved over the years as one of the main tools to achieve this goal. . . . Initially, the developed countries led the UN force deployment but since the 1980s there has been a decline in their troop contribution—barring the missions in the Middle East. Since then, the contribution of developing nations increased with the predominance of South Asian nations, including Bangladesh. The number of TCCS has also increased considerably (from 34 in 1965 to 115 in 2011), displaying its importance and acceptability. UN peace-keeping has been most responsive to conflicts in Europe, Latin America and Africa but least responsive in Asia.

Bangladesh, as a top TCC, has participated since 1988 in 46 UN peacekeep-ing missions in 32 countries with approximately 100,000 uniformed person-nel. Currently, 10,621 personnel are deployed in 11 missions (in 10 countries), mostly in Africa—ranking top amongst TCCs (as of May 26, 2011).

Though Bangladesh entered the UNPKO from the Second Generation of UN Peacekeeping (1988), she has proved to be an invaluable partner to the UN. Bangladesh troops went through many critical situations in many missions where they held the UN flag high and steadfast—like in Cambodia, Somalia, DRC [Democratic Republic of Congo], Sierra Leone, Cote D'Ivoire, Liberia and Sudan. Bangladesh's commitment to global peace has not been without a price. A hundred and three of her brave peacekeepers died and 116 were wounded in maintaining world peace far away from home. On this auspi-cious day, the country salutes them and remembers their valour and sacrifice.

UNPKO has provided Bangladesh forces a unique opportunity to work in environments that are evolving, complex and multidimensional, and undertake military, quasi-military and civic actions. It has also facilitated them to gain immense experience and exposure to conflict management, modern weapons and equipment, international operating procedures, com-mand and control systems, etc. Their experiences and best practices in various national development activities, disaster management, and counter-insurgency operations have also positively contributed to UNPKO. The fac-tors that contributed to their wide acceptability and credibility include their professionalism, discipline, neutrality, compliance of mission mandate, cor-dial relations with host populations, etc.

Peacekeeping operations demand a multidimensional approach. Hence, our forces need to constantly revise and update policies and practices in order to maintain their meaningful presence and lead role in future UNPKO. Back home, there should be continuous institutional study and research on the evolving policies and best practices of UN peacekeeping at all levels, i.e., tactical, operational and strategic. Our forces should be more conver-sant with local languages, especially French and Arabic for the missions in French and Arabic speaking countries.

As top TCC, Bangladesh must vigorously pursue proportionate represen-tation in leadership positions and thus ensure implementation of [the UN] Resolution (Paragraph 215 of General Assembly Resolution A/61//19 Part II dated 5 June 2007), which emphasises this issue. Bangladesh representation in the civil dimension of peacekeeping is far less than it is in uniformed representation.

Garment Workers' Rights

Clean Clothes Campaign

In the 1980s a new industry developed in Bangladesh: ready-made garments for export overseas. Based on very cheap labor, the industry grew explosively. In 1983–84 the value of exported garments amounted to US$32 million, or 4 percent of Bangladesh's total exports. By 2008–9 the value had gone up to more than US$1.23 billion, and its share of Bangladesh's total exports to a whopping 79 percent.

The working conditions of the (mostly female) garment workers soon raised international concern. Global campaigns were launched to improve their rights. Among the campaigners is an alliance of organizations in thirteen European countries— the Clean Clothes Campaign. Members include trade unions and NGOs that cover a broad spectrum of approaches, such as women's rights, consumer advocacy, and poverty reduction. Working closely with organizations in Bangladesh, they lobby companies that source garments from Bangladesh. Here is an example.

April 11 [2010] marks the fifth anniversary of the collapse of the Spectrum/ Shahriyar Sweater factory in Bangladesh, which killed 64 workers and injured 80, 54 of whom were seriously injured. The Spectrum collapse focused global attention on the chronic safety problems in the Bangladesh garment industry. To mark the anniversary of the Spectrum collapse, the Clean Clothes Campaign, the Maquila Solidarity Network (Canada), and the International Labor Rights Forum (USA) call upon all buyers sourcing garments in Bangladesh to take proactive, sustained, and coordinated measures to help eliminate these systemic problems.

In February this year, a large fire at the Garib & Garib Sweater Ltd factory in Bangladesh sadly took the lives of 21 workers and injured another 50. This new drama is a brutal reminder that five years since the Spectrum disaster, effective and proactive action is still lacking to ensure that garment workers in Bangladesh can go to work without fearing for their lives.

The Bangladeshi garment [industry] is notorious for its bad safety record. Within a year of the Spectrum collapse around 65 workers in KTS Textiles and Sayem Fashions lost their lives. Two weeks after the Garib & Garib fire

After the collapse of the Spectrum factory, garment workers' unions demonstrate against unsafe working conditions. Photograph by Jenneke Arens, 2005. Used by permission of the photographer.

another worker lost her life in yet another factory, Matrix Sweater. Between 2005 and 2010, at least 172 workers were killed. Most of the victims were producing clothes for well-known international brands when they died.

More could have been done by all concerned to prevent these disasters from occurring. More needs to be done to ensure further disasters are prevented. In consultation with Bangladeshi unions and the US-based Worker Rights Consortium, and incorporating proposals developed earlier by the International Textile, Garment and Leather Workers Federation (ITGLWF), we have compiled a list of actions that companies sourcing garments from Bangladesh should take within their own supply chain to prevent future tragedies. We are also asking that companies . . . collectively press the Government of Bangladesh and the Bangladesh Garment Manufacturers & Exporters Association (BGMEA) to take specific actions to address these problems industry-wide in Bangladesh. We have sent this list to all brands known to have sourced garments from factories where major health and safety incidents have occurred in recent years. We also call upon international brands sourcing from factories where recent disasters occurred to ensure that victims and their families receive fair and timely compensation.

Companies sourcing at factories where major health and safety incidents occurred:

3 Suisses—Arcandor—Bestseller—Bluhmod—Carrefour—Cotton Group—El Corte Ingles—Gap—H&M—HBC—Inditex—JC Penny—Kirsten Mode—Li & Fung—Lindex—Littlewoods—Marks Work Wearhouse—New Wave Group—New Yorker—Otto—Pimkie—Provera—Scapino—Solo Invest—Steilmann—Tahagroup/Tema—Teddy—Ulla Popken—Wal-Mart.

International Mother Language Day

UNESCO

In 1999 the Bangladesh government proposed to the General Conference of UNESCO
*(United Nations Educational, Scientific and Cultural Organization) the introduc-
tion of an annual celebration of mother languages. The International Mother Language Day was to be celebrated on 21 February, to commemorate the people who
were killed on 21 February 1952 as they demanded that their mother tongue, Bengali,
be declared a state language in Pakistan. The General Conference adopted a resolution to that effect and the day has been celebrated since 2000.*

*Amendment to the Draft Programme and Budget for 2000–2001 (30 C /5),
Submitted by Bangladesh*

PROPOSED MODIFICATION

An International Mother Language Day will be proclaimed with a view to
pursuing the Organization's work in favour of linguistic and cultural diversity and multilingualism in all fields of competence and that the proposed
International Mother Language Day be observed on 21 February every year
in the Member States and at UNESCO Headquarters.

EXPLANATORY NOTE

Considering that languages are at the very heart of UNESCO's objectives and
that they are the most powerful instruments of preserving and developing
our tangible and intangible heritage.

Bearing in mind also that all moves to promote the dissemination of
mother tongues will serve not only to encourage linguistic diversity and
multilingual education but also to the development of fuller awareness of
linguistic and cultural traditions throughout the world and to inspire solidarity based on understanding, tolerance and dialogue.

Considering consequently that one of the most effective ways to promote and develop mother tongues is the establishment of an "International

International Mother Language Day
Languages matter!
February 21, 2009

Journée internationale de la langue maternelle
Les langues, ça compte!
21 Février 2009

For the tenth International Mother Language Day in 2009, UNESCO launched a poster competition. This design, titled "Diversity Brings Us Together," is by the Italian finalist Angela Morelli. Poster "Diversity Brings Us Together" © 2009 Angela Morelli, www.angelamorelli.com. Used by permission.

Mother Language Day" with a view to organizing various activities in the Member States and an exhibition at UNESCO Headquarters on that same day.

Recognizing the unprecedented sacrifice made by Bangladesh for the cause of mother language on 21 February 1952.

Noting that this idea has not yet been adopted at the international level.

Proposes that 21 February be proclaimed "International Mother Language Day" throughout the world to commemorate the martyrs who sacrificed their lives on this very date in 1952.

Grameen in Russia

Staff correspondent, The Daily Star

One of Bangladesh's most notable exports is an idea that goes by the name of Grameen. The Grameen Bank (Village Bank) is an institution that provides small loans to poor people who do not qualify for traditional bank loans because they lack collateral. This approach became known globally as microcredit or microfinance and was picked up by development and banking organizations all over the world. It also became an important element in rebranding Bangladesh—from a world icon of grinding poverty and dependence to a self-confident nation that has things to teach the world. Grameen itself has been very active in setting up microfinance schemes in various locations beyond Bangladesh, and increasingly in the developed world. This article, originally titled "Global Financial Meltdown: Russia to Intensify Microcredit to Offset Adverse Effects," appeared in a Bangladesh newspaper in 2009.

Russia wants to intensify its microcredit programme to cushion the adverse effects of the global financial meltdown, said the visiting Russian Deputy Minister for Economic Development Anna Popova at a press conference at Grameen Bank Bhaban in the city yesterday. "The global financial crisis has affected many small businesses in Russia while the conventional banks are not willing to finance them for risk involvement in such financing," she added at the press conference attended by Nobel Laureate Prof Muhammad Yunus, managing director of Grameen Bank.

Popova said under such situations, microfinance will help those affected by the economic recession and people also want to develop new enterprises in the new circumstances. Popova arrived in Dhaka on Wednesday on a four-day visit to learn about operations and legal structure of Grameen Bank and to replicate the structure in Russia.

She was leading a 10-member high profile delegation which is due to leave Bangladesh today [21 February 2010]. The Russian delegation told the press conference that presently there are around 2,000 microfinance institutions in Russia that distribute some US$1 billion annually and cover around one million people.

Though many microfinance institutions are operating in Russia, there is a huge demand for microcredit in remote parts of the country where the conventional banking system is yet to be developed, said Mikhail Mamuta, president of National Association of Microfinance Market Stakeholders. "As there is a huge demand for microcredit products in Russia, we through this visit wanted to learn different aspects of this financing," he added.

The press conference was informed that microfinance has been operating in Russia for around a decade. Speaking on the occasion, Prof Yunus said after the collapse of the Soviet Union it was the highest Russian delegation to visit Bangladesh, and this visit would open a new door of cooperation between the two countries. The arrival of a high profile delegation suggests that Russia is very willing to expand its microcredit activities, he added.

Prof Yunus was invited by the delegation to visit Russia in November this year to witness the development of microfinance activities in that country.

He is scheduled to be the chief guest at the national microcredit convention in Russia in November.

Speaking at the press briefing, Alexey Savatyugin, director of [the] financial policy department at the Russian Ministry of Finance, said the delegation has learned a lot through this visit and Prof Yunus will be able to witness the application of their experiences during his November visit. When asked by journalists whether the global financial meltdown will affect Bangladesh, Savatyugin said the countries having [the] most developed credit and banking systems would be the most affected by economic downturn. He, however, cautioned that the economic tension might touch Bangladesh if it affects those countries where Bangladeshi expatriates are at work.

Suggestions for Further Reading

General Histories

Baxter, Craig, and Syedur Rahman. *Historical Dictionary of Bangladesh*. Lanham, MD: Scarecrow Press, 2003.

Islam, Sirajul, ed. *History of Bangladesh 1704–1971*. 3 vols. Dhaka: Asiatic Society of Bangladesh, 1992.

Islam, Sirajul, and Sajahan Miah, eds. *Banglapedia: National Encyclopedia of Bangladesh*. 10 vols. Dhaka: Asiatic Society of Bangladesh, 2003. Online version available at http://www.banglapedia.org.

Novak, James J. *Bangladesh: Reflections on the Water*. Bloomington: Indiana University Press, 1993.

van Schendel, Willem. *A History of Bangladesh*. Cambridge: Cambridge University Press, 2009.

Voices from Bangladesh

Bangladesh online newspapers: http://www.onlinenewspapers.com/banglade.htm.
Drishtipat Writers' Collective: http://dpwriters.wordpress.com.

Early Histories

Chakrabarti, Dilip K. *Ancient Bangladesh: A Study of the Archaeological Sources*. Delhi: Oxford University Press, 1992.

Eaton, Richard M. *The Rise of Islam and the Bengal Frontier, 1204–1760*. Berkeley: University of California Press, 1993.

Moudud, Hasna Jasimuddin. *A Thousand Year Old Bengali Mystic Poetry*. Dhaka: University Press Limited, 1992.

Raychaudhury, Tapan. *Bengal under Akbar and Jahangir: An Introductory Study in Social History*. Delhi: Munshiram Manoharlal, 1966.

Stewart, Tony K. *Fabulous Females and Peerless Pīrs: Tales of Mad Adventure in Old Bengal*. New York: Oxford University Press, 2004.

Colonial Encounters

Ahmed, Rafiuddin. *The Bengal Muslims 1871–1906: A Quest for Identity*. Delhi: Oxford University Press, 1981.

Bandyopadhyay, Sekhar, ed. *Bengal: Rethinking History—Essays on Historiography*. Delhi: International Centre of Bengal Studies/Manohar Publications, 2001.

Chatterjee, Partha. *A Princely Impostor? The Strange and Universal History of the Kumar of Bhawal*. Princeton: Princeton University Press, 2002.

Chaudhuri, Nirad C. *The Autobiography of an Unknown Indian*. London: Macmillan and Co., 1951.

Greenough, Paul R. *Prosperity and Misery in Modern Bengal: The Famine of 1943–44*. New York: Oxford University Press, 1982.

Hashmi, Taj ul-Islam. *Pakistan as a Peasant Utopia: The Communalization of Class Politics in East Bengal, 1920–1947*. Boulder, CO: Westview Press, 1992.

Hossain, Rokeya Sakhawat. *Sultana's Dream and Padmarag: Two Feminist Utopias*. Edited and translated by Barnita Bagchi. Delhi: Penguin Books, 2005.

Iqbal, Iftekhar. *The Bengal Delta: Ecology, State and Social Change, 1840–1943*. Houndmills, UK: Palgrave Macmillan, 2010.

Openshaw, Jeanne. *Seeking Bāuls of Bengal*. Cambridge: Cambridge University Press, 2004.

Partition and Pakistan

Jahan, Rounaq. *Pakistan: Failure in National Integration*. Dhaka: University Press Limited, 1994.

Kamal, Ahmed. *State against the Nation: The Decline of the Muslim League in Pre-independence Bangladesh, 1947–54*. Dhaka: University Press Limited, 2009.

Nasrin, Taslima. *Meyebela—My Bengali Girlhood: A Memoir of Growing Up Female in a Muslim World*. Moreton-in-Marsh, UK: Arris, 2003.

Umar, Badruddin. *The Emergence of Bangladesh: Class Struggles in East Pakistan (1947–1958)*. Vol. 1. Oxford: Oxford University Press, 2004.

———. *The Emergence of Bangladesh, Vol. 2: Rise of Bengali Nationalism (1958–1971)*. Oxford: Oxford University Press, 2006.

van Schendel, Willem. *The Bengal Borderland: Beyond State and Nation in South Asia*. London: Anthem Press, 2005.

Zaheer, Hasan. *The Separation of East Pakistan: The Rise and Realization of Bengali Muslim Nationalism*. Karachi, Pakistan: Oxford University Press/Dhaka: University Press Limited, 1994.

War and Independence

Anam, Tahmima. *A Golden Age*. London: John Murray, 2007.

Gill, John H. *An Atlas of the 1971 India-Pakistan War: The Creation of Bangladesh*. Washington, DC: Near East South Asia Center for Strategic Studies, 2003.

Imam, Jahanara. *Ekattorer Dinguli*. Dhaka: Shondhani Prokashoni, 1986. Translated by Mustafizur Rahman as *Of Blood and Fire: The Untold Story of Bangladesh's War of Independence*. Dhaka: University Press Limited, 1990.

Karim, S. A. *Sheikh Mujib: Triumph and Tragedy*. Dhaka: University Press Limited, 2005.

Maniruzzaman, Talukder. *The Bangladesh Revolution and Its Aftermath.* Dacca: Bangladesh Books International, 1980.

Maswani, A. M. K. *Subversion in East Pakistan.* Lahore, Pakistan: Amir Publications, 1979.

Niazi, A. A. K. *The Betrayal of East Pakistan.* Dhaka: University Press Limited, 1999.

Siddiqi, Abdul Rahman. *East Pakistan—The End Game: An Onlooker's Journal 1969–1971.* Karachi, Pakistan: Oxford University Press, 2004.

Sisson, Richard, and Leo E. Rose. *War and Secession: Pakistan, India, and the Creation of Bangladesh.* Berkeley: University of California Press, 1990.

Zaman, Niaz, and Asif Farrukhi, eds. *Fault Lines, Stories of 1971.* Dhaka: University Press Limited, 2008.

Dilemmas of Nationhood

Ali, S. Mahmud. *Understanding Bangladesh.* New York: Columbia University Press, 2010.

Bal, Ellen. *They Ask If We Eat Frogs: Garo Ethnicity in Bangladesh.* Singapore: Institute of Southeast Asian Studies, 2007.

Chtnews.com: http://www.chtnews.blogspot.com.

Jahan, Rounaq, ed. *Bangladesh: Promise and Performance.* London: Zed Books, 2000.

Mamoon, Muntassir, and Jayanta Kumar Ray. *Civil Society in Bangladesh: Resilience and Retreat.* Dhaka: Subarna, 1998.

Mohaiemen, Naeem, ed. *Between Ashes and Hope: Chittagong Hill Tracts in the Blind Spot of Bangladesh Nationalism.* Dhaka: Drishtipat Writers' Collective, 2010.

Mohsin, Amena. *The Politics of Nationalism: The Case of the Chittagong Hill Tracts, Bangladesh.* Dhaka: University Press Limited, 1997.

Riaz, Ali. *God Willing: The Politics of Islamism in Bangladesh.* Lanham, MD: Rowman and Littlefield, 2004.

———. *Islamist Militancy in Bangladesh: A Complex Web.* Oxford: Routledge, 2008.

Seabrook, Jeremy. *Freedom Unfinished: Fundamentalism and Popular Resistance in Bangladesh Today.* London: Zed Books, 2001.

Shehabuddin, Elora. *Reshaping the Holy: Democracy, Development, and Muslim Women in Bangladesh.* New York: Columbia University Press, 2008.

Uddin, Sufia M. *Constructing Bangladesh: Religion, Ethnicity, and Language in an Islamic Nation.* Chapel Hill: University of North Carolina Press, 2006.

Umar, Badruddin. *The Emergence of Bangladesh, Vol. 2: Rise of Bengali Nationalism (1958–1971).* Oxford: Oxford University Press, 2006.

van Schendel, Willem, Wolfgang Mey, and Aditya Kumar Dewan. *The Chittagong Hill Tracts: Living in a Borderland.* Bangkok: White Lotus, 2000.

Contemporary Culture

Ahmed, Rafiuddin, ed. *Understanding the Bengal Muslims: Interpretive Essays.* New Delhi: Oxford University Press, 2001.

Azim, Ferdous, and Niaz Zaman, eds. *Infinite Variety: Women in Society and Literature.* Dhaka: University Press Limited, 1994.

Glassie, Henry. *Art and Life in Bangladesh.* Bloomington: Indiana University Press, 1997.

Harder, Hans. *Sufism and Saint Veneration in Contemporary Bangladesh: The Maijbhandaris of Chittagong.* Oxford: Routledge, 2011.

Hashmi, Taj I. *Women and Islam in Bangladesh: Beyond Subjection and Tyranny.* Houndmills, UK: Palgrave, 2000.

Jalais, Annu. *Forest of Tigers: People, Politics and Environment in the Sundarbans.* London: Routledge, 2010.

Janeja, Manpreet K. *Transactions in Taste: The Collaborative Lives of Everyday Bengali Food.* London: Routledge, 2010.

Kirkpatrick, Joanna. *Transports of Delight: The Ricksha Arts of Bangladesh.* Bloomington: Indiana University Press, 2003.

Murshid, Tazeen M. *The Sacred and the Secular: Bengal Muslim Discourses, 1871–1977.* New York: Oxford University Press, 1995.

Zaman, Niaz. *Under the Krishnachura: Fifty Years of Bangladeshi Writing.* Dhaka: University Press Limited, 2003.

The Development Gaze

Adnan, Shapan, and Ranajit Dastidar. *Alienation of the Lands of Indigenous Peoples in the CHT of Bangladesh.* Dhaka: Chittagong Hill Tracts Commission and International Work Group on Indigenous Affairs, 2011.

Arens, Jenneke, and Jos van Beurden. *Jhagrapur: Poor Peasants and Women in a Village in Bangladesh.* New Delhi: Orient Longman, 1980.

Bertocci, Peter J. *The Politics of Community and Culture in Bangladesh: Selected Essays.* Dhaka: Centre for Social Studies, 1996.

Crow, Ben, with Alan Lindquist and David Wilson. *Sharing the Ganges: The Politics and Technology of River Development.* New Delhi: Sage Publications, 1995.

Faaland, Just, and J. R. Parkinson. *Bangladesh: The Test Case of Development.* London: C. Hurst and Co., 1976.

Faraizi, Aminul, Taskinur Rahman, and Jim McAllister. *Microcredit and Women's Empowerment: A Case Study of Bangladesh.* London: Routledge, 2011.

Gardner, Katy. *Discordant Development: Global Capitalism and the Struggle for Connection in Bangladesh.* London: Pluto Press, 2012.

Hartmann, Betsy, and James K. Boyce. *A Quiet Violence: View from a Bangladesh Village.* London: Zed Press, 1983.

Karim, Lamia. *Microfinance and Its Discontents: Women in Debt in Bangladesh.* Minneapolis: University of Minnesota Press, 2011.

Lewis, David. *Bangladesh: Politics, Economy and Civil Society.* Cambridge: Cambridge University Press, 2011.

Messerli, Bruno, and Thomas Hofer. *Floods in Bangladesh: History, Dynamics and Rethinking the Role of the Himalayas.* Tokyo: United Nations University Press, 2006.

Shahaduz Zaman. *Broken Limbs, Broken Lives: Ethnography of a Hospital Ward in Bangladesh*. Amsterdam: Het Spinhuis, 2005.

Bangladesh beyond Borders

Gardner, Katy. *Age, Narrative and Migration: The Life Course and Life Histories of Bengali Elders in London*. Oxford: Berg, 2002.

Hazarika, Sanjoy. *Rites of Passage: Border Crossings, Imagined Homelands, India's East and Bangladesh*. New Delhi: Penguin Books, 2000.

Kabeer, Naila. *The Power to Choose: Bangladeshi Women Workers and Labour Market Decisions in London and Dhaka*. London: Verso, 2000.

Kibria, Nazli. *Muslims in Motion: Islam and National Identity in the Bangladesh Diaspora*. New Brunswick, NJ: Rutgers University Press, 2011.

Sobhan, Rehman, ed. *Bangladesh-India Relations: Perspectives from Civil Society Dialogues*. Dhaka: Centre for Policy Dialogue/Dhaka: University Press Limited, 2002.

Yunus, Muhammad. *Banker to the Poor: Micro-lending and the Battle against World Poverty*. Philadelphia: Public Affairs, 2003.

Acknowledgment of Copyrights and Sources

Part I. Voices from Bangladesh

"Becoming a Village Photographer," an interview with Sabina Yasmin Sathi, from *Shubidhabonchiter Srijonshil Uddyog, Onushondhan, Prochar o Proshar*, edited by Quratul-Ain Tahmina, Shishir Morol, Prisila Raj, et al. (Dhaka: Research Initiatives, Bangladesh, 2010), vol. II, 168–69. Translation © 2013 Meghna Guhathakurta. Used by permission of Research Initiatives, Bangladesh.

"Wait for a While, Death!" by Abdul Gofur Hali, from *Der verrückte Gofur spricht: Mystische Lieder aus Ostbengalen von Abdul Gofur Hali*, translated by Hans Harder (Heidelberg: Draupadi Verlage, 2004), 75–77. Used by permission of Hans Harder.

"Telephone Ladies and Social Business," statement by Laureate Professor Muhammad Yunus delivered at the ITU World Information Society Award Ceremony, 17 May 2006. Available at http://www.itu.int/wisd/2006/award/statements/yunus.html.

"I Work in a Clothing Factory," testimonial by Shana K., from "Testimony of a Bangladeshi Garment Worker," *Institute for Global Labour and Human Rights*, June 15, 2010. Institute for Global Labour and Human Rights. Available at http://www.nlcnet.org/alerts?id=0170. Accessed 27 August 2010. Reprinted by permission of the Institute for Global Labour and Human Rights, formerly National Labor Committee.

"Bengali New Year," from "Traditions That Transcend Differences—Interview," by Shamsuzzaman Khan and Kajalie Shehreen Islam, edited by Mahfuz Anam, *The Star—Stories behind the News*, 16 April 2010. *The Daily Star*. Available at http://www.thedailystar.net/magazine/2010/04/03/interview.htm. Accessed 15 March 2012. Reprinted by permission of *The Daily Star*.

"The Fundamentalist," by Abdul Qader Mullah, from *Freedom Unfinished: Fundamentalism and Popular Resistance in Bangladesh Today*, by Jeremy Seabrook (London and New York: Zed Books, 2001), 116–17. Reprinted by permission of Zed Books.

"This Land Is Your Land, This Land Is Our Land," by Farah Mehreen Ahmad, adapted from "This Is Your Land," by Farah Mehreen Ahmad in *Between Ashes and Hope: Chittagong Hill Tracts in the Blind Spot of Bangladesh Nationalism*, edited by Naeem Mohaiemen (Dhaka: Drishtipat Writers' Collective, 2010), 13–14. Used by permission of the author.

"How They Discriminate Me," interview with Roshni Rani, translated from Bengali by Sushmita Hossain Natasha, in *Antaj Jonogoshtir Shonglap*, no. 4, Special Edition on Women and Independence (March 2009), 7. Used by permission of Research Initiatives, Bangladesh.

Part II. Early Histories

"The Earliest Inscription," by anonymous, previously published as "The Mahasthan
Brahmi Inscription," in *Banglapedia: National Encyclopedia of Bangladesh* (Dhaka:
Asiatic Society of Bangladesh, 2003), vol. 6, 350. Translated by Jean-François Salles.
Reprinted by permission of The Banglapedia Trust and the Asiatic Society of
Bangladesh, Dhaka.

"A View from the Sea," by anonymous, from *The Periplus of the Erythraean Sea: Travel
and Trade in the Indian Ocean by a Merchant of the First Century*, edited and translated
by Wilfred H. Scholl (New York: Longmans Green, 1912), 47–48.

"Jackfruits and a Jade Buddha," by Xuanzang, from *Si-Yu-Ki: Buddhist Records of the
Western World, Translated from the Chinese of Hiuen Tsiang (A.D. 629)*, translated by
Samuel Beal (London: Trubner & Co., 1884), II, 194–95, 199–200.

"Songs of Realization," by Bhusuku-pada, Sabara-pada, and Kukkuri-pada, from
A Thousand Year Old Bengali Mystic Poetry, by Hasna Jasimuddin Moudud (Dhaka:
University Press Limited, 1992), 53, 75, 95. Used by permission of The University
Press Limited and Hasna Jasimuddin Moudud.

"A King's Gift of Land," by anonymous, from "New Copperplate Grant of Śrīcandra
(no. 8) from Bangladesh," in *Bulletin of SOAS* 73, no. 2 (2010), 234–38. © School of
Oriental and African Studies, published by Cambridge University Press. Translated
by Benjamin J. Fleming. Reprinted by permission of Cambridge University Press
and Benjamin Fleming.

"A Visit to Sylhet," by Ibn Battutah, from *The Travels of Ibn Batūta*, translated by the
Rev. Samuel Lee (London: The Oriental Translation Committee, 1829), 194–98
(abridged).

"The Rise of Islam," by Richard M. Eaton, from *The Rise of Islam and the Bengal Frontier,
1204–1760* (Berkeley, etc.: University of California Press, 1993), xxi–xxvii (abridged).
© 1993 by The Regents of the University of California. Reproduced by permission
of University of California Press and by permission of Oxford University Press,
New Delhi.

"Poor and Rich in Mughal Bengal," by Tapan Raychaudhuri, from *Bengal under Akbar
and Jahangir: An Introductory Study in Social History* (Delhi: Munshiram Manoharlal, 1966 [1953]), 217–27 (abridged). Used by permission of Munshiram Manoharlal
Publishers.

"Washed Ashore," by Frans Jansz van der Heiden and Willem Kunst, from *Vervarelyke
Schip-Breuk van 't Oost-Indisch Jacht Ter Schelling onder het Landt van Bengale* (Am-
sterdam: Joannes van Someren, 1675) (abridged). Translation © 2013 Willem van
Schendel.

"Origin of the Sak in Bangladesh," by the Headman of Baishari, from *Les Cak: Contri-
bution à l'étude ethnographique d'une population de langue loi*, by Lucien Bernot (Paris:
Éditions du Centre National de la Recherche Scientifique, 1967), 13 (abridged).
Translation © 2013 Willem van Schendel. Used by permission of CNRS Editions.

"Mahua and Naderchand Fall in Love," by Dvija Kanai, from *Eastern Bengal Ballads—
Mymensing, Vol. I*, edited and translated by Dinesh Chandra Sen (Calcutta: University of Calcutta, 1923), 5–7.

"The Path That Leads to You," by Modon Baul, from *Folklore of Bangladesh*, edited by Shamsuzzaman Khan (Dhaka: Bangla Academy, 1987), vol 1., 297. Reprinted by permission of Bangla Academy and Shamsuzzaman Khan.

Part III. Colonial Encounters

"A Tax Rebellion in Rangpur," by Ratiram Das, previously published as "Rangpurer Jager Gan," by Ratiram Das, *Rangpur Shahitya Parishad Patrika* (1315 BE–1907 CE). Reprinted, with an English translation by Amiya Bose, in Narahari Kaviraj, *A Peasant Uprising in Bengal 1783: The First Formidable Peasant Uprising against the Rule of East India Company* (New Delhi: People's Publishing House, 1972), 97–104. Reprinted by permission of the People's Publishing House.

"Making Sense of Hill People," by Francis Buchanan, previously published as "An Account of a Journey Undertaken by Order of the Board of Trade through the Provinces of Chittagong and Tiperah, in Order to Look Out for the Places Most Proper for the Cultivation of Spices," by Francis Buchanan (manuscript ADD. 19,286, British Library). Published in *Francis Buchanan in Southeast Bengal (1798): His Journey to Chittagong, the Chittagong Hill Tracts, Noakhali and Comilla*, edited by Willem van Schendel (Dhaka: University Press Limited, 1992), 68–75 (abridged). Used by permission of The University Press Limited.

"Rhinos among the Ruins" by A. Magon de Clos-Doré, from *Souvenirs d'un voyageur en Asie, depuis 1802 jusqu'en 1815 inclusivement* (Paris: Nepveu, 1822) 75–84 (abridged). Translation © 2013 Willem van Schendel.

"A Woman Teaches Herself to Read," by Rashsundari Debi, originally published as *Amar Jiban*, by Rashsundari Debi (1897) in *Words to Win: The Making of* Amar Jiban: *A Modern Autobiography*, translated by Tanika Sarkar (New Delhi: Kali for Women, 1999), 168–73. Used by permission of Kali for Women/Zubaan Books.

"What Is Lalon's Faith?," by Fakir Lalon Shah, translated by Sudipto Chatterjee. Parabas Translation. Available at http://www.parabaas.com/translation/database/translations/poems/lalon_sudipto2.html and http://www.parabaas.com/translation/database/translations/poems/lalon_sudipto3.html. Reprinted by permission of the translator.

"Blue Devil," by George Dowdeswell, Bhobonath Joardar, Panju Mulla, and Maibulla, from *Copies of the Circular Letters Sent on the 13th and 20th of July 1810 by Orders of the Governor General in Council of Fort William to the Magistrates under That Presidency; Ordered, by the House of Commons, to Be Printed, 27th April 1813* (London: His Majesty's Stationery Office, 1813), and from *Report of the Indigo Commission, 1860* (Calcutta, 1861), 178, 204, 207 (abridged).

"Fundamentalist Reform and the Rural Response," by Rafiuddin Ahmed, from *The Bengal Muslims 1871–1906: A Quest for Identity* (Delhi: Oxford University Press, 1981), 39–50 (abridged). Reproduced by permission of Oxford University Press India, New Delhi.

"Wage Holy War—or Leave!," by Moulvi Mirza Jan Rahman, Haji Budaruddeen of Dhaka, from *Tattva* [Spiritual principles] (Dhaka: Dacca Vernacular Press).

"The Great Famine Strikes the Land," by Tushar Kanti Ghosh and others, from *The Bengal Tragedy* (Lahore: Hero Publication, 1944), 94, 101–2.

"Pakistan as a Peasant Utopia," by Taj ul-Islam Hashmi, from *Pakistan as a Peasant Utopia: The Communalization of Class Politics in East Bengal, 1920–1947* (Boulder, CO: Westview Press, 1992), 263–64, 266. Used by permission of the author.

Part IV. Partition and Pakistan

"Creating an International Border," by Sir Cyril Radcliffe, chairman of the Border Commissions, *Report of the Bengal Boundary Commission*, New Delhi, August 12, 1947, annexure A to appendix II to no. 488 L/P & J/10/17: ff 40–47; found in the B. Proceedings; Political Branch confidential records, December 1948, Home Department of Government of East Bengal, record group 3R-12, National Archives of Bangladesh, Dhaka.

"Joy, Hope and Fear at Independence," by Ahmed Kamal from *State against the Nation: The Decline of the Muslim League in Pre-independence Bangladesh, 1947–54* (Dhaka: University Press Limited, 2009), 11–12, 23–25, 27. Reprinted by permission of The University Press Limited.

"Where Is the Border?" (1) By Indian and Pakistani Officials, from the proceedings of the conference held between the District Magistrate Rajshahi and District Magistrate Murshidabad, Rajshahi Circuit House, June 6–7, 1953; found in the B. Proceedings, Political Branch confidential records, June 1954, Home Department of Government of East Bengal, record group CR 1B1–4/53. (2) By S. M. Lutfullah, Superintendent of Dinajpur Police, report of the kidnapping of a constable and four embodied Ansars with arms and ammunition from Dinajpur border; found in the B. Proceedings, Political Branch confidential records, January 1955, Home Department of Government of East Bengal, record group CR 1B2–54/51, National Archives of Bangladesh, Dhaka.

"Teenage Migrant," an interview with Hasan Azizul Huq, from "'I Am *Not* a Refugee': Rethinking Partition Migration," by Md. Mahbubar Rahman and Willem van Schendel, translated by Willem van Schendel, *Modern Asian Studies* 37:3 (2003), 565–66. © Cambridge University Press. Reprinted with permission of Cambridge University Press and Willem van Schendel.

"Establishing the Communist Party of Pakistan," by Moni Singh, from *Jibon Shongram* (Dhaka: Bortoman Shomo, an imprint of Jatiyo Prokashoni, 1983), 91–96. Translation © 2013 Meghna Guhathakurta. Used by permission of Jatiyo Prokashoni.

"Broken Bengal," by Taslima Nasrin, from *Behula Eka Bhasiyechilo Bhela* (1993), English translation published in "Porous Borders, Divided Selves: A Symposium on Partition," *Seminar, The Monthly Symposium* 510 (2002), 38. Translation © 2002 Subho-Ranjan Dasgupta. Reprinted by permission of the translator.

"The Pakistan Experiment and the Language Issue," by Willem van Schendel, from *A History of Bangladesh* (Cambridge: Cambridge University Press, 2009), 107–14. © Cambridge University Press. Reprinted with permission of Cambridge University Press and Willem van Schendel.

"A Vernacular Elite," by Rounaq Jahan, from *Pakistan: Failure in National Integration* (Dhaka: University Press Limited, 1994 [1972]), 38–41. Reprinted by permission of The University Press Limited.

"East and West Pakistan: Economic Divergence," by Rehman Sobhan, from "The Problem of Regional Imbalance in the Economic Development of Pakistan," *Asian Survey* 2:5 (1962), 31–33, 36–37.

"Architectural Masterpiece in Dhaka," by Andrée Iffrig, LEED AP, from "Capital Complex in Bangladesh: Louis Kahn's Architectural Masterpiece for Dhaka," *Architecture@suite101*, August 8, 2008. Suite101. Available at http://architecture .suite101.com/article.cfm/capital_complex_in_bangladesh. Accessed 18 August 2010. Reprinted by permission of the author.

"Lake Kaptai," an interview with Shilabrata Tangchangya and Nripati Ranjan Tripura, from *Bara Parang: The Tale of the Developmental Refugees of the Chittagong Hill Tracts*, by Hari Kishore Chakma, Tapash Chakma, Preyasi Dewan, and Mahfuz Ullah (Dhaka: Centre for Sustainable Development, 1995), 26–27 (abridged). Used by permission of Hari Kishore Chakma.

"What Do I Pay My Cook?," by Ellura Winters and Robert Winters and Peggy Becker and Maxwell Becker, from "Dear Potential Chittagonger . . . ," in *Letters from Chittagong: An American Forestry Couple's Letters Home, 1952–54,* edited by Margaret W. Andrews, John L. Baker, and Fritz Blackwell (New Delhi: Arnold Publishers, 1992), 201, 203–4 (abridged). Used by permission of Margaret W. Andrews.

"The Garo Exodus of 1964," by Ellen Bal, from "Becoming the Garos of Bangladesh: Policies of Exclusion and the Ethnicisation of a 'Tribal' Minority," *South Asia: Journal of South Asian Studies* 30:3 (2007), 447–51. © South Asian Studies Association of Australia. Reprinted by permission of Taylor & Francis Ltd, http://www.tandf .co.uk/journals, on behalf of South Asian Studies Association of Australia, and by permission of the author.

"Elusive Villages," by Peter J. Bertocci, from "Elusive Villages: Social Structure and Community Organization in Rural East Pakistan" (Ph.D. dissertation, Michigan State University, 1970), 16–17, 19–20, 22. Used by permission of the author.

"Effects of the India-Pakistan War of 1965," by Badruddin Umar, from *The Emergence of Bangladesh. Vol. 2: Rise of Bengali Nationalism (1958–1971)* (Oxford: Oxford University Press, 2006), 101–5. Reprinted by permission of Oxford University Press, Pakistan.

"Six Points towards a Federation," proposal by the Awami League, from "The Awami League in the Political Development of Pakistan," by M. Rashiduzzaman, *Asian Survey* 10:7 (1970), 583. Reprinted by permission of University of California Press.

"This Time the Struggle Is for Our Independence!," by Sheikh Mujibur Rahman, from *Bangladesher Swadhinota Juddho: Dolilpottro/History of Bangladesh War of Independence: Documents* (Dhaka: Ministry of Information, Government of the People's Republic of Bangladesh, 1982), vol. 1, 46.

Part V. War and Independence

"The Declaration of Independence (25–26 March 1971)," by Sheikh Mujibur Rahman. Text can be found in *The History of the Freedom Movement in Bangladesh, 1943–1973*, by Jyoti Sen Gupta (Calcutta: Naya Prokash, 1974).

"A Radio Message from Kalurghat (27 March 1971)," by Ziaur Rahman, from *Bangladesher Swadhinota Juddho: Dolilpottro/History of Bangladesh War of Independence: Documents* (Dhaka: Ministry of Information, Government of the People's Republic of Bangladesh, 1982), vol. 3, 4–6.

"Mujibnagar: Proclaiming a New Country (17 April 1971)," by the Elected Representatives of the People of Bangladesh. Full text of the Proclamation of Independence is available at http://www.banglapedia.org/httpdocs/HT/P_0289.HTM.

"Operation Searchlight," by Siddiq Salik, from "Witness to Surrender: 26th April–2nd May, 1971," in *Bangladesher Swadhinota Juddho: Dolilpottro/History of Bangladesh War of Independence: Documents* (Dhaka: Ministry of Information, Government of the People's Republic of Bangladesh, 1984), vol. 7, 4–8.

"I Was Just a Kid Then," by Odhir Chandra Dey, from *Historicizing 1971 Genocide: State Versus Person*, by Imtiaz Ahmed (Dhaka: University Press Limited, 2009), 76–78. Reprinted by permission of The University Press Limited.

"A Telegram and a Phone Call." (1) By Archer Blood. Telegram 959 from the Consulate General (Blood) in Dacca to the Department of State, March 28, 1971, 0540Z, National Archives, record group 59, Central Files 1970–73, POL 23–9 PAK, Confidential, National Archives Building, Washington, DC; originally declassified as "Document 125," from "Documents on South Asia, 1969–1972," in *Foreign Relations of the United States, 1969–1976*, volume E–7 (United States Department of State, 2005). Available at http://history.state.gov/historicaldocuments/frus1969-76ve07/d125. (2) By Richard Nixon and Henry Kissinger. Transcript of a telephone conversation between President Nixon and his Assistant for National Security Affairs (Kissinger); Library of Congress Manuscript Division, Kissinger Papers, Box 367, Telephone Conversations, Chronological File, Library of Congress, Washington DC; originally declassified as "Document 14," from "South Asia Crisis, 1971," in *Foreign Relations of the United States, 1969–1976* (United States Department of State, 2005), vol. XI. Available at http://history.state.gov/historicaldocuments/frus1969-76v11/d14.

"From Counter-Insurgency to Defeat," by A. A. K. Niazi, from *The Betrayal of East Pakistan* (Dhaka: The University Press Limited, 1999), 58–60. Reprinted by permission of The University Press Limited.

"A Father's Letter to His Daughter," by Ataur Rahman Khan Kaysar, from *Ekattorer Chithi*, edited by Salauddin Ahmad et al. (Dhaka: Prothoma Prokashan, 2009), 39–40 (abridged). Translation © 2013 Meghna Guhathakurta. Used by permission of Prothoma Prokashan.

"Powdered Pepper," by Shaheen Akhtar, originally published as "She Knew the Use of Powdered Pepper," in *Fault Lines, Stories of 1971*, edited by Niaz Zaman and Asif Farrukhi (Dhaka: The University Press Limited, 2008), 76–83. Translated by Shabnam Nadiya. Reprinted by permission of The University Press Limited.

"A Raja's Protection," by Raja Tridiv Roy, from *The Departed Melody (Memoirs)* (Islamabad: PPA Publications, 2003), 218–21. Reprinted by permission of the author.

"To the People of West Pakistan" by K. K. Sinha, from *Bangladesh Revolution for Liberation* (Calcutta: Firma KLM Private Limited, 1973), 18–20. Reprinted by permission of Firma KLM Private Limited.

"A Missionary Family in the War," by Jim McKinley, from *Death to Life: Bangladesh— As Experienced by a Missionary Family* (Kentucky: Highview Baptist Church, 1978), 123–36 (abridged). Used by permission of Highview Baptist Church.

"The Diary's Final Pages," by Mahbub Alam, from *Guerrilla Theke Shommukh Juddhe* (Dhaka: Shahityo Prokash, 1993), 576–78. Translation © 2013 Meghna Guhathakurta. Used by permission of Shahityo Prokash.

"The Jagannath College Concentration Camp," by Basanti Guhathakurta, from *Ekattorer Smriti* (Dhaka: The University Press Limited, 1991), 145–46. Translation © 2013 Meghna Guhathakurta. Used by permission of The University Press Limited.

"Stranded Pakistanis ('Biharis')," by Ben Whittaker, from *The Biharis in Bangladesh* (London: Minority Rights Group, 1972), 8–9. Reprinted by permission of Minority Rights Group International.

"Party over State," by Willem van Schendel, from *A History of Bangladesh* (Cambridge: Cambridge University Press, 2009), 176–79. © Cambridge University Press. Reprinted with permission of Cambridge University Press and Willem van Schendel.

Part VI. Dilemmas of Nationhood

"What Makes Us a Nation?," by Abdur Razzaq, from *Bangladesh, State of the Nation: Muzaffar Ahmed Choudhuri Memorial Lectures* (Dhaka: University of Dacca, 1981), 13–22. Reprinted by permission of Dhaka University Press.

"Perceptions of Cultural Identity," by Salma Sobhan, previously published as "Internal and External Perceptions of Cultural Identity," in *Bangladesh in the 1990s: Selected Studies*, edited by Willem van Schendel and Kirsten Westergaard (Dhaka: The University Press Limited, 1997), 33–42. Reprinted by permission of The University Press Limited.

"Creating a Symbol of the Nation," by Sayeed Ahmad, from "It Is My Mother's Face," in *Novera*, edited by Hasnat Abdul Hye (Dhaka: Shohityo Prokash, n.d.), 195–200. Reprinted by permission of Shohityo Prokash.

"Suppressing Student Protests in Dhaka," by Meghna Guhathakurta, in "Democracy and the War of Symbols" (2002). © 2002 Meghna Guhathakurta. Accessed 11 October 2011 at http://www.meghbarta.org/. No longer accessible; see new website: http://meghbarta.info.

"Chittagong Hill Tracts Peace Accord (1997)," by Parbattya Chattagram Jana Sanghati Samiti and the Government of Bangladesh (Dhaka: Government of the People's Republic of Bangladesh and The People of the Chittagong Hill Tracts, 2 December 1997) (abridged).

"Gender, Ethnicity, and the Nation," by Kalpana Chakma, originally published as "Addressing the Delegates of the First National Representatives Conference of the Hill

Women's Federation," in *Kalpana Chakma Diary* (Dhaka: Hill Women's Federation, 2001), 23. Translation © 2013 Meghna Guhathakurta. Used by permission of the Hill Women's Federation.

"The Two Meanings of 'Bangladeshi,'" by Amena Mohsin, from *The Politics of Nationalism: The Case of the Chittagong Hill Tracts, Bangladesh* (Dhaka: The University Press Limited, 1997), 67–68. Reprinted by permission of The University Press Limited.

"Secularism as Religious Tolerance," by Amena Mohsin, from *The Politics of Nationalism: The Case of the Chittagong Hill Tracts, Bangladesh* (Dhaka: The University Press Limited, 1997), 60–61. Reprinted by permission of The University Press Limited.

"The Tablighi Jama'at," by Yoginder S. Sikand, previously published as "The Tablighi Jama'at in Bangladesh," in "Bangladesh: Three Decades of Liberation," edited by Karan R. Sawny, *Peace Initiatives* 7:1–3 (2001), 103–6 (abridged). Used by permission of the author.

"Islamist Women Activists Discuss Jihad," by Maimuna Huq, originally published as "Talking *Jihad* and Piety: Reformist Exertions among Islamist Women in Bangladesh," by Maimuna Huq, *Journal of the Royal Anthropological Institute (N.S.)* (2009), s163–s182. © John Wiley & Sons, Inc. Used by permission of John Wiley & Sons.

"The Nation and the Military," by Ayesha Siddiqa, originally published as "Fighting for the Soul of Bangladesh," *The Daily Times*, 17 December 2007. Available at http://www.dailytimes.com.pk/default.asp?page=2007\12\17\story_17-12-2007_pg3_4. Accessed 13 November 2010. Used by permission of *The Daily Times*.

"Amending the Constitution," by Saqeb Mahbub, originally published as "Judgment of the Appellate Division," *The Unheard Voice: All Things Bangladesh* (blog), 28 July 2010. Available at http://unheardvoice.net/blog/2010/07/28/judgment/. Accessed 22 March 2012. Used by permission of Saqeb Mahbub, Partner, Mahbub & Company, Dhaka, Bangladesh. Special thanks to Syeed Ahamed, CEO at Institute Informatics and Development (IID), for inspiring the article.

"The Bengali Sense of Victimhood," by Rahnuma Ahmed, originally published as "Chittagong Hill Tracts and the Bengali Sense of Victimhood," *New Age*, 5 April 2010. Reprinted by permission of the author.

Part VII. Contemporary Culture

"The Raw, Frank, Funny Eid Parade," by Henry Glassie, from *Art and Life in Bangladesh* (Bloomington and Indianapolis: Indiana University Press, 1997), 54–56, 58–60. Copyright © 1997, Indiana University Press. Reprinted with permission of Indiana University Press.

"A Visionary of Rural Beauty," by Burhanuddin Khan Jahangir, from *The Quest of Zainal Abedin* (Dhaka: International Centre for Bengal Studies, 1993), 21–25. Translation © 1993. Meghna Guhathakurta. Reprinted by permission of the International Centre for Bengal Studies.

"A Dancer's Mission," by Bulbul Chowdhury, from "Bangladeshe Nrittochorcha o Moulobad," special issue on the rise of fundamentalism, *Shomaj Nirikkhon* 26 (1987), by Meghna Guhathakurta. Translation © 2013 Meghna Guhathakurta. Used by permission of Meghna Guhathakurta.

Part VIII. The Development Gaze

at http://www.thedailystar.net/forum/2007/march/modhurpur.htm. Accessed 10 December 2011. Reprinted by permission of *The Daily Star.*

Part IX. Bangladesh beyond Borders

"Dispersing Partition Refugees in India," by Joya Chatterji, from "'Dispersal' and the Failure of Rehabilitation: Refugee Camp-Dwellers and Squatters in West Bengal," *Modern Asian Studies* 41:5 (2007), 997–1007, 1031–32 (abridged). © Cambridge University Press. Used by permission of Cambridge University Press and Joya Chatterji.

"The Nellie Massacre," by Makiko Kimura, from "Memories of the Massacre: Violence and Collective Identity in the Narratives on the Nellie Incident," *Asian Ethnicity* 4:2 (2003), 227–28, 230–31. Reprinted by permission of the publisher (Taylor & Francis Ltd., http://www.informaworld.com) and Makiko Kimura.

"Operation Pushback," by Sujata Ramachandran, from "'Operation Pushback': Sangh Parivar, State, Slums and Surreptitious Bangladeshis in New Delhi," *Economic and Political Weekly* 38:7 (15 February 2003), 641–42. Reprinted by permission of the author.

"Snake Charmers in Limbo," by Satadru Sen, originally published as "Border of Insanity: Deporting Bangladeshi Migrants," *Economic and Political Weekly* 38:7 (15 February 2003), 611–12. Reprinted by permission of the author.

"The Green Passport," by Zakir Kibria, *Forum, a Monthly Publication of The Daily Star* 3:11 (November 2009). Available at: http://www.thedailystar.net/forum/2009/november/passport.htm. Accessed 18 March 2012. Reprinted by permission of *The Daily Star.*

"Fast-Footed Sylhetis," by Katy Gardner and Zahir Ahmed, from *Place, Social Protection and Migration in Bangladesh: A Londoni Village in Biswanath* (Brighton: Development Research Centre on Migration, Globalisation and Poverty, University of Sussex, 2006), 7–10 (abridged). Used by permission of the Moving Out of Poverty Research Consortium and Katy Gardner.

"Sending Money Home," by Alastair Lawson, originally published as "Bangladeshi Bank Tackles Illegal Money," *BBC News*, 8 May 2003. BBC. Available at http://news.bbc.co.uk/2/hi/business/3008343.stm. Accessed 27 August 2010. Reprinted by permission of *BBC News* at bbc.co.uk/news.

"Bangladeshi Activists in London," by John Eade and David Garbin, from "Changing Narratives of Violence, Struggle and Resistance: Bangladeshis and the Competition for Resources in the Global City," *Oxford Development Studies* 30:2 (2002), 139–43, 145, 147–48 (abridged). © International Development Centre, Oxford. Used by permission of the publisher (Taylor & Francis Ltd., http://www.informaworld.com) on behalf of International Development Centre, Oxford, and by permission of the authors.

"A Lungi with a Zip!," by Emdad Rahman, originally published as "Thoughts on the Lungi from a Londoner," in *The Daily Star Book of Bangladeshi Writing*, edited by Khademul Islam (Dhaka: Daily Star, 2006), 253–56. Reprinted by permission of *The Daily Star.*

Index